Buildings and society

Edited by Anthony D. King

Buildings and society

Essays on the social development of the built environment

ROUTLEDGE & KEGAN PAUL
London, Boston and Henley

First published in 1980
by Routledge & Kegan Paul Ltd
39 Store Street, London WC1E 7DD,
9 Park Street, Boston, Mass. 02108, USA and
Broadway House, Newtown Road,
Henley-on-Thames, Oxon RG9 1EN
Set in 11/13 Baskerville by
Rowland Phototypesetting Ltd, Bury St Edmunds, Suffolk
and printed in Great Britain by
Lowe and Brydone Printers Ltd, Thetford, Norfolk

British Library Cataloguing in Publication Data

Buildings and society.
1. Architecture and society
I. King, Anthony Douglas
720   NA2543.S6   80-40938

ISBN 0 7100 0616 0

Contents

Acknowledgments   x
Introduction   1

Part I

1   A convenient place to get rid of inconvenient   *Andrew Scull*   37
    people: the Victorian lunatic asylum

2   The modern hospital in England and France: *Adrian Forty*   61
    the social and medical uses of architecture

3   Design and reform: the 'separate system' in   *Heather Tomlinson*   94
    the nineteenth-century English prison

Part II

4   The Hindu temple in south India   *Susan Lewandowski*   123

5   The apartment house in urban America   *John Hancock*   151

Part III

6   A time for space and a space for time: the   *Anthony D. King*   193
    social production of the vacation house

7   Places of refreshment in the nineteenth-   *Robert Thorne*   228
     century city

8   Office buildings and organisational change   *Francis Duffy*   255

     Part IV

9   Vernacular architecture and the cultural   *Amos Rapoport*   283
     determinants of form

     Contributors   306

     Index   309

Illustrations

		facing page
1.1	The original building of the York Retreat, opened 1796	45
1.2	Ground floor plan of the Claybury County Asylum at Woodford, Essex, begun 1887	46
1.3	Cheshire County Asylum, built 1828	48
1.4	'Twelfth Night Entertainments at Hanwell Lunatic Asylum', a picture taken from the *Illustrated London News*, 1848	50
1.5	Colney Hatch Lunatic Asylum, opened 1851	53
1.6	Design for asylums at Leavesden Woodside, near Watford, and Caterham, near Croydon, 1868	55
1.7	Floor plan of the general, infirmary and administrative blocks of the asylums for the chronic insane at Caterham and Leavesden, 1868	54
2.1	Plan of La Charité Hospital, Paris, 1788, from Tenon's *Memoires sur les Hôpitaux de Paris*	65
2.2	Engraving of the elevation and plan of The London Hospital, 1752	70
2.3	Plan of the 1801 extension to the Newcastle-upon-Tyne Infirmary	77
2.4	Plan of ward for the new wing of St Thomas's Hospital, London, 1840–2	78
2.5	Aerial view of St Marylebone Workhouse Infirmary, 1879–81, drawn and published by the architect, H. S. Snell	82
2.6	Interior of a ward at the Glasgow Western Infirmary (built in 1881) shortly before 1909	87
2.7	Interior of a single-bed ward in the private patients' block for the Royal Northern Hospital, designed by Adams, Holden and Pearson, and photographed shortly after completion in 1935	86
2.8	The hospital as office block: University College Hospital, London, 1895 and 1964	88

3.1 Design for cell, Pentonville Prison, 1844   100
3.2 Aerial view of Strangeways Prison, Manchester   102
3.3 Interior of the House of Detention, Clerkenwell   104
3.4 Pentonville Prison, ground plan   107
3.5 Chapel on the 'separate system', Pentonville, during divine service   106
3.6 Partitioned pews, Lincoln Prison Chapel   109
3.7 Masked convicts exercising at Pentonville   108
3.8 Holloway Prison, London: main gateway   110

4.1 Examples showing the evolution of temple form in India   128
4.2 Minakshi temple and Madurai City, c. 1977   131
4.3 Map of Madurai City, 1937   132
4.4 Plan of Minakshi temple, Madurai City   134
4.5 Shri Mahalakshmi temple, Tiruvanmiyur, Madras City, 1980   139
4.6 Street temple, Georgetown, Madras City, 1977   144

5.1 Chicago: from slum to Gold Coast   155
5.2 The Stuyvesant, New York City (1869, razed 1957)   160
5.3 Architect's drawing of 1107 Fifth Avenue, New York City (1924)   162
5.4 The Dakota, New York City (1884)   164
5.5 Marina City, Chicago (1964–7)   168
5.6 Middle-class apartment house district, Chicago (1934)   172
5.7 Robert R. Taylor Homes, Chicago (1959–63)   179

6.1 A horizontal container for the consumption of surplus free time: the
     bungalow as purpose-built vacation house, 1895   206
6.2 Space for time: the prefabricated weekend cottage, 1905   210
6.3 Stages in the transformation of a temporary to a permanent settlement:
     the self-built bungalow, New Shoreham Beach, Sussex, c. 1910–75–80   215
6.4 Weekend cottage as the idealisation of rural life, 1933   218

7.1 Painting of the Cock Tavern, Fleet Street, by Philip Norman   235
7.2 Simpson's, the Strand   236
7.3 Purssell's Coffee Saloon, Cornhill, 1849   239
7.4 Ground floor and grand hall floor plans of the Criterion, Piccadilly,
     1871   243
7.5 The Goat in Boots public house, Fulham Road, 1889   247
7.6 Prince's Restaurant, Piccadilly, photographed in 1896   249

8.1   Interior of the Bank of England, London, early nineteenth century   255
8.2   The Sun Insurance Office, London, 1849   260
8.3   The Sun Insurance Office, London, 1949: interior   263
8.4   Oriel Chambers, Liverpool, 1864: floor plan   262
8.5   Oriel Chambers, Liverpool, 1864: elevation   265
8.6   Larkin Company Administration building, Buffalo, New York, 1904   267
8.7   Clerical desk, Larkin Administration building, Buffalo, New York, 1904   269
8.8   The Guaranty building, Buffalo, New York, 1895, exterior   271
8.9   The Guaranty building, Buffalo, New York, 1895, floor plan   270
8.10 Empire State building, New York City, 1940: part plan of section from window wall to building core   272
8.11 Exterior of the Seagram building, New York City, 1953   275
8.12 Seagram building, New York City, 1953: interior of management office   274
8.13 Ninoflax offices, Nordhorn, West Germany, 1963: interior   277
8.14 Ninoflax offices, Nordhorn, West Germany, 1963: plan   276

Acknowledgments

My thanks are first due to Professor Peter Gleichmann for the invitation to develop the ideas behind this book in the Architectural Sociology Seminars of the Technical Universities of Hanover and Aachen in November–December 1976. I am also grateful to Professor John Burnett for instigating me to work further on them and prepare the scheme for publication. My principal thanks, however, must go to the contributors who first helped me to develop the outline and, in many subsequent conversations, letters and drafts, stimulated many further ideas. Their patience and co-operation in working within a somewhat demanding framework are greatly appreciated.

Adrian Forty did more than his share of work in reading the Introduction and my own essay, making many valuable suggestions and also providing help in other ways, all of which I appreciate. My thanks too, to Vere Hole for reading the outline and the Introduction and for the many ideas, not all of which I have been able to incorporate. Apart from making valuable suggestions on the original scheme and other parts of the book, and in discussing – on innumerable occasions – everything from concepts of time to Hindu temples, my wife, Ursula King, has helped in other ways too numerous to mention. Mike Bartholomew provided a very good piece of advice and David Page, as always, gave help of many different kinds. To past students in the Department of Building Technology at Brunel, and to many other friends at various conferences or departmental seminars in sociology, architecture and planning where I have been able to discuss some of the issues in this book, I extend my warm appreciation. I should also like to thank Peter Hopkins, Eileen Wood and other staff at Routledge & Kegan Paul for their co-operation and advice and especially, Brent Curless for his sympathetic approach to the design of this book. Finally, to Ursula, Frances, Karen, Anna and Nina go my sincerest thanks and love for their patience and stolen time.

Anthony D. King
30 June 1979

Introduction

What can we understand about a society by examining its buildings and
physical environment?
What can we understand about buildings and environments by examining the
society in which they exist?

These two questions are at the core of this book. The assumption behind it is that
buildings, indeed, the entire built environment, are essentially social and
cultural products. Buildings result from social needs and accommodate a variety
of functions – economic, social, political, religious and cultural. Their size,
appearance, location and form are governed not simply by physical factors
(climate, materials or topography) but by a society's ideas, its forms of economic
and social organisation, its distribution of resources and authority, its activities,
and the beliefs and values which prevail at any one period of time.

As changes in society occur, so too does change in its built environment. New
building types emerge and existing ones become obsolete. Some buildings are
modified, extended and take on different functions; others may simply disappear.
Society produces its buildings, and the buildings, although not producing
society, help to maintain many of its social forms.

If these are sweeping generalisations, then the aim of the essays in this volume
is to question, qualify or refute them. The statements formed the opening paragraphs of the initial working brief prepared by the editor and circulated among
potential contributors and others in 1977. In different ways, the nine essays
explore the relationship between social forms and built forms, between society
and the built environment it produces. Of the questions suggested above, the
second is considered first.

The background

To have yet another book with 'environment' in its title needs an explanation. One way of giving this would be to refer to 'the urban crisis', city centre re-development or 'problems of access to limited and scarce resources in the city'. Yet this would be false. This book is *not* about policy – or at least not explicitly so – but about an approach or method, a way of understanding society and the buildings it produces. Only this can explain the inclusion of topics as apparently unrelated as the Hindu temple, American apartment house and British prison. An alternative explanation might be through a discussion of the many academic subjects or disciplines that deal with society, the built environment and the relationship between them. Yet because of the vast amount of literature in these fields, not only would this be unrealistic, but, for the readers for whom this book is intended – not just sociologists, architects or historians but for the very many people interested in the built environment and especially its historical develop-ment – it would also be tedious. A third way might be to give the reasons for how I myself became interested in the approach. If this seems an excessively personal explanation, it is none the less an honest one and, for this reason at least, it is the one I shall adopt. In this way, problems of a wider, more general, interest will be thrown up and the logic of the collection explained.

Some years ago, as a sociologist–historian interested in the built environment (a loosely defined concept which includes most aspects of the physical environ-ment and especially the spheres of building, architecture and planning), I began, after five years' residence in Delhi, a study of the recent development of the city. As any visitor would recognise, Delhi consists of at least two very different cities: Old Delhi, the original walled town, and New Delhi, which was once the imperial capital of the British Raj. These two cities stand amidst the ruins of earlier settlements and, more especially, the enormous accretion of urban de-velopment which has taken place since Independence in 1947.

Despite sharing the same climate and location, two more different cities are hard to imagine. One, with shady, narrow, treeless streets, full of bustling activity; traditional three- or four-storeyed courtyard houses; temples, mosques, bazaars; dense throngs of people, traditionally dressed, walking, cycling, pulling carts or riding rickshaws; a myriad of things being made and sold in one of the most densely populated cities in the world. The other, with vast, tree-lined avenues, often empty of traffic; huge, single-storey, white-painted 'classical' bungalows in three-acre compounds, surrounded by trees; impressive ceremonial spaces and huge office blocks, international hotels, modern cars and 'Western'-dressed inhabitants milling round new supermarkets. How did I explain what I saw? And what social significance did these different physical environments have?

The initial aims of the study were relatively simple: why was the physical and spatial urban form like it was? Moreover, what was the relationship, if any, between these forms and the social structure, way of life and everyday activities of the various inhabitants of Delhi? What difference had the building of this vast new capital and the social mix to which it gave rise made to the traditional caste system of India? Yet finding a suitable way, and, more especially, an appropriate framework in which to answer these questions, was less simple. In the first instance, it was clear that the two main cities were products of at least two very different cultures – one Indian (both Hindu and Muslim), the other British – each with its own language (or languages), religion, institutions, values, ideas and world views. Moreover, New Delhi had been built as the capital of the British Raj: both the city itself and its relationship to Old Delhi were the product of colonialism. Third, not only were the two cities products of different historical times (mainly seventeenth to nineteenth century for Old Delhi, early twentieth century for the new city) but, more importantly, they were based on different economic and technological premises: one, on the assumptions of a pre-industrial society; the other, on those of the industrial society. Finally, the actual plan and architectural form of New Delhi had, according to the available books on the history of the city, been based on the ideas of two particular representatives of this colonial culture, the architect-planners Edwin Lutyens and Herbert Baker. There are no doubt other explanatory factors but these appeared to be the main ones.

In short, the task of the study was to explain the historical development of a city that was the product of particular cultures (English and Indian), of a particular political and economic system (modern industrial colonialism) and a particular industrial technology (based on inanimate sources of energy) and to relate it to the society of which it was a part. These seemed to be the essential prerequisites to establish before any attempt could be made to assess the contribution of individual 'designers' to the form of the city. It was from this and subsequent work that my interest in the relationship between social and cultural forms on the one hand, and built and spatial forms on the other, has developed (one could, of course, say 'between society and culture and architecture and urban form', though this phrase is less specific than the original). How have these relationships been investigated? As a comprehensive and accurate answer to this question is far beyond the scope of this introduction, the following comments must be necessarily selective.

Explaining the transformation of landscape and the physical environment as a product of culture has long been the task of cultural geography. Similarly, though with a different intention and focus, studies in social and cultural anthropology have shown, for example, how forms of social organisation are expressed in spatial form on the ground, how buildings carry symbolic meaning or how the religious beliefs and world view of particular social groups are represented in settlement form.

While traditionally many of these questions were incidental rather than central to anthropological research, in the last decade there has been a growing interest in them, much of it generated by the pioneer work of Amos Rapoport, whose *House Form and Culture* (1969) draws on anthropological and other studies to show how dwellings and settlement form relate to culture as a way of life, world view and form of social organisation. In subsequent work, Rapoport has pursued these themes, suggesting a wide range of categories in which the study of building and spatial organisation can be related to social variables, including not just how social factors affect the physical and spatial environment, but also how people are affected by their environments (1976, pp. 12–17). In a rich fund of writing, Rapoport's aim has been to stress the socio-cultural, psychological and related aspects of the built environment, leaving to others (as he states in his latest book) questions of 'social planning, political process and economic matters' (1977, p. 6). Rapoport has also drawn on historical research, although the focus of his own work has been on comparative studies across cultures rather than across, or through time. Yet, as he states in his essay here, historical studies are a further way of broadening the sample of environments in order to arrive at a more valid theory.

Since Rapoport's earlier work, others, whether in anthropology, geography, architecture or planning, have produced a growing body of research relating architecture and built form to social and cultural variables. A fairly recent addition to this literature, for example, aims to show that 'important social and religious elements in tribal life are reflected in a community's domestic buildings and usually symbolically expressed in their design and decoration'. It explains 'how dwellings come to be erected for particular social purposes such as menstrual lodges or the bachelor houses built by the Trobriand Islanders, and how kinship and household structures gave rise to house types such as the *molucas* of Amazonia . . . and how tribal man has shaped . . . his domestic space' (Duly, 1979). These (mainly architectural) studies, however, have often had two characteristics. They reflect the traditional interest of anthropologists in 'exotic', pre-literate, non-Western cultures (e.g. Oliver, 1969, 1973, 1975; Denyer, 1978; Duly, 1979) and they have generally (for obvious reasons) concentrated on dwelling form. Yet there is a need to bring this approach to the study of modern industrial societies and to apply it to the study of other, non-domestic, building forms. It was with this in view that the study of colonial urban forms in India attempted to see the British colonial community, and the environment that they produced, as others have seen the Trobriand Islanders (King, 1976).

Cities and buildings, however, are not explained simply by reference to social and cultural variables. They also reflect a distribution of power. Like similar cities, Delhi was first and foremost the result of the political, economic and social processes of colonialism. As such, it had its own institutions, and to understand the city as a social (rather than a physical) entity meant understanding the society of which it was a part. This view of the city as a social, political and economic system has traditionally been the concern of urban sociology and, more recently, the 'new urban sociology', better described, because it encompasses other scholars from geography, economics, politics and history, as the 'political economy of cities and regions' (represented, for example, by the work of Harvey, 1973; Castells, 1977, 1978; Harloe, 1977; Pickvance, 1976).

Here, the perspective is quite different. Though the relation of spatial structure to social structure is discussed, as also, for example, the political and economic processes leading to the establishment of factories, banks, shops or the provision of housing and schools, the actual built forms of these are not considered. A further issue deals with the question of public access to limited and scarce resources (Pahl, 1975) such as housing, urban space, education or shopping facilities. The main impetus of much of this essentially theoretical work, with its Marxist perspective, has been to develop a theory 'which effectively relates urban development to the development of society as a whole' (Harloe, 1977, p. 5).

While this research brings out the economic and social processes governing the development of the city under capitalism, examining, for example, the interest groups behind urban redevelopment and the logic of commercial or industrial location, its focus is at the scale of the city rather than the building and is not on the physical, built environment actually produced. Just why buildings emerge with the particular shape, location and appearance that they have, or what meaning such forms have for their inhabitants is not within the province of such studies. And while in every society economic and political power is a major – probably the major – factor explaining the actual form of the built environment, the way such power is expressed varies from culture to culture. So far, much of this new work has concentrated on European and North American cities and the cultural variable has tended to be minimised. It seems likely, however, that future work on these lines will extend both to other areas as well as address the question of culture (see, for example, the *International Journal of Urban and Regional Research*, 3, 1, 1979).

In many other urban sociological studies, the built environment as such has often tended to be incidental rather than central to the research, except, of course, in studies of urban imagery (e.g. Strauss, 1968). In many cases, built form is seen as the province of urban or social geography rather than sociology. Where included, it has generally been to relate quality and type of housing to social stratification (e.g. Stacey, 1960) or, receiving greater attention, to the more sophisticated understanding of class and urban conflict by reference to distinct 'housing classes' (Rex, 1971; Rex and Moore, 1967). In general, however, the attempt to relate other, non-domestic elements in the built environment (factories, farms, hospitals, prisons, shops, churches, office blocks) to forms of economic, social and political organisation in a broader sociological understanding of social development seems to be relatively rare. Here, though it is perhaps not the most appropriate point, reference might be made to the work of Foucault (e.g. 1973, 1977), though the frame of reference is too complex for brief discussion.

A third very broad category of research relating to the built environment consists of historical studies. These, including work in urban, social and economic history, urban and historical geography, the history of housing and planning, and architectural and building history, each with their distinctive approach and focus, have – since the pioneer work of Lewis Mumford in the USA or Asa Briggs and the late H. J. Dyos in Britain, grown profusely in the last two decades, contributing greatly to the understanding of urban development. Among these, the historical study of buildings as discrete units in the built environment has, with some exceptions in urban history (e.g. Ravetz, 1974; Jackson, 1973; Sutcliffe, 1974), frequently been the province of building history and, more especially, of architectural history. While in the former the emphasis has usually been on materials and technology, the scope of the latter has encompassed a wide variety of styles, and more recently the most widely read have increasingly taken account of social factors (e.g. Girouard, 1975, 1978). Yet as Rapoport (1969, p. 1) and others have pointed out, the approach of architectural history is often selective, the decision to investigate and explain any particular element in the built environment, whether building or landscape, based in the first instance on evaluative, aesthetic criteria: is it 'aesthetically important'? (the criteria used to answer this question being based on the particular social and cultural values prevailing at any one period of time). In practice this has generally meant, to use Rapoport's terms, that only 'high style', architect-designed buildings are deemed appropriate for attention, and in some, if not all, cases the explanation for these is based primarily on ascertaining the identity of the architect, his perceived intentions and their relation to a given 'style'. What social or economic changes gave rise to the need for the building in the first instance, what explains its function, location, the activities it is meant to house, the spatial arrangements within it, its social and especially economic base or its relationship to the larger society and culture, are questions which too rarely receive sufficient attention. The response to the building by its occupants or its effect on the larger society (difficult enough questions to examine in relation to present-day environments, let alone past ones) are other issues which none the less might be pursued.

In this context, as the work (like this volume) is on building types, it is appropriate to mention Nikolaus Pevsner's *History of Building Types* (1976), which, while giving many interesting insights into the social function of the buildings discussed and including a wealth of valuable data, relies primarily for explanation on the contribution of individual architects and prevailing styles. The selection of buildings is principally from the work of known architects, and there is no general explanation of why the form of building types changes beyond an implicit evolutionary model; there is also no explanation of why buildings serving the same function have different forms in different societies. To some extent, this issue is avoided by limiting the book's compass to European and American society (i.e. parts of the world dominated by Western tradition or civilisation). The questions of change and cultural variation are avoided. (I am indebted to Adrian Forty for these insights.)

What this collection attempts, even with the very limited selection of different built forms discussed, is to break down the distinctions often made between different items in the built environment and the ways in which they are discussed. It is an attempt to see *all* as built form, whether this is a vast Hindu temple or a self-built mountain hut.

As suggested above, too often decisions whether to examine particular items in the environment are based on narrow criteria. One reason for this is the ever-increasing fragmentation of knowledge, not only in the existence of different disciplines (history, sociology) and sub-disciplines (urban history, urban sociology) but in the specialisations within these (history, and sociology of housing). These divisions are then made even more complex by social factors influencing research and practice. Thus, members of particular socioeconomic groups, with their own values as to what they consider important, are recruited to particular institutes of learning and research and socialised into distinct styles of scholarship. The result of this disciplinary specialisation and these social factors means that there are big gaps in communication between people who, effectively, are interested in the same field. The outcome is that one set of scholars, prompted perhaps by 'aesthetic' motives, produce lavishly illustrated scholarly books on individual architects or styles, to be appreciated by one social group; while another set of scholars, recruited from different social backgrounds, and prompted by social and political motives, produce equally scholarly books on economic fluctuations in the production of working-class housing which are read by another social group.

While this over-simplified view will be recognised as a caricature, it none the less helps to explain the profusion of studies and knowledge about the work of 'great architects' on one hand and about 'housing' on the other. A genuine sociology of architectural knowledge which attempted to explain why certain subjects are researched and others are not, and in what way, and how this knowledge is transmitted would need to take account of these and many other issues.

There are, of course, other approaches to the study of buildings and environments, particularly more recent developments in such fields as architectural and environmental psychology or man–environment studies, though as yet these two approaches have not been much used in historical studies. Each has its own focus and all have their contribution to make. Yet are all these approaches complementary, mutually exclusive or, at worst, contradictory? More specifically, can they (or at least, some of them) be coherently combined in a genuinely inter-disciplinary approach? The answer, clearly, must lie with each of us as individuals and with the background we bring to our problem. Ideally, however, the frame of reference ought to be one which would help explain the characteristics and development of built form as it relates to society and culture which would be equally valid, whether in New York or New Guinea, in medieval Europe or twentieth-century Japan. It is to help in the development of this comparative and historical frame of reference that this collection of essays has been compiled.

This objective is shared not only by the contributors but by others. Some years ago, the editors of the *Journal of Architectural Research* argued for 'the need to put much greater emphasis on an historical understanding of the economic, functional and cultural aspects of built form and the social conditions within which particular types of built form have evolved' (vol. 5, no. 2, August 1976). Or, in discussing the design process, 'architects translate from social ideas (like "school", "need", "community") into real buildings and aggregates which means that research must be concerned not only with the social ideas on one hand and the physical building on the other but with the relations between the two. This is currently one of our greatest areas of ignorance' (vol. 4, no. 2, August 1975).

This book, therefore, should be of interest to practitioners as well as those who teach them. Today, in schools of architecture, building, planning and design, varying amounts of economics, history, sociology and political economy often figure in the curriculum alongside more 'technical' subjects. Yet frequently these subjects are quite unrelated, the biggest gap perhaps being between the sociologist's approach to the built environment and that of the architectural historian. Can this gap be reduced? This is discussed in more detail below.

It is the aim of this book to throw some light on these issues. By deliberately choosing a selection of built forms from a wide range of historical and cultural experience, the aim is to emphasise the approach and method, the paramount necessity that, if we are to understand buildings and environments, we must understand the society and culture in which they exist. With this approach, by focusing our attention on built form and spatial organisation, we can understand much more about the society in which such forms exist – much, indeed, that might otherwise escape us. In this way, the relationships between society and its built environment could be explored and clarified. It is essentially an inter-disciplinary approach, and for this reason the essays in this volume are by sociologists/anthropologists, historians and architects, each with an interest in the methods of the others. If other scholars in the field are interested in this approach I should be glad to hear from them.

The aims and method

Based on the above premises, therefore, the volume has three main, and no doubt ambitious objectives:

1 to demonstrate the relationship between social forms and built forms;
2 to develop new methodological approaches for understanding the historical development of the built environment;
3 to suggest, as an outcome of the above, a preliminary framework for the understanding of the built environment both through time and between different cultures.

It is conventional practice in sociology and social anthropology to approach the study of society through a study of its institutions (see, for example, Eisenstadt, 1968, p. 409). Though there may be disagreement about the definition, there is widespread agreement that all societies share certain common institutions – the spheres of family and kinship, economy, polity, education, religion, social stratification (Eisenstadt, 1968, p. 410). Thus, for Bierstedt *et al.* (1964) an institution is 'a definite, formal and regular way of doing something, an established procedure', pp. 148–9). Different societies, however, institutionalise different activities: in very simple societies institutions are relatively undifferentiated, and priest, medicine man and political leader may be undistinguishable. As societies grow, differentiation occurs, and with it the growth of institutions. Hence, in modern society we can speak of leisure as a social institution.

Institutions depend on particular associations to sustain them: wherever we find an institution there will also be an association, or a number of them, whose function it is to pursue the institutionalised activity. Bierstedt lists a number of institutions and their related associations, i.e. business, a corporation; war, an army; education, a college; religion, a church; government, a government.

The understanding of institutions is, of course, far more complex than is presented here but, for present purposes further discussion is unnecessary at this point. In the framework developed for this book, what sociologists would describe as a straightforward functionalist approach has been adopted; this assumes that institutions can be related to basic human needs.

By assuming, therefore, that some kind of religion or belief system exists in every society, we may ask what are the particular built forms with which it is associated, and how can they be explained? Or, as all societies have some form of family and kinship, how do these various forms, and the ideas and beliefs surrounding them, relate to dwelling form? However, because institutions are interdependent, it is clear that any particular building will not relate solely to one institution. For example, while a dwelling might seem to be most obviously related to family and kinship, it is equally evident that its production is related to the economy; it can have religious meaning; it is a major symbol of social stratification; and, in terms of tenure, it can be a means of social control. Similarly, the institutions of religion, economy or social stratification can be expressed in all aspects of the built environment.

While there is inadequate space to develop this discussion here, the basic framework provided a useful device for structuring this book. More importantly, it explains the particular choice of topics included within it. Initially, these were meant to cover some of the main institutions, their associations and related building forms and could, for example, have included any of those in column (A) below, a small selection of many which could be used.

	(A)	(B)
family and kinship	the house	American apartment house, the Islamic house*, the vacation house
the economy	factory, office, warehouse, farm	the office, refreshment buildings, vacation house, laboratory*
religion	the temple, church, cemetery	the Hindu temple, the Islamic house*
the polity, social control	courthouse, town hall, prison	the prison, asylum, hospital
social stratification	housing estate, house form, residential area	all types
culture and social-isation	school, museum, library, college	laboratory*

In this way, it might be possible to see how the ideas, values, beliefs, activities, relationships and forms of social organisation of particular institutions were related to the form and plan of particular buildings, and also to see how changes in institutions were reflected in changed building form.

For example, the associated activities of the *polity* include those of government, law and social control, which, in modern societies, give rise to government buildings, administrative offices, embassies, courts, police stations and military camps – and many others; socialisation and culture, with their associated activities of education, or the creation, storage and distribution of knowledge, give rise to schools, colleges, libraries, laboratories and museums.

Originally, the intention was to include building forms or types that relate primarily, though not solely, to some of the major social institutions. Hence, there was a very wide scope of possible building types which might be included; nor was it important from which culture they were drawn – at this stage, an Islamic mosque was as relevant as a Quaker meeting house as the principal religious building. In the event, the topics indicated under column (B) were arranged, though for the reasons indicated below those marked by an asterisk could not be covered.

While this was the logic behind the framework, it is clear from the essays that it was a good deal too rigid to accommodate all the topics. Nevertheless, the generosity and flexibility of the contributors have enabled them to work within it – donning the raiment, as it were, as a loose cloak rather than as a fitted suit. Moreover, by the juxtaposition of explanations for particular building types, a large number of questions have been raised about the society that produced them.

A final note is necessary on the mechanics involved in the preparation of this collection. Following discussions with potential contributors, the initial draft outline of the scheme was prepared, discussed again with about half the authors, and revised. Other contributors were subsequently invited on the basis of this revision. The following extract from the outline suggested a possible framework for the essays and, though repeating some of the above discussion, is included for the sake of clarity.

> The suggested framework is that of 'modern' industrial society as it has emerged in the Western hemisphere over the last 100–150 years. This pre-supposes the existence of 'pre-industrial', 'industrialising' and 'post-industrial' phases which, in some societies, are ongoing processes and in others, are part of their historical past. . . .
>
> Though comparison of the institutions and building types discussed with those of other cultures would be ideal, the lack of published research and space make such comparisons difficult in every case. However, it is expected that some contributors will refer to developments in other societies.
>
> Two levels of explanation are envisaged. The first would deal with the larger socio-economic environment and discuss the various changes – economic, technological, cultural, scientific, political, social, religious, demographic – which give rise to either a 'new' social need, or the modification of society's arrangements for existing needs, which results either in a new building type (e.g. a community health centre, labour exchange or research laboratory) or the substantial modification of an existing building form. Once such a need or function is identified, the second level of explanation might focus more on the building type itself, indicating how, over time, 'needs' change according to changing theories and other social factors and lead to changes in the building form.

Obviously, each contributor will need – in discussing the evolution of the particular built form – to emphasise some aspects of explanation more than others. Likewise, depending on contributor and subject matter, greater or lesser attention might be given to the economic–political basis of society and the implications of this for the social and class structure and the reflection of this in the built environment.

From the synopses submitted, however, three or four elements seem to be common to the structure of each paper. Though greater or less attention might be given to each of these elements by individual contributors, their retention will obviously help in giving coherence to the volume:

> an introductory reference to the basic social function accommodated by the building type in 'pre-modern' society and the existing architectural/built form provision for it (with some reference to the factors determining this), if any (i.e. the 'traditional' built form provision, where this exists);

> the new or changed circumstances giving rise to a new building type or the modification of existing built form;

> the social factors determining the new or modified form discussed in detail at the macro- (i.e. location, number, scale, appearance) level and the micro- (internal design, space and room arrangements, equipment, contents) level;

> where possible, the social effects and changes brought about by the new or modified building form.

Various questions might suggest themselves for each building type, both at the first and subsequent levels, and these will clearly vary for each type and the way it relates to particular social institutions. For example, for buildings primarily related to the economy (e.g. bank, vacation house, supermarket, office), first-level questions might include: what is the economic basis of society, its energy sources, its technology? How do methods of production, distribution, relate to location and building form? How are resources distributed in society? How has change in the economic structure in industrial society led to change in the occupational structure, social structure and nature of social organisation?

At the second level, questions would relate primarily to the building form. Why, in the first place, does the building type exist? What functions does it fulfil? What previous social arrangements were made to accommodate these functions, if any? What governs its location, size and contents? For which social institution does it primarily cater? What is the economic and financial basis of the building? Who owns it and controls its use?

Further questions at this level might relate to 'social space'; e.g., what are the cultural, social, scientific, welfare, technical and other presuppositions ('theories') assumed in its layout? What activities does it accommodate? What are the social divisions represented both by the building itself and by the organisation of its internal space? What is the basis of the social categories used and are such categories represented in the spatial nomenclature? What are the corresponding rules/regulations governing the use of such spaces, who enforces them and how?

How is the 'architectural style' to be explained? What symbolic aspects are used, from where are they derived and what do they represent? To whose universe of meaning do such symbolic aspects refer?

If, in the course of tracing the development of a particular built form, it is possible to identify 'firsts' (i.e. the first purpose-built health clinic or apartment house, or the first substantial modification of a prevailing design), this might be highlighted as the *formal* acknowledgment of a change in society's arrangements for meeting a particular social need.

That this volume has been completed in just over eighteen months is largely due to the willingness of the contributors to work within this rather demanding framework.

The essays

The essays are arranged in four parts. In the first – all from one culture, society and period – two essays, on the asylum and prison, clearly relate to the control of deviance in society (social control); the third, on the hospital, as its author shows, also fits in here though less obviously so. That these essays all draw primarily on the experience of nineteenth-century Britain is a result of a happy accident rather than conscious editorial decision.

Part II includes essays on subjects from totally contrasting cultures, yet pursuing the same general theme and approach of the book. That on the temple in South India relates primarily to the institution of religion, but also to the polity and economy; that on the apartment house in America relates less to family and kinship than to social stratification. A third essay, on the Islamic house in western Asia, examining the dwelling form in the light of continuities and change in religion and family organisation, was also planned but could not be researched because of the contributor's subsequent illness.

Part III most clearly relates to the economy, although both refreshment places and the vacation house might also be subsumed under the institution of leisure. A further essay (relating to culture and socialisation), examining the growth of scientific knowledge and its relation to the development of the laboratory and other building forms, could unfortunately not be completed on account of the author's other commitments. In Part IV further issues relating to the cultural determinants of form are discussed in the essay by Amos Rapoport.

I

Of all the essays, that of Andrew Scull on the asylum gives most attention to the transformations in society and economy which eventually gave rise to the emergence of a particular building form. Scull's earlier work on this subject, recently published (1979), was not on the asylum building as such but on the social organisation of insanity in nineteenth-century England (1974). In this, he explored the change in societal arrangements by which certain types of behaviour became identified and categorised as deviant and 'insane'; there was, in his words, 'a redefinition of the moral boundaries of the community by which insanity was transformed from a vague, culturally defined phenomenon . . . into a uniquely and essentially medical problem'.

The reasons for the rise of this 'segregative response to madness' Scull locates firmly in the 'direct and indirect effects of the advent of a mature capitalist economy and the ever more thoroughgoing commercialisation of existence'. The establishment of a market in labour provided the initial incentive to distinguish more carefully than hitherto between different categories of deviance and to make a distinction between the able-bodied and non-able-bodied poor. At first, workhouses and the like were a practical way to achieve this, but later further segregation was necessary, particularly of the insane. Initially, these were transferred to 'madhouses', which were not purpose-built, where people were kept in chains and manacles. Subsequently, however, it was shown that the danger and frenzy anticipated from maniacs was a consequence of rather than an occasion for their harsh treatment, and new arrangements were necessary. With the emergence of an institutional ideology came the development of new professional experts in the management of the mad. In the course of the nineteenth century these evolved from mad doctors to alienists and, subsequently, psychiatrists. With these developments emerged also the belief that a special building was required for the treatment of the insane.

As with the treatment of the sick in hospital and the criminal in prison, so also the logic of the asylum placed immense importance on classification as a means of control and socialisation. This formed the basis of the purpose-built architecture which continued to be employed long after the ideas behind the system were abandoned. At first, the emphasis was on small numbers, with asylums for between 100 and 200; later, economic considerations prevailed and asylums – where, in the second half of the nineteenth century, the number of inmates multiplied five times while the population doubled – were to accommodate 2,000 inmates.

It was, Scull maintains, the very existence and expansion of the asylum system which created an increased demand for its own services. By the late nineteenth century, the different types of asylum had simply become 'receptacles for the storage of imbeciles'. The message of this essay is cogently contained in the comparison of the Retreat at York in the late eighteenth century (Figure 1.1) and Claybury Asylum (Figure 1.2) built less than one hundred years later.

Scull's essay provides a useful lead into that on the hospital by Adrian Forty. With some types of building, such as the vacation house, office or restaurant, there is virtually no secondary literature on either their architectural or their social development. This is not the case with the hospital. Yet as Forty points out, none of this literature satisfactorily explains the more fundamental questions that he poses. Why was there a rapid growth in hospital building in the nineteenth century, and what explanations can be given for the immense changes in size, location, form, plan and internal arrangements in hospitals over the last two centuries?

In looking more particularly at the social function of hospitals, Forty examines the motives of those who founded them, especially in the eighteenth century, when the governors were as much interested in finding methods for rationalising the labour market as they were in curing the sick. These considerations affected the design of hospitals, as also did the social hierarchy of those who built, ran and worked in them. Indeed, the fact that mid-eighteenth-century hospitals, asylums and prisons were all accommodated in a superficially similar building form, and that form – the Palladian villa – was the model most favoured by the aristocracy for their own dwellings (as well, of course, for many other public buildings), is an interesting if not sufficient clue to the understanding of their social function. It demonstrates the dominant social and political influence of the aristocratic ruling class in the same way that the much altered forms of nineteenth- and twentieth-century hospitals (and other buildings) demonstrate the increasing social power of new professional groups – in medicine, architecture and science. This argument could, of course, be extended: the interwar council estate as an expression of both shifts in political power and the triumph of professional architect-planning ideology; the office block as the representation of finance capital; government buildings as the growth of bureaucracy; the supermarket as symbolic of collective consumption.

In this essay, Forty draws on recent historical and sociological studies of the emergence of the medical profession to show that changes in the form of hospitals were due not just to changes in medical science but rather to the increasing social position and power of doctors. The 'pavilion plan', with its large numbers of widely separated ward blocks based on the 'miasmic' theory of infection (which held that disease was transmitted by polluted air), was the result. Like the cosmological ideas behind the Hindu temple, this is an interesting example of specific cultural knowledge which results in a very distinct environment (see also King, 1976, chapter 5). As with the other essays, Forty amply demonstrates that the understanding of hospital building demands an understanding not only of architectural form but also of much larger changes in society.

What, indeed, do hospitals tell us, not only about scientific and medical ideas but about society? How are a society's divisions represented in the social organis-ation of the sick? Currently, for example, London hospitals are categorised according to age (for children, the elderly); illness (infectious diseases, TB), parts of the body (eye, ENT), gender, nationality (Italian, German), religious beliefs of patrons (Jewish, Catholic); in earlier colonial societies by racial divisions (for Europeans, 'natives'); in the nineteenth century and today by socioeconomic status (for the poor; for National Health Service and 'private' patients). Forty's essay clearly brings out these social divisions and their importance in understanding the environment of hospitals. He ends with the ironic observation that, despite public ownership, the hospital buildings of the last two hundred years are surviving monuments to the transfer of power from lay to professional control.

Of all building types most graphically demonstrating the relationship between ideas, beliefs and architectural form, the Victorian separate system prison, the subject of an increasing amount of attention (Evans, 1975; Tomlinson, 1975; Foucault, 1977; Howe, 1977; Ignatieff, 1978, Fitzgerald and Sim, 1979), is probably the best known. In this particular treatment, however, Heather Tomlinson's essay, unlike the two previous ones, concentrates less on the 'macro' social changes leading to the rebuilding of prisons in the late eighteenth century and more on the ways in which particular social and religious ideas were embodied in their design and the rebuilding programme that this necessitated. In particular, where others have investigated the ideology behind penal archi-tecture (Evans, 1975), much of Tomlinson's own research has been on the administrative mechanisms by which the new prisons were introduced and operated. For their proper functioning, all environments – whether purpose-built or otherwise – require a system of rules, formal or informal, to ensure that they work, and this is illustrated by this essay.

The emphasis of the ideology was on reformation: central to this idea was the process of classification in order to prevent different types of prisoner from corrupting one another. Early nineteenth-century prison policy developed increasingly elaborate classification systems, each level representing a different grade of moral corruption. Evans (whose study provides a valuable extension of the themes considered here) speaks of the 'moral geography' of Derby prison which was 'as precisely arranged and graduated as that of any medieval purga-tory or hell' (1975, p. 286). But as Tomlinson points out here, classification could not continue indefinitely, and ideas of the separate system – the ultimate in classification, with each prisoner in his own category – were introduced.

The basis of separate confinement (not to be confused with solitary confine-ment, which was a form of punishment) were threefold: it provided opportunity for reflection as the starting point for reformation; by preventing communication it also prevented corruption; and it deterred through terror (Evans, 1975, p. 339). As the aim of the separate system was to induce reflection all external stimulations, visual and aural, if not olfactory – had to be prevented. Much of Tomlinson's chapter describes how this was done.

Few better examples exist to show how not only planning but also the choice of building materials, construction methods and services (heating, lighting, ventilation, sewerage) were subordinated to a set of social and moral ideas. Particularly interesting are the lengths to which the designers went to achieve acoustic control. And where prisoners were moved to other parts of the prison for school, chapel or exercise, elaborate physical arrangements continued to ensure total separation. In the overall design of the building the architect's contribution was limited to the facade, though even this was governed by the symbolic meaning associated with prevailing styles. Behind the facade, everything resulted from the moral ideas of the reformers (Evans, 1975, p. 353).

While each of these three essays prompts its own questions, the issues raised by reading them together are immense and, going far beyond the more limited aims of this book, can hardly be dealt with here. One obvious subject for further research is the emergence of the state as patron of building development and its alliance with new (i.e. nineteenth- and twentieth-century) professional groups, especially where the latter have an interest in the development of specialised knowledge (such as architects in the design of particular building types) in order to establish their professional identity – and monopoly – as professionals. (On professionalism, see Larson, 1978; Illich, 1978.)

All three types demonstrate the widespread nineteenth-century belief in architectural determinism. And where the ideology and logic behind the three types has changed drastically in this century, the least changed building (apart, that is, from those that have been newly built) is – for whatever reason – the prison. Here, where penal theories discarded the idea that moral qualities could be induced by particular surroundings, the separate system prison building continues to function, and, according to a recent account (Fitzgerald and Sim, 1979), all aims of education and rehabilitation in such prisons are subordinated to those of security. In the 1980s our society is still imprisoned by Victorian environments in more ways than one. What the essays also demonstrate is the ephemeral nature of the social basis of design and the outcome that results when economic and political power is strong enough to put such ideas into practice.

Tomlinson discusses the rapid spread of the separate system prison in England; it was also widely adopted in Europe in the mid-nineteenth century, with an exact replica of Pentonville Prison built at Moabit (Berlin) (Evans, 1975, p. 354). Moreover, as a result of imperial expansion in Asia, Africa and elsewhere, prisons, asylums, hospitals, as well as many other built forms and whole environments, were established around the globe (King, 1976, 1978). The consequences of the transfer of these institutions and their related built forms pose massive problems for what are now independent countries of the 'Third World'.

II

Most of the essays in this volume deal with 'new' forms of economic and social organisation and the physical and spatial forms built to contain them – the asylum, restaurant or vacation house. Susan Lewandowski focuses on what is probably one of man's most ancient building forms, the temple, to show how both continuity in the Hindu religious tradition and economic and political change have influenced the location, size and appearance of the temple in South India. Here again we have an example of how cultural values persist despite immense social and political change.

For some readers the ideas of Hinduism as well as Indian culture as a whole will be unfamiliar, and this, indeed, is one of the main reasons for including an essay in this area. Susan Lewandowski first discusses some of the basic tenets of Hinduism as they relate to the development of the temple, and shows how these were expressed in the traditional temple complex of the Minakshi Temple in Madurai, South India. Apart from its religious and symbolic meaning, however, the temple obviously also had important political, social and economic functions. In a culture where the sacred and secular are totally fused, temple building was a means to legitimise political authority, and the pre-industrial temple complex of Madurai was the product of the Nayaka ruler, Vishvanata. The elaborate spatial order of the complex both expressed and helped to sustain the equally elaborate social and ritual order of the inhabitants of the town.

Lewandowski then moves her focus from the traditional city of Madurai to the more modern urban context of Madras, discussing the impact of British colonial rule on the administration and form of Hindu temples. With the British conquest, there was a disassociation of religious and political spheres, and not only a break in traditional urban form but also new patterns of urbanisation. Modern forms of political authority and economic institutions penetrated the new, secular city, modifying both the location and architecture of temples. Though the institution persisted, new forms arose: in the traditional sacred city of Madurai, space for ritual circumambulation was horizontal, surrounding the main temple building; today, in the modern, more secular city of Madras, in one of the newest suburban temples, economic constraints such as the price of land have modified this form: ritual space is now vertical, incorporated as an upward spiral within the main building. The sacred tank, processional streets for the Jagannath-type temple car (from which our contemporary term 'juggernaut' is derived), and special residential quarters for the temple priests and Brahmins – all part of the traditional temple complex – have now disappeared. Where once the temple complex gave rise to and accommodated the city, now the city accommodates the temple.

Yet the modern temple maintains its important social and political functions. Surplus wealth in India, whether that of the barons of modern business or of stars in the flourishing Indian film industry, is invested in temples. In this way, they continue to fulfil their traditional function of legitimising the status of the newly arrived. Here is a very different use of an economic surplus than in the contemporary industrial West.

On one hand, suburban sprawl leads to the growth of new temples which cater for the expanding population; on the other, as in earlier times, the direction of urban development can also follow the location of existing temples. Particularly fascinating is the way in which wayside shrines, beginning perhaps only as a brick or stone painted with religious symbols, suddenly develop into small, then large, temples, despite municipal legislation supposedly prohibiting such developments. These temples, sustained by the persistence of religious beliefs, continue to meet the requirements of a modern urban population whose members are under pressure from very contemporary, secular needs – to pass exams, gain promotion or recover their health.

As Lewandowski shows how the temple symbolises the enduring values of Hinduism, despite immense economic and social change, so John Hancock's study of the apartment house in America demonstrates the persistence of residential segregation as a fundamental principle in the ordering of American social life.

Since its introduction in the late nineteenth century, the social function of the apartment house has literally been 'to house people apart', whether these have been the very rich (as in its early history), the middle class or, increasingly, the state-subsidised urban poor. In a culture where the dominant values overwhelmingly favour owner-occupied, single-family, detached (and usually suburban) housing, both the image and the reality of the apartment house (defined by the author as a building with at least three and generally a larger number of households living under one roof, arranged on at least two and usually more floors) has been suspect: apartment house occupants are predominantly *renters* and, generally speaking, are people in a *transient* social state. Where the social attitudes of the dominant class coincide with market practices and government regulations, the apartment house is confined to the edge of preferred, single-home residential neighbourhoods: in a classic judgment of the 1920s, it was referred to as a 'mere parasite', living off what were assumed to be 'superior' residential neighbourhoods.

For the British reader, the obvious comparisons are with housing in the private, owner-occupied (and often detached or semi-detached) sector and the public, local authority sector which, especially since the 1960s, was built in the form of multi-storey flats (Cooney, 1974): the form of dwelling and form of tenure are fused in what Perin, quoted by Hancock, refers to as 'a primary social sign' like race, income or gender. Here, there is a close parallel with Rex's concept of 'housing class' (1971; Rex and Moore, 1967), which, though defined in terms of ownership and tenure, in fact is frequently related to actual house type and form (Reid, 1977, p. 156) and, more specifically, to the amount of control exercised by tenants over the external appearance of the dwelling.

In the USA, however, where public housing plays a much smaller role than in Britain, privately built but subsidised apartment houses have been used to decant city centre populations, completing and formalising the 'ghettoisation' of the poor. Earlier in the introduction, it was suggested that building forms, as well as the larger built environment, help to maintain social forms. There is evidence in this essay of the widespread existence of perceptions that apartment houses connote 'a lack of community' and 'a shallowness of social roots', and in this they apparently symbolise for mainstream American culture a class of people 'living apart'.

III

While the subjects of the next three essays might be seen as being primarily related to the economy, none are mainly discussed in these terms. However, there are other reasons for grouping them together. Though all three types (vacation house, restaurant and office) have predecessors in pre-industrial society, in their contemporary number and form they are all very much products of modern, Western, capitalist–industrial society. As with the vacation house, the proliferation and development of offices and public eating places has apparently resulted from the creation of a massive economic surplus created by industrial capitalism, and it is not without significance that the main development of all three forms occurred at the time of the major growth phase of capitalism, the third quarter of the nineteenth century (Hobsbawm, 1975).

Moreover, unlike the public or state institutions of the asylum, or prison, the vacation house, restaurant and, in part at least, the office are products of the private sector. This has many implications, one of which is that the social function they house has not, in general, as Robert Thorne points out, been the subject of public inquiry, investigation and theorising, at least until relatively recent times. This itself raises interesting questions about the development of society and its man-made environment. Why is knowledge generated, at any one time, about particular social functions and the built forms in which they are housed? Here, the temptations to make massive – and shaky – interpretations are great. If, as Scull, Forty and others argue, the emergence and rebuilding of the asylum, hospital and prison in the late eighteenth and early nineteenth centuries, largely by the state or dominant social groups, was part of the process by which the labour market was organised for capitalist production, can the 'successful' outcome of this process – the creation and investment of surplus

capital – be seen in the development and proliferation of private leisure institutions, with the emphasis on consumption, and the built environment with
which they were connected (e.g. vacation houses, resorts, spas, restaurants,
shops, etc.) in the later nineteenth century (cf. for example, Hobsbawm, 1975;
Pickvance, 1976)? If these observations are far too crude, they none the less
demonstrate the very considerable possibilities of understanding society by
examining its built environment. Why does a new building type emerge at any
one period of time? An eminent architectural historian has deliberately eschewed
the practice of identifying 'firsts' (Banham, 1969), yet as the first example of a
new building form often provides a bench-mark indicating a significant shift in
the arrangements by which society organises its needs, the social importance of
firsts is not so easily dismissed.

There are two further reasons for grouping these essays together. The social
function which these three building types perform were and are easily accommodated in non-purpose-built shells, in the 'anonymous architecture' or building,
the use of which can change overnight. What then, are the other factors that
cause purpose-built environments to emerge? Some of the answers are found in
Frank Duffy's essay.

Some of these themes are taken up in my own essay on the social production of
the vacation house. Drawing on studies in sociology and geography, it attempts
to explain why the modern mass vacation house emerged just when it did and
the social and cultural factors that govern its location and form. In developing
this theme, it might seem to some readers that I go to unnecessary lengths
(though to others, not far enough) to discuss the processes of differentiation and
specialisation that characterise both the development of industrial society and its
physical and spatial environment. Hopefully, however, the other essays will help
to vindicate this discussion and demonstrate the need to develop a more con-
vincing theory linking social development to the evolution of building form and
environment. Someone, somewhere, might indeed be tempted to develop a
'grand theory' which links up theories of society with a satisfactory explanation
of the development of building forms.

One possible entry into this task might be through the analysis of the terminology used at different times to describe buildings, spaces, rooms, etc., at all
levels (King, 1974, 1976; Rapoport, 1976). For example, the subject index of the
Royal Institute of British Architects Library catalogue (Mason and Thompson,
1968) lists over a thousand terms, from abattoirs to zoos, describing building
forms that have identifiable, culturally significant differences; a quick glance
through these enabled almost all to be readily associated with one of six basic
social institutions. The architectural profession itself uses a taxonomy (SFB
Index) of ten basic categories subdivided into ninety-nine further functional
divisions. It is often quoted that Eskimos, because of the significance of drifting
snow in their everyday life, have a large number of different terms to describe its

various types. How many names are there for dwellings in Britain, and what are the culturally significant criteria by which they are distinguished? More important, how have these meanings developed over time, and what do they show? In more general terms, how are social and cultural categories reflected in the terminology of the built environment?

One of the main themes explored in the essay on the vacation house is the way in which time is organised in society and then sustained both by spatial organisation and by the built form in which particular 'units' of time are contained. The weekend country cottage is a particular building for a particular time and particular place. This is a theme also mentioned in Rapoport's essay, and, in the way in which mealtimes were reorganised (probably because of the changing spatial organisation of the city), by Robert Thorne. What the study of the vacation house shows is the propensity for society to create certain patterns of organisation, whether social, spatial or temporal, and then to live within the constraints that they impose. In an article predicting the microelectronic life-style of the future ('The Day after Tomorrow', *Guardian*, 17 February 1979), with everything done through silicon chips, the heroine walks along the beach organising a world-wide newspaper with the aid of a pocket computer terminal. It is still *she*, however, who uses electronic robots to do the household chores; and in their country cottage in Cornwall her husband comes home at weekends. Despite revolutionary technological change, traditional values persist (see also Berry, 1970).

Robert Thorne's pioneering essay on places of refreshment has unearthed a wealth of empirical data on a subject where there was virtually no previous research. Because of this, he rightly holds to the historian's brief first to establish a verifiable descriptive account of some of the principal institutions for eating and drinking in Victorian London as a representative modernising city.

As Thorne points out, eating is a universal human activity, yet how, when and what people eat, and with whom, are questions determined by social and cultural considerations: in India, for example, the rules governing commensality are an integral part of the traditional caste system (Mayer, 1960; Dumont, 1972). The major difference between pre-industrial or 'simple' societies, whose eating activity is usually restricted to domestic groups (though with some provision for travellers), and our own is the extent to which public eating away from the home has developed. And where many religions tend to have elaborate regulations concerning social and dietary behaviour, in most societies influenced by Christianity, the factors governing who eats with whom are principally social and economic rather than specifically religious.

Hence, in the rapid development of public eating facilities in the nineteenth-century city, a central question is, what are the most important social groupings within which food and drink are taken, and how does built form provision both reflect and help to sustain these groupings? Most obviously, these are based on social and economic criteria, on gender (with teashops and special types of food for women), on dietary and ideological considerations (temperance hotels, vegetarian restaurants), on religious beliefs (Jewish restaurants) and partially on criteria of ethnicity and nationality (with a vast twentieth-century growth in ethnic/national eating places reflecting the increasing cosmopolitanism of the city). Of interest here is the extent to which economic, social, technological and cultural change promotes new behaviour, new social groupings and new or modified buildings and building types, and how the existence of these helps to institutionalise new social forms and patterns of behaviour. These are not just interesting theoretical questions but, in recent years, have become controversial social and political ones. For example, persistent social divisions are represented in the 'works canteen', 'staff restaurant' and 'directors' bar' or the 'junior' and 'senior common rooms' and 'students' bar'; a recent legal judgment upheld the right of a public bar to refuse to serve unaccompanied women. Non-British patrons of pubs are still intrigued by the taken-for-granted distinction between the public bar and the saloon, or by the age discrimination which leaves adolescent children out in the street.

In recent years, high finance and business mergers have considerably changed both the nature and number of refreshment places, as has, for example, the growth of the business function and 'ceremonial eating' by professional institutions, corporations and other associations. In the ethnography of urban behaviour, the eating place has a central role, whether the 'transport caff' of the Hell's Angels of the 1960s or the Lyons' teashop rendezvous for courting couples between the wars. What social meaning can be deduced (if any) from changes over time in the size, shape and arrangement of tables for 'singles', 'pairs' or larger groups? (Scheflen, 1976; Girouard, 1978).

What are the distinctive social functions served by the English pub compared, for example, to those of the Korean tea-room, Turkish coffee house, African beer-bar or Paris café (Rapoport, 1977, pp. 305–15) and how have changing functions been reflected, over time, in its particular physical and spatial characteristics? How, if at all, are the characteristics of a particular social area, the city centre or commuter suburb, or even the changing day or night-time clientèle mirrored in the design, form and lay-out of refreshment places?

Robert Thorne's essay provides the starting point for these explorations. He shows how, in the early nineteenth-century city, existing social divisions were reflected in the commercial provision for refreshment. With economic and social changes, not least in transport, and the introduction of modern forms of business organisation (the limited company and hotel chain) there was created, for growing numbers of middle- and upper middle-class patrons, the large commercial restaurant. Towards the end of the century, transport changes, suburbanisation, changes in occupational structure (with a large growth in clerical and especially women's employment), new technologies and social movements such as temperance and vegetarianism were some of the main factors that led to modern mass catering and the new environments in which this was contained.

As is evident from the illustrations, Thorne concentrates primarily on the social factors affecting the internal form of refreshment places. In tracing the emergence of the modern restaurant, he identifies a gradual shift from the traditional 'semi-communal' boxes of the old tavern and coffee-house (with their important business function) to the separate tables and chairs of the modern restaurant. Surplus wealth, widening social divisions and an increasing concern with privacy in mid-Victorian London, together with the rising proportion of women patrons attracted to the West End by cultural and shopping opportunities, were probably also responsible. (The shift, from what may or may not have been a more 'collective sociability' of the long tables and benches in the nineteenth-century seaside boarding house to the 'privatised apartness' of the small table and individual chairs in the twentieth-century private hotel, has also been commented on by Walton, 1978.)

In accounting for the development of the elaborate tableware and lavish furnishings of the new restaurants, Thorne examines two representative firms of entrepreneurs who, by 'investing capital, time and initiative for the satisfaction of the needs and wants of the time' (Eisenstadt, 1968, p. 427), made significant contributions to the development of refreshment places. Just what were the 'needs and wants of the time' must be researched elsewhere.

At the close of the nineteenth century, much might possibly be explained by reference to the increasingly elaborate social rituals of the London 'Season' and the celebrations attached to rites of passage, especially the 'coming of age' parties and dances (Davidoff, 1973). One of the most glittering restaurants of the period, the Café Royal, developed in association with the growth in cultural activities (the poets, artists, authors, actors and *bon viveurs*) sustained by economic development (Hobsbawm, 1975). Like the West End shops, theatres, museums and galleries, the restaurant represented a growth in consumption, amply demonstrated by the combination of restaurant and theatre in the innovative Criterion discussed in this essay.

Cities, as 'aggregates' of built form, both reflect and contain social forms, as do the buildings discussed in this book. And as house form is both socially and spatially related to settlement form (Rapoport, 1977, pp. 305–15; 1969, p. 69), so other building types and the social function they contain are related to the larger system of settlement. The development of public eating places, high-rise apartments and the 'country cottage' are all, to a greater or lesser extent, the result of spatial and social forces of city growth.

As the growth of towns marked the transition from an agricultural to an industrial economy, so the growth of offices in these towns characterised the transformation of an industrial to a post-industrial society. The structural shift in the economy, from one where the workforce is largely in the primary sector (agriculture, fishing, etc.), to a concentration in the secondary (industry) and then in the tertiary sector (commerce, administration) is a process characteristic of all industrialising societies. A few facts should help bring this point home.

In 1970, 1.5 per cent of the working population of Britain were engaged in agriculture compared with 22 per cent in 1840 (today, India has about 73 per cent in agriculture and the USSR, about 25 per cent). Of the rest, about 42 per cent were in industry and about 48 per cent in commerce and administration (Hurd, 1978, p. 13). Between 1851 and 1966, the percentage of clerks in the British workforce increased from 1 to 13 per cent (Hurd, 1978, p. 146). In the USA, where the shift from production to service employment has gone much further, the percentage of white-collar workers in the labour force grew from less than 18 per cent in 1900 to over 36 per cent in 1950 (Bell, 1974, p. 134); between then and 1975 it grew to 49 per cent (Armstrong, 1979, p. 64). As a percentage of total employment, the tertiary sector in the USA (trade, finance, services, transportation, government) represented 69 per cent in 1975 (Armstrong, 1979, p. 65).

Such facts only partly explain the emergence of the 'office city' such as Frankfurt, London or New York where, in the latter for example, over 50 per cent of all employment is in office-type, white-collar occupations (Schwartz, 1979, p. 215). A more comprehensive explanation would clearly need to deal with the entire political economy of cities in free market, capitalist societies where land and property speculation ensures the near monopoly of central city sites by business corporations (Ambrose and Colenutt, 1975; Marriott, 1967). Yet failing fundamental technological innovation or equally revolutionary political change (as, for example, has been tried in de-urbanisation policies in parts of South-East Asia), the office is likely to be the most typical work environment of the future, at least in the industrialised West.

The function of the office, like the city itself which was its predecessor, is communication and administration. The development of separate offices, whether in connection with trade, government or banking, is a classic case of differentiation. With the demands of industrialisation and the development of communications (railways, post, telegraph, telephone), specialised management systems arose and specialised offices to contain them. Early purpose-built offices seem to have become increasingly common from the 1840s and in the third quarter of the nineteenth century, the emergence of the central business district in many large cities was already reflecting the increasing dominance of the tertiary sector, finance capital and growing government activity. Bureaucracy, as Weber pointed out, was to become a characteristic feature of modern society (Gerth and Mills, 1977).

So far, few scholars have examined the social and economic development of the office within this framework, though a recent publication (Delgado, 1979) traces some of the social aspects. On other dimensions of office growth and location, there is now an increasing body of literature (see bibliographies in Daniels, ed., 1979). In this essay, however, Frank Duffy, a practising architect and space planner, explores an ares of office developments hitherto untouched – the relationship between the form of office buildings and the organisation they contain.

As implied above, the variables explaining the size, form, location, number and appearance of office buildings are far too complex to be discussed in one essay. But as far as form and internal design are concerned, Frank Duffy looks especially at four factors: office organisation (including theories and the social context of the office), office technology, building technology and real estate practice. To investigate his theme, he takes three pairs of buildings, constructed at intervals of sixty years between the 1840s, 1900s and 1960s, showing how each reflects such factors as the level of economic development, representative types of business, size of organisation, existing levels of technology and prevailing social ideas and theories of organisation. Where the Sun Life Assurance office catered for about fifty people in the 1850s, today's large multinational headquarters can accommodate over 3,000.

Yet more important than mere size is the social basis of office design. In mid-Victorian Britain, what might now seem a stable, almost domestic, organisation was contained (as the illustrations show) in an office building only slightly different from a grand town house in Mayfair. By the early twentieth century, however, the introduction of the ideas of 'scientific management' had brought the rationalisation of space, activity and movement which, combined with technological innovation, introduced a specialised, controlled environment. Office workers were 'plugged in' to a socio-technical system with seats hinged to desks and all technology at hand.

The logical sequence of the 'human relations', social engineering school was the open-plan, landscaped office of the 1960s, with vegetation sprouting from all sides. Giving maximum supervisory power to management and a reduction of individual privacy and autonomy to office staff, it was changing power relationships that put a brake on its further development. With organised staff gaining more control over their conditions of work, current anti-office landscaping and highly cellular projects in Scandinavia are the direct consequence of new participative labour laws. Here, the analogy with the Victorian prison is close: the ideology behind the basic form determines the shape of the building rather than any contribution from the individual architect. The question of office design also raises interesting issues with regard to the organisation of lay opinion (in hospitals, factories, housing estates, institutions of all kinds) against the dominance of professional control (Illich, 1978).

As Duffy points out, we need far more knowledge of organisations, their rise, their corporate images, their cultural differences, to explore the many questions he raises in this paper.

IV

Amos Rapoport's essay on vernacular architecture and the cultural determinants of form provides a fitting conclusion to the collection. In the previous papers, the authors have taken a particular building type and shown how changes in *one* culture resulted in changes in building form and the larger built environment, discussing also the effects of those changes. In these studies there is a comparison of institutions and building form *over time*: though institutions persist, the ideas, activities and relationships associated with them change, leading to change in form and spatial organisation.

This diachronic approach, across time, can be matched by a synchronic approach, comparing institutions and built form across space or, more accurately, *across cultures*. We might, with a somewhat simplistic conception of time and space, say that in the first case we look 'backwards' and in the second 'sidewards'. In this context Amos Rapoport, who stimulated many such comparisons in *House Form and Culture* (1969), here takes further some of the issues first raised in that book and pursued in later writings. Of the numerous insights contained in his essay, many relate to issues discussed by other contributors such as the social meaning of architecture, differentiation in environments and the importance of what anthropologist Mary Douglas simply refers to as *Rules and Meanings* (1973).

Thus, whether the subject is vernacular architecture in general or the spatial morphology of the prison, Indian temple or office, the end product can be seen to result from the application of a set of cultural rules. People build environments to create a particular kind of order: 'a particular set of cognitive schemata or "templates" representing some vision of an ideal is given form'. The tendency of the human mind is to impose order on the world through schemata and naming; thus, as mentioned earlier, spatial categories are often reflected in linguistic categories, and although questions of nomenclature and terminology are not systematically discussed in these essays, some of the authors (Hancock, King, Thorne) refer to them, touching on what are apparently important distinctions for the cultures under discussion.

To understand built environments it is essential to know both the codes and systems which order the environment as well as those which order behaviour; this is as true for making sense of the Australian aboriginal camp as of the Indian temple or Victorian hospital. What Rapoport's essay brings out is that behaviour and environment cannot be separated but form part of a single system. Built environments encode or give expression to a particular set of cultural rules and also influence both social and cognitive environments. How people build not only results from but also influences how people think.

Particularly useful in the context of these essays is Rapoport's comprehensive conceptualisation of 'design' and his discussion of the four elements that he suggests are organised when any environment is being designed: communication, time, space and meaning. 'The specific organisation of space, meaning and time reflect and influence the organisation of communication. Who communicates with whom, under what conditions, how, when, where and in what context, is an important way in which built environments and social organisation are related.' This theme runs through each essay, irrespective of the scale of environment discussed, whether it is the prison cell, hospital ward, asylum, temple complex, apartment house, restaurant, vacation house or office. Each environment, moreover, has a particular social meaning which is often expressed through 'signs, materials, colours, shapes, size, furnishings or landscaping' – a meaning which only makes sense for its own cultural group. This point can be equally applied to the understanding of the late Victorian restaurant interior or to the 'ideal' form of the vacation house.

A persistent theme, then, of this essay is that built environments communicate meaning: to try and understand these, whether in the societies of the present or past, is one aim of this book.

One final point. Where vernacular architecture is created by its users and is easily understood by them, modern or 'high style' architecture results from four separate groups: architects, builders, clients and the actual users who adapt it to fit their own purposes. Historically, this division emerged largely in the industrial period: we see in many of these essays how the development of specific forms of cultural knowledge, created by newly emerging professional groups (doctors, psychiatrists, architects, planners, human relations experts), gave rise to built environments which could not be understood without reference to the beliefs and ideologies of these groups. The industrial and post-industrial building forms discussed in this book are far more complex than the great majority of pre-industrial buildings: hence, an adequate explanation of them requires reference to a much wider range of social and other factors. It is only within this much more comprehensive framework that the development of the built environment can be understood.

Conclusion

The aim of comparative and historical studies is to try and establish what is common to all men as human and social beings and what is unique to them as individuals, or as members of any one society or culture. This is an assumption that underlies this book. The essays have explored not only the possible social explanations of built form but the way in which built form can be used to understand society and its institutions. This approach, and the interdisciplinary context in which it is made, needs further development.

If certain institutions are common to all societies, do they give rise to common building types? If so, how do such types vary from culture to culture? The office block, for example, may be a universal building type in modern societies, yet how does its form and internal arrangements vary between Germany and Cuba, or Canada and Kenya? Many tribal villages may have a granary to store their surplus product, but what is done with the economic surplus in Rome or Katmandu? Is Nuffield College or the Rockefeller Center the modern equivalent of the medieval wool church? Some buildings, such as the menstrual lodge of the Trobriand Islands mentioned earlier, may be almost if not totally unique to one culture, telling us much about the way particular human needs are met. Equally culture-specific perhaps are the purpose-built 'funeral homes' of North America or the English 'club' in ex-colonial societies around the globe.

There are different ways of applying this 'institutional' approach to the study of building form (e.g. King, 1976, chapter 3). For example, one institution and its associated built form (e.g. the family and dwelling) might be examined historically or across cultures. We might ask, whether historically in any one society or cross-culturally with respect to many, which institutional sphere (i.e. the family, polity, religion) catered for which social need. For example, Forty shows in his essay the changes in form and plan of the hospital consequent upon its shifting from being primarily associated with the institution of religion (with ward plans oriented to an altar) to that of the secular control of the state. Likewise, we can examine what has happened to built form provision for education as this particular social need has been transferred from the sphere of family, to the church and ultimately to the state.

How far are buildings instruments of cultural imperialism or simply of cultural control? In many developing societies today, and especially in the rapidly changing oil states of the Middle East, modern, Western-style hotels, hospitals and apartments are being built with the implicit assumption that the ideas, values and social forms that they embody are either already present or will develop. Yet their 'proper' functioning will require appropriate behaviour and the adoption of social and cultural rules which are assumed in their design. In short, it is not just buildings that are imported but an entirely new way of life. The built environment becomes an essential component in the total – and, one may add, Western, capitalist – transformation of the culture.

This, of course, raises other issues. All environments are adapted by their users. In these essays, the emphasis has been on the social production of *new* building types, on innovations produced by social and cultural change. Yet in many cases, changes do not give rise to new building types but are met by modifications in *existing* building forms. These may involve major structural alterations or only slight changes in behaviour or the use of space. What can be understood about a man from the way he reorganises an office, or an organisation that modifies a building? Another collection of essays might deal with such adaptations or, indeed, with the question of permanence. If a proper understanding between institutions and built forms is to be developed, we need to know what aspects of the built environment have changed least over the years. Where do traditional values persist? Despite cut-throat competition in land, the dead are still buried in horizontal rather than vertical positions: though crematoria are more numerous, over the years cemeteries have only marginally changed their form.

What are the stages in the emergence of a purpose-built environment catering for any identified social need? First, the activity occurs at a particular *place*, which may be either an existing building or simply a location on the ground, and then becomes institutionalised. Next perhaps, property rights are established and boundary markers drawn; a form of shelter is constructed, or an existing building is adapted for use. Next, there is a rationalisation of activities, theorising, the construction – to use Rapoport's phrase – of 'an ideal': the environment is 'thought before it is built'. Finally, the particular built form is constructed.

In some cases, the process described may take days; in others – for example, the development of a market place and hall – it may span centuries. Within this process, the problem is to identify the point at which what was previously only an abstraction, present in the form of repeated human activities or as a model in the actors' heads, is translated into built form on the ground. How, indeed, are such abstractions as 'social structure' transformed into physical and spatial forms on the ground (as for example, the social structure of a colonial society: King, 1976, chapter 10)? Such is the social importance of the first example of a new building type: it marks a change in the way society accommodates its needs. Where will be the first purpose-built marriage guidance clinic or women's commune, and what forms will it take?

If one overriding impression emerges from these essays, it is the importance and use of spatial segregation as an ordering principle of social life. This segregation may be at the scale of the room (restaurant or office), building (hospital or temple) or urban area (apartment house or vacation home); it can be enforced (prison), adopted by agreement (office) or a personal choice (vacation house). In different circumstances, it can mean 'solitary confinement', 'isolation' or 'privacy'. Yet, as Rapoport points out in his essay, in different cultures, privacy is achieved in a wide variety of ways, many of them not requiring the use of physical barriers. And how far does physical segregation depend on authority and the concept of property rights?

The importance of technology as an independent factor contributing to the shape of the built environment has not been stressed in these essays. And this is correct. Technology is a cultural product, invented by man to meet identified cultural needs. None the less, changes in technology have also been instrumental in the production of particular built forms, enabling, for example, the enclosure of vast numbers in building complexes or stadiums, and in this way helping to create new forms of social organisation; or in the vertical stacking of human beings in high-rise blocks, creating (as Hancock points out) new ways in which social stratification can be expressed. The transfer of technology between cultures (particularly in the context of 'Third World' cities mentioned earlier) is another important subject, though one far too complex to discuss here.

The essays also suggest the extent to which architecture as well as the larger built environment is used as an instrument of social control. It is not just a question of 'society's' ideas and beliefs being incorporated into built form. True, some ideas and behaviour are shared by *all* members of a particular society (indeed, it is partly these that distinguish them as belonging to the same culture); others, however, are not. The social distribution of ideas, knowledge or values is equally important. On the basis of *whose* ideas, *whose* beliefs, *whose* values or *whose* view of the world are decisions based? These questions can be asked equally about the 'Nightingale Ward', the open plan office, the re-development of city centres or about any aspect of the built environment today; and these, clearly, are questions about the distribution of economic and political power in society, whether this is capitalist or socialist, or in the East, West or South.

What these essays demonstrate, therefore, are some of the taken-for-granted assumptions on which all of us, not just designers or planners, operate. To try and understand them seems important not only for practitioners who need to be aware of the social and cultural assumptions on which their decisions are based, but also for those who teach, write or decide policy in regard to the built environment, as well as those who simply use it. Hopefully, this volume will help provide a more comprehensive framework with which to understand that environment *and* society as a whole.

References

Ambrose, P. and Colenutt, B. (1975), *The Property Machine*, Penguin, Harmondsworth.

Armstrong, R. B. (1979), 'National trends in office construction, employment and headquarter location in US metropolitan areas', in Daniels (1979), pp. 61–94.

Banham, P. R. (1969), *Architecture of the Well-tempered Environment*, Architectural Press, London.

Bell, D. W. (1974), *The Coming of Post-Industrial Society*, Heinemann, London.

Berry, B. J. L. (1970), 'The geography of the United States in the year 2000', *Transactions of the Institute of British Geographers*, vol. 51, pp. 21–54.

Bierstedt, R. *et al.* (1964), *Modern Social Science*, McGraw-Hill, London.

Castells, M. (1977), *The Urban Question*, Edward Arnold, London.

Castells, M. (1978), *City, Class and Power*, Macmillan, London.

Cooney, E. W. (1974), 'High flats in local authority housing in England and Wales since 1945', in Sutcliffe (1974), pp. 151–80.

Daniels, P. W. (ed.) (1979), *Spatial Patterns of Office Growth and Location*, John Wiley, Chichester/New York.

Davidoff, L. (1973), *The Best Circles. Society, Etiquette and the Season*, Croom Helm, London.

Delgado, A. (1979), *The Enormous File. A Social History of the Office*, Murray, London.

Denyer, S. (1978), *African Traditional Architecture*, Heinemann, London.

Douglas, M. (1973), *Rules and Meanings*, Penguin, Harmondsworth.

Duly, C. (1979), *The Houses of Mankind*, Thames & Hudson, London.

Dumont, L. (1972), *Homo Hierarchicus*, Paladin, London.

Eisenstadt, S. N. (1968), 'Social institutions', in *International Encyclopaedia of the Social Sciences*, Macmillan, New York, pp. 409–29.

Evans, R. (1975), 'Prison design, 1750–1842. A study of the relationship between functional architecture and penal ideology', PhD dissertation, University of Essex.

Fitzgerald, M. and Sim, J. (1979), *British Prisons*, Blackwell, Oxford.

Foucault, M. (1973), *Madness and Civilisation. A History of Insanity in the Age of Reason*, Vintage Books, New York.

Foucault, M. (1977), *Discipline and Punish. The Birth of the Prison*, Allen Lane, London.

Gerth, H. and Mills, C. Wright, *From Max Weber: Essays in Sociology*, Routledge & Kegan Paul, London.

Girouard, M. (1975), *The Victorian Country House*, Country Life, London.

Girouard, M. (1978), *Life in the English Country House*, Yale University Press, New Haven, Conn.

Harloe, M. (ed.) (1977), *Captive Cities*, John Wiley, Chichester/New York.

Harvey, D. (1973), *Social Justice and the City*, Edward Arnold, London.

Hobsbawm, E. J. (1975), *The Age of Capital, 1850–1875*, Weidenfeld & Nicolson, London.

Howe, A. (1977), 'The spatial morphology of the reformed prisons', MSc dissertation (Architecture), University College London.

Hurd, G. (ed.) (1978), *Human Societies*, Routledge & Kegan Paul, London.

Ignatieff, M. (1978), *A Just Measure of Pain. The Penitentiary in the Industrial Revolution, 1750–1850*, Macmillan, London.

Illich, I. (1978), *The Right to Useful Unemployment*, Marion Boyars, London.

Jackson, A. A. (1973), *Semi-detached London*, Allen & Unwin, London.

King, A. D. (1974), 'The language of colonial urbanisation', *Sociology*, vol. 8, no. 1, pp. 81–110.

King, A. D. (1976), *Colonial Urban Development. Culture, Social Power and Environment*, Routledge & Kegan Paul, London.

King, A. D. (1978), 'Exporting "planning": the colonial and neo-colonial experience', *Urbanism Past and Present*, Winter-Spring, vol. 5; revised in Cherry, G. E. (ed.) (1980), *Shaping an Urban World. Planning in the Twentieth Century*, Mansell, London.

Larson, M. S. (1978), *The Rise and Fall of Professionalism*, University of California Press, Berkeley and London.

Marriot, O. (1967), *The Property Boom*, Pan Books, London.

Mason, B. M. and Thompson, A. (1968), *List of Subject Headings on Architecture and Related Subjects as Used in the Periodicals Subject Index of the RIBA Library*, RIBA, London (first published 1953).

Mayer, A. C. (1960), *Caste and Kinship in Central India*, Routledge & Kegan Paul, London.

Oliver, P. (ed.) (1969), *Shelter and Society*, Barrie & Jenkins, London.

Oliver, P. (ed.) (1973), *Shelter in Africa*, Barrie & Jenkins, London.

Oliver, P. (ed.) (1975), *Shelter, Sign and Symbol*, Barrie & Jenkins, London.

Pahl, R. E. (1975), *Whose City?*, Penguin, Harmondsworth.

Pevsner, N. (1976), *A History of Building Types*, Thames & Hudson, London.

Pickvance, C. G. (ed.) (1976), *Urban Sociology. Critical Essays*, Tavistock, London.

Rapoport, A. (1969), *House Form and Culture*, Prentice-Hall, Englewood Cliffs, NJ.

Rapoport, A. (1971), 'Some observations regarding man-environment studies', *Architectural Research and Teaching*, vol. 2, no. 1, pp. 4–14.

Rapoport, A. (1976), *The Mutual Interaction of People and Their Built Environment. A Cross-cultural Perspective*, Mouton, The Hague.

Rapoport, A. (1977), *Human Aspects of Urban Form*, Pergamon, London.

Ravetz, A. (1974), *Model Estate*, Croom Helm, London.

Reid, I. (1977), *Social Class Differences in Britain*, Open Books, London.

Rex, J. (1971), 'The concept of housing class and the sociology of race relations', *Race*, vol. 12, pp. 293–301.

Rex, J. and Moore, R. (1967), *Race, Community and Conflict*, Oxford University Press, London.

Scheflen, A. E. (1976), *Human Territories. How We Behave in Space–Time*, Prentice-Hall, Englewood Cliffs, NJ.

Schwartz, G. G. (1979), 'The office pattern in New York City, 1960–75', in Daniels (1979), pp. 215–38.

Scull, A. T. (1974), 'Museums of Madness. The Social Organisation of Insanity in Nineteenth-Century England', PhD dissertation, Princeton University.

Scull, A. T. (1979), *Museums of Madness. The Social Organisation of Insanity in Nineteenth-Century England*, Allen Lane, London.

Stacey, M. (1960), *Tradition and Change*, Oxford University Press, London.

Strauss, A. L. (ed.) (1968), *The American City. A Sourcebook of Urban Imagery*, Aldine Publishing Company, Chicago.

Sutcliffe, A. (ed.) (1974), *Multi-Storey Living. The British Working-Class Experience*, Croom Helm, London.

Tomlinson, H. (1975), 'Victorian prison administration and architecture, 1835–77', PhD dissertation, University of London.

Walton, J. (1978), *The Blackpool Landlady. A Social History*, Manchester University Press.

Part I

1 A convenient place to get rid of inconvenient people: the Victorian lunatic asylum*

Andrew Scull

Were we to draw our opinions on the treatment of insanity from the construction of the buildings destined to the reception of patients, we should conclude that the great principle adopted in recovering the faculties of the mind was to immure the demented in gloomy and iron-bound fastnesses; that these were the means best adapted for restoring the wandering intellect, correcting its illusions, or quickening its torpidity: that the depraved or lost social affections were to be corrected or removed by coldness or monotony.[1]

Scattered widely across the English landscape, sometimes surrounded now by urban and suburban sprawl, sometimes still incongruously installed in the midst of sylvan countryside, are to be found one of the most notable architectural curiosities inherited from the nineteenth century, the Victorian 'loony bins'. Huge, ramshackle, decaying structures, once hailed as 'the most blessed manifestation of true civilization the world can present',[2] they now apparently exist on borrowed time – a collection of 'doomed institutions' merely awaiting the setting of 'the torch to the funeral pyre'.[3] Not that they go unused in the meanwhile: on the contrary, mental hospital admission rates have seldom been higher. But the number of patients under treatment on any given day falls remorselessly, as the mentally disturbed are processed and discharged at an ever more rapid rate. And as the targets of a mounting attack on their therapeutic failings and harmful effects on those they treat, the asylums steadily lose ground to newer, 'community-based' alternatives.

Still, the association between mental disorder and these grim relics of

* Portions of the research on which this paper is based were made possible by a grant from the American Philosophical Society.

Victorian humanitarianism remains indelibly fixed in our minds. For almost two centuries, madness and the built form within which it has been contained have been virtually synonymous. The link will not easily be obliterated. Nor, I suspect, will the buildings themselves. In this chapter, I shall examine the social forces which lay behind the emergence of asylums as the dominant response to madness, and I shall explore some of the factors which led to the transformation of these institutions into museums for the collection of the unwanted.

Capitalism and the transformation of society

The rise of the asylum forms part of a much larger transformation in social control styles and practices which took place in England roughly between the mid-eighteenth and mid-nineteenth centuries. Prior to this, the control of deviants of all sorts had been an essentially communal and family affair. The amorphous class of the morally disreputable, the indigent, and the helpless – including such elements as vagrants, minor criminals, the insane and the physically handicapped – was managed in essentially similar ways. Characteristically, little effort was made to segregate such 'problem populations' into separate receptacles designed to keep them apart from the rest of society. Instead, they were dealt with in a variety of ways which left them at large in the community. Most of the time, families were held liable to provide for their own, if necessary with the aid of temporary assistance or a more permanent subsidy from the community. Lunatics were generally treated no differently from other deviants:[4] only a few of the most violent or troublesome cases might find themselves confined in a specially constructed cell or as part of the heterogeneous population of the local gaol.

By the mid-nineteenth century, however, virtually no aspect of this traditional response remained intact. In the course of a century or so, a remarkable change in social practices and a highly significant redefinition of the moral boundaries of English society had taken place. Insanity had been transformed from a vague, culturally defined phenomenon affecting an unknown, but probably small, proportion of the population into a condition which could be authoritatively diagnosed, certified, and dealt with only by a group of legally recognized experts; and which was now seen as one of the major forms of deviance in English society. Finally, and of critical importance for my present concerns, whereas in the eighteenth century only the most violent and destructive among those now labelled insane would have been segregated and confined apart from the rest of the community, with the achievement of what is conventionally called 'lunacy reform', the asylum was endorsed as the sole officially approved response to the problems posed by mental illness. Throughout the length and breadth of the country, huge specialized buildings had been built or were in the process of being built to accommodate the legions of the mad.

What had happened to bring about these profound changes? It is frequently suggested that the shift towards institutional modes of handling deviance represents no more than a quasi-automatic response to the realities of life in an urban–industrial society. Supposedly, the sheer scale of the problems associated with the advent of the Industrial Revolution proved beyond the adaptive capacity of a community and household-based relief system, prompting the resort to the asylum and the workhouse. In practice, however, not only is this account excessively mechanistic, but, in addition, no clear-cut connection exists between the rise of asylums and the growth of large cities. The drive to institutionalize the lunatic begins too soon to be simply a response to the problems created by urbanization; and at a very early stage in the process rural areas exhibit a marked enthusiasm for the asylum solution.

Instead, as I have argued at greater length elsewhere,[5] the main driving force behind the rise of a segregative response to madness (and to other forms of deviance, come to that) can much more plausibly be asserted to lie in the direct and indirect effects of the advent of a mature capitalist market economy and the associated ever more thoroughgoing commercialization of existence. While the urban conditions created by industrialization initially had an impact which was quite limited in geographical scope, the market obeyed few such restrictions. Rather, it had increasingly subversive effects on the whole traditional rural and urban social structure – changes which, as I shall suggest below, in turn prompted the abandonment of long-established techniques for coping with the poor and troublesome.

Quite obviously, of course, the origins of capitalism in England lie much further back in time than the end of the eighteenth century. One may trace commercialized production back at least as far as the 1400s, and by 1750 England was already on some definitions a single national market economy.[6] But for all the importance of these earlier developments, it remains incontrovertible that, until the latter part of the eighteenth century, the market continued to exercise 'only a weak pull on the economy' and had only a limited impact on English social structure.[7] This, in turn, allowed the persistence, until well into the eighteenth century, of a relatively unchanging agriculture and a social order which exhibited substantial continuities with the past. The mass of workers were not yet fully proletarianized; and notions of the just price and the just wage co-existed with and at times inhibited market determination of wages and prices.[8] Put another way, though the rationalizing impact of capitalism was present, it operated only within strict limits.[9]

Beginning in the late eighteenth century, however, capitalism broke the social bonds which had formerly held it in check. There occurred a massive reorganization of society as a whole along market principles – a development Karl Polanyi has termed 'the running of society as an adjunct to the market'.[10] The old social order was undermined and then destroyed, and profound shifts took place in the relationships between superordinate and subordinate classes: changes which we may sum up as the movement from a paternalistic social order dominated by rank, order and degree to a society based on class.[11] The sources of this transformation are too many and complex to go into here,[12] particularly since my present concern is rather with the social impact of the process than with its origins. Turning to these consequences, in the first place, the rationalization of production increasingly forced the closing off of all alternatives except wage work as a means of providing for subsistence. And wage-earners, whether agricultural labourers or industrial workers, shared a similar incapacity to make adequate provision for periods of economic depression. Yet employers increasingly convinced themselves that they owed the workers only wages, and that once these had been paid the men had no further claim on them.[13] To make matters worse, one of the most notable features of the economy in this period was its tendency to oscillate wildly between conditions of boom and slump. Thus, for the lower classes, family members unable to contribute to their own subsistence became a serious drain on resources. Such dependent groups as the aged and children became a much greater burden – as, of course, did the insane.

These changes in structures, perceptions and outlook provided a direct source of bourgeois dissatisfaction with the traditional, non-institutional response to the indigent. There were others, however. Most notably, the dislocations of the social structure associated with the transition to an industrial economy led to a sizeable rise in the proportion of the population in receipt of poor relief – at precisely the time when the growing power of the bourgeoisie and their increasing dominance of intellectual and cultural life was reducing the inclination to tolerate this. In the circumstances, the upper classes readily convinced themselves that laxly administered household relief *promoted* poverty rather than relieved it (a position for which they found ample ideological support in the writings of Malthus and others).[14] In its place, they were increasingly attracted towards an institutionally based system. For, in theory at least, workhouses and the like enabled a close and continuing watch to be kept on who was admitted. They could be used to punish idleness. Moreover, their quasi-military authority structure seemed ideally suited to instil 'proper' work habits among those resisting the monotony, routine and regularity of industrialized labour. In Bentham's caustic phrase,[15] they would function as 'a mill to grind rogues honest and idle men industrious'; and in this way the whole system would be rendered efficient and economical.

If the general receptivity of the English ruling class to institutional responses to indigence can be traced to these underlying structural transformations of their society, what in turn accounts for the tendency not merely to institutionalize, but to divide up and categorize the previously amorphous class of the indigent, the troublesome and the morally disreputable? More specifically for our present concerns, how and why was insanity differentiated in this way? The establishment of a market economy, and, more especially, a market in labour, provided the initial incentive to distinguish far more carefully than hitherto between different categories of deviance. If nothing else, under these conditions, stress had to be laid for the first time on the importance of distinguishing the able-bodied and non-able-bodied poor. For a labour market was a basic prerequisite of capitalism,[16] and to provide aid to the able-bodied threatened to undermine that market in a radical fashion and on many different levels. As Adam Smith pointed out,[17] relief to the able-bodied interfered with labour mobility; it created cost differentials between one town and region and another; and it had a wholly pernicious effect on labour discipline and productivity. Instead, it was felt that want ought to be the stimulus to the capable, who must therefore be distinguished from the helpless. The significance of this distinction thus increases in direct relationship to the rise of the wage labour system.

One can see the primitive beginnings of this process even in the Elizabethan Poor Law of 1601, which distinguishes between the able but workless, the aged and impotent, and children. But until much later than this, the boundaries between what today would be termed the unemployed, the unemployable, and the employed remain much more fluid than the modern reader is apt to realize.[18] Moreover, while the Tudors and Stuarts did not scruple to invoke harsh legal penalties to force the poor to work, their efforts were inspired at least as much by the need to defuse the political threat posed by a landless 'army' of vagrants as by more directly economic considerations.[19]

As economic considerations grow in importance, so does the pressure to separate the able-bodied and to force them to work. At first the compulsion to work came through threats of judicial punishment, but gradually this approach was abandoned in favour of an approach best summed up by the Quaker pamphleteer, John Bellers:[20] 'The Sluggard shall be cloathed in Raggs. He that will not work shall not eat.' The superiority of the whiplash of hunger over legal compulsion was clear. Not least, it appeared as a purely economic and 'objective' form of compulsion, a supra-human law of nature. As that well-known humanitarian Thomas Robert Malthus put it:[21] 'when Nature will govern and punish for us, it is a very miserable ambition to wish to snatch the rod from her hands and draw upon ourselves the odium of the executioner.'

In this way, then, the functional requirements of a market system promoted a relatively simple, if crucial, distinction between two broad classes of the indigent. Workhouses and the like were to be an important *practical* means of making this vital theoretical separation, and thereby of rendering the whole system efficient and economical. Notwithstanding the intentions of their founders, however, workhouses quickly became filled with the decaying, the decrepit and the unemployable; and an unintended consequence of this concentration of the deviant in an institutional environment was to exacerbate the problems of handling at least some of them – most notably those who could not or would not abide by the rules of the house.

Among the most important of these were the acutely disturbed and refractory insane. The problems presented by madmen gathered together in an institution were quite different from those they had posed when scattered through the community. The order and discipline of the whole establishment were threatened by the presence of people who, even by threats of discipline and punishment, could not be persuaded or induced to conform. Hence the adoption of an institutional response to all sorts of problem populations greatly increased the pressures and incentives to differentiate among them. Under the impact of multiplying complaints from both administrators and inmates of workhouses, gaols and hospitals, efforts were made to exclude the insane.

Initially, this provided simply an opportunity for speculation and profit for those willing to traffic in this species of human misery. Those involved with 'the disposal of lunatics' increasingly placed them with individual entrepreneurs 'in private dwelling houses which gradually acquired the description of "mad" houses'.[22] Large as some madhouses became, and lucrative as the 'trade in lunacy' often was, few of these places were purpose-built. The resulting structural deficiencies of the buildings, together with the lack of restraints on entry into or conduct of the business, undoubtedly had some connection with the widespread reliance upon chains, manacles and physical coercion to manage patients. Their importance in this respect should not be exaggerated, however. Alongside the profit-making madhouses, and in addition to the ancient establishment of Bethlem (which had been rebuilt in 1676),[23] the eighteenth century also saw the foundation of a number of charity asylums supported by public subscription. And though these institutions were housed in buildings *built* to contain lunatics, here too madness was considered to be 'a display of fury and violence to be subdued and conquered by stripes, chains, and lowering treatments'.[24]

'Lunacy reform'

Beginning in the early years of the new century, however, a movement began to replace the private madhouses and to accommodate those lunatics still housed in gaols, poor law institutions or in solitude, in state-supported asylums. Particularly in its early stages, lunacy reform formed part of a much broader movement of 'philanthropic' social reform characteristic of the late eighteenth and early nineteenth centuries. Borrowing both personnel[25] and ideas from these related movements, it was at first a somewhat confused and ill-defined enterprise. Those involved in it shared in varying degrees a concern to protect society from the disorder threatened by the raving; a desire to simplify life for those charged with administering the local poorhouses and gaols; and an equally unfocused and unsystematic feeling that the insane themselves deserved to be treated in a more 'humane' fashion; but they possessed no clear ideological vision of what could or should be put in their place. This lack of clarity was evident both in the first parliamentary inquiry the reformers instituted into the treatment of the insane, which at once found little but insufficient institutional provision to complain about and bestowed considerable praise on precisely the existing madhouses and asylums the reformers were shortly to criticize so vehemently;[26] and in the vague, weak permissive legislation of 1808 which the reformers then secured. Counties were now allowed (although not required) to provide asylum accommodation at public expense; but even the reformers appeared to have little conception at this point of why the asylum was desirable or what kind of institution it should be.[27]

Within less than a decade, they possessed answers to both questions. A hitherto obscure provincial Quaker institution, the York Retreat, attracted national attention and provided the reformers with both a model to be copied and an account of the superiority of properly run asylums as a treatment setting.[28] Sharply departing from traditional practices, the staff at the Retreat insisted upon 'the superior efficacy . . . of a mild system of treatment'. External, physical coercion was minimized and, in its most blatant forms – 'gyves, chains, and manacles' – done away with entirely. In its place came an emphasis on 'treating the patient as much in the manner of a rational being as the state of mind will possibly allow'; and carefully designed measures to induce the inmate to collaborate in his own recapture by the forces of reason [29] (Figure 1.1).

The Retreat was an outstandingly successful experiment. It had demonstrated, to the reformers' satisfaction at least, that the supposedly continuous danger and frenzy to be anticipated from maniacs were the consequence of rather than the occasion for harsh and misguided methods of management and restraint; indeed, that this reputation was in great measure the self-serving creation of the madhouse keepers. It apparently showed that the asylum could provide a comfortable and forgiving environment which not only spared the insane the neglect which would otherwise have been their lot, but which played a vital role in restoring a substantial proportion of them to sanity.

Having before them a practical realization of their own half-formulated ideals, the reformers' reaction to conditions in most existing madhouses became one of fierce moral outrage. Since the free trade in lunacy simply multiplied the opportunities and incentives for keepers to maltreat the mad (or so they now concluded), only a system of state-supported, rigorously inspected asylums would allow the extension of the benefits of moral treatment to all the insane. As early as 1815, therefore, they were seeking legislation to secure these ends.

Any such measures, however, threatened a transformation in political relationships whose importance extended far beyond the narrow sphere of lunacy reform. If enacted, it would have set the precedent for a notable expansion of the central coercive machinery at the disposal of the state. Opposition to such a concentration of power at the national level remained, however, extraordinarily widespread and well entrenched at both the structural and ideological levels,[30] with the consequence that it took some thirty years for the lunacy reformers to secure legislative enactment of their plans. (Indeed, they succeeded only after the obstacles to central administration had been confronted and dealt a decisive defeat, not over the marginal issue of the treatment of lunatics, but over the critically important issue of Poor Law reform.) In the interim, the reformers devoted themselves to winning over public opinion, through the periodic exposure of the evils necessarily attendant upon the continued operation of the private madhouse system; and through the development of a steadily more elaborate ideological account of the virtues of properly constructed and run asylums.

Though it was further developed and refined by the newly emerging class of professional 'alienists', the new institutional ideology drew heavily on the York Retreat for inspiration.[31] It was insistently proclaimed that in the successful

1.1 The original building of the York Retreat, opened in 1796.
The domestic architecture reminded one early visitor of 'une grande ferme rustique'. In the early nineteenth century, the institution (at first, with only thirty patients) acted as a model for lunacy reformers.
(from D. H. Tuke, *Reform in the Treatment of the Insane*, London, Churchill, 1892, p. 18. Courtesy of the Wellcome Trustees)

treatment of insanity, the requisite 'means and advantages can rarely, if ever, be united in the private habitations even of the opulent'.[32] In part, this simply reflected the much greater experience of asylum personnel with the shapes and forms of mental disturbance, which allowed them to handle the insane more easily and skilfully, in situations where the well-meaning but clumsy and misdirected interventions of relatives only aggravated the condition. But, beyond this, the public must recognize that 'a private dwelling is ill-adapted to the wants and requirements of such an unfortunate being'. Experience had convinced the experts charged with curing lunatics of 'the improbability (I had almost said moral impossibility) of an insane person's regaining the use of his reason, except by . . . a mode of treatment . . . which can be fully adopted only in a Building constructed for the purpose'.[33] The very physical structure, as this implied, was 'a special apparatus for the cure of lunacy . . .'[34] quite as important as any drugs or other remedies in the alienist's armamentarium. In the words of Luther Bell,[35] a leading American member of the fraternity,

> An Asylum or more properly a Hospital for the insane, may justly be considered an architectural contrivance as peculiar and characteristic to carry out its designs, as is any edifice for manufacturing purposes to meet its specific end. It is emphatically an instrument of treatment. . . .

Designing the purpose-built asylum

Many aspects of the asylum's physical structure and siting contributed to its value as a therapeutic tool. In the first place, Tuke and his followers placed a wholly new emphasis on the importance of classification as a means of control and resocialization.[36] Segregation of inmates by other than social class was largely ignored in the eighteenth century. When John Howard visited Bethlem in 1788, for example, he discovered that:[37]

> The patients communicate with one another from the top to the bottom of the house, so that there is no separation of the calm and the quiet from the noisy and turbulent, except those who are chained in their cells.

By contrast, in the reform institutions, separation was a key management device, the technique which made possible the discarding of cruder, more obvious ways of inducing a measure of conformity from the asylum's inmates. Once 'the patients are arranged into classes, as much as may be, according to the degree in which they approach to rational or orderly conduct',[38] the asylum authorities had a powerful weapon at their disposal with which to prevail upon the patients to exercise self-restraint: '[the insane] quickly perceive, or if not, they are informed on the first occasion, that their treatment depends in great measure on their conduct.'[39] If a patient misbehaved, he was simply demoted to a level where 'this conduct is routinely dealt with and to a degree allowed', but where the available social amenities were sharply curtailed. Only by exhibiting a suitable willingness to control his disagreeable propensities was he allowed to obtain his former privileges, always with the implied threat that their grant was purely conditional and subject to revocation. As Goffman has pointed out, 'What we find here (and do not on the outside) is a very model of what psychologists might call a learning situation – all hinged on the process of an admitted giving in.'[40] The importance of this as a mechanism for controlling the uncontrollable is perhaps indicated by the persistent employment of architecture to permit classification, long after its use for the other purposes the reformers had in mind had been abandoned. (Figure 1.2).

For beyond the utility of physical barriers to enforce moral divisions in the patient population, the building's design was important for the reformers in countless other ways. Their ideal institution was to be a home, where the patient was known and treated as an individual, where his mind was constantly stimulated and encouraged to return to its 'natural' state. Such a nicely calibrated treatment could be administered only in an institution of manageable size. The Retreat itself had begun with only thirty patients, though later expansion almost doubled that number. For the new pauper asylums to be built at public expense, it was felt that these standards could be relaxed, though not by much. 'It is evident,' said Ellis,[41]

> that for the patients to have all the care they require, there should never be more than can, with comfort, be attended to: from 100 to 120, are as many as ought to be in any one house; where they are beyond that the individual cases cease to excite the attention they ought; and if once that is the case, not one half the good can be expected to result.

Others thought that the number might be raised to 200, or even 250, but all the

1.2 Ground floor plan of the Claybury County Asylum at Woodford, Essex, begun 1887. (Opposite page)
The Claybury Asylum was designed for 2,000 patients. In addition to its four 'curative' asylums (of which this was one), Middlesex also made use of two asylums for incurables at Caterham and Leavesden (Figures 1.6, 1.7), each taking approximately 2,500 patients. As with the hospital and prison, the architecture of the asylum developed in association with the system of classifying and organising the inmates.
(based on drawings from *The Builder*, vol. 57, 23 November 1889 and H. C. Burdett, *Hospitals and Asylums of the World*, London, Churchill, 1893, p. 158)

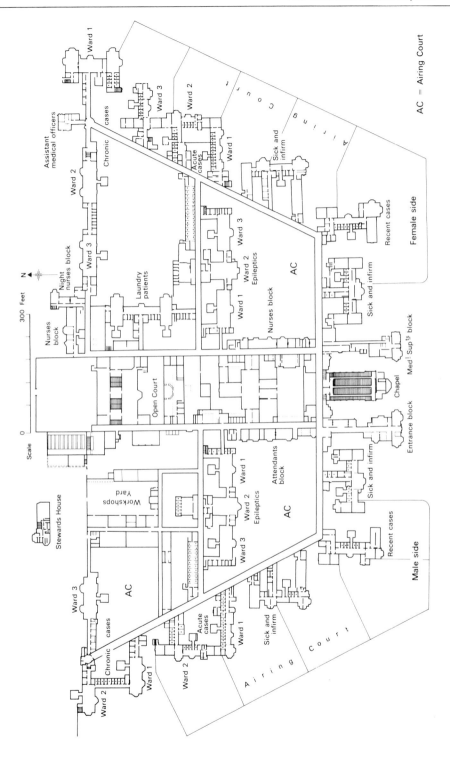

major authorities agreed that it should not rise beyond this point.[42]

The building itself should emphasize as little as possible the idea of imprisonment or confinement. It should be sited where the patients could enjoy the benefits of fresh, bracing country air, and where there was an extensive and pleasing view of the surrounding countryside to divert the mind from its morbid fantasies. The insane were very sensitive to their surroundings, and though 'some have been disposed to contemn as superfluous the attention paid to the lesser feelings of the patients, there is great reason to believe it has been of considerable advantage'.[43] It was thus not an extravagance to design and build institutions which emphasized cheerfulness by being aesthetically pleasing. The architect could help to secure these ends even through small and apparently insignificant details: for example, by substituting iron for wooden frames in the sash windows, security could be maintained without the need for iron bars.[44] Similarly, patients ought to be able to change rooms in the course of the day to get a change of scenery, and provision ought always to be made for extensive grounds to be attached to an asylum. These features would allow scope for recreation and harmless diversions, the kinds of mental and physical stimulation which would counteract the tendency of insanity to degenerate into outright fatuity.

'Monasteries of the mad'

Such utopian reveries bore little relationship to reality. During the first twenty years after the passage of the permissive County Asylums Act of 1808, the ten asylums built were all of moderate size, averaging 115 inmates each. (Cheshire County Asylum, built for 110 patients (Figure 1.3) is typical of the asylums built in this period.) Thereafter, however, county asylums rapidly and inexorably grew ever larger. By the mid-1840s, the average size was in the region of 300 inmates; the Lancashire Asylum contained over 600 inmates; and the Middlesex Asylum at Hanwell as many as a thousand.[45] Thus, almost from the outset, local magistrates exhibited a profound scepticism about the reformers' arguments in favour of small institutions. Faced with the problem of providing for a horde of derelict paupers, they opted for the concrete economies of scale over the hypothetical savings small curative institutions would allegedly produce.

Subsequent events only stiffened their resolve. Over the last half of the nineteenth century, the number of certified madmen increased dramatically, multiplying more than five times, from 20,809 in 1844 to 117,200 in 1904, while the population merely doubled. In part this massive increase reflected the failure of the asylum doctors to cure more than a fraction of those they treated, with the consequent accumulation of chronic cases. But beyond this, the very existence and expansion of the asylum system created an increased demand for its own services. The availability of the 'humanitarian' and 'scientific' alternative of treatment in a specialized institution operated steadily to reduce family and community tolerance, encouraging the abandonment of the struggle to cope with the troublesome, and thereby inducing both the experts and their public to take a more expansive view of what constituted madness. In Andrew Wynter's words,[46]

> The very imposing appearance of these establishments acts as an advertisement to draw patients towards them. If we make a convenient lumber room, we all know how speedily it becomes filled up with lumber. The county asylum is the mental lumber room of the surrounding district; friends are only too willing, in their poverty, to place away the human encumbrance of the family in a palatial building at county expense.

Even the experts in the magistrates' employ, the asylum superintendents, conceded that a steadily dwindling proportion of this enormous mass of lunatics – drawn overwhelmingly from the lower classes – was susceptible of cure. By 1875, they were estimating that fewer than eight in a hundred of their charges would recover,[47] a prophecy that proved remarkably accurate.[48] The doctors were disposed to blame this not on the bankruptcy of their own therapeutic techniques,[49] but on the failure of their patients to seek treatment soon enough

1.3 Cheshire County Asylum, built 1828.
Accommodating 110 patients, the asylum already looks more 'institutional' than its supposed inspiration, the York Retreat. Within a generation, such small-scale asylums had vanished.
(engraving by Dean after Musgrave. Courtesy of the Wellcome Trustees)

following the onset of insanity, coupled with the deleterious effects of their employers' parsimony. But such complaints, while useful for bolstering the alienists' sagging morale, had no discernible impact on the authorities' actions.

If magistrates were unwilling to spend 'extravagant' sums of money on pauper lunatics, they were still less inclined to do so for *incurable* pauper lunatics. Propelled by the overriding desire to economize, local justices almost everywhere adopted the practice of tacking wing after wing, story upon story, building next to building, in a haphazard and fortuitous fashion, as they strove to keep pace with the demand for accommodation for more and more lunatics. In the weary words of one asylum administrator, 'Once christen the disease insanity, and the cost of treatment shrinks in the public estimation, to less than that of living in health.'[50] Remorselessly, the size of the average asylum grew, climbing to 542 beds by 1870 and to 961 beds by 1900. By the last quarter of the nineteenth century, asylums such as the one at Claybury in Essex (Figure 1.2), the fourth county asylum for Middlesex, were almost commonplace. Accommodating up-wards of 2,000 patients and several hundred staff, these places were 'more like towns than houses' and partook 'rather of the nature of industrial than medical establishments,'[51] but they sufficed to 'herd lunatics together . . . where they can be more easily visited and accounted for by the authorities'.[52]

Despite their failure to live up to their original promise, asylums remained a convenient place to get rid of inconvenient people. The community was used by now to disposing of the derelict and troublesome in an institution, where, as one doctor put it, 'they are for the most part harmless because they are kept out of harm's way'.[53] In other respects, too, confinement provided its own rationale. Why else were lunatics locked up in the first place, unless it was unsafe for them to be at large? Since the public were convinced (not without supporting 'evidence' supplied by the asylum doctors) that 'these establishments are the necessary places of detention of troops of violent madness, too dangerous to be allowed outside the walls',[54] asylums were now seen as an essential guarantor of the social order, as well as an important symbolic reminder of the awful consequences of non-conformity. Reflecting these related demands for 'economy. . . , safe custody, and physical repression', the asylum designers produced a 'bald and monotonous architecture, which has scarcely recognized more than physical necessities'.[55]

Homogeneous in these respects, asylum design did vary in others. In particular, it is possible to distinguish three basic architectural types, though some institutions took on intermediate forms. In the first place, some asylums were what has been termed 'irregular or conglomerate' in construction, by which is meant little more than that they were a hodge-podge of miscellaneous structures, exhibiting little or no unity of style and often composed of buildings of widely varying age. A number of asylums of this sort were housed in buildings converted from other uses. Such was the case at the Suffolk County Asylum, for example. Originally a conversion of an existing workhouse, it opened in 1827; with additions and further remodelling, it was still being used to house over 500 patients at the end of the nineteenth century. Other asylums were originally purpose-built to a more or less symmetrical design and only gradually acquired this higgledy-piggledy appearance. Typical of these last was the Gloucester County Asylum, which by 1890 had grown from its original 120 to some 780 inmates. As its superintendent confessed,[56]

> In order to defer as long as possible the evil day of building a second asylum, all sorts of queer, fantastic additions have been made to the original building, until it now resembles nothing so much as a rabbit warren.

1.4 'Twelfth Night Entertainments at Hanwell Lunatic Asylum', a picture taken from the Illustrated London News, 1848.
The illustration was designed to display the achievements of lunacy reform to the public at large. The group in the right foreground is the Asylum Committee and their guests. Behind them stretches the cavernous corridor which, save on this festive occasion (a Christmas party), served as a day room for male patients.
(from the *Illustrated London News*, vol. 12, 1848, p. 27)

Certainly the most frequently used asylum design, in England at least, was the corridor type. As its name suggests, these asylums consisted of a series of corridors with wards and other rooms opening off them, connected together in wings at right angles to one another, or in echelon. Usually, as at Hanwell (Figure 1.4), these corridors doubled as the day rooms, to which the patients were consigned on being expelled from their sleeping quarters. While some asylums had rooms on only one side of the corridors, others had rooms on both, adding to the problems of securing sufficient ventilation and light. At Colney Hatch (Figure 1.5), built on the latter plan, 'the wards were tunnel-like and dark at the centre, ill-heated, sparsely furnished, and unpainted, with lavatories opening directly into the gallery, and deficient wash and bath facilities.'[57] Here, as in other institutions built on this plan, the central portion of the building contained the main entrance and administrative department, as well as a large centre hall for exercise in wet weather.[58] Regarded on its completion as the most modern asylum in Europe, it was from the outset designed for more than 1,000 patients. In consequence, its wards and passages taken together were more than six miles long. Subsequently, it grew still more enormous: within a decade and a half it had expanded to contain over 2,000 inmates.[59] Contemporaries remarked that the exterior was 'almost palatial' in character:[60]

Its facade, of nearly one third of a mile, is broken at intervals by Italian campaniles and cupolas, and the whole aspect of the exterior leads the

1.5 Colney Hatch Lunatic Asylum, opened 1851.
The original building, with its facade of a third of a mile, accommodated over 1,000 patients on the corridor plan, the second main type of asylum design and the most frequently used in mid-nineteenth-century England. According to one report, its interior was characterised by 'long cold corridors, huge wards, and a general aspect of cheerlessness'.
(wood engraving by Laing, n.d. Courtesy of the Wellcome Trustees)

visitor to expect an interior of commensurable pretensions. He no sooner
crosses the threshold, however, than the scene changes. As he passes
along the corridor, which runs from end to end of the building, he is
oppressed with the gloom; the little light admitted by the loopholed
windows is absorbed by the inky ashphalte paving, and coupled with the
low vaulting of the ceiling gives a stifling feeling and a sense of detention
as in a prison. The staircases scarcely equal those of a workhouse; plaster
there is none, and a coat of paint, or whitewash, does not even conceal the
rugged surface of the brickwork. In the wards a similar state of affairs
exists: . . . of human interest they possess nothing.

'Long, narrow, gloomy and comfortless', each room contained as many as
eight inmates. And from their dormitories and dayrooms the inmates escaped
only for brief periods into 'airing courts [which], although in some instances
carefully planted, are uninviting and prison-like'.[61] The consequences of this
situation were recorded even in the reports of the official supervisors of the whole
asylum enterprise, the Lunacy Commissioners. Such structures were characterized by[62]

the utter absence of any means for engaging the attention of the Patients,
interesting them in any occupations or amusements, or affording them a
sufficient variety of exercise outdoors. Besides a large number crouching
on the floors, many were in or upon their beds, some for very trivial
causes, and some as if they had merely sought relief there from the noise
and monotony of the galleries.

Finally, in the late 1860s, a third basic building type made its appearance –
the so-called pavilion asylum (See Figure 1.6). This was characterized by the
replication of uniform blocks in two parallel rows, each housing between 150 and
200 patients, one row for male patients and the other for females. Between the
buildings assigned to each sex was a third row of buildings, containing the
administration, accommodation for the superintendent and staff, and that
critical part of every well-wrought Victorian asylum, the chapel, in which the
inmates could be brought the consolations of organized religion. The first
asylums of this type, those at Caterham and Leavesden, were identical institutions explicitly designed to siphon off the most hopeless and decrepit cases
from the existing metropolitan asylums. Scarcely any of these 'patients' were
expected to recover, and few did (less than one per cent in an average year).
Here, then, the drive for economy reached its apotheosis, in institutions which
housed more than 2,000 inmates accommodated in huge, barn-like dormitories
of eighty beds apiece, two to a building. As the floor plan reveals (Figure 1.7),
even at the outset each dormitory was partitioned once only, into two groups of

forty beds, with scarcely room for passage between them; and subsequently, they were to be 'adapted' to cram in still more patients. Apart from this barren, featureless room, the inmates' only change of scene was to be removed *en masse* to the building's single day room, 105 feet long by 36 feet wide and 14 feet high – 'home' for some 160 human beings.[63]

Everything was now 'well arranged for the storage (we use the word advisedly) of imbeciles'.[64] The rapid collapse of the asylum's pretensions to provide cure in the post-1845 era had been matched by the decay and disappearance of all the crucial features of moral treatment – those elements which were supposed to distinguish the asylum from the prison. Nowhere was this more apparent than in the physical appearance of these institutions. The cheerful and pleasing architecture, which in the initial formulations of moral treatment was to have played such a vital role in creating and sustaining the optimistic and family-like atmosphere so essential to success, had come to be considered an 'unnecessary

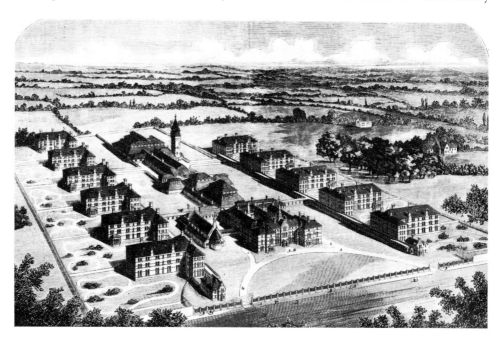

1.6 Design for asylums at Leavesden Woodside, near Watford, and Caterham, near Croydon, 1868.

This shows a typical example of the pavilion asylum, the third basic type developed in the late nineteenth century to provide efficient storage for pauper lunatics. The emphasis on a healthy environment in a 'country setting', as well as social distance from the town, is well illustrated in this drawing.

(from *The Builder*, vol. 26, 25 July 1868, p. 551)

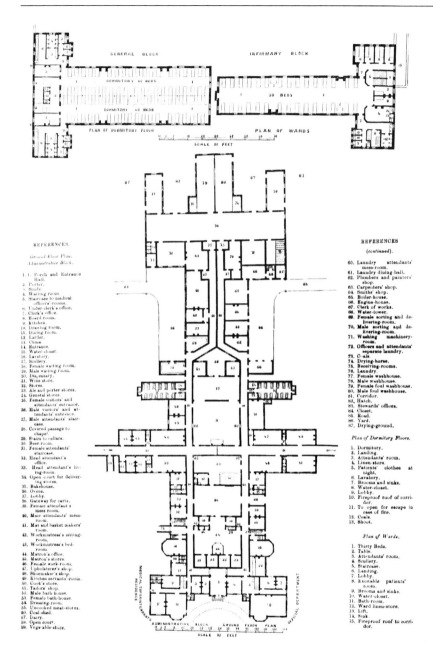

1.7 Floor plan of the general, infirmary and administrative blocks of the asylums for the chronic insane at Caterham and Leavesden, 1868.
Note the spacing of the beds in the dormitories. For lack of room, the patients' clothes were stored outside each dormitory at night.
(from *The Builder*, vol. 26, 25 July 1868, p. 550)

cost', so that the buildings themselves now offered mute testimony to the fact that the asylum was now 'a mere refuge or house of detention for a mass of hopeless and incurable cases'.[65] The distressing truth which thus confronted those who looked back on the work of the reformers in the early part of the century was 'how closely the complaints and aims of the reformers, in the days when there were few county and borough asylums, resemble our own. It is in respect to the very evils these institutions were designed to remedy that they are themselves conspicuously defective.'[66]

Notes and references

1 'Lunatic Asylums', *Westminster Review*, vol. 43, 1845, p. 167.
2 G. E. Paget, *The Harveian Oration*, Cambridge, Deighton, Bell, 1866, pp. 34–5.
3 The words are Enoch Powell's, spoken when he was Minister of Health in the 1959–64 Macmillan Government.
4 A. Fessler, 'The Management of Lunacy in Seventeenth Century England', *Proceedings of the Royal Society of Medicine, Historical Section*, vol. 49, 1956, pp. 901–7.
5 See A. Scull, *Museums of Madness: The Social Organization of Insanity in Nineteenth-Century England*, London, Allen Lane, 1979, on which I have drawn at various points throughout this paper.
6 E. J. Hobsbawm, *Industry and Empire*, Harmondsworth, Penguin, 1969, pp. 27–8.
7 L. A. Clarkson, *The Pre-Industrial Economy in England 1500–1750*, London, Batsford, 1971, p. 22 and *passim*.
8 E. P. Thompson, 'The Moral Economy of the English Crowd in the Eighteenth Century', *Past and Present*, vol. 50, 1971, pp. 76–136.
9 K. Polanyi, *The Great Transformation*, Boston, Beacon, 1957, *passim*, esp. p. 70; Clarkson, op. cit.
10 Polanyi, op. cit.
11 A. Briggs, 'The Language of "Class" in Early Nineteenth Century England', in A. Briggs and J. Saville, eds, *Essays in Labour History*, London, Macmillan, 1960, pp. 43–73; A. Briggs, *The Making of Modern England*, New York, Harper & Row, 1965; Harold Perkin, *The Origins of Modern English Society 1780–1880*, London, Routledge & Kegan Paul, 1969.
12 Among the most important were: improvements in transport and the widening of internal markets; the rise in domestic population and the associated expansion of demand, further fuelled by the growing industrial sector of the economy; and the additional stimulus to domestic food production resulting from the Napoleonic Wars. For further discussion, see E. J. Hobsbawm and G. Rude, *Captain Swing*, Harmondsworth, Penguin, 1969, chapters 1 and 2; Hobsbawm, op. cit.; Briggs, *The Making of Modern England*, op. cit.
13 P. Mantoux, *The Industrial Revolution in the Eighteenth Century*, London, Jonathan Cape, 1928, p. 428.
14 T. R. Malthus, *An Essay on the Principle of Population*, London, Johnson, 1798, esp. chapter 5.

15 Bentham to Brissot, in J. Bentham, *Works*, vol. 10 (ed. J. Bowring), Edinburgh, 1843, p. 226.

16 K. Marx, *Capital*, vol. 1, New York, International Publishers, 1967, pp. 578, 717–33; M. Weber, *The Protestant Ethic and the Spirit of Capitalism*, London, Allen & Unwin, 1930, p. 22.

17 A. Smith, *The Wealth of Nations*, New York, Modern Library, 1937, pp. 135–40.

18 Polanyi, op. cit., p. 86.

19 D. Marshall, *The English Poor in the Eighteenth Century*, London, Routledge, 1926, p. 17.

20 J. Bellers, *Proposals for Raising a College of Industry*, London, 1696, p. 1.

21 T. R. Malthus, *An Essay on the Principle of Population*, 6th edn, London, Murray, 1826, book II, p. 339.

22 W. Ll. Parry-Jones, *The Trade in Lunacy*, London, Routledge & Kegan Paul, 1972, p. 7.

23 Bethlem was a mediaeval foundation which for centuries had been the only special- ized institution for the insane, albeit a small one. In 1632 it contained only 27 inmates, and in 1642, 44. The new building, for about 150 inmates, opened in 1676, and was further enlarged in the 1720s.

24 R. A. Hunter and I. MacAlpine, *Three Hundred Years of Psychiatry*, London, Oxford University Press, 1963, p. 475. One should note, however, that it scarcely makes sense to describe even these charity asylums as 'purpose-built' in the sense in which this term becomes applicable in the nineteenth century. Little connection was seen at this time between architecture and 'cure' – the latter being held to depend primarily upon physical treatments of various sorts. Apart from its uses for decorative purposes or for show (the exterior of Bethlem, for example, was modelled on the Tuileries), the architecture of these places was primarily designed to secure 'the safe confinement and imprisonment of lunatics' (House of Commons, *Report of the Select Committee on Madhouses*, 1815, p. 76), something which led later generations to comment on 'the prison-mindedness of eighteenth-century insane asylum designers'. (The words are J. D. Thompson and G. Goldin's, taken from their recent study of hospital design, *The Hospital: A Social and Architectural History*, New Haven, Yale University Press, 1975; but such sentiments were a commonplace in nineteenth-century reform circles.) It is perhaps of interest to recall, therefore, that the architect of St Luke's Hospital – perhaps the most influential of the eighteenth-century charity asylums – was George Dance the Younger, who was also responsible for the design of the new Newgate Prison.

25 E.g., Romilly, Whitbread, and Wilberforce at the parliamentary level; and Sir G. O. Paul and the Rev. J. T. Becher at the local level.

26 House of Commons, *Select Committee on Criminal and Pauper Lunatics*, 1807.

27 Magistrates were provided with scarcely any guidance concerning the construction or administration of the new asylums, other than the advice that they should be placed 'in an airy and healthy situation, with a good supply of water, and which may afford the probability of the vicinity of constant medical assistance' (Preamble to 48 Geo III c96) – simply an adaptation of John Howard's prescription for the proper site for a reform prison: 'It should not be cramped among other buildings, but should be in open country – perhaps on a rise of a hill to get the full force of the wind, and it should be close to a running stream'. (See R. Evans, 'Prison design, 1750–1842. A

study of the relationship between functional architecture and penal ideology',
unpublished Ph.D. dissertation, Essex University, 1975, chapter 4.)

28 Particularly important in drawing attention to the Retreat, which had been opened
in 1796, were the book by the founder's grandson, Samuel Tuke (*Description of the
Retreat*, York, Alexander, 1813), and its review in the *Edinburgh Review* (1814) by
Sydney Smith. One should note that, though it was the Retreat's experience which
became the reformers' model, the approach adopted here was not unique. A number
of other madhouse proprietors were independently experimenting along similar lines
in this period: cf. E. L. Fox, *Brislington House: An Asylum for Lunatics*, Bristol, 1806; J.
Ferriar, *Medical Histories and Reflections*, vol. 2, London, 1795.

29 Tuke, op. cit. For a critical re-examination of this decisive shift in our characteristic
ways of responding to and coping with the mentally disturbed, and an exploration of
its links to larger social movements and processes, see A. Scull, 'Moral Treatment
Reconsidered: Some Sociological Comments on an Episode in the History of British
Psychiatry', *Psychological Medicine*, 9, 3, August 1979, pp. 421–8.

30 E. P. Thompson, *The Making of the English Working Class*, New York, Vintage Books,
1963, p. 82 *et passim*.

31 The emerging institutions provided on the one hand a guaranteed market for an
emerging profession, and on the other the opportunity for an occupational group to
develop empirically based skills in coping with madmen. The asylums thus formed
the breeding ground for a new group of 'experts' in the management of the mad, first
known as 'mad-doctors', later as 'alienists', and only in the latter part of the nineteenth century referred to as 'psychiatrists'. For discussions of the growth and
consolidation of the English psychiatric profession in this period, see W. F. Bynum,
'Rationales for Therapy in British Psychiatry: 1780–1835', *Medical History*, vol. 18,
1974, pp. 317–34; A. T. Scull, 'From Madness to Mental Illness: Medical Men as
Moral Entrepreneurs', *European Journal of Sociology*, vol. 16, 1975, pp. 218–61; A. T.
Scull, 'Mad-doctors and Magistrates: English Psychiatry's Struggle for Professional
Autonomy in the Nineteenth Century', *European Journal of Sociology*, vol. 17, 1976, pp.
279–305.

32 W. Ellis, *A Letter to Thomas Thompson Esq., M.P.*, Hull, Topping & Dawson, 1815,
p. 8.

33 R. G. Hill, *A Lecture on the Management of Lunatic Asylums*, London, Simpkin, Marshall,
1839, pp. 4–6.

34 Cited in J. M. Granville, *The Care and Cure of the Insane*, vol. 1, London, Hardwicke &
Bogue, 1877, p. 15.

35 Cited in D. Dix, *Memorial Soliciting Adequate Appropriations for the Construction of a State
Hospital for the Insane in the State of Mississippi*, Jackson, Miss., Fall & Marshall, 1850,
p. 20.

36 Wholly new as applied to lunatics, that is: for criminals, classification was the key
disciplinary tool to be used in the new penitentiaries from the time of John Howard
onwards. Here too, therefore, 'The programme of reformatory discipline outlined by
the philanthropists . . . could only be implemented in a building designed for the
purpose. Because reformation relied so much on demarcation and division, to isolate
prisoner from prisoner, architecture was acknowledged to be the crucial factor in
setting the whole process in motion.' Evans, op. cit., p. 179.

37 Cited in Thompson and Goldin, op. cit., p. 69.

38 Tuke, op. cit., p. 141.

39 Ibid. For further discussions of the importance of classification, see, *inter alia*, M. Jacobi, *On the Construction and Management of Hospitals for the Insane*, London, Churchill, 1841; and W. A. F. Browne, *What Asylums Were, Are, and Ought to Be*, Edinburgh, Black, 1837.

40 E. Goffman, *Asylums*, Garden City, NY, Doubleday, 1961, pp. 361–2.

41 W. Ellis, *A Treatise on the Nature, Symptoms, Causes, and Treatment of Insanity*, London, Holdsworth, 1838, p. 17.

42 See, e.g., Jacobi, op. cit., p. 23; *Report of the Metropolitan Commissioners in Lunacy, 1844*, Sessional Papers of the House of Lords, vol. xxvi, 1844, p. 23.

43 Tuke, op. cit., p. 102.

44 At the Retreat itself, the use of this device 'and the garden in front being defended from the road only by a neat common hedge, prevent, entirely, the appearance of a place of confinement': ibid, p. 94.

45 *Report of the Metropolitan Commissioners*, pp. 23–4; 209.

46 A. Wynter, 'Non-Restraint in the Treatment of the Insane', *Edinburgh Review*, vol. 131, 1870, p. 221.

47 House of Commons, *Report of the Select Committee on the Operation of the Lunacy Laws*, 1877, p. 386.

48 Commissioners in Lunacy, *Annual Report*, 1891, pp. 96–9.

49 In fact, however, even in private asylums geared to the upper classes, with no shortage of money, staff or facilities, reported cure-rates declined to abysmally low levels. Between 1880 and 1890 they fluctuated between 6 and 7½ per cent per year of those under treatment.

50 P. J. Bancroft, 'The Bearing of Hospital Adjustments upon the Efficiency of Remedial and Meliorating Treatment in Mental Diseases', Appendix to H. C. Burdett, *Hospitals and Asylums of the World*, vol. 2, London, Churchill, 1891, p. 271.

51 House of Commons, *Select Committee on the Care and Treatment of Lunatics*, 1859, p. 99, evidence of Lord Shaftesbury; J. T. Arlidge, *On the State of Lunacy and the Legal Provision for the Insane*, London, Churchill, 1859, p. 36.

52 J. C. Bucknill, *The Care of the Insane and their Legal Control*, London, Macmillan, 1880, p. 122.

53 Hanwell County Asylum, *25th Annual Report*, 1870, p. 36.

54 Wynter, op. cit., p. 224.

55 Bancroft, op. cit., p. 271.

56 Cited in Burdett, op. cit., vol. 2, p. 61.

57 R. A. Hunter and I. MacAlpine, *Psychiatry for the Poor*, London, Dawsons, 1973, pp. 30–1.

58 In the standard plan, the central structure also contained reception rooms, dining hall, kitchens, and perhaps the superintendent's accommodation.

59 Commissioners in Lunacy, *Annual Report*, 1867, p. 62.

60 'Lunatic Asylums', *Quarterly Review*, vol. 101, 1857, p. 353.

61 Granville, op. cit., vol. 1, p. 154; Edward Pierce, 'Report on a Visit to some European Asylums', *Massachusetts State Board of Charities Tenth Report*, 1873, pp. 114–15.

62 Commissioners in Lunacy, *Annual Report*, 1862, p. 138.

63 *The Builder*, vol. 26, 1868, pp. 541–2.
64 Burdett, op. cit., vol. 1, p. 103.
65 Granville, op. cit., vol. 1, p. 8.
66 Ibid., p. 86.

2 The modern hospital in England and France: the social and medical uses of architecture

Adrian Forty

Hospitals are in some degree the measure of the civilization of a people.[1]

Almost no other type of building has produced more varied and opinionated ideas about its proper form than the hospital. As a result, over the last two centuries, the appearance of the typical hospital has been through a succession of major changes. In the late eighteenth century, most were in large single blocks which superficially resembled mansions. A hundred years later, hospitals were generally designed on the 'pavilion' plan, and, consisting of a number of separate blocks connected by corridors, they were recognizable instantly as hospitals. In the twentieth century, hospitals have reverted to large single blocks, whose closest resemblance is to office or industrial buildings (Figures 2.2, 2.5, 2.8). How can these changes be explained?

Of the several studies of the history of hospital architecture,[2] none deals specifically with the problem of why the form of hospital buildings has changed over time. The customary explanation is that their development resulted from advances in medical and scientific knowledge, but this seems inadequate for several reasons. In the first place, it ignores the question of why scientific knowledge develops at all. Moreover, there is no reason why scientific knowledge should be applied to buildings, or to anything else, unless it is in someone's interest to do so. In the history of society, knowledge matters less for what it is than for the use that is made of it. In the development of hospital buildings, some scientific discoveries led to changes in their design but others did not; equally, changes occurred independently of any revision of prevailing scientific beliefs. This lack of any clear causal relationship between scientific discovery and innovation in building form suggests that more attention should be given to the motives of those who controlled hospitals than to the development of science.

A further objection to the 'scientific' explanation for change in the form of hospital buildings is that it exaggerates the extent to which hospitals were concerned solely with the cure of the sick and ignores their other functions. In practice, hospitals served many other purposes, and for many years effective cure was not the most important among them.

In examining the development of the general hospital in England and France since the mid-eighteenth century, this chapter suggests that, apart from any purpose they may have had in curing the sick, hospitals also served more fundamental social functions. For the eighteenth and much of the nineteenth century, hospitals were dominated by lay authorities. Under this control, they were used to complement the system of poor relief, and were instrumental in introducing a new social morality, now often called the 'work ethic', which attached great importance to self-help and stigmatized the receipt of charity. In the nineteenth century, as medicine developed into an organized and socially powerful profession, doctors started to make use of hospitals to advance their professional prestige and social standing. With their greater influence, the design and management of hospitals began increasingly to incorporate specifically medical ideas, besides the moral principles they had embodied formerly. In more recent times, despite attempts to introduce more lay control, doctors continue to have great authority over the utilization of hospital buildings, although their general management is in the hands of bureaucrats. It is the purpose of this chapter to trace these developments and show how they gave rise to radical changes in the design of hospital buildings.

The hospital and its alternatives

Hospitals represent only one way of dealing with the sick. In China today, where more importance is attached to the treatment and care of the patient at home, hospitals play a smaller part in medical care than in the West. But even within Western society, support for the hospital has not always been universal. Until the end of the nineteenth century, they were almost without exception only for the poor, and it was expected that anyone who could afford to do so would be treated at home where the chances of recovery were much greater. Not only did the middle and upper classes avoid hospitals, but throughout the eighteenth and for much of the nineteenth century objections were also made to their use for the poor. In 1794 the French Legislative Assembly passed a law closing all the provincial hospitals. They were said to be repositories of privilege, inefficient and, because of their unhealthiness, a cause of increased mortality. The intention was to replace them by a national system of domiciliary care which, it was believed, would be more effective, cheaper and more democratic.[3] Although the law never took effect, the argument that hospitals did more harm than good continued to be raised throughout the nineteenth century. The two principal objections were that they discouraged the poor from relying on their own providence in times of sickness, and that patients stood less chance of recovery in them than they did at home.[4]

With hindsight, it is clear that, if the best possible care of every sick person had been a principal goal of European society in the eighteenth and nineteenth centuries, few if any hospitals would have been built until the twentieth.[5] The fact that they were built in ever-increasing numbers through the two preceding centuries, at a rate faster than the growth of population, needs to be explained. Evidently the causes of their proliferation had less to do with their record of therapeutic success than with the other contributions they were able to make to the economic and social order.

The secularization of the hospital

Hospitals had existed in considerable numbers throughout mediaeval Europe, inspired by the Christian duty to perform 'acts of mercy', which included nursing the sick.[6] Some were run as adjuncts to monasteries; others were charitable foundations staffed by nursing orders. None were hospitals in the modern sense, as they were operated primarily to secure the spiritual salvation of their benefactors and of those who carried out the nursing. Medical treatment seems to have been of secondary importance, for they were staffed exclusively by members of religious orders and only occasionally employed physicians.[7]

The purpose of the mediaeval hospitals was to dispense charity. Their fundamentally religious nature was reflected in the composition of the staff and in the form of the buildings. Since as much importance was attached to spiritual comfort as to medical care, a major priority in the ward layout was that the sick should be able to see and hear religious ceremonies from their beds. Normally, therefore, hospitals had large open wards with an altar, and sometimes a chapel, either at the end or in the middle. In Catholic countries, unaffected by the Reformation, this form persisted until the end of the eighteenth century and, in some cases, into the twentieth. In France, the religious character of both wards and staff survived until the Revolution. In 1788 the Charité Hospital (Figure 2.1), thought to be the best in Paris, had, for 208 patients, a nursing staff of fifty monks and novices – but only one physician and one surgeon with seven apprentices.[8] The ward layout was based on the mediaeval principle of providing as many beds as possible with a view of the oratories.

In England the mediaeval religious hospitals were closed at the Reformation, with the exception of St Bartholomew's and St Thomas's, which were put under secular control. When new hospitals were built in the eighteenth century they were financed and run by private individuals whose motives were only to a

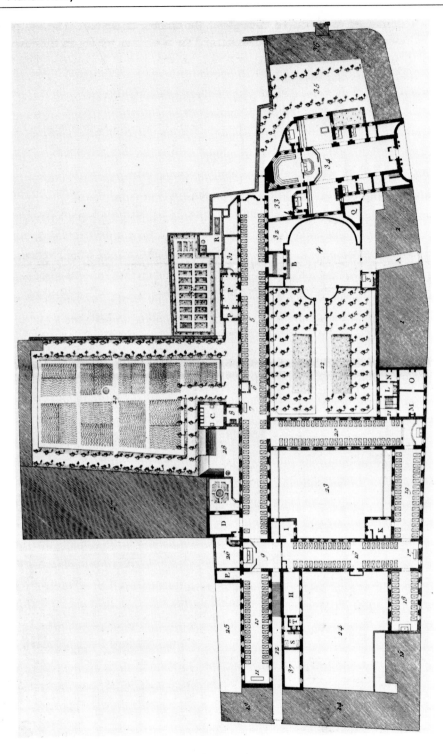

limited extent religious, and they developed a new plan form suited to their secular purposes. In France the secularization of hospitals occurred very rapidly during the Revolution. In both countries, the establishment of secular management was an essential step towards the form of the modern hospital.

The motives for eighteenth-century hospitals: instruments for moral cure

In Europe, and particularly in Britain, the eighteenth century was a period of increased activity in hospital building. There were various reasons for this and the motives of those concerned had considerable effect on the shape of the new buildings.

2.1 Plan of La Charité Hospital, Paris, 1788, from Tenon's 'Mémoires sur les Hôpitaux de Paris'. (Opposite page)
The building dated from the early seventeenth century. The Charité was a religious institution and the need to provide oratories (at *9* and the intersection of *19* and *20*) within sight or hearing of all the patients was an important determinant of the plan. As a result, wards were large and they interconnected; the design was criticised on hygienic grounds by Tenon because of the proximity of the fever ward (*18*) and the surgical ward (*19*), with the risks of cross-infection by infected air.
The key is as follows:

A Main entrance
1, 2, 13, 14, 15, 27, 36 Adjoining houses belonging to the Brothers of La Charité
3 Verger's lodging
4 First main courtyard
B Porch leading to sick wards
5 Ward St Louis, for ordinary fever cases
6 Night duty room
7 Large fixed table
8 Vestibule leading to the room for emptying commodes, called the *Timbre*
C Timbre (or sluice room)
9 Oratory
E Head nurse's room
10 Ward St Augustin, for convalescents
11 Fixed table
12 Passage to the rue Jacob

H Heated room for the sick Here are done certain operations, like cutting for the stone
I Room for the preparation of dressings
16 Ward of the Virgin, for ordinary casualties
17 Fixed table
18 Ward St Raphael, for putrid and malignant fevers
19 Ward St Jean, for the most serious surgical cases
20 Ward St Michel, for ordinary fever cases
21 Closet
K Receiving room, used for heating
L Antechamber to the Father Provincial's apartment
M Meeting room
N Closet

O Father Provincial's room
22 Promenade for the sick
23 Second main courtyard
24 Back courtyard
25 Small courtyard
26 Dispensary courtyard
28 Cleaners' courtyard
29 Monks' garden
30 Botanical garden
PP Rooms for the natural history collection
31 Courtyard of the natural history collection
Q Large water reservoir
R Small water reservoir
32, 33 Small yards
34 Church
35 Courtyard adjoining the rue Taranne, and which connects with the ward St Louis
37 Granary
S Bath for the poor
T Monks' bath

(reproduced by permission of the Trustees of the British Library)

The principles of mercantilism, which dominated economic thinking in western Europe at the end of the seventeenth century, laid great stress on population as the source of national wealth.[9] Statesmen gave considerable attention to the means of increasing population, and, although the principal object was to raise the birth rate, the reduction of mortality was also important. Two Englishmen, Sir William Petty (1623–87) and John Bellers (1654–1725), both argued the economic cost of ill health to the nation, and proposed that hospitals should be established to improve medical knowledge and train doctors who could treat the sick poor in their own homes at public expense.[10]

Concern with the size of population and the need to keep it economically active was not in itself an argument for hospitals. In practice they occupied only a minor part of the schemes to reduce mortality; more importance was attached to quarantine regulations, lazarettos, sanitary police and efforts to establish health care as a function of the family.[11] The wars of the eighteenth century provided a more pressing reason for hospitals. The maintenance of an adequate supply of men for the services was a constant problem when there were not only high casualties but also frequent outbreaks of camp and shipboard fever. The European armies and the British navy were compelled to provide hospitals for the sick and wounded lest they either die or desert, a common occurrence when they were nursed in billets. In England the Admiralty built large naval hospitals at Portsmouth and Plymouth in response to the problem.[12] Probably because the need to secure the rapid and effective recovery of the sick was a high priority, the Admiralty took a much more innovatory and experimental approach to the design of hospitals than the civil authorities of the time. The hospital at Stonehouse, Plymouth, completed in 1762, was designed on a plan at that time unique (it had detached pavilions connected by an open arcade) and appears to be the first hospital design to make use of *medical* ideas. It was widely admired in England and abroad and was regarded, for reasons discussed below, as an exemplary and model design.[13]

However, neither military nor political motives can explain the growth of English voluntary hospitals in the eighteenth century. These were founded and supported by private subscribers who administered the hospitals, appointed the doctors and controlled the admission of patients.

Any explanation for the form of the voluntary hospitals must refer to the motives of the subscribers. Although these varied from place to place, some were common to all hospitals.[14] Statements of philanthropic intent figure large among the acknowledged motives of the founders. However, hospitals were not the only outlets for philanthropy, nor were they necessarily the most effective means of securing the best medical care. This was recognized in some towns where a desire to improve the population's health led to the foundation not of hospitals, but of out-patient dispensaries and systems of home visiting which generally provided more widespread and effective care than any hospital could offer.[15] The question remains, therefore, why, in the eighteenth century, individuals should have chosen to endow hospitals rather than other institutions.

Even if there were such a thing as disinterested philanthropy, the voluntary hospitals cannot be counted among its products. The founders themselves put forward many material justifications to explain their decision. Following Beller's arguments, the desire to advance medical knowledge was often given as a reason. Although hospitals might have served this purpose in theory, in practice doctors (who might have been expected to show most interest in their educational function) did not invariably appear on the lists of founders, nor did they carry much influence (at least not in their capacity as doctors) in eighteenth-century hospitals. While there are exceptions, medical interests seem to have been subordinate to the secular interests of the governors.[16]

It has been suggested that an important motive for many subscribers was the social prestige gained by being a hospital governor.[17] Subscribers had their names associated with the aristocracy who generally headed the subscription lists, and the hospital provided opportunities to appear in company with them. There was also the chance to take part in the management of the hospital, while the right to nominate patients was a useful form of patronage in the local community.[18]

However, by far the most important motive for the founding of hospitals was dissatisfaction with existing methods of dealing with the sick poor. As Andrew Scull has shown in chapter 1 above, one effect of the growth of capitalism was the development of a morality which denied the validity of all other alternatives to wage work as a means of subsistence. To contemporaries, the problem was that this principle, the 'work ethic', conflicted with the two usual methods of relieving the poor at this time, personal charity and the Poor Laws. The Poor Law system was organized on a local basis so that each parish looked after its own poor out of poor rates collected from the residents of the parish. At the beginning of the eighteenth century, the most general form of relief was the distribution of allowances of food or money, but these were criticized because they gave the poor no incentive to seek their own means of support. On the contrary, many people believed that the system encouraged dependency and was a disincentive to work, and, far from reducing poverty, actually increased it. The sick poor presented a special problem for, while care was necessary, since their sickness deprived themselves of wages and their employers and the nation of the wealth created by their labour, it was important not to encourage dependence on relief. The eighteenth-century hospital was developed as a solution to this problem. This is an aspect of the hospital that so far has been neglected by historians, although statements by the founders show that they intended hospitals to be part of a general reform of the poor relief system.

There were two particular shortcomings of the Poor Laws that the hospitals were designed to remedy. The first was due to the Settlement Law which restricted the right to relief to the parish of birth. The rapid growth of London and, to a lesser extent, other cities created the problem of migrants who, if they fell sick, did not qualify for relief. Voluntary hospitals, which could provide care without reference to the Poor Law, were one answer to this problem.[19]

The second shortcoming of the Poor Law was its manner of caring for the sick. From the little known about this subject, it appears that the sick poor occasionally were tended by doctors paid out of the poor rates; alternatively, they were given monetary relief and left to shift for themselves.[20] These practices gave rise to the same complaints held against the treatment of poverty by the Poor Laws: relief was expensive and encouraged idleness, itself believed to be the main cause of poverty. In the administration of poor relief, these complaints led to repeated attempts throughout the history of the Poor Laws to distinguish between the 'deserving' and the 'undeserving' poor. In the early eighteenth century, attention shifted to possible means of testing the authenticity of an individual's poverty, and with this as its object, the Poor Law Act of 1723 was passed to enable parishes to build workhouses and restrict relief to those who entered them. Since the conditions inside the workhouses were to be austere and uninviting, the 'undeserving' poor would be deterred from seeking relief, and the costs of poor relief thus reduced.[21] Although only about 150 workhouses were built under the act, the principle of 'testing' poverty was popular in the early eighteenth century, and it was not surprising that reformers sought to extend it to the treatment of the sick poor. Contemporaries in fact described hospitals as supplements or alternatives to the workhouse, and it seems that hospitals were meant to do for sickness what workhouses were to do for poverty.[22]

The hospital made possible a number of improvements in the administration of sick relief. It economized on the cost of care by concentrating the sick in one place; it could ensure that the prescribed treatment was followed, and it enabled the discovery of malingerers. Above all, the hospital changed the basis of sick relief from a money allowance, which was always in danger of being spent improvidently, to relief in the form of food, medicine and nursing, none of which could be abused so easily. In these various ways, hospitals might reduce the costs of sick relief to the ratepayers, from whose ranks the subscribers came. Since the subscribers also controlled the admissions, they could ensure that relief went only to the 'deserving' sick, who were more often industrious artisans than the totally indigent. Moreover, the austere regimen of the hospitals, similar to that of the workhouses, guaranteed that only the genuinely ill would seek admission. In the Radcliffe Infirmary in Oxford, for example, patients were forbidden to smoke, swear, play cards, dice or any other game; and it was generally recommended that visiting should be limited to no more than twice a week.[23]

By these various means, the hospital acted as an instrument for controlling sick relief; it overcame the faults of money allowances, and it ensured that only genuine and deserving cases received relief. Since care of the sick was necessary for both economic and humanitarian reasons, the problem was to provide that care without disturbing the values on which the developing capitalist society was believed to rest. The hospital solved the problem in ways that the alternative, domiciliary care, did not.

For patients in eighteenth-century hospitals, 'cure' was intended to include not simply physical recovery from illness but also moral reform. As the founders of the Winchester Hospital put it, one of the intended effects of the hospital on patients was that it 'by degrees may recover them out of that profligate State of Life which is the general complaint of these Times, and of the utmost consequence to the Well-being of the whole Kingdom'.[24] Hospitals were designed to educate their inmates in the economic and moral principles which had made it necessary to build them; the generally unattractive conditions inside were meant to teach patients the virtues of providence and self-help. 'Getting better' had more than one meaning in the eighteenth-century hospital.

'Objects of repulsive awe': the design of English eighteenth-century hospitals

In many respects, the pattern of development of the eighteenth-century English hospitals conformed to principles which have been found to apply in later centuries. All the voluntary hospitals were built in towns or cities, though their development did not correspond to the pattern of urbanization in the eighteenth century. The majority were built in older towns, before the rapid growth of the new industrial centres, which were in many cases slow to build hospitals of their own. In their locations, the voluntary hospitals followed principles which have continued to hold true.[25] With the exception of some provincial examples built in or close to town centres to satisfy civic pride, the majority were on sites which were, at the time of building, on the outskirts of towns; these were the places in which it was easiest to assemble sufficiently large plots of land, and where, according to prevailing medical beliefs, there was least risk of atmospheric pollution. Their size was controlled mainly by the size and nature of their funds, and as they relied on annual subscriptions rather than large original endowments, the splendid buildings characteristic of royal or state investment were out of the question. Most began in adapted private houses and then moved to purpose-designed buildings when funds permitted.

Superficially, the design of English eighteenth-century hospital buildings resembled that of Palladian mansions. However, there were important differences. The extensive use of corridors in hospitals made the organization of interior space rather different; and the elevations of hospitals often had several storeys of equal height, unlike the Palladian model, where a high middle storey was sandwiched between the lower heights of the rustic storey below and the attic storey above.

The reason for equal storey heights in the hospital was that the different floors often served the same functions; the upper floor plans often simply duplicated those below, unlike the mansion where the different floors represented different degrees of social importance. Similar considerations controlled the layout of rooms in the mansion. Those nearest the main entrance, the hall and the saloon, were the most public and admission to them carried the least discrimination; the further away from the entrance, the more exclusive the rooms became and the more privileged the access to them. There were often several sets of rooms laid out in this sequence; the rooms interconnected and the principal circulation was through them, although many houses also had corridors as a secondary system for unseen access by servants.[26] In most hospitals, however, the principal circulation was a corridor, and though there were often interconnecting rooms as well, these were merely a secondary system. In the ground floor plan of The London Hospital (Figure 2.2), the building was divided in half by a corridor which connected all the staff rooms on the north side, and the wards on the south side.

The use of corridors was a reflection of the social organization of the hospital: a hierarchy of authority extended down from the governors and their resident member, the house visitor, to the medical staff, the apothecary, the nursing staff, the servants and, finally, the patients. Each group had a separate identity and different requirements, although it was necessary for all to be able to communicate with each other, and for the governors to be able to exercise their authority over everyone. The corridor, offering the advantages of independence, privacy and supervision, made it possible to maintain this complex set of relationships.

At The London Hospital, the committee room occupied the most prominent space in the building, the middle of the first floor. The staff rooms were arranged along the two corridors leading from it in an order which corresponded to the social hierarchy of the occupants: medical staff closest to the centre, and nurses at the end. The wards were all on the south side of the building, and on each floor the access to them was by two single doors at either end of the corridor. Each door opened into a ward lobby from which three large wards of about fifteen beds each gave off; this arrangement made it possible to supervise three wards at once, and to control entry to and exit from the wards. Since patients at The London were often inclined to absent themselves from the wards, and the hospital itself (which was against the rules), the ward lobby arrangement was a valuable means of enforcing hospital discipline. This was necessary partly for medical reasons and partly to make the hospital an effective deterrent against 'that profligate State of Life'.[27]

The plans of eighteenth-century hospitals, of which The London was fairly typical, were designed to serve the governors' interests: they combined adequate

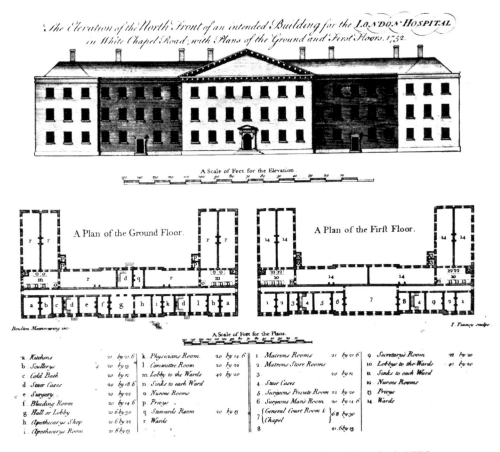

The Elevation of the North Front of an intended Building for the LONDON HOSPITAL in White Chapel Road, with Plans of the Ground and First Floors. 1752.

A Scale of Feet for the Elevation

A Plan of the Ground Floor.   A Plan of the First Floor.

A Scale of Feet for the Plans.

a. Kitchens	21 by 21.6	k. Physicians Room	20 by 14.6	1. Matrons Rooms	21 by 21.6	9. Secretary's Room	12 by 10
b. Scullery	20 by 13	l. Committee Room	20 by 22	2. Matrons Store Rooms		10. Lobby to the Wards	42 by 20
c. Cold Bath	20 by 12	m. Lobby to the Wards	42 by 20	3.	20 by 12	11. Sinks to each Ward	
d. Stair Cases	20 by 18.6	n. Sinks to each Ward		4. Stair Cases		12. Nurses Rooms	
e. Surgery	20 by 22	o. Nurses Rooms		5. Surgeons Private Room	22 by 20	13. Privys	
f. Bleeding Room	20 by 14.6	p. Privys		6. Surgeons Mans Room	20 by 14.6	14. Wards	
g. Hall or Lobby	21.6 by 30	q. Stewards Room	20 by 13	7. General Court Room & Chapel	68 by 30		
h. Apothecary Shop	21.6 by 22	r. Wards		8.	21.6 by 13		
i. Apothecary Room	21.6 by 21						

Boulton Mainwaring inv.   I. Toms sculp.

2.2 Engraving of the elevation and plan of The London Hospital, 1752. (On the plan, North is at the bottom.)

The purpose of this engraving was to advertise the hospital and attract subscribers. The superficially Palladian front elevation of the building conveyed the impression of a fine and noble institution; the rather oppressive mass of the actual building appears much reduced in the illustration owing to the heavily shaded areas between the projecting bays. The plan, not at all like that of a Palladian mansion, shows in detail the way in which the hospital was to work, and in particular, the close surveillance intended over the patients by the ward lobby arrangement at *m* and *10*.
(by courtesy of The London Hospital)

accommodation for medical attention with excellent conditions for what were thought to be its necessary adjuncts, strict discipline and moral reform. There was a similar compromise in the appearance of the buildings. Association with members of the aristocracy was one of the subscribers' motives, and Palladian forms and motifs in the design enhanced this by identifying the patrons with aristocratic taste (Figure 2.2). Ornament, however, was generally eschewed except for the committee room and sometimes the main façade on the grounds that it was a misuse of charitable funds.[28] Consequently, most voluntary hospitals looked austere and institutional, a point not ignored by contemporaries. A description of 1819 contrasted the fine appearance of St Thomas's with that of other hospitals:[29]

> Instead of that heavy sombre appearance, which is so frequently complained of as making a hospital resemble a prison or a place of punishment, and striking a repulsive awe in the sufferers who apply for relief, it [St Thomas's] bears a striking similitude to an agreeable private mansion.

The unlikely combination of the penal and the gracious in the appearance of hospital buildings was the result of the governors' own conflicting motives. On one hand, they desired a fine building, a noble institution that would beautify the town, advertise their philanthropy and attract more funds. On the other, they wished to deter undeserving cases, reduce the costs of sick relief, and moralize the poor out of their habit of reliance on the charity of others.

Doctors in hospitals

Doctors did not carry much authority in hospitals either in England or in France in the eighteenth century. In England the hospitals were run by lay governors, in France by a combination of religious and civic authorities, and these bodies laid down the conditions under which doctors worked in the hospitals. The doctors' lack of influence there corresponded to their lack of prestige in society generally. They had almost no professional organization or identity, and although individual doctors might be respected in society, it was not by virtue of being doctors, but for their personal qualities.[30]

The progress of doctors' status from the lowly position of the eighteenth century to the high social esteem in which they are now held was a long drawn-out process. Beyond saying that doctors first began to show concern about professional status in the late eighteenth century, and that by the beginning of the twentieth century they had become one of the most highly respected groups in society, it is hard to attach many dates to the changes. One difficulty is that over this period the criteria of success for a doctor also changed. In the eighteenth century, the standing of a doctor depended on his ability to maintain the qualities of a gentleman; by the early twentieth century, however, a doctor's reputation rested largely on his record of clinical success. For much of the nineteenth century doctors themselves were divided on which criterion of success mattered most, which confuses the issue further. In general, though, it was true that over that time doctors were concerned with improving their professional status, and they resorted to a variety of means to achieve this. In Britain they formed professional associations which strengthened their corporate power. With the Medical Act of 1858 they achieved legitimation of their status by registration. At the same time, their improved knowledge and skills enabled them to command greater public respect and also, since they acquired a monopoly of a branch of knowledge, made them more able to resist lay interference. All three aspects were important for the improvement of their status in society but it is the last, the increase in medical knowledge and therapeutic skill, that has most relevance to this discussion.

Hospitals played an essential part in the development of medical skills. They provided good conditions for scientific experiment and for the development of the cures that were essential if doctors were to achieve professional, and hence social, recognition. However, to be able to study and cure patients successfully in hospitals, doctors had to have some control over their management. One particular requirement was for them to be reasonably healthy, since the high incidences of cross-infection and mortality, for which many were notorious, were direct obstacles to the doctors' desire to increase their knowledge and skills. Consequently, from the late eighteenth century some doctors became increasingly interested in the application of scientific ideas to hospital design. Their object was to make hospitals healthier, improve the patients' chances of recovery, and thereby enhance their reputations individually and, ultimately, as a profession.

That individual doctors were able to influence the design of hospitals from the end of the eighteenth century is in itself evidence of their growing power and ability to command respect. However, the extent of their influence was limited and generally was confined to changes in the use of space within the buildings and to details of ward layout. Although certain doctors had formulated wholly new principles for the design of entire new sets of buildings, it was not until the latter part of the nineteenth century that doctors gained sufficient authority to have these schemes carried out.

Although hospital appointments in eighteenth- and nineteenth-century Britain were generally honorary and unpaid, they were nevertheless valued by doctors as a means of building up a private practice, as they practically guaranteed a clientele among the governors and their circle. Particularly in provincial towns, a hospital appointment was almost an essential requirement

for a successful local practice.[31] Moreover, as the posts were restricted to quali-
fied men, they were a means of establishing superiority over the large numbers of
quacks who practised in eighteenth- and early nineteenth-century England.[32]
Although the posts were less valued for their medical than for their social advantages, the practice of medicine in hospitals was to have a considerable effect
on the development of medical science and was ultimately to greatly enhance the
prestige of doctors.

Hospitals affected medical science in two ways. They concentrated cases together, thereby facilitating study, and they changed the nature of the doctor's
relationship with the patient. The low status of doctors in the eighteenth century
meant that the private client had considerable authority in the consultation.
Doctors did not normally examine patients physically, and patients were in a
position to dictate the terms of both diagnosis and treatment. Medical patronage
of this type led to a style of medicine since called 'bedside medicine', which was
concerned mainly with the observation and classification of symptoms, and
where experiments were not encouraged. In the hospital, by contrast, patients
were not clients but the recipients of charity, and doctors had more control over
them. This permitted a more experimental style of medicine, for not only could
doctors examine patients freely, but if they wished to watch a condition develop
they could delay diagnosis and treatment; equally, they could prescribe treatment, or undertake surgery, regardless of the patient's wishes. Hospital conditions were more favourable to empirical clinical medicine than were the
constraints of 'bedside medicine', and for this reason it has been argued that
hospitals (particularly those in Paris) played a major part in the development of
modern medicine.[33]

Of the first doctors to propose reforms in the design and management of
hospitals the two most influential were, in England, John Aikin, whose *Thoughts
on Hospitals* was published in 1771, and, in France, J. R. Tenon, whose *Mémoires
sur les Hôpitaux de Paris* appeared in 1788. Both were well aware of the novelty of
doctors taking an interest in hospitals.[34]

The main innovation in their writings was the proposition that the hospital
building itself could function as an instrument of cure independently of the
therapy practised within it.[35] This important principle, which provided the
rationale for doctors to intervene in the design of buildings, dominated the design
of hospitals, as also of prisons, lunatic asylums and schools, for the whole of the
nineteenth century. The idea seems to have originated in the experiences of
eighteenth-century military doctors. In *Observations of Diseases of the Army in Camp
and Garrison* (1752), Sir John Pringle described the effects of different environments on patients, noticing that soldiers nursed in draughty barns or tents
recovered more quickly than those in conventional hospitals.[36] Pringle's discovery of the healthy effects of ventilation was made much of by the prison
reformer, John Howard, and by Aikin, Tenon and others, and it became a

fundamental principle not only for hospitals but for all nineteenth-century institutional buildings. Stonehouse Royal Naval Hospital had been designed as a naturally self-ventilating building, possibly under Pringle's influence, and the same principle appeared in many of the designs proposed for rebuilding the Hôtel Dieu, the major Paris hospital, burnt down in 1772. However, none of those schemes was ever realized, and no hospitals incorporating the ideas were built in France until the 1820s or in England until the 1850s. That it took so long for medical ideas to affect the design of hospitals may have been due partly to the fact that scientific views carried little weight at the time; but the delay can also be explained by the low status of doctors, from whom the ideas originated, by their lack of influence in hospitals, and by the lack of interest among the leaders of the profession, more concerned with their private practices than with hospital work.

Nevertheless, even if medical interest did not succeed in creating totally new hospitals, it did lead to some important changes in existing ones. The principal developments were the segregation of patients suffering from different illnesses, the introduction of smaller wards, the addition of space for out-patient consultations and teaching, and some changes to the internal environment.

One of Tenon's principal objections to the old Hôtel Dieu and other older hospitals was the confusion of different cases, medical and surgical, chronic and acute, in the same wards. In hospitals whose function was care and charity this hardly mattered, but in a hospital concerned with effective cure and the acquisition of knowledge, the segregation of patients with different conditions was important. The probability of cross-infection in an unsegregated ward reduced chances of recovery and made it difficult to give effective treatment or to isolate and study the development of a particular case. The separation of medical from surgical cases, and of different diseases from one another, reduced the risks of secondary infections. Segregation in the large open wards (Figure 2.1) of the old hospitals was impossible except by partitioning, which was unsatisfactory because it interfered with the ventilation; and consequently a major feature of the designs for the new Hôtel Dieu proposed by Tenon and others was the separate wards for different categories of patient. Although the principle was not fully applied in new buildings until later, some attempts at segregation were made, and early nineteenth-century Paris hospitals were organized spatially according to the classification of symptoms.[37] In English hospitals doctors tried to persuade the governors to segregate medical and surgical cases, but were apparently not often successful before the 1820s.[38]

One exception was the Newcastle-upon-Tyne Infirmary. Here, in 1801, the infirmary's progressive physician, Dr Clark, persuaded the governors to replace the large wards, the size of which he blamed for the high incidence of cross-infection, with smaller wards and to segregate patients with different conditions[39] (Figure 2.3). This change was typical of the changes made to hospitals in the first half of the nineteenth century. That the supposedly healthier small wards became more common was the result of certain doctors showing more interest in hospital design and carrying more influence with the lay governors than formerly.

A further reason for the rebuilding programme at Newcastle was to create additional rooms for the medical staff. This development, common to many other hospitals in the early nineteenth century, while in general indicative of the doctors' desire to spend more time working there, was usually associated with two specific causes. The first was to provide space for out-patient consultations which became more common in the nineteenth century. To doctors out-patient work had great value, since besides increasing the number of patients to whom they could offer treatment it extended their catchment of cases from which to learn. Moreover, it was through the out-patient departments that doctors acquired the power, originally denied them, to admit patients. The other reason for the additional space for medical staff was connected with changes in the methods of teaching medicine. Traditionally, doctors were trained by apprenticeship to individual physicians or surgeons, but in the first half of the nineteenth century this system was superseded by hospital medical schools, run by the medical staff. Although generally the schools were accommodated in separate adjoining buildings, clinical teaching required additional space within the hospital itself for students to observe operations and physical examinations. The

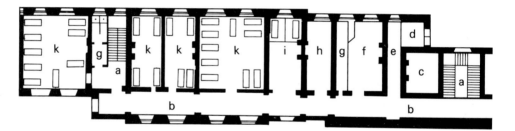

2.3 Plan of the 1801 extension to the Newcastle-upon-Tyne Infirmary.
This extension illustrates the application of at least two ideas held by progressive doctors at the beginning of the nineteenth century: the use of small wards to segregate patients with different conditions, and the isolation of fever patients. The isolation ward was at the left-hand end of the corridor (*b*), where there was a door that was normally kept locked; access to the ward, when in use for fever patients, was from the outside only.
Key: *a* stair-case; *b* corridor; *c* store room; *d* lift for coals; *e* passage; *f* scullery; *g* water closet; *h* nurses' room; *i* dining and bathroom; *k* ward. (based on drawing from Newcastle-upon-Tyne Infirmary, *An Account of the Plan for the Internal Improvement of the Infirmary at Newcastle*, Newcastle, 1801)

creation of new spaces within the buildings for the out-patient and teaching functions anticipated changes in the balance of power between consultants and governors, for it has been argued that it was the conduct of these activities by the doctors that led to the great increase of their authority within the hospitals later in the nineteenth century.[40]

The last main effect of medical intervention in the early nineteenth century was on the internal environment of the hospital. For doctors, one of the main advantages of hospital work was the authority it gave them over patients. In Paris hospitals in the early part of the century patients had to submit to examination and treatment on pain of punishment or discharge. A contemporary description stated that:[41]

> in some hospitals, more or less severe punishments, such as the privation of food or wine, even prison itself, are inflicted on those patients who disturb in some way the established order or who resist the will of the doctor, even when these demands are not immediately relevant to the treatment of their illness. In the venereal disease hospital, for example, where one is accustomed, for the instruction of students, to expose patients of both sexes to their observation, all resistance on this point is rigorously punished.

Significantly, these punishments were for refusal to submit to medical authority and not for the social or moral misdemeanours described in English hospital regulations.

The effect of the discipline was to render the patients powerless, and this sense was enhanced by changes in the internal appearance of the hospital. In the interests of hygiene, reformers recommended improvements to the interiors of the wards. They should be whitewashed regularly, contain nothing but what was strictly essential to the care of patients, have beds of a uniform design (and, in English opinion, without curtains around them); windows should be at regular intervals and of a specified size to allow the best ventilation and, according to some, designed so that they could not be closed by patients or nurses in rebellion against the constant draught of fresh air.[42] The effect of these changes was to give the hospital a distinctly medical setting.

Recent research has shown that when very ill and dying patients are allowed to have personal belongings and pictures in the ward, nurses find it harder to maintain professional detachment and are more affected emotionally by the patients' condition.[43] If clinical surroundings strengthen professional and medical authority, it suggests that, although the efforts of the reformers to set new standards for the ward interior were hygienic in intention and aimed directly at improving the cure, they also had other social effects which were greatly to the doctors' advantage. For doctors, the new environment of the wards, combined with strict rules, increased the value of the hospital by putting patients in a weak position, less able to resist their directions than if they were being treated at home.

All the changes in hospital design that have been described were initiated by doctors. Although doctors relied for their income on private consultations in their patients' homes or in their own consulting rooms, for them to improve their professional and social standing it was, among other things, seen as necessary for them to increase their knowledge and become more skilled at effecting cures. Because of the potential power and freedom it gave doctors, the hospital was a means to these ends, and to make it more efficient ideas based on scientific theory were introduced to replace the religious and moral principles which had dominated hospital design and management up to that time. Before the mid-nineteenth century the actual effects of the medical principles on the design of new buildings were slight, and the new ideas generally appeared only in alterations and additions to existing buildings. Not until the second half of the century did the prestige and authority of the profession rise to a level at which it was able to influence the form of entire new sets of hospital buildings.

The triumph of professionalism: the pavilion plan

With the exception of Stonehouse, the pavilion plan hospital was an invention of the 1780s and first appeared in the designs prepared by doctors for the new Hôtel Dieu.[44] The plan type was the result of the application of medical principles to design, and its introduction depended on the extent to which doctors were able and wanting to influence the design of hospitals. By the last quarter of the nineteenth century the pavilion plan had become orthodox; it was the first type to be unmistakable as a hospital building, and some believed it was the perfect solution.[45] Its supremacy was achieved through the combined aspirations of three professional groups: doctors, nurses and architects. It represented a triumph of professional over lay authority.

The first pavilion hospitals to be built were, apart from Stonehouse, at Bordeaux (1821–9), Beaujon (1837–44), and the Lariboisière in Paris (1846–54). None of these was outstandingly successsful in reducing hospital mortality, but they were admired in England in the 1850s because their design resolved some of the difficulties caused by changes already taking place in English hospitals.

From about 1840 the small wards of the early part of the century began to go out of favour. At the Newcastle Infirmary, for example, the wards built in 1801 were enlarged in 1852, and elsewhere large wards became more common.[46] When the old St Thomas's building was extended in 1840–2 the new wards (Figure 2.4) were lit and ventilated by windows in both walls and beds were

There were several reasons why patients were able to influence hospital environments. As hospitals began to offer a higher standard of medical care than was possible in the patient's home, they became patronized by the rich and powerful. Moreover, from the end of the nineteenth century it became increasingly common for patients to contribute towards the cost of their stay, either directly or through insurance, and this gave them some right to make demands on the hospital. More recently, the nationalization of the hospitals in Britain by the National Health Service in 1948 gave the public, at least in theory, some control over the hospitals.

The widening social class background of patients had several effects. Wealthier patients shunned large open wards where there were patients of a lower social class and an ethos of charity. By the late nineteenth century British hospitals had begun to provide alternative accommodation, usually in single-bed private wards, for paying patients. This introduced a new system of classification into the hospital. Formerly patients had been segregated by sex and ailment; now they were segregated by social and economic status as well. To meet the spatial requirements of this classification, many hospitals gave over sections of the building to private patients or built special blocks. The presence of this class of patient from the end of the nineteenth century greatly enhanced the prestige of hospitals and improved their funds.

It has been argued that the more the members of a society value material wealth, the more importance they attach to good health.[63] If this is so, it would explain the growth of investment in health services in the twentieth century. It does not, however, explain why such a large share of that investment has been spent on hospitals rather than other forms of health care.[64] At least part of the answer must lie with the increased social influence of hospital consultants. Their ability to perform medical wonders, made possible by the hospital facilities, raised their social prestige and gave them power to divert health expenditure into hospitals. Within that system, the greater part of those funds was allocated, through the influence of consultants, not into the improvement of the accommodation for patients but into research facilities and diagnostic and therapeutic equipment, the 'instruments of cure' which provide the means to still greater medical successes and further public esteem.

Typically, within a teaching hospital today there are about three staff per bed. (In comparison, the Charité in 1788 had 0.5 staff per bed.) This enormous increase in the number of staff, due partly to the emphasis on research and technology and partly to the expansion of out-patient work, has had far-reaching effects on the design of new hospitals, as well as on the modification of old ones. Wards, which were the basic units of nineteenth-century hospitals, have only a subsidiary place in the design of modern hospitals and are normally grouped around the medical services which constitute the core of the building.[65] The same need to house the proliferation of medical services explains the landscape of huts and semi-permanent buildings surrounding most older hospitals. These

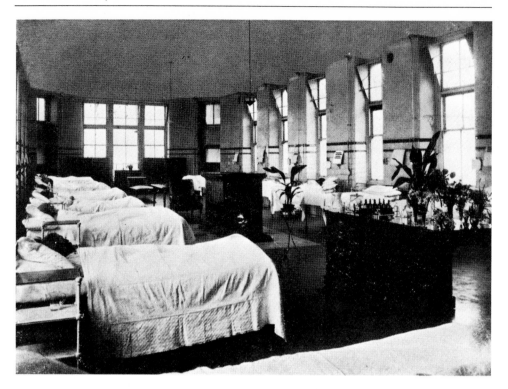

2.6 Interior of a ward at the Glasgow Western Infirmary (built in 1881) shortly before 1909.

The photograph reveals a high level of medical influence on the design: the dado of the ward is lined with easily washable white glazed bricks and the only relieving feature of the otherwise clinical atmosphere are the two aspidistras in the middle. Here, as in most late nineteenth-century hospitals, the doctors' desire for hygiene converged with the governors' social objectives, which were to teach the poor habits of providence and discourage reliance on charity. The result was an environment at once both hygienic but also thoroughly uninviting to the patient. Evidently the photograph was posed: the patients lie rigidly in their beds and the bedside shelves have been cleared of personal possessions.

(from D. J. Mackintosh, *Construction, Equipment and Management of a General Hospital*, Edinburgh and London, 1909. Courtesy of the Wellcome Trustees)

2.7 Interior of a single-bed ward in the private patients' block for the Royal Northern Hospital, London, and photographed shortly after completion in 1935.
The difference between this and the public ward in Figure 2.6 is spectacular. Furnished in the style of contemporary middle-class taste, this ward was intended for patients paying the full cost of their stay (between 5 and 10 guineas in 1935) and shows no trace of the clinical environment of a hospital. It could equally well have been a domestic or hotel bedroom. (from E. C. O. Jewesbury, *The Royal Northern Hospital, 1856–1956*, London, 1956. Reproduced by permission of H. K. Lewis & Co.)

changes, designed to improve the quality of medical care, are not due simply to advances in medical science; their direct cause is the ability of the medical profession to convince hospital administrators of the benefits the new facilities will bring.

Although the major changes in twentieth-century hospitals are the results of medical prestige, it can be argued that at least some of the changes within the hospital have been due to patients' influence. Above all, it was the development of payment by patients as an important source of income to the hospitals that made governors and administrators more sensitive to patients' opinions. Hospitals began to take payments from patients in the late nineteenth century for a variety of reasons: their own insolvency, the growth of a middle class that believed itself above charity but could not afford home care, and the widespread belief that people should not receive something free if they could afford to pay for it.[66] Payment changed the terms of the patients' stay, and in recognition of this hospitals began in the 1930s to remove some of the more obvious marks of charity and make the décor more appealing.[67] In practice, however, the division of patients into two economic groups meant that it was only the private ones paying the full cost of their stay who benefited to any great extent from the attempts to remove the medical ethos (Figures 2.6, 2.7). In public wards, where the professional setting has remained important to the medical and nursing staff, the changes have been more limited and the environments of those wards have continued to be overtly clinical.

This very brief discussion of recent hospital buildings has suggested that, in spite of greater public influence on their management and design, they have remained medical territory. Only with new research would it be possible to establish more precisely the relative importance of outside political pressures, doctors, architects and the bureaucratic management of the hospitals on the form of new buildings. However, the irony has been that wider public patronage of hospitals has led not to greater public control but to more influence by medical consultants: in Britain it was the very measure designed to democratize medical care, the National Health Service Act of 1946, that gave consultants represen-tation on the management of hospitals for the first time.[68] In the two previous centuries hospitals had been administered by lay authorities who had used them

2.8 The hospital as office block: University College Hospital, London, 1895 and 1964. (Opposite page)
On the left is one of the distinctive sanitary turrets of the original main building, designed in 1895 and completed in 1906. The new outpatients' and accident building (1964–71) is in the middle of the picture and resembles more closely the office building behind it than the main hospital. (photograph, Adrian Forty)

to educate society in a new economic morality. In the twentieth century that authority was displaced, not by a new form of lay control with democratic objects, but by the authority of the professions which had both made the reputation of the hospitals and had also made their own reputations through them. The hospital buildings of the last two centuries are surviving monuments to the transfer of power from lay to professional control.

Notes and references

1 J. R. Tenon, *Mémoires sur les Hôpitaux de Paris*, Paris, 1788, p. 1.

2 See J. D. Thompson and G. Goldin, *The Hospital: A Social and Architectural History*, Yale University Press, New Haven and London, 1975; N. Pevsner, *A History of Building Types*, Thames & Hudson, London, 1976, chapter 9, 'Hospitals'; B. Duncum, 'The Development of Hospital Design and Planning', in F. N. L. Poynter (ed.), *The Evolution of Hospitals in Britain*, Pitmans, London, 1964. Although not specifically about hospital architecture, the two following works contain much useful information related to buildings: B. Abel-Smith, *The Hospitals*, Heinemann, London, 1964; and G. Rosen, 'The Hospital: Historical Sociology', in G. Rosen, *From Medical Police to Social Medicine, Essays on the History of Health Care*, Science History Publications, New York, 1974.

3 G. Rosen, 'Hospitals, Medical Care and Social Policy in the French Revolution', *Bulletin of the History of Medicine*, vol. 30, 1956, pp. 124–49.

4 Thompson and Goldin, op. cit., p. 102; Sir James Simpson in D. Galton, *An Address on the General Principles which should be observed in the Construction of Hospitals*, Macmillan, London, 1869, pp. 65–6.

5 Fever hospitals were one exception: by isolating fever cases they did increase the chance of survival for the whole population. On the minimal therapeutic value of hospitals, see T. McKeown and R. G. Brown, 'Medical Evidence Related to English Population Change in the Eighteenth Century', *Population Studies*, vol. 9, 1955, pp. 119–41; T. McKeown and R. G. Record, 'Reasons for the Decline of Mortality in England and Wales during the Nineteenth Century', *Population Studies*, vol. 16, pp. 94–122; T. McKeown, R. G. Brown and R. G. Record, 'An Interpretation of the Modern Rise of Population in Europe', *Population Studies*, vol. 26, no. 3, 1972, pp. 345–82. The negative effect of hospitals argued in these articles has been questioned by E. M. Sigsworth, 'Gateways to Death? Medicine, Hospitals and Mortality, 1700–1850', chapter 5 in P. Mathias (ed.), *Science and Society*, Cambridge University Press, London, 1972.

6 Thompson and Goldin, op. cit., p. 6.

7 Rosen, *From Medical Police to Social Medicine*, p. 287.

8 Tenon, op. cit., p. 35.

9 E. F. Heckscher, *Mercantilism*, Allen & Unwin, London, 1935, vol. 2, pp. 158–9.

10 J. Woodward, *To Do the Sick No Harm. A Study of the British Voluntary Hospital System to 1875*, Routledge & Kegan Paul, London, 1974, pp. 6–10.

11 M. Foucault, 'La Politique de la Santé au Dix-Huitième Siècle', in M. Foucault (ed.), *Les Machines à Guérir*, Institut de l'Environnement, Paris, 1976, pp. 11–21.

12 C. Lloyd and J. S. Coulter, *Medicine and the Navy 1200–1900*, E. &. S. Livingstone, Edinburgh and London, 1961, vol. III, chapters 14, 16 and 17.

13 For a description of Stonehouse, see Thompson and Goldin, op. cit., pp. 142, 146. Also Tenon, op. cit., pp. liii–iv; J. Howard, *State of the Prisons in England and Wales, with preliminary observations and an account of some Foreign Prisons and Hospitals*, 4th edn, J. Johnson, London, 1792, pp. 389–90 (1st edn 1784); and L. S. Greenbaum, 'The Commercial Treaty of Humanity. La Tournée des hôpitaux anglais par Jacques Tenon en 1787', *Revue d'Histoire des Sciences*, vol. 24, 1971, pp. 317–50, p. 342.

14 On the local differences between voluntary hospitals, see C. Webster, 'The Crisis of the Hospitals During the Industrial Revolution', in E. G. Forbes (ed.), *Human Implications of Scientific Advance (Proceedings of the XVth International Congress of the History of Science)*, Edinburgh University Press, 1978, pp. 214–23.

15 Ibid., pp. 217–20.

16 There were exceptions, for example in the person of John Lettsom. See Woodward, op. cit., p. 145.

17 Ibid., pp. 17–22.

18 Ibid., p. 21.

19 Ibid., p. 11.

20 This in inferred from statements by the founders. For example, for Winchester Hospital, see Woodward, op. cit., p. 149; for Bristol see G. Munro Smith, *A History of the Bristol Royal Infirmary*, J. W. Arrowsmith, Bristol, 1917, p. 6.

21 S. Webb and B. Webb, *English Local Government: English Poor Law History. Part 1: The Old Poor Law*, Longmans, Green, London, 1927, pp. 243–5.

22 See the statement by founders of the Winchester Hospital, *An Account of the Establishment of the County Hospital at Winchester*, 1737, reprinted as Appendix 2 in Woodward, op. cit., pp. 149–52.

23 A. G. Gibson, *The Radcliffe Infirmary*, Oxford University Press, London, 1926, p. 195; J. Howard, *An Account of the Principal Lazarettoes in Europe*, T. Cadell, London, 1789, p. 81.

24 *An Account of the Establishment of the County Hospital at Winchester*; reprinted in Woodward, op. cit., pp. 151–2.

25 Webster, op. cit.; the English experience contradicts the theory of a relationship between hospitals and urbanization put forward in R. F. Bridgman, *L'Hôpital et la Cité*, Editions du Cosmos, Paris, 1963, pp. 3–4. On the location of hospitals, see P. Cowan, 'Hospitals in Towns: Location and Siting', *Architectural Review*, vol. 137, June 1965, pp. 417–21.

26 M. Girouard, *Life in the English Country House*, Yale University Press, New Haven and London, 1978, chapter 5. The comparison between the mansion and the hospital made by Thompson and Goldin, op. cit., pp. 87–9, is not borne out by the evidence of the plans they illustrate on p. 89.

27 A. E. Clark-Kennedy, *The London*, Pitmans, London, 1962, vol. 1, pp. 105, 154.

28 Thompson and Goldin, op. cit., p. 87; F. Oppert, *Hospitals, Infirmaries and Dispensaries*, Churchill, London, 1867, p. 8.

29 B. Golding, *Historical Account of St Thomas's Hospital*, Longman, London, 1819, pp. 120–1; quoted by Thompson and Goldin, op. cit., p. 86.

30 M. J. Peterson, *The Medical Profession in Mid-Victorian London*, University of California Press, Berkeley, Los Angeles and London, 1978, pp. 38–9. The following paragraphs on the development of the medical profession are mainly from the same book.

31 Abel-Smith, op. cit., p. 6; Peterson, op. cit., pp. 123, 127–8.

32 *An Account of the Establishment of the County Hospital at Winchester*, reprinted in Woodward, op. cit., p. 151; Abel-Smith, op. cit., p. 6; Peterson, op. cit., p. 34.

33 I. Waddington, 'The Role of the Hospital in the Development of Modern Medicine: A Sociological Analysis', *Sociology*, vol. 7, 1973, pp. 211–24; N. D. Jewson, 'Medical Knowledge and the Patronage System in Eighteenth Century England', *Sociology*, vol. 8, 1974, pp. 369–85; N. D. Jewson, 'The Disappearance of the Sick Man from Medical Cosmology', *Sociology*, vol. 10, 1976, pp. 225–54; M. Foucault, *The Birth of the Clinic*, Tavistock, London, 1973.

34 John Aikin, *Thoughts on Hospitals*, 1771, p. 19; Tenon, op. cit., p. viii; letters from Tenon published in Foucault, *Les Machines à Guérir*, pp. 124, 176.

35 Letter from Tenon in Foucault, *Les Machines à Guérir*, p. 176.

36 Sir John Pringle, *Observations on Diseases of the Army in Camp and Garrison*, 1752, pp. 104–6.

37 F. Dagognet, *Le Catalogue de la Vie*, Presses Universitaires de France, Paris, 1970, pp. 153–4.

38 There were still unsegregated wards at the Radcliffe Infirmary in 1839; see Gibson, op. cit., p. 200.

39 Newcastle-upon-Tyne Infirmary, *An Account of the Plan for the Internal Improvement of the Infirmary at Newcastle*, Newcastle, 1801; W. E. Hume, *The Infirmary, Newcastle-upon-Tyne, 1751–1951*, Newcastle, 1951, pp. 24–31; Webster, op. cit., pp. 220–2. See also Aikin, op. cit., p. 15, on the defects of large wards.

40 Peterson, op. cit., chapter IV.

41 *Dictionnaire des Sciences Médicales*, Pancoucke, Paris, 1818, vol. 28, p. 107; quoted in K. Figlio, 'The Historiography of Scientific Medicine: An Invitation to the Human Sciences', *Comparative Studies in Society and History*, vol. 19, 1977, pp. 262–86, on p. 284.

42 Howard, *State of the Prisons*, p. 183; Tenon, op. cit., pp. 160–8, 186–90.

43 E. Kübler-Ross, *On Death and Dying*, Macmillan, New York, 1970, p. 251.

44 Thompson and Goldin, op. cit., pp. 125–42.

45 F. J. Mouat and H. S. Snell, *Hospital Management and Construction*, Churchill, London, 1883. The entire work was a vindication of the pavilion plan.

46 Newcastle-upon-Tyne Infirmary, *Report of the Deputation of the Building Committee of the Newcastle-upon-Tyne Infirmary, being the result of their inspection of several of the London and Provincial Hospitals*, Newcastle, 1852.

47 Ibid., p. 8.

48 See A. King, 'Hospital Planning: Revised Thoughts on the Origin of the Pavilion Principle in England', *Medical History*, vol. 10, 1966, pp. 360–73.

49 B. Abel-Smith, *A History of the Nursing Profession*, Heinemann, London, 1963, chapters 1–3.

50 F. Nightingale, *Notes on Hospitals*, J. W. Parker, London, 1859, pp. 96, 102.

51 Ibid., p. 16.

52 *Nursing Times*, 3 August 1978, pp. 1279–84.

53 Peterson, op. cit., chapter I. Peterson argues that at the same time a hierarchical division between practitioners and consultants was created.

54 The first major nineteenth-century investigation of British hospitals and their buildings was undertaken by two doctors, Dr J. S. Bristowe and Mr T. Holmes. Their report was published as Appendix 15 to the *Sixth Report of the Medical Officer of the Privy Council, 1863*, in *Parliamentary Papers*, vol. 28, 1864. Dr J. S. Billings was responsible for the design of Johns Hopkins Hospital (see Thompson and Goldin, op. cit., pp. 175–87); Dr V. Poore was responsible for the design of University College Hospital (see W. R. Merrington, *University College Hospital and its Medical School: a History*, Heinemann, London, 1976, pp. 58–9).

55 B. Kaye, *The Development of the Architectural Profession in Britain*, Allen & Unwin, London, 1960; F. Jenkins, *Architect and Patron*, Oxford University Press, London, 1961.

56 Abel-Smith, *The Hospitals*, p. 46.

57 Ibid., chapters, 4, 5 and 6.

58 Ibid., p. 86.

59 Florence Nightingale's influence over the LGB is suggested by Mouat and Snell, op. cit., pp. 71–2.

60 Manuscript letter from Florence Nightingale to Saxon Snell, dated 10 January 1882, in the Wellcome Institute for the History of Medicine, London.

61 *Parliamentary Papers*, vol. 28, 1864, pp. 65, 491, 499.

62 The Nuffield Provincial Hospitals Trust, *Studies in the Functions and Design of Hospitals*, Oxford University Press, London, 1955, should be seen in this context.

63 S. W. F. Holloway, 'Medical Education in England 1830–1858: A Sociological Analysis', *History*, vol. 49, 1964, pp. 299–324, on p. 319; Peterson, op. cit., p. 28.

64 R. Pinker, *English Hospital Statistics 1861–1938*, Heinemann, London, 1966, Table xxxi, p. 149, shows that hospital income, at constant prices, approximately doubled between 1891 and 1938.

65 The disproportionate growth of space for diagnostic and medical services is shown by P. Cowan and J. Nicholson, 'Growth and Change in Hospitals', *Transactions of the Bartlett Society*, vol. 3, 1964–5, pp. 63–88.

66 H. C. Burdett, *Hospitals and Asylums of the World*, Churchill, London, 1893, vol. III, pp. 55, 845–9; Abel-Smith, *The Hospitals*, chapters 9, 21 and *passim*.

67 Abel-Smith, *The Hospitals*, p. 402.

68 Ibid., p. 478.

3 Design and reform: the 'separate system' in the nineteenth-century English prison

Heather Tomlinson

Between 1835 and 1877, the number of prisons either closed down, reconstructed or newly built in England was phenomenal. At the beginning of the period, there were some 230 local prisons; in 1878 there were only sixty-eight. And in the eight years between 1842 and 1850, just over fifty were rebuilt or remodelled: by 1877 a further ninety or so had been altered.[1]

The key to the immense changes during these years was a particular method and ideology of imprisonment known as the 'separate system'. At a time of increasing centralisation of government and the introduction of administrative uniformity in many spheres, it was a system which was to have immense and far-reaching implications. Broadly speaking, the prisons that were entirely rebuilt during this period are those which are still in use today. As a case study in how social ideas were embodied in a particular built form, this chapter examines the separate system prison and the process by which it was institutionalised in nineteenth-century England.

The background

From the sixteenth century the prison began to assume a greater importance in England's criminal law, with increasing numbers of petty offenders being imprisoned rather than hanged, whipped or branded.[2] The old places of temporary confinement – castle towers and dungeons, monastic gatehouses, old mills, town hall cellars, even dwelling houses – rapidly became overcrowded and unhealthy. In the seventeenth and eighteenth centuries the situation deteriorated further: the population rose, criminal activity increased, the number of capital offences was rapidly augmented and, almost equally rapidly, the sentences, when passed, were commuted to imprisonment. With the revolt of the American colonies in the 1770s, the transportation of convicts to the colonies came abruptly to an end; now even more people convicted of crime had to be crammed into the gaols at home.

The movement for prison reform developed in the late eighteenth century out of a revulsion against what were seen as the appalling conditions prevailing in the prisons. These were caused by the tradition of farming out the management of houses of correction to private enterprise, and by the corruption and apathy of the magistrates in control. The results were insecure and fever-ridden prisons, where the inmates used a system of privilege and extortion as their means of survival. At almost the same time as John Howard compiled his notes on the conditions he saw in British and European prisons,[3] Sir William Eden was attempting to examine the structure and principles of English criminal law in order to find a comprehensive plan for its reform. With the researches of these two reformers and the writings of other thinkers in this 'Age of Enlightenment', a debate developed about the nature of punishment.[4] What was punishment supposed to achieve, and what, in particular, was the purpose of imprisonment?

The answer to these questions and the solutions posed varied according to the basic philosophy of the reformer. There were two main movements for reform: the evangelical, represented by such people as Howard, William Blackburn, the architect, and Sir William Eden, and those who adopted the utilitarian principles of Jeremy Bentham. There was, however, a wide area of consensus between the two groups. Both agreed that deterrence was a primary aim of punishment, and both were affronted by what Henriques[5] calls the 'idleness, corruption, drunkenness and profane jollity' of eighteenth-century prison life. The remedies they proposed, however, differed radically. While both aimed at reformation, the evangelicals stressed solitude, reflection and prayer to convert those they saw as sinners; the utilitarians, on the other hand, hoped to create honest and industrious citizens by submitting criminals to the discipline of an industrial and self-supporting prison.

The debate on the virtues of these two approaches continued unresolved throughout the remainder of the eighteenth and the first half of the nineteenth century. Yet new prison buildings were essential, and, stemming from the work of Howard and Blackburn (who concentrated on improving hygiene and ventilation rather than instituting any particular philosophy), forty-two new gaols and 'houses of correction' were under construction by the 1790s. During the Napoleonic Wars, this first major reform movement suffered a setback, but after 1815, and more particularly after 1820, rebuilding began once more.

Many of the new prisons in the 1820s and 1830s were influenced by the classification system, common in the late eighteenth century and officially approved in the new Gaol Act of 1823. The rationale of this system was that different kinds of criminals corrupted each other and hence should be kept apart. Prisoners were therefore grouped not only according to age and sex but also according to the degree of criminality. Ideally, vagrants would be kept apart from felons, felons from misdemeanants, untried prisoners from convicted prisoners, and so on. Debtors, still frequently found in local prisons, were also to be segregated from the rest. Such a scheme necessitated the provision of a complex series of wards, classes, workrooms, dayrooms, exercise yards and sleeping cells. However, as the number of categories or classes of prisoner could be multiplied almost indefinitely, it was simply not feasible to duplicate separate facilities in the smaller prisons which housed only a handful of inmates. This was recognised by the government, for the 1823 Act was applied only to the county prisons and the seventeen principal city and borough gaols. Classification, as a system of imprisonment, was not uniformly implemented, however, even in these major prisons, for the Act did not provide for any means of enforcement. Moreover, new and more fundamental changes were in the air.

About this time, penal experiments which were to have a great influence in England were taking place in America. Two rival American schemes resembling those proposed by the utilitarians and the evangelicals in the eighteenth century came into prominence: the solitary or Pennsylvanian system, and the silent or Auburn system. In solitary system prisons, inmates were kept in single cells day and night throughout the length of their sentences; in silent system prisons, prisoners were congregated and set to work in total silence by day, and were separated in individual cells at night. Soon both systems were being avidly discussed in England, the advocates of each seeking to have them adopted in the existing penal establishments.

By the early 1830s, therefore, the English prison system was in a state of confusion. There still remained the centuries-old gaols such as St Albans, situated in the gate of a monastery where it had been since 1558; there was Louth Borough Gaol, a dark unventilated dungeon 9ft 6in square, furnished with two straw-covered wooden beds and one pail; and there were the two or three dark cells attached to the town hall or workhouse, common in many towns such as Canterbury, Winchelsea, Richmond and Scarborough.[6] In other places stood the purpose-built 'reformed prisons' dating from Howard's era and the post-1823 establishments, many of which had been designed to carry out some minimal degree of classification. Superimposed upon this diversity, and often ill-befitting their physical environment, the varying prison disciplines of hard labour, silence and solitude struggled for supremacy.

The separate system adopted

The solitary or separate system involved keeping each prisoner in his own cell, day and night, except for exercise and chapel services, for the length of his sentence or at least a large part of it. By the mid-1830s, the exponents of this system were strongly in the ascendant. The campaign had begun with the winning over of the major pressure group in penal matters, the Prison Discipline Society. The next step was to gain the government's support and convert influential public opinion. These objectives were achieved through that instrument of 'manipulated inquiry',[7] the Select Committee, which in 1835 came out in favour of the separate system.[8]

However, the then Home Secretary, Lord John Russell, was afraid to go too far too quickly. As widespread insanity and prevalent suicide attempts had followed in the wake of the early American experiments in solitude, he contented himself with framing legislation for 'increasing uniformity in prison discipline', which included the appointment of the first five prison inspectors. Two of these, William Crawford and William Whitworth Russell, staunch representatives of prevailing evangelical ideas, were to be instrumental in getting the separate scheme adopted. Crawford, the foremost among these five,[9] was a prominent member of the Prison Discipline Society and had been a confirmed enthusiast for the solitary system ever since his visit to the Eastern Penitentiary, Philadelphia, in 1833. For the rest of their lives, Crawford and Russell dedicated themselves to the establishment of the separate system in England, even though its implementation involved reconstructing nearly every prison in the country at enormous cost. What they wanted was efficiency and economy. What is money, they argued, compared with morals, religion, civilisation and public security? The forty-two cellular prisons dating from the nineteenth century still in use today bear witness to their achievement.

One reason for Crawford and Russell's success was their total confidence in the cause. They knew, with a certainty and optimism lacking in later reformers, that the separate system could cure all criminal ills. They saw crime increasing at a frightening pace in newly industrialising England, and the growing passion for collecting statistics apparently proved it.[10] The most readily available area for its containment seemed to be at the punishment stage. In the inspectors' opinion, the answer was to improve prison discipline by ensuring that it embodied four essential principles: the protection of the untried and possibly innocent prisoner from contact with the convicted; the prevention of cross-fertilisation of criminal ideas; deterrence; and, most importantly and optimistically of all, the reformation of as many wrong-doers as possible.[11]

True, there were other prison systems which sought to attain some or all of these ends, but according to Crawford and Russell they were doomed to failure. Classification, it was argued, could never be foolproof. A hardened criminal, for example, might be convicted for a comparatively minor offence and thus serve his sentence among young first-time offenders who would be corrupted by his influence; moreover, reformation was impossible while prisoners lived in association, for any good effect the chaplain might have on an inmate would be immediately undone by the ridicule of his fellows.

The silent system, by forbidding all conversation between prisoners, was devised to eradicate the defect of contamination. The inspectors, however, thought that it was impossible to prevent all communication and this was demonstrated by the high number of punishments meted out in such prisons for the breaking of the silence rules.

The system of hard labour was similarly dismissed, despite claims that the 'habits of industry' enforced in prison would become second nature to the criminal. In the first place, the inspectors suspected that prison officials were influenced more by the cash profits to be gained by industrial labour than by any moral benefit bestowed by the system. They deemed the drawbacks of hard labour, moreover, to be great: for example, profitable labour could not easily be organised in single cells, so prisoners generally worked in association, with the inevitable contamination which that implied; equally important, hard labour left little time for religious instruction and introspection, and so minimised the possibility of reformation.

Worse than industrial labour was the system of 'useless' hard labour, such as the hours spent on the treadwheel or turning a capstan. The theory was that such labour, being valueless and known by the prisoner to be so, would be more irksome and therefore more of a deterrent. Crawford and Russell, however, believed that such a regime would merely build up insupportable resentment in the criminal, and would result in violence rather than reform.

Only the separate system – keeping each prisoner alone in his cell throughout his sentence – could fulfil the requirements of good prison discipline. An untried prisoner would never have to see or mix with the convicted ones, and the first-time offender would not be contaminated or further corrupted by the company of evil-doers. The deterrent nature of solitude was undeniable, especially for criminals who, it was thought, relied heavily on the support and encouragement of their fellows. Most important of all, at a time when evangelical religious fervour was at its height, the separate system was seen to provide the optimum conditions for reformation. The bases of this assumption were moral and religious.

Nowhere was this more forcefully expressed than in the review of a book by John Thomas Burt, chaplain of Pentonville:[12]

> The first hours of the cell are hours of great anguish; all the stimulants of crime are gone, there is no voice nor fellowship in the passionless walls, no sympathy, no love, no hate, nothing present but the past; how can the mind resist and not be subdued? Then arise the cravings of the social instinct: the trade-master's hour of lesson, the visit of the minister of religion, the chapel with its common worship, the school with its common instruction, are privileges not lightly to be forfeited. The heart imperceptibly yields up its impurities and is cleansed. Kindness compels belief and gratitude, many a casual word gives issue to feelings long concealed under the lava-crust of vice.

Here, in the separate cell, a prisoner had time and peace for religion and was most susceptible to the chaplain's ministrations: 'In the quiet of the prison cell and when humbled by correction, the warnings, promises and consolation of the gospel come home to the conscience with redoubled force.'[13]

Moreover, separation not only reformed, it also deterred. 'There is nothing so terrible and so effectual in its tendency to deter as solitude', declared Crawford. Russell agreed: 'The greatest deterrent is strict solitude with religious instruction.'[14]

Solitude gave the prisoner the opportunity to reflect on his misdeeds. It excluded all distractions – save the presence of a Bible in each cell – and therefore left no alternative to introspection. It was likely to break down a rebellious spirit, leaving a mind more receptive to the ministrations of the chaplain, whose importance in the prison was next only, if not equal, to the governor. It was this claim, sincerely held by the early protagonists of separation, that solitude could reform the errant and bring him back to the flock, which elevated the system above the brutal and repressive, giving it the air of a moral crusade.

The architecture of separation

The building which emerged to incorporate the ideas of the system was carefully and intricately planned. Nothing was left to chance. The ideal site for the prison, the optimum size of the cell, the thickness of the door, the types of bolts, locks and hinges, the dimensions of the windows – everything was minutely investigated. 'The enforcement of the separate system of prison discipline is dependent, in a great measure, on the construction of the prison admitting of its being carried into effect', wrote Crawford[15] who, with Russell and a military engineer, Joshua Jebb, as their architect, set out to devise a building which embodied their social and religious ideas. The original blueprint was for a gaol holding 208 prisoners, details of which were published in their third report (1838). But this was followed in 1840–1 by the construction of the Model Prison at Pentonville, where all their theories could be put into practice.[16]

Fundamental to the idea of the separate system was the prevention of all communication between inmates. Further than this, expectations about reformation required as near total silence as possible in each cell to induce necessary reflection and introspection. Before work began on the Model Prison, therefore, the first task was to construct a totally soundproof cell. Not only did these ideas require a different prison plan; they also demanded research into new construction techniques as well as building services.

Experiments were begun inside the perimeter wall at Millbank Prison. The inspectors first tried cell walls 31in thick consisting of two 13in jagged walls separated by a 5in space. As these were not totally soundproof, two thicknesses of sailcloth were hung in the 5in space, but this was difficult to accomplish; moreover, the sailcloth rotted in the damp air. The inspectors then tried building two 9in brick walls, with two spaces of 3¾in divided by a 4½in brick wall in the middle. This prevented intelligible communication but resulted in considerable reverberation when the side walls were struck, so the 3¾in gaps were filled with sand. Yet, while diminishing the vibration, this experiment made the cells less soundproof. The same experiments were repeated with Bath stone instead of brick; ultimately, the inspectors settled for 18in walls, double doors, arched ceilings and concrete floors, to prevent the penetration of any comprehensible noise.

There were, however, other conditions that had to be fulfilled. Foremost among these was the preservation of the inmates' health. One lesson learned from the American experiments was that space should not be too confined if the prisoner was to sleep, eat and work in his cell without suffering mental disorders. The inspectors, therefore, decreed that the cell should be 'large, light and airy', which in practice meant 12ft by 8ft by 10ft high, or 13ft by 7ft by 10ft high. This was lit by a window, 42in by 11in high, located sufficiently high up the wall to shut out the outside world. As the prisoner's solitude was not to be broken by visits to the privy or wash shed, plumbing had also to be provided. In each cell both water closet and wash basin were fitted, and a towel and a comb provided for every prisoner (Figure 3.1). Cleanliness, after all, was not only next to godliness, it was also an essential precaution against bad smells which, according to the 'miasmic' theory, were thought to cause disease. Cells were lit by gas to allow prisoners to read or work in the long winter evenings. Whether the gas was installed on grounds of humanity or with the object of keeping the prisoners at work for longer hours is not altogether clear.[17] What is known is that the lighting was believed to be costly to run and some prison authorities who went to the expense of having it installed turned it off early to cut down on their gas bills.[18]

3.1 Design for cell, Pentonville Prison, 1844. (Opposite page)

The idea of separate confinement was based on a belief in reformation through reflection, as well as deterrence. Hence, cells were bare, providing minimum distractions, the window located sufficiently high in the wall to give light but exclude the outside world. Prevention of the transmission of sound as well as security required thick walls and ceilings. As prisoners were kept separate at all times, sleeping, eating and working in their own cells, each was provided with individual sanitary facilities. Attention to physical health required careful ventilation arrangements which posed problems for the maintenance of acoustic control.
(from *Parliamentary Papers*, 1844, vol. 28 (594), p. 171; reproduced by permission of the Trustees of the British Library)

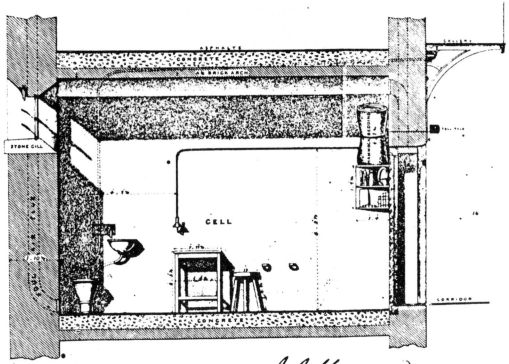

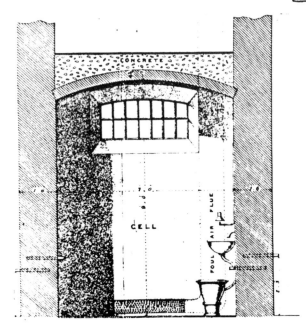

A more serious difficulty was the problem of heating and ventilation, particularly if the cells were to remain soundproof. An inmate could scarcely take enough exercise to keep warm in the confined space of his cell, nor – as the windows were fixed to prevent prisoners communicating with each other – could he open them to admit fresh air. Equally important was the need to remove the smells associated with having a WC in the cell. Efficient ventilation, therefore, was essential.

Previous nineteenth-century heating and ventilating systems had been extremely rudimentary. Many prison windows were not even glazed in the 1830s, but had shutters for night-time use. Presumably there were no ventilation problems in such gaols, although heating them obviously posed difficulties. In some of the old 'associated' prisons, inmates warmed themselves round the open fires placed in the day rooms and occasionally in the dormitories. More modern heating devices included the 'Arnott' stoves placed in the corridors at Hereford and Northallerton, and other patent warming and ventilating apparatus installed at Derby, Nottingham and King's Lynn. These systems were rarely efficient. The stoves, for example, might well have raised the temperature in the corridors, but it is unlikely that much heat percolated into the cells through the perforated bricks and holes drilled in the doors: these holes, in any case, reduced the soundproofing of the cells. The patent heating system at King's Lynn had to be discontinued as a result of pipes exploding, almost suffocating the inmates with steam.[19] These cases emphasise the rudimentary nature of prison heating preceding Pentonville, and the ambitiousness of the system devised for the Model Prison. Nothing else even approaching its complexity was undertaken in the first half of the nineteenth century, except for the attempted ventilation of the Houses of Parliament – and that was considered an abysmal failure.

This system, developed by Messrs Haden of Trowbridge, worked on the following principles. Boilers and pipes were installed in the basement of each wing. Cold fresh air was drawn into the prison basement through a fresh-air shaft, and in winter was made to pass over heated pipes. The fresh air or heated air was then carried along a series of flues into the top of each cell. The object of making the point of entry at the top instead of at the bottom of the cell was to prevent draughts and also frustrate any prisoner's attempt to block up the hole. The foul air was then to be extracted through a flue at the bottom of the cell, diagonally opposite the fresh-air entrance. It then passed along the walls and into the outer air via the main foul air flue which, in summer, was to have a fire burning in it so as to aid the withdrawal of the foul air.

This attempt to overcome some of the basic laws of physical science to accommodate the moral ideas of the prison inspectorate, and therefore to keep the separate system intact, inevitably ran into trouble. Just why the system failed so frequently is open to question, but fail it did. Even at the Model Prison, Pentonville, it took two weeks to raise the temperature in the cells, and at least

3.2 Aerial view of Strangeways Prison, Manchester.
The typical radial plan of the reformed prison.
(reproduced by permission of Aerofilms Library)

ten days to lower it again once the fires were extinguished.[20] At Aylesbury Prison the situation was worse. With the temperature in the cells varying between 50° and 78°F, there was only one way to make the extracting flues work – by opening the cell doors.[21] The failure was quite possibly a matter of pure science, for despite the so-called 'descending principle', hot air persisted in rising and thus evaded the foul air flue near the floor. Either the engineering required for its successful working was inadequately developed or the prison's maintenance staff lacked the necessary expertise to operate it. Many prison governors failed to realise that the fires in the chimney were required in summer to create a draught to pull through the foul air. All too frequently they associated fires with heating in winter, and had them extinguished in summer when the need for them was most pressing.

Within the cell, furnishings were sparse – a stool, a table and a shelf for the prisoner's personal items. As a concession to those wishing to inculcate in-dustrious habits, some cells were fitted with a loom, which left no space for anything else. At night a hammock was slung for the prisoner to sleep in, but to prevent any temptation to lounge in it during the day, this was to be rolled up each morning, together with the prisoner's bedding, and stacked on his shelf. The only remaining item in the cell, other than a Bible and library books, was a mechanical alarm enabling the prisoner to summon an officer in case of emergency.

The individual cells, therefore, were designed with the twin aims of instituting, as far as humanly possible, the total separation of one prisoner from the next,[22] and also incorporating those features thought necessary for maintaining health. The layout of the prison, on the other hand, was arranged with the primary aim of maintaining security and ease of control. Cells were arranged on either side of open corridors, generally two or three stories high, lit by a large window at the far end, and often by skylights in the roof. Cells on the upper floor opened out on to iron galleries (Figure 3.3). These wings radiated from one central observation point from which the whole prison could be surveyed at once (Figure 3.4). This layout reflected the rationalisation of administration which had gone into the prison design and owed much to the experiments of Jeremy Bentham in the late eighteenth century. It made the warder's task far easier than in the old-style prison, where he had been required to patrol numerous wards, rooms and yards, connected by corridors and passageways. Supervision of the prison was absolute. Not only did a turnkey have all the cell doors within his field of vision, but minute inspection windows in each cell door meant that he could observe the prisoner, without in turn being seen by him. The advantages in terms of control which the radial-plan, cellular prison gave the prison staff were immense.

Security, of course, was as important as control. Cell walls had iron loops set into them at narrow intervals to guard against anyone chipping his way through to the outside; the double doors were heavily locked and bolted; the 11 in high window near the top of the cell had a sloping sill and was barred on the outside. The 15ft perimeter wall with its even, smooth surface and semi-circular, projection-free coping was built with foundations too deep to be undermined in the course of one night. Though escapes did occur from separate system gaols, the built-in obstacles deterred all but the most ingenious inmate.

Central to the moral and religious elements in the separate system ideology was the role of the chaplain and the chapel where he preached. Yet how was the attendance of prisoners at chapel to be reconciled with the demands of total separation? Every day (and twice on Sundays) all prisoners attended chapel service. Here, too, total isolation was maintained. Each row of seats was divided into separate stalls, with a high partition door between each prisoner on the same row (Figures 3.5, 3.6). The rows ascended steeply in tiers, so that the back of each row of seats would be high enough to intercept communications between rows when the prisoners were standing up, yet not so high as to conceal them

3.3 Interior of the House of Detention, Clerkenwell.
The interior shown here was similar to that of the re-formed prison. The separate system was the ultimate form of classification, with each prisoner assigned to his own category, confined in his own cell and stacked horizontally and vertically in the radiating wings of the prison. The figures in the illustration are apparently middle-class visitors inspecting the establishment.
(from H. Mayhew and J. Binny, *The Criminal Prisons of London*, 1862; by permission of the publishers of the 1968 impression, Frank Cass, London)

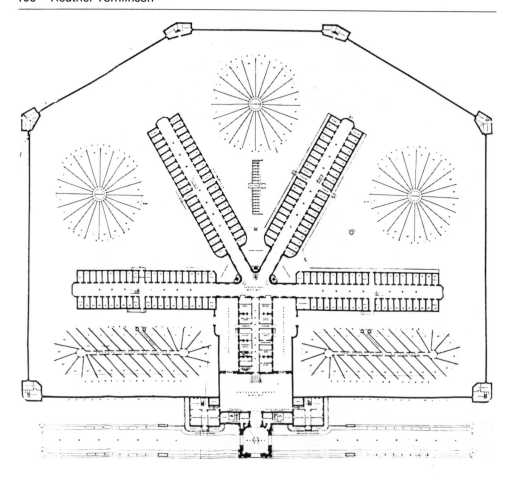

3.4 Pentonville Prison, ground plan.
Blocks of separate cells radiated from the central hall from which all internal corridors could be observed. Exercise yards between the wings and at the front of the prison were divided by high partitions to prevent contact between prisoners. The houses of the governor and chaplain, located on either side of the main gate, symbolised the dual functions of discipline and reform.
(from *Parliamentary Papers*, 1844, vol. 28 (594), p. 159; reproduced by permission of the Trustees of the British Library)

from the chaplain's and officers' sight when sitting down. This posed problems. As the steeply ascending rows of seats made heavy demands on the available volume of a normal room, chapels tended to be stuffy and airless, especially for those prisoners sitting in the highest rows, their heads only inches from the ceiling. Hence, fainting was common and presented difficulties for the officers when the unconscious prisoner was situated in the middle of a row.

The schoolroom, similarly partitioned, was another instrument for reformation. The education provided was not necessarily restricted to a grounding in the basic Christian precepts. Some larger prisons employed a schoolmaster to teach the 'three Rs', for the prison statistics showed that most convicted criminals had lower than average educational attainments. Thus, the link between ignorance and crime seemed confirmed, and the remedy of education validated. Despite objections from some quarters, education became an intrinsic part of the prison system, few denying a prisoner the right to learn to read his Bible.

3.5 Chapel on the 'separate system', Pentonville, during divine service.
Like reflection in the cells, daily chapel service (twice on Sunday) was an instrument of moral reform. To prohibit the moral contamination of one prisoner by another, wooden partitions to each side and at front and rear prevented all communication. The chaplain is at the left; elsewhere, warders exercise supervision.
(from H. Mayhew and J. Binny, *The Criminal Prisons of London*, 1862, by permission of the publishers of the 1968 impression, Frank Cass, London)

The prisoner left his cell not only for chapel and school, but also for daily outdoor exercise. Again, the separate system had to remain inviolate. The exercise yard, usually situated in between the prison wings (Figures 3.2 and 3.4), were divided by high walls into individual areas for each prisoner. Here, he was expected to take sufficient exercise to maintain health. In practice the system was not enforced, and by 1850 the separate exercise yards in many prisons were being abolished.

One further detail was required to preserve the separate system intact. The only time when prisoners might see and recognise each other was when leaving their cells for chapel or exercise. It was feared that, once released from prison, this knowledge of another man's criminal past might be used for extortion or for planning some future crime. Hence, to ensure anonymity outside his cell, each prisoner was required to wear a mask – a long peaked cap with eye-holes (Figure 3.7).

If the separate system was to work, it was essential that, in addition to the

3.6 Partitioned pews, Lincoln Prison Chapel.
(by permission of Reece Winstone, photographer)

purpose-built environment, a set of rules be devised to ensure that it was properly used. Above all, the prisoner's health, vitality and sanity were to be maintained. For the inspectors knew that if disasters on the lines of the early American experiments occurred at Pentonville, their hopes of having separation adopted throughout the country would be finished. As a supplement to their architectural design, therefore, they devised a code of regulations to ensure the prisoners' wellbeing.[23] These stipulated that each prisoner should be visited daily by both the governor and chaplain, and at regular intervals by the medical officer – both as a precaution against insanity, and as a means of quickly discovering it should it occur. They recommended that prisoners were to receive three meals a day, at least two of which were to be hot. As communal dining halls were ruled out, all meals were eaten in total isolation in the cells. Again, this proposed a particular problem in design. Kitchens were therefore constructed in the basement, and a series of lifts and trolleys installed to carry the meals up to the cells. Each cell door had a trap door let into it, which, when lowered, formed

3.7 Masked convicts exercising at Pentonville.
Between individual cells and separated exercise yards, or where the latter were not used, prisoners were required to wear peaked cap masks to preserve anonymity and prevent recognition by other prisoners once outside the gaol.
(from H. Mayhew and J. Binny, *The Criminal Prisons of London*, 1862, by permission of the publishers of the 1968 impression, Frank Cass, London)

a shelf on which the prisoner placed his mug and plate ready to receive his food. Such was the high level of organisation that Henry Mayhew, who visited Pentonville in 1856, saw breakfast served by these means to 367 prisoners in less than ten minutes.[24]

Cleanliness and hygiene were considered equally important, and detailed regulations set out the procedure for maintaining good health. Prisoners were to be bathed on reception into the prison, and at monthly intervals thereafter. Baths were accordingly fitted in the prison basement, and the number of prisoners to be bathed in the same water (which was to be tepid) was precisely laid down. Cells were to be kept clean. Brooms were issued each morning and were used – at least at Pentonville, where Mayhew observed a 'Dutch-like', even 'dainty', cleanliness.[25] It was hoped that the sweeping routine, together with early rising, would help counteract 'slovenly habits'.

The public image

In his article on Newgate Prison, Kalman[26] suggests that it was not until after the mid-eighteenth century that a positive prison architecture emerged. Before then, newly built gaols differed little from large houses either in plan or elevation but were simply a series of large rooms extending from corridors or small courts. After the rebuilding of Newgate (1783–5) architects attempted to make prisons look like prisons as opposed to palaces or hospitals. Prison architects of the nineteenth century had two models to follow: the massive solidity of Newgate, with fetters overhanging the gates to emphasise its use as a place of incarceration, or the turrets and crenellation of a mediaeval castle. It was the latter of these two styles which found most favour in the nineteenth century.

To the outside world, a separate system prison presented a daunting, even repelling, sight: the high boundary wall revealed only an occasional glimpse of long cell blocks, punctuated by low, barred windows. A tall ventilating tower was often the only major feature seen from the road. The inspectors recommended that the outside of a prison should be plain and simple: 'the absence of ornament, and the utmost simplicity, will not only be in accordance with the object of the building, but it will be the most economical.'[27] Many prison authorities, however, chose to ignore this advice. The main gateway, flanked by the governor's and chaplain's houses – symbolic of the dual function of discipline and reform – was erected in every shade of revived gothic architecture: domestic gothic at Portsmouth, Byzantine gothic at Strangeways (Manchester), castellated gothic at Holloway (Figure 3.8). The turrets and crenellation prompted much criticism. Reading was accused of 'resembling more a ducal seat than a penitentiary', with a style 'at once castellated and collegiate',[28] and Jebb held that such ornamentation was responsible for the high cost sustained in the building of new gaols.[29]

3.8 Holloway Prison, London: Main gateway.
The use of castellated facades in the design of the Victorian prison was a conscious attempt to make prisons appear repulsive, symbolising on the outside the terrors to be expected within. In this way, it was hoped that potential wrongdoers would be deterred.
(by permission of the Greater London Council)

But not all comments on the castellated style were unfavourable. The association of prisons with castles dated back to 1166, when sheriffs were told they must site their gaols in one of the king's boroughs or castles, and many Victorians felt this was an association worth exploiting. One writer explained:[30]

> Thus York Castle, Norwich Castle, Lancaster Castle and Carlisle Castle speak with the sound of captivity, and their well-known towered and battlemented forms are as thoroughly and achitecturally exponent of gaols to the public eye as anything that can be devised.

If an architect, he continued, chose not to use an existing castle, or to copy the castellated style in designing his prison, he was 'depriving himself and his employers of a vantage ground of association and situation, which of themselves afford character and expression so desirable in architecture'. In other words, revised gothic architecture used in the context of prison building was designed not to make the structure attractive – indeed, quite the reverse. It was to symbolise on the outside the terrors to be expected within, and thus to deter any potential evil-doer from ever entering its portals. Not all architects chose gothic styles to achieve this end, and classical designs – massive, strong and foreboding – were also adopted. The prison system might aspire to reform the criminals within its walls, but outside it was firmly intended to deter.

The nineteenth-century cellular prison was conceived out of the need to reduce the criminal population, in a period when a new humanity restricted the use of the gallows, and out of the pious optimism that religious instruction in conditions of solitude could reform. There was no doubt that the discipline was meant also to be a punishment and a deterrent, although a simple restriction of freedom fulfils those requirements, without the hours of solitude in a comfortless cell, the 'wholesome' but plain unvaried food,[31] coarse prison clothing and a timetable regulated with clockwork precision. Underlying the prison regime, therefore, were various assumptions about the character of the prison population: that it was coarse, idle and slovenly; that it needed to learn habits of cleanliness, hard work and good order; that it was primarily lower-class and ignorant, and therefore capable of being influenced and improved; and that, irrespective of the crime, no criminal deserved to leave prison broken in health owing to his confinement.

Many of the ideas the regime embodied were far from original. The notion of reformation by solitude, for example, dates back to the ecclesiastical prisons of the mediaeval period;[32] that of total supervision and control from a central vantage point was developed in Jeremy Bentham's scheme for his panopticon. But although it was influenced by the past, the nineteenth-century prison was a structure of its own time. The improved technology of the era can be seen in the use of iron – the galleries on the upper floors, the lifts and trolleys, the bolts and hinges – gas lighting, hot water heating, steam cooking and a running water supply.

The prisons transformed

So far this chapter has treated the ideology behind the separate system prison regime, and its translation into the built form. Yet how did the ideology become accepted by the prison administrators of the period, and how were they persuaded to undertake the vastly expensive task of rebuilding their gaols? The merits of the separate system were not necessarily self-evident; and those who had formerly preferred the silent system, or enforced labour, did not spontaneously change their views on reading the findings of the 1835 Select Committee. Nor were the prison administrators easily susceptible to Home Office control. On the contrary, they were principally magistrates or councillors,[33] jealous of their traditional independence and guardians of the ratepayers out of whose money prison construction was financed.[34]

They were met, however, by a government guided by two leading assumptions of Benthamite thought: the value of uniformity of administration throughout the country, and the impossibility of attaining it without a large increase in the activity of central government. The most important step it took was the appointment of the prison inspectorate – although it must be added that the other three prison inspectors were not as enthusiastic for separation as Crawford and Russell, who visited the prisons every year, exhorted magistrates to rebuild their gaols, castigated in their annual reports all failures to do so, re-affirmed the principle of separation and drew up plans to demonstrate its implementation.[35] The inspectors were involved with Jebb, as Surveyor General of Prisons, in designing and constructing the Model Prison at Pentonville and were associated with him in the inspection and correction of plans submitted for approval by the local authorities.[36]

Crawford and Russell both died in 1847, but by then their work had been done. The separate system of prison discipline had become an orthodox belief, inextricably linked with the need for uniformity in prison administration. More importantly, the best part of fifty prisons were in the process of being reconstructed or substantially altered to admit of cellular confinement. Once that was done, the system became self-perpetuating.

The campaign for separation, however, did not end with the inspectors' death. The process of advice and admonishment through the reports and visits of the other inspectors continued. By the 1860s most of those prison authorities who were willing to institute separation had been won over, but there were still others who were not conforming. Following a third Select Committee in thirty years,[37] the government finally resorted to compulsion. The 1865 Act was passed compelling the institution of separation and hard labour throughout the prisons of England and Wales, and threatening the withdrawal of Treasury grants-in-aid (which covered about one-fifth of the prisons' expenses) from those authorities which did not comply.[38] In 1877 the government finally transferred the administration and finance of local prisons from the magistrates to a newly created Prison Commission.[39]

It was therefore through advice, persuasion and finally compulsion that the largest prison building programme in England's history was achieved, and the separate system established. Yet, as early as the 1850s, the theory of deterrence through hard labour was challenging once more that of reformation through solitude. But it was already too late; too many cellular prisons were already in existence. The only solution was to modify the system by legislation. The 1865 Prison Act incorporated hard labour into the existing system and adapted the cellular prisons to meet the challenge. Crank machines were installed in the separate cells and prisoners set to turn the handles 12,000 times a day; more treadwheels fitted with partitions were erected for inmates in the prison yards; individual sheds were built where criminals spent their day breaking stones; and picking oakum resumed its earlier popularity as it could easily be performed in a single cell. (It also provided excellent material for stopping up the ventilating system.) With these adaptations, the pattern was set. From then until the end of the century, the emphasis lay in enforcing the system of separation and hard labour which the buildings had all too adequately accommodated.

As a principle of penal policy, separation survived into the third decade of the twentieth century. In the intervening period little rebuilding was considered necessary, for the nineteenth-century prisons adequately served the purpose of shutting criminals away. Not until after the end of the Second World War did people awake to the gulf between the new concepts of criminal training and the nineteenth-century establishments in which they had to be carried out.[40] It was not possible in the immediate postwar economic climate to establish a new prison system at a stroke, and so in an attempt to provide the workshops, classrooms, gymnasiums, libraries and hospitals now deemed necessary makeshift buildings were fitted into nearly every corner of space enclosed within the high prison walls.

By the end of the 1950s it was once more possible to contemplate a new prison building programme. But there were two major stumbling blocks, one ideological, the other financial. First, it was no longer clear what imprisonment was trying to achieve. The three general planning considerations were listed as security, functional efficiency and economy. Security and economy were familiar friends: it was the question of functional efficiency that required closer study. What was ultimately envisaged was the building of thirty new establishments, embracing five or six different functions – secure training prisons; observation centres; borstals; detention centres; a psychiatric prison; a prison for women; open prisons – at a cost of £12 million. Blundeston and half a dozen others were under construction or already completed when the second obstacle was met – finance. Government economy cuts and soaring prices brought that particular programme to a sudden end.

Since then, prison building in England has continued in a piecemeal fashion, but nothing which could be termed twentieth-century prison architecture has developed. There has been much more discussion on the purpose of imprisonment, but no consensus of opinion has emerged. For a while the rehabilitation theory offered hope for the future, and facilities to achieve it were built into the system. But the physical and vocational training, mental and physical medicine, recreational provision, productive work and spiritual and welfare support have not reduced recidivism. In consequence, the term 'rehabilitation' is now becoming as outmoded as 'reformation', its nineteenth-century counterpart. It is still acceptable for prisoners to be 'treated' and 'trained', but now there are also demands for them to be members of a 'normal community'.

These demands are finding shape in a women's prison, Cornton Vale, in Scotland. Here, the aim is to create an institution which, far from cutting off the outside world by a high perimeter wall, would become part of the total community of central Scotland. The 'treatment' includes 'character-building', the improvement of the self-image, and the application of social skills.

The prison buildings segregate five different categories of offender into separate blocks, each divided into 'family' units for seven inmates. The units are provided with a separate entrance, and comprise bedrooms, living room, storeroom, utility room, kitchen, toilets, bathroom, shower and officer's room. For a month at a time an inmate serves as the 'homemaker' to her 'family'. She cooks, cleans, washes, mends and irons clothes, and generally performs the tasks of a housewife while the other six members go out to work or training each day. In addition to the family units, there are communal facilities in the central block; there is also a perimeter fence and window grilles (instead of bars), but the aim is to make conditions in prison as 'normal' as possible.

The concepts of 'community' and 'normality', however, for obvious reasons, are already criticised, although this most recent area of debate is too vast to embark on here. The result of controversy over ideology is that there is no agreement as to what constitutes an acceptable prison form. Everyone calls for more discussion, participation and research. There is a conviction that big is not beautiful, and that the prison of the future must be smaller than that of the past. But there is disagreement on every other issue, from where to house long-term potentially dangerous criminals to the optimum size of the 'residential modules'. Caution is recommended on all sides. 'We do not want', wrote D. L. Howard in the 1960s,[41] 'at vast expense, to erect buildings which are destined to be as great a handicap to our successors as early Victorian prisons are to us now'; more recently, Leslie Fairweather emphasised that 'Each problem demands a different solution, and not, as in the past, the same solution. . . . Empiricism and experiment should be the order of the day.'[42] The experimental institutions of the late twentieth century will tell future generations as much about the social awareness and uncertainty of the 1970s as the Victorian prisons tell us of earlier aspirations and ideals.

Notes and references

1 See M. H. Tomlinson's unpublished thesis (PhD dissertation, University of London, 1975), 'Victorian Prison Administration and Architecture, 1835–77' (from which this chapter is largely drawn), p. 99. For an introduction to prison architecture see N. Johnstone, *The Human Cage: A Brief History of Prison Architecture*, Walker, New York, 1973.

2 The use of imprisonment as a punishment was, of course, not new in the sixteenth century. In *Imprisonment in Medieval England*, Cambridge University Press, 1968, R. B. Pugh has shown that the use of imprisonment in the medieval period extended far more widely than the mere detention of criminals before trial and pending sentence. See, for example, pp. 2, 9, and 26–30.

3 From which he wrote *The State of the Prisons in England and Wales*, 2nd edn, Warrington, 1780.

4 For a full account of the criminal law reform movement, see L. Radzinowicz, *A History of English Criminal Law*, Stevens, London, 1948, vol. 1.

5 U. R. Q. Henriques, 'The rise and decline of the separate system of prison discipline', *Past and Present*, vol. 54, 1972, pp. 63–4.

6 See Appendix D to Tomlinson, op. cit., for details of the site, construction, size, cost and architect of these prisons, and the others in existence between 1835 and 1877.

7 S. E. Finer, 'The transmission of Benthamite ideas, 1820–50', in Gillian Sutherland, ed., *Studies in the Growth of Nineteenth Century Government*, Routledge & Kegan Paul, London, 1972, pp. 11–32.

8 Reports of the Select Committee of the House of Lords, Appointed to Enquire into the Present State of Prisons in England and Wales. *Parliamentary Papers* (hereafter *P.P.*) 1835, vol. 11, (438), (439); vol. 12, (440), (441).

9 Crawford and Russell were jointly appointed inspectors for the Home District, and were entrusted with special duties and received higher pay than the other three. Officially there was no chief inspector, but there is little doubt that Crawford was *primus inter pares*.

10 There is disagreement between J. J. Tobias, *Crime and Industrial Society in the Nineteenth Century*, Batsford, London, 1967, and V. A. C. Gatrell and T. B. Hadden, 'Criminal Statistics and their Interpretation' in E. A. Wrigley, ed., *Nineteenth Century Society. Essays on the use of Quantitative Methods for a Study of Social Data*, Cambridge University Press, 1972, on the usefulness of the criminal statistics which began in 1805, and were

subsequently improved in 1836 and 1857. Whatever their value may be to the historian today, there is little doubt that they were extremely influential in the 1830s and 1840s, and that the apparent – and probably real – increase in crime which they showed over the previous quarter-century caused widespread alarm.

11 The inspectors' views on the merits and defects of the various prison systems, including the separate system, have been taken principally from their first three annual reports, *P.P.* 1836, vol. 35, (117), pp. 79–82, *P.P.* 1837, vol. 32 (89), pp. 5–36; *P.P.* 1838, vol. 30 (141), pp. 5–103.

12 R. Fergusson, 'Results of the system of separate confinement as administered at the Pentonville Prison, *Quarterly Review*, vol. 92, 1853, p. 500.

13 *P.P.* 1837, vol. 32 (89), p. 18.

14 *P.P.* 1835, vol. 11 (438), pp. 14, 41.

15 *P.P.* 1838, vol. 30 (141), p. 117.

16 The following details on the design and construction of separate system prisons have been taken from the second, third and fourth inspectors' reports, *P.P.* 1837, vol. 32 (89), pp. 25–7; *P.P.* 1838, vol. 30 (141), pp. 117–24; *P.P.* 1839, vol. 21 (210), pp. 11–18; The report of the Surveyor General on the construction, ventilation and details of Pentonville Prison, *P.P.* 1844, vol. 28 (594), pp. 129–99.

17 The inspectors' attitude to labour was ambivalent. Ideally they would have preferred prisoners not to work: an occupation took the edge off their solitude, giving them something to think about other than their sins. In practice, however, they recognised the value of labour as a safety valve against insanity. Equally important, they accepted that many prison authorities sought to exploit prison labour either as a workforce to provide items for prison use, such as shirts and shoes, or to make articles for sale. Such authorities would be reluctant to adopt the cellular system if they thought it would prohibit them from using such means of reducing maintenance costs. Though against their principles, the inspectors even implicitly accepted the use of the treadwheel but they made rules governing its use (for example, setting a maximum of 14,000 steps a day for any prisoner) and recommended that prisoners working on it should be separated from each other by partitions, to maintain the integrity of the system.

18 For example, Hereford City Gaol. See Inspector's Report, *P.P.* 1852, vol. 24 (1495), p. 21.

19 The examples have been taken from inspectors' reports. See *P.P.* 1839, vol. 22 (199), p. 205; *P.P.* 1842, vol. 21 (420), pp. 23, 79, and 96; and *P.P.* 1842, vol. 32 (63), p. 68.

20 Report by the Medical Officer on the plan of ventilating the cells of the Pentonville Prison, *P.P.* 1844, vol. 28 (536), p. 85.

21 Aylesbury County Record Office, QAG 14/182, Report by Inspector Russell, 3 March 1847.

22 It proved quite impossible to prevent all communication between prisoners. Punishments were meted out throughout the century for the offence of communicating, either through the waterpipes or by tapping on the walls and doors.

23 The first set of regulations was circulated by the inspectors in 1843, and published in the Parliamentary Papers, *P.P.* 1843, vols 25 and 26 (457), pp. 15–29. These were amended in 1849 (see Public Record Office, Home Office series 158/2, Home Office

Circular Book, 10 December 1849). There were also rules embodied in each successive Gaol Act from Peel's Act (4 Geo IV Cap 64, 1823) onwards. See especially 2 & 3 Vic Cap 56 (1839); 28 & 29 Vic Cap 126 (1865) and 40 & 41 Vic Cap 21 (1877).

24 Henry Mayhew and John Binny, *The Criminal Prisons of London*, 1862; new impression, Frank Cass, London, 1968, pp. 134–5.

25 Ibid., p. 119.

26 H. D. Kalman, 'Newgate Prison', *Architectural History*, vol. 12, 1969, p. 57.

27 *P.P.* 1838, vol. 30 (141), p. 114.

28 'Prison Building', *Building News*, vol. 25, 1873, p. 587.

29 See Jebb's evidence to the 1850 Select Committee on Prison Discipline, *P.P.* 1850, vol. 17 (632), p. 35.

30 'Prison Architecture', *Building News*, vol. 3, 1857, p. 227.

31 See H. Tomlinson, 'Not an instrument of punishment: prison diet in the nineteenth century', *Journal of Consumer Studies and Home Economics*, vol. 2, 1978, pp. 15–26.

32 Johnston, op. cit., pp. 8–10.

33 The county gaols, generally speaking, were administered by the county magistrates, although the sheriff had one or two residual duties. The borough gaols were run by the borough magistrates, but financed by the town council – a situation fraught with problems. There also still existed in the 1830s bishop's prisons at York and Ely, a liberty prison at Peterborough, a prison governed by a royal charter at Bath and a penitentiary regulated by its own Act of Parliament at Gloucester. These, and other anomalies in the Channel Islands, did not seriously hinder the cause of prison reform.

34 The government took financial responsibility only for those criminals convicted of the more serious offences, and sentenced to transportation or penal servitude. Those who were sentenced to imprisonment for from three days to about two years were maintained in the local prisons at the ratepayers' expense.

35 For example, it was necessary to pass a new Act, 2 & 3 Vic Cap 56 (1839), An Act for the Better Ordering of Prisons, to define separate confinement and differentiate it from solitary confinement. Solitary confinement, being a prison punishment, was tightly restricted in its use.

36 The role of Jebb and the inspectorate is discussed at greater length in Tomlinson, op. cit.

37 See *The Report of a Select Committee on Prison Discipline*, *P.P.* 1863, vol. 9 (499).

38 The Prison Act, 28 & 29 Vic Cap 126 (1865), moreover, took a large stride towards increasing uniformity, simply by closing down 80 of the existing 193 prisons.

39 This was achieved through the Prison Act, 40 & 41 Vic Cap 21 (1877). There were reasons other than the lack of uniformity which prompted this drastic measure, the most important being the Tory pledge to reduce the burden of the rates.

40 I am deeply indebted to Leslie Fairweather for much of the material on postwar prisons and penal policy. See his articles, 'Prison architecture in England', *British Journal of Criminology*, vol. i, no. 4, April 1961, pp. 339–61, and 'The evolution of the prison' in *Prison Architecture*, Architectural Press, London, 1975, pp. 13–40. I have also taken ideas and information from Johnston, op. cit.; from Peter Dickens, Sean McConville and Leslie Fairweather, eds, *Penal Policy and Prison Architecture*, selected papers from a symposium held at the University of Sussex, Barry Rose, Brighton,

1978; from A. W. Peterson 'The prison building programme', *British Journal of Criminology*, vol. 1, no. 4, April 1961, pp. 307–16; and *H.M. Institution Cornton Vale*, HMSO, London, 1974.

41 D. L. Howard, *The English Prison*, Methuen, London, 1960; quoted by Fairweather, 'Prison architecture in England', pp. 358–9.

42 Fairweather, 'The evolution of the prison', p. 40.

Part II

4 The Hindu temple in south India*

Susan Lewandowski

The ethnoenvironment

Stand by a street in an Indian city and watch the endless variety of people who pass: men in slacks and sports shirts or Western suits; men in loosely wrapped dhotis with a cloth draped over bare shoulders; women in saris, some of rough peasant cloth and some silk, in constantly changing colors and styles; a few boys, some in blue jeans, with a Beatles record; a [Hindu] holy man in loincloth and sandals and long tangled hair; a Sikh, with turban and beard; a group coming from a nearby [Hindu] temple, with flowers in hand and fresh spots of red powder on their foreheads; priests from the Ramakrishna Mission in long saffron robes; a funeral party, led by drummers, carrying a corpse on a palanquin. . . .[1]

What makes this cultural diversity work is the Hindu religious tradition, shared by one-fifth of the world's population. The words 'India' and 'Hindu' derive from the same linguistic root, *Sindhu*, the Sanskrit name for sea as well as the major river flowing in what is now Pakistan.[2] The civilization that grew up around the river and spread throughout the Indian subcontinent was distinct from that of Persia to the west and central Asia to the north, but it incorporated elements from both; it was a composite culture, reflecting the different peoples who settled there. Yet the new did not drive out the old; it merely supplemented it. Historically, both India and the Hindu tradition have assimilated ideas and

* The research for this essay, carried out in India during 1976–7, was made possible by grants from Amherst College, the American Institute of Indian Studies, and the Joint Committee on South Asia of the American Council of Learned Societies and the Social Science Research Council. I wish to thank Dennis Hudson, Indira Shetterly and Gary Tartakov for their comments on this paper.

beliefs from many different parts of the world, and although to a Westerner these may at times seem contradictory, they have all found a place in the whole. It is this ability to absorb and transform ideas that has enabled India, along with China, to remain one of the two primary world civilizations that still exist today.[3] Although much of the world, including China, has become secular in its transformation to a modern way of life, an important characteristic of the Hindu tradition is that 'there is no dividing line between sacred and secular, no area of belief or custom that is alien to religious influence.'[4] For this reason, religious institutions such as the temple continue today as living forces for both the village and urban Indian.

This chapter is in three parts. It begins by briefly discussing the basic tenets of Hinduism as they relate to the development of the temple. In particular, it focuses on the symbolism and evolution of its traditional form as a metaphor for the religious beliefs of the people in a largely monarchical, agrarian-based society.

The second section, on the Minakshi temple of Madurai, shows how these traditional principles were embodied in the largest temple complex in south India, built in the sixteenth and seventeenth centuries.

The final and main part of the essay examines changes in the location, scale and form of temples in Madras since the eighteenth century. In recent years, new industrial wealth, modern engineering and (especially transport) technology have brought subtle changes, with new suburban temples having an impact both on their neighborhoods and on the city as a whole. A surge of Hindu revivalism has also brought a move away from traditional, external ritual towards more personal devotional forms of worship.

Although the paper focuses on south India, and specifically on Tamilnadu as the heart of Dravidian culture, the issues it raises relate to Indian society as a whole. The south, with less Islamic influence than the north, has remained more traditional in its religious beliefs. Here one can most clearly ask: what role does the temple play in contemporary India? How is it adapting to the needs of a modern society? Can it be argued that the modernization of cultures results in a linear transformation from sacred to secular?

The Hindu religious tradition

Hinduism is more than a religion; it is a way of life. At the heart of the belief system is the underlying principle that all things are one, and this is expressed in the cosmic ideal of Brahman, 'the Absolute beyond name and form.' To attain the universal oneness of Brahman, the Hindu believes that he must be released from an endless cycle of births and rebirths, for although the soul is eternal, it is tied by the body to its actions (*karma*). Good acts mean an ascent on the spiritual ladder of rebirth and eventual union with the godhead. Here is one of the important characteristics of the Hindu religious and social system – the concept of *hierarchy*. All things in the Hindu cosmology are placed on a continuum from low to high, from inanimate objects (rocks) through plants, animals and humans to gods.

The caste system follows from this general principle. Human beings are part of a continuum, and although each has a soul and a potential for union with the supreme godhead, not all people, because of their actions, are alike. Therefore, the untouchable, who has traditionally performed impure occupations within the socio-economic hierarchy, holds a lower status than a *shudra* (cultivator), *vaishya* (merchant and artisan), *kshatriya* (warrior), and *brahmin* (priest). Yet, within each of these categories, there are innumerable hierarchically organized subdivisions (*jatis*) that fill out the continuum of the caste system. The *brahmin* is at the top of the hierarchy because he has historically been an interpreter of the sacred Vedas, and the keeper of religious rituals, such as the fire sacrifice, and it is he who has prescribed a way of life leading to spiritual progress for the other castes.

For over 1,000 years before Christ, the Vedas (scriptures or hymns of praise that outlined the way to realizing the Truth) were handed down orally among the priestly community and formed the basis for the Hindu tradition. At the center of Vedic worship was the fire sacrifice; the need to control fire, to propitiate it and to personify it as a deity through the offering of food is a common characteristic of primitive belief systems. In Vedic times, the philosophical orientation of the religion limited worship to the elite and educated strata of society, that is, the ruling classes and the priesthood. By the first and second centuries BC there increasingly appeared a number of popular gods who were seen as manifestations of the universal essence, Brahman. In the process, new deities whose origins could often be traced to village religious traditions were incorporated along with the Vedas into the body of what has since become known as Hinduism, and in the process, the peasant joined in religious worship. It took almost another 1,000 years for the synthesis of Brahmanical and popular religion to take place, and it is only in the period since AD 900 that the Hindu tradition, as we know it today, has existed.

Hand in hand with the development of a theistic religion came changes in religious worship. One of the major shifts in ritual was from the earlier Vedic sacrifice to the performance of *puja*. *Puja*, the most common form of worship today in India, has been described by one writer as 'a hospitality ritual.'[5] During *puja*, the deity, often personified as a king, is called to the ritual and given water for washing his feet and hands; he is bathed, clothed, anointed with sandalwood or other fragrances, and given offerings such as flowers and food; then the worshipper circumambulates the deity to show his humility to the god, reciting hymns of praise. The *puja* ends with the devotee taking his departure from the deity. This personal form of worship could now be performed by family members in their own home, or by an officiating priest in the house of god, the Hindu temple.

Gods and temples were subject to hierarchy as were humans and other living creatures. The more important gods resided in larger temples, while lesser or more localized village deities lived either in small temples or in shrines. Today, some of the smallest temples resemble the earliest structures that first appeared in India around the third century BC, while the largest date from the medieval period when kings and rich merchants provided capital for colossal temple construction. By the sixth century AD, temples made of permanent materials, such as stone, had become an important source of financial investment and a visible reflection of artistic development in the society. Although the priesthood had control over religious matters, they were dependent on the kings and nobles for financial support. And while Hindu society was segmented into different castes who performed different functions, they were interdependent on one another, together forming a whole. It was this interdependence, in part, that sustained a religious system which had no over-arching ecclesiastical structure, in contrast with religions such as Christianity.[6]

> The Hindu temple is the sum total of architectural rites performed on the basis of its myth. The myth covers the ground and is the plan on which the structure is raised.[7]

It is impossible to discuss the Hindu temple without emphasizing the symbolic elements of its form. Here, an attempt will be made to interrelate not only the architectural aspects of the form but also the symbolic aspects of the site, plan, rites and modular parts of the temple.

There were essentially two prototypes for the form of the temple in India, the house and the palace. The earliest shelters provided for the gods were small in size and originally constructed of wattle supported by posts and beams.[8] One of the first stone temples echoed the simplicity of the hut shelter on which it was modeled. It consisted of a single square room (the god's residence), fronted by an open veranda, whose roof was supported by four stone pillars.[9] On entering, the devotee passed through the door, under the lintel, and into the inner recesses of the god's 'home' (Figure 4.1). Although the family who performed *puja* to the deity in their home treated the god as an honored guest, in the temple he was increasingly seen as a king. From the sixth century onwards, the temple 'homes' of the deities became correspondingly palatial, as the wealth of royal empires was invested in monumental architecture.

The sixth-century manual of architecture (*Vastu-Sastra*) prescribes where and how temples should be built. One of the requirements for the site is that it be a place where the gods are at play[10] such as the seashore, the banks of a lake or river or the junction of two rivers, but they were also found on mountain tops, in forests or gardens and in areas of habitation such as villages, towns or cities. Since water was an intrinsic part of the gods' play, as well as essential for the ritual purification of the devotee, on sites where no natural water source existed man-made ponds or tanks were built on the auspicious locations to the left or front of the temple.

Once the site was chosen, the ground was prepared by drawing a geometrical design called a *vastu-purusha-mandala*. The derivation of the words, *mandala* (circle), *purusha* (universal essence) and *vastu* (to dwell), signifies the attempt to delimit sacred from profane space, and to prepare the dwelling place of the god by ridding it of 'unpredictable forces.'[11] Before the diagram was drawn, the priest recited a number of magical formulas (*mantras*) to encourage every living creature to leave the space being purified. This ensured that the architect (*stapathi*) would be able to perform his work without interference from malevolent forces. Traditionally, a symbolic ploughing and sowing of the ground with different types of grain guaranteed the fertility of the site.

Although the *mandala* was in theory a circle, in actuality it formed a square, for the drawing of the *mandala* was determined by the four cardinal directions.[12] After laying out the axes of the diagram, the perimeter was located, and lines were drawn linking the corners of the *mandala*. The completion of the sacred diagram involved its division into plots (*padas*) where the different deities resided, the central location being reserved for Brahman. In order to breathe a life-force into the diagram, an anthropomorphic image representing *purusha*, the universal spirit, was laid beneath the *mandala*. After drawing the *vastu-purusha-mandala*, offerings were made to the god Brahman and other lesser deities, and the ordering and controlling of space was completed.

The configuration of parts of the temple, like the ritual controlling the use of space, was carefully prescribed in the texts. At the center of the traditional south Indian temple was the sanctuary (*vimana*) which housed the essential part of the institution, the *garbha-griha*, a Sanskrit word meaning womb house. This was a small, square, windowless, cave-like room, devoid of any ornamentation, where the presiding deity, representative of the universal essence, resided in the form of an idol. It was here in the interior recesses of the temple that an officiating priest performed *puja*, lighting the face of the deity with an oil lamp, and offering scented flowers and incense during the ritual. Devotees were not allowed into this central shrine but waited for a vision of the god at the doorway to the *garbha-griha*, which was kept closed when the priest was not in attendance.

Beneath this house of god the *vastu-purusha-mandala* had been drawn to define the sacred space, and above the inner shrine the superstructure of the dome (*shikhara*) stretched skyward.[13] The arch of leaves or bamboo that originally provided protection for the deity in India forms the prototype for this cupola-like exterior structure. In the larger temples of India there is an ambulatory (*garbha-*

griha) that surrounds the central shrine, allowing the devotee ritually to circumambulate (*pradakshina*) the deity. As Stella Kramrish has pointed out, this rite allows the worshipper 'a communion by movement with the images stationed on the walls,'[14] for although the interior of the shrine is devoid of ornamentation, its outer walls may be filled with stone-carved images meant to inspire the devotee. Circumambulation (*pradakshina*) is also performed out in the open, around the *vimana* as a whole.

A pillared hall (*mandapa*), traditionally located at the eastern approach to the temple, served the function of a waiting area for pilgrims about to enter the main shrine. Although in some of the earliest temples the *mandapa* was a detached structure, during the medieval period it was structurally joined to the *vimana*. Around AD 700 a further elaboration of the temple took place in south India with the construction of a series of cells built into a wall (*prakara*) that enclosed the courtyard in which the temple was located. As temples expanded after the twelfth century, additional halls, or *mandapas*, and subsidiary shrines were often constructed in courtyards beyond the initial temple wall, and additional walls

4.1 Examples showing the evolution of temple form in India. (Opposite page)
Top left:
Elevation and plan, Sanchi, *c.* AD 450
Top right:
Temple of Durge, Aihole, *c.* AD 550
Bottom:
Kailasanatha temple, Kanchipuram, seventh century
Key:
A Main shrine; B Vimana; C Prakara; D Mandapa; E Gopura

The *vimana* ('sanctuary') is at the heart of the traditional South Indian temple; here, the presiding deity resides in the form of an idol and the priest performs the *puja* or ceremony of worship. A pillared hall (*mandapa*) serves as a waiting area for pilgrims. In some of the earliest temples this was detached, but later it was structurally joined to the *vimana*. Another elaboration of the structure occurred with the construction of a series of cells built into a wall (*prakara*) enclosing the courtyard where the temple was located. The outer gateways (*gopurams*) were later to increase in size relative to the height of the *vimana*.
(based on Charles Fabri, *An Introduction to Indian Architecture*, Asia Publishing House, New York, 1963, p. 16; Andreas Wolwahsen, *Living Architecture*, Grosset & Dunlap, New York, 1969, p. 136; Percy Brown, *Indian Architecture* (Buddhist and Hindu Periods), D. B. Taraporevala Sons & Co., Bombay, 1956, plate lxiii. Drawing by John Robertshaw)

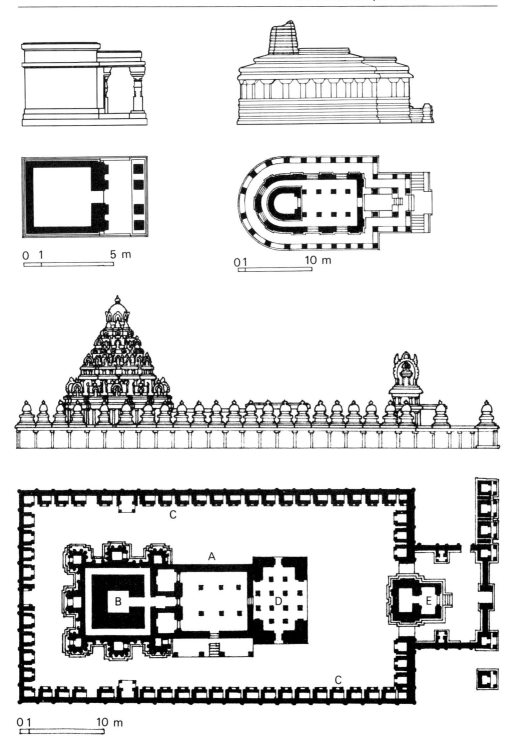

0 1   5 m

0 1   10 m

0 1   10 m

enclosed these courtyards. By the later medieval period *kalyana mandapas*, for the celebration of the wedding of the god and his consort and, by extension, the weddings of worshippers, were also built in the outer courtyards. Music concerts and dance performances were held in the *mandapas*, as were readings from the sacred texts, and during this period the temple emerged as an important cultural institution.

The Indian temple replicates again and again the Hindu beliefs in the parts mirroring, and at the same time *being*, the universal whole. On examining the superstructure of the temple one is made visually aware that it rests on 'an organism of repeating cells.'[15] The sanctuary in north and south India or the gate-tower in south India is composed of replicas of itself that form the basic ornamentation of the entire structure, rising in many stories from a wide base to a narrower apex (Figure 4.2).

Another original model for temple building was based on the image of the cosmic mountain of Meru or Kailasa in the Himalayas where the gods were thought to reside.

4.2 Minakshi temple and Madurai City, c. 1977.
For description, see pp. 131–4.
(photograph by courtesy of Gary Tartakov)

In the northern part of the Indian subcontinent during the medieval period, the sanctuary (*vimana*) rose in size and proportions, emphasizing the centrality of the cosmic mountain imagery. In the south, after the year AD 1000, the height of the *vimana* decreased relatively in size compared with the outer gateways (*gopurams*) located in the center of the concentric walls that ringed the temple. This pattern of evolution allowed for the continuing expansion of the temple complex; the addition of pillared halls, pavilions and subsidiary shrines; the accommodation of newly emerging administrative institutions whose functions were incorporated within the temple complex; and the creation of processional car streets that grew up around the central shrine. Now the walls with high gate-towers defining the doorways were 'like the mythical mountains rimming the Indian world.'[16] But the temple was more than a religious, symbolic and architectural structure; it also had important political, social and economic functions. To illustrate these we will briefly look at the growth of the temple of Minakshi, located at the traditional center of the city of Madurai, one of the oldest temple complexes in south India.

The temple complex of Madurai

The great temple complexes of south India emerged during the medieval period as a result of both kingly patronage and increasing wealth within the society. The practice of rulers endowing temples as an affirmation of their political status and ritual purity can be traced back to the Pallava period from the sixth and ninth centuries, when permanent stone temples began to be built in Madurai.[17] However, it was not until the twelfth century, when the Brahmanic priestly community had become well established in this region of the south, that one can document a temple dedicated to the god Siva in the center of the city of Madurai.[18] The temple city today, representing a culmination of Dravidian architecture in south India, is largely a product of the sixteenth and seventeenth centuries, when Nayaka warriors from the region to the north of Madurai established a semi-independent dynasty, with Vishvanatha, the first Nayaka ruler, focusing their rule on the city. These warriors were 'most often men of low ritual origin whose participation in temple-oriented Hinduism reflected their pretensions to higher rank commensurate with their political power.'[19] Local merchants also contributed to the construction of temples, and their status rose as their wealth buttressed the power of the new warrior rulers. Symbolically, the temple patron – whether ruler or merchant – became a *Yajamana*, literally, a sacrificer, a term that can be traced back to the role of the patron in Vedic sacrifice. Through his association with the temple priest and architect, he was drawn into a direct relationship with the universal essence, Brahman.

The Nayaka ruler, Vishvanatha, allegedly had his civil architect redesign the city of Madurai in strict accordance with the principles laid down in the ancient texts (*Silpa-Sastras*) dealing with urban planning.[20] For this reason, Madurai expresses a sense of unitary planning not visible in ceremonial cities such as Benares. The city was laid out in the shape of a square with a series of concentric streets (squares within squares) culminating in the great temple of Minakshi Sundaresvarar. These squares continue to retain their traditional names, Adhi, Chitrai, Avani-moola, and Masi Streets. The street names correspond to the Tamil months in which the most important temple deities are taken in procession along the streets surrounding Minakshi temple.[21] Along these, quarters were laid out for the different castes and professional groups. The streets around the king's palace, located to the south-east of the temple, contained the houses of the royal ministers and merchants, whereas the brahmin community resided in a special quarter in the city[22] (Figure 4.3).

In the *Manasara Silpa-Sastra* there are elaborate prescriptions for the expansion and reconstruction of ancient cities. Where a temple city is to be rebuilt, it is important to begin with the central shrine and to fashion the city around it.[23] The design of the Minakshi Sundaresvarar temple in Madurai has been attributed to Vishvanatha Nayaka, who began construction of the walls surrounding the original shrines of the god and goddess, the oldest part of the temple. Further additions were made by princes, nobles and merchants who competed with one another to complete the structure without changing the original design of Vishvanatha for whom economic investments in the temple yielded increased social prestige.

The temple, as well as the city, faced east – for the direction of the rising sun holds the greatest cosmological significance for the Hindus. In accordance with orthodox principles of urban planning in India, the city's axes were aligned with the four quarters of the compass, and four gateways gave access to it. One might argue, in effect, that the city, and the temple at its center, were microcosms of the Hindu universe, for they both followed similar plans. The temple of Madurai had gate-towers (*gopurams*) facing the car street; and at times of procession the presiding deity would be drawn past these gates as it circled the temple, symbolic of the universe. The vertical dimension of the temple was striking. One of the gate-towers which allowed access to the temple was 150ft high and was visible for miles outside the city, thus attracting pilgrims to the deity and place of worship.[24] If one were to look at the temple from above, one would see a square within a square; the cardinal points on the compass defined by these eight *gopurams*, with the central shrine marked by a dome (*shikhara*). What is important here is that the outer *gopurams* were the last ones to be built, symbolizing an infinitely expandable temple universe[25] (Figure 4.4).

The physical and spatial growth of the temple complex corresponded to an expansion of temple ritual and ceremonies. One of the most important innovations made by the rulers of the city were the festival processions linking 'the

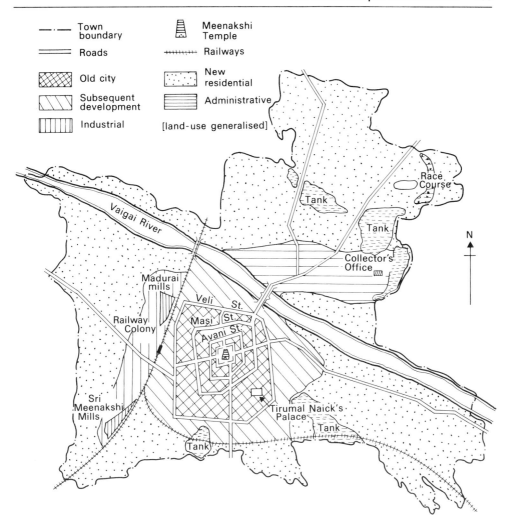

4.3 Map of Madurai City, 1937.

The city was planned in accordance with the principles stated in the ancient texts (Silpa Sastras). It is laid out in the shape of a square with a series of concentric streets culminating in the temple of Minakshi Sundarasvarar. Along these were quarters for different castes and professional groups. The streets around the King's Palace (to the south-east of the temple) contained the houses of the royal ministers and merchants; the Brahmin community resided in a special quarter of the city.

(drawing by John Robertshaw)

sacred diagram and the secular landscape.'[26] If a Hindu were asked, 'Who owns and controls the temple?' the response would most likely be, 'the deity-king'. Although the Nayakas were the ones who reshaped the temple complex, instituted a new processional cycle and gained the support of the temple priesthood in charge of administration, this was all done in the name of the presiding deity. Temple ritual, as well as the festival cycle, symbolically affirms the role of the deity as royal sovereign.[27] Whereas the stone images of the god Siva and his consort Meenakshi reside in the inner recesses of the temple, in the course of the festival cycle (particularly the main Chitrai Festival that occurs during the first month of the Ṭamil year (April/May) and lasts for a period of twelve days), the bronze processional forms of the deities are taken into the secular world, and are proclaimed rulers of the city. By the end of the annual festival cycle, the god and his consort have processed through all the concentric streets surrounding the temple complex, and have redefined the sacred geometry of the traditional city.[28]

The city of Madurai was a product of a particular Hindu world view that stressed both the sacred and secular aspects of the political capital of an empire. It was created and developed by Hindu rulers and the wealthier stratum of urban society which saw the city as a symbolic expression of the empire. Like the deity who circled the temple on processional occasions, the king theoretically circled his capital city at the time of his coronation, accepting the obligation to protect the kingdom over which he ruled.[29] At a time when Nayaka rule was extending itself in south India, Madurai was remodeled on a monumental scale. But the form chosen was a unitary one expressive of the complementary relationship of deity and king in Hindu society, with the first position given to the former, as signified in the divine palace, the Great Minakshi temple. As one moved away from the symbolic center, one moved down the Hindu hierarchy of caste, with the wealthiest and ritually purest stratum in closest proximity to the temple and palace, and the poorest on the urban fringes. The city was a visual reflection of the world view of those who occupied it, and whose values were mirrored in its functions and residential patterns. It was also a reflection of the infinite expandability of such a universe.

With the coming of the British, however, Madurai ceased to be the capital city of Hindu rulers. In the course of the nineteenth and twentieth centuries, it became the district headquarters of a larger colonial political complex and an industrial town. Madurai no longer retained its unitary form but became a

4.4 Plan of Minakshi temple, Madurai City. (Opposite page)
For description, see pp. 131–4.
Key: A Temple tank; B Shrine of Minakshi; C Shrine of Sundaresvara; D Thousand-Pillar Mandapa; E East Gopura
(drawing by John Robertshaw)

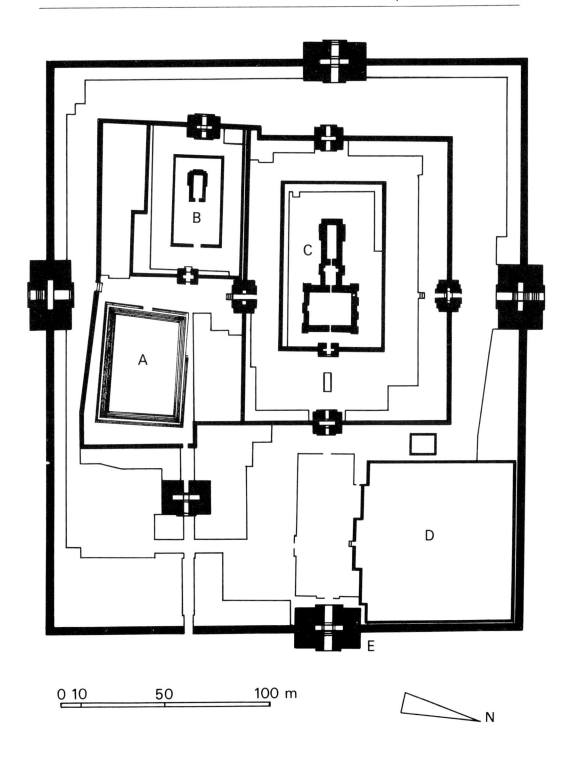

0 10   50   100 m

N

collection of urban nuclei functionally related to one another, with the old temple complex representing but one sector of the city, albeit the most important for Hindus.

Changes in the south Indian urban temple

Colonial rule led indirectly to important changes in the administration of Hindu temples, and to modifications in their built form. The British arrival in the seventeenth century marked the end of a period of large-scale temple building, for there were no longer independent kings with substantial wealth that could be invested in temple construction. Initially, the British gave endowments to temples on a small scale as a means of integrating themselves into the socio-political structure of south India. Lord Clive, Governor of Madras from 1798 to 1803, generously donated jewels taken from the loot of Seringapatam by East India Company troops to temples in Kanchipuram and Madras.[30] Company troops participated in temple festivals, and the governor of Fort St George in Madras City assumed the trappings of state associated with Hindu royalty on ceremonial occasions. In the late seventeenth century when the heads of the Madras settlement and the Dutch settlement at Pulicat exchanged visits, the former carried a royal umbrella, symbolizing the king-like role demanded of the British by their Madras subjects, and signifying their complicity in such a role.

Although the British were initially involved in activities that focused on temple centers, by the nineteenth century they were withdrawing from their role of temple patron. In 1820 the Court of Directors of the East India Company ordered the Madras government to stop troops firing salutes at Hindu festivals in Madras Presidency.[31] Subsequently, they also forbade the presentation of offerings to temples on the gods' birthdays. Temple lands under the control of the British collectors of Madras were now handed over to the trustees of the temples, and cash payments were made to priests or trustees for land that had been incorporated into the rent rolls of the British government.[32] In the process, the religious sphere became increasingly disassociated from the colonial political sphere, representing an important break with indigenous patterns of urbanization.

Yet one important characteristic that carried over from pre-colonial times was the tendency for indigenous merchants to invest their wealth in urban temples. This practice was evident in the colonial city of Madras, founded in 1640 and today the largest city in south India.[33] During the seventeenth and eighteenth centuries, as indigenous merchants migrated to Madras to take up jobs as interpreters and middlemen for the supply of cloth to the East India Company, they

used the wealth earned in the mercantile sphere for the building and maintenance of temples, which served to legitimize their newly earned socio-political
status.[34] In the environs of Madras, there existed two ancient temple complexes,
later incorporated within the city limits, that became a focus for temple reno-
vation, but the building of new temples in what were then the developing
suburbs of the city became a major activity of the eighteenth century.

There were two constraints placed on temple construction during this period
that remain factors in the building of new temples today: urban wealth and
urban space. Although the basic form of the temple has not been modified as a
result of these constraints, many non-essential trimmings have been pared down
in the process of modernization. Since Hinduism specifies a prescribed way of
doing things, to deviate from the tradition in the essential would mean changing
the nature of the institution. Urban temples built during the eighteenth century,
when there was considerable wealth generated by the expansion of the colonial
commercial economy, resembled on a smaller scale the type of temple that
existed during the pre-colonial period. For example, the Chennakesava temple,
the first temple founded in Madras City, dates from the 1640s when two merchants employed by the East India Company gave endowments to support its
growth.[35] The layout of the early town of Madras was similar to that of Madurai
in that the temple provided a focal point for indigenous urban settlement and
cultural activities. The streets were laid out in a rectangular grid pattern a little
more than a mile and a half in circumference and were settled on the basis of
caste and occupational criteria. The temple was located near the center.

However, in the middle of the eighteenth century, the British, fearing a French
attack on the city, demolished the temple for military reasons. Land was subsequently granted to their East India Company *dubash* (or middleman) for constructing a new temple complex in 1762, consisting of two temples within the
same compound, one dedicated to Shiva (Chennamalleeswarar) and the other to
Vishnu (Chennakesava Perumal). Subsequently, the numerous *mandapas* or halls
that now comprise the complex were built, as well as the temple tank for
purification before entering the inner shrines. Unlike Sri Minakshi temple in
Madurai, urban space did not allow for car (processional) streets surrounding
the complex, and processional deities had to compete with traffic at the times of
festivals. Although the wealth of these temples cannot rival Madurai Minakshi,
this temple complex is one of the best endowed in Madras City.[36]

If we compare this eighteenth-century temple with a very recent twentieth-
century example in the same city, important changes in the built form become
apparent, resulting from constraints of space and wealth. Non-essential elements
have disappeared and changes in building materials, engineering techniques and
temple patronage have brought other modifications.

A modern Hindu temple

The Mahalakshmi temple, located in one of the developing suburbs of Madras, is a building of the 1970s, and the basic characteristics revealed in the form are reflected in other temples built since independence in 1947. What is different about this temple compared with many other modern urban structures is, first, the architectural form chosen for the house of the deity, and, second, its location by the sea. These factors, in part, have already made the temple an urban pilgrimage center (Figure 4.5).

4.5 Shri Mahalakshmi temple, Tiruvanmiyur, Madras City, 1980.
In comparison with the earlier south Indian examples, this modern temple in a rapidly growing suburb of Madras has shed many non-essential features. Spatial and other constraints mean that ritual circumambulation is now incorporated as a 'vertical' and 'spiral' activity within the main structure, rather than horizontally along pathways surrounding the temple as in the traditional form. As before, however, the temple is an important ritual centre for legitimising newcomers, in this case wealthy industrialists. (photograph by G. Gourishankar, courtesy of P. V. Indiresan)

The eight-sided *form* of the temple (the *Ashtanga Vimanam*) was apparently chosen for two reasons. It was hoped that such an unusual structure would draw curious devotees, and also it allowed for the construction of an elaborate temple complex with eight shrines dedicated to Lakshmi, the goddess of wealth, all within the same building. Instead of having a series of subsidiary shrines within the temple courtyard taking a lot of space, this design allows the devotee to receive the grace of eight different forms of the deity for the price of one.

The temple, standing a little more than 60ft high, has been built on three levels.[37] One enters the building on the east, through a portico, and after climbing a series of steps reaches the first level, where four shrines facing the cardinal points on the compass are located. The most important shrine, looking eastward out to the sea, is dedicated to Mahalakshmi (the Great Lakshmi) and her consort, Maha Vishnu. It is the largest shrine in the temple, and is made of black granite, the same material traditionally used for temple icons. After worshipping Mahalakshmi, the devotee walks clockwise to the south, west and north where the subsidiary shrines are located, dedicated to forms of Lakshmi that are believed to destroy hunger and poverty. An ascent of nine steps (one of the sacred numbers in Hinduism) brings the worshipper to the second level of the temple, and to four additional shrines dedicated to the goddess; the third and final level contains a single shrine to Dhanalakshmi, believed to bring monetary as well as spiritual wealth. When the devotee has reached the last of the Lakshmis at the apex, he has circled the temple three times, itself a form of devotion in the Hindu belief system (i.e., *pradakshina*). Instead of moving horizontally into the deep inner recesses of the temple, here the vertical dimension is stressed as the devotee continually climbs the great Mount Kailasa until he arrives at the summit.

The model for the temple, although unique in the city of Madras, appears in several medieval temple centers in south India, such as Uttiramerur in Chingleput district and Koodalazhagar temple in Madurai City.[38] However, these temples are not located by the sea; and those responsible for the Mahalakshmi temple are in the process of building an elaborate mythology that links the *site* of this temple with other famous shore temples on the east coast of India.[39] Since the goddess, Mahalakshmi, was believed to have originally emerged from the sea, the site of the temple overlooking the Bay of Bengal is claimed to be particularly auspicious. But the location of the temple also serves another purpose. As a number of visitors to the temple have explained, its proximity to the sea, and the ability to climb the temple and view the shoreline, provide an escape from the crowded congestion of the city where many of the middle-class devotees reside.

The plot of land on which the temple is now located is relatively small (about one-half acre) and this has been an important factor determining its size.[40] Mahalakshmi temple now has gate-towers (*gopurams*) at two of its four corners, and plans for the expansion of the temple complex include a proposal for the building of a royal gate-tower (*rajagopuram*), standing 108ft high, at the entrance to the temple with steps leading into the Bay of Bengal. In 1977 the courtyard surrounding the temple was essentially bare, except for two treasuries (*nidhis*) shaped like *vimanas* standing 36ft high, and containing cash boxes (*hundials*) for the collection of money offered the goddess by devotees. There was also a thatched structure (*madapalli*) with a kitchen attached, used by the temple priests for preparing food for the gods; this will be made permanent as the wealth of the temple increases. There was also speculation about building an independent shrine in the courtyard to one of the lesser deities associated with Vishnu. Urban land costs throughout the city have limited the sites on which new temples have been constructed in the post-colonial period, and the constraints of space will continue to play a role in temple construction in the future. However, since Mahalakshmi temple is located in a rapidly developing suburb of the 1970s, there is considerable open land still available adjacent to the site; in 1977 eleven additional grounds (between three-fifths and four-fifths of an acre) were donated by a wealthy patron for the construction of a school for the study of the Vedas (*Veda sala*), and two additional shrines.[41]

What aspects of this temple are characteristic of the modernizing process? A number of non-essential elements of temple construction have been shed in the course of the twentieth century. Owing to spatial constraints, a tank is not part of most modern temples. Although the symbolic presence of water remains important, a tank is no longer considered essential.

Two other extensions of the temple have also disappeared recently. The first is the *agraharam* or brahmin residential quarter where temple priests traditionally lived; the second is the car or processional street surrounding the temple. Since temples are now smaller, they do not require as large a staff to administer, and the priest's house located within walking distance of the temple, is not necessarily set apart from the houses of non-brahmins. The temple office usually consists of one room built into the wall surrounding the courtyard. Further, although festivals remain an important part of the ritual calendar of Hindu temples, only the oldest Madras temples own the enormous and rickety wooden cars pulled by devotees during annual processions. Deities are now borne on palanquins (seats) on the backs of devotees, and streets wide enough to accommodate a bulky temple car are no longer required. Car streets began to disappear with the arrival of the British in south India and the scaling down of the temple complex.

Traditionally, the auspiciousness of the site of the temple was believed to be an important consideration in its *location*; today, limitations of space no longer allow the temple builder to be so choosy. A number of temples have been built in Madras during the last two decades on land that the donors had originally designated for house sites. However, with recent legislation limiting urban landholding, some plots have been given by wealthy patrons to temple building committees. Owing to limitations of space, one newly constructed temple has two subsidiary shrines built into the back wall of the courtyard, so that there is no room for devotees to circumambulate the deities. Although traditionally there should be enough space to perform *pradakshina*, circumambulating even the minor temple deities, constraints of space have led to innovations in both the built form and ritual activities.[42]

There are also important innovations in the use of building materials and technology. Whereas granite was used during the medieval period of temple building in south India, modern structures, such as the Mahalakshmi temple, use this only for inner shrines and the fashioning of temple idols. Traditionally, the Indian mason worked at the stone quarry, rather than on the construction site, and it was there that stone was shaped to the size needed for building.[43] Blocks of stone were faced by hammer and chisel, a method that can still be seen in south Indian villages specializing in the making of stone idols. After the pieces were completed, they were assembled at the temple site. Today it is cheaper, though perhaps not as attractive or permanent, to use reinforced concrete and to work at the site. The cream-colored temple of Mahalakshmi reflects this shift in building materials.

Although Mahalakshmi was constructed by a *stapathi*, trained in the traditional art of temple building, its overall supervision was in the hands of two civil engineers, hired to control sand erosion by the use of modern engineering techniques.[44] Now, Western-trained architects and engineers are getting contracts to build temples along with more traditionally trained *stapathis*. Since the nineteenth century, a decrease in the demand for traditional skills in south India has paralleled a decrease in the construction of temples under British rule and an occupational shift to modern building industries. Fathers who once taught their sons the hereditary skills of stonemasonry, architecture and idol-making are now encouraging them to look elsewhere for employment,[45] and this has led to a decline in the number of specialists capable of reproducing traditional arts. In an attempt to control this process, the government of Tamilnadu has established a school of traditional sculpture and architecture at Mahabalipuram, in Chingleput district, an ancient Pallava town which has remarkable rock-cut and free-standing temple remains dating from the seventh and eighth centuries.

Temple patronage and the power of the deity

Apart from the impact of new building materials and techniques, there have also been important changes in the patronage of temples. Sponsorship in the twentieth century has increasingly come from the barons of modern industry. In the case of the Mahalakshmi temple, textile mill owners have been in the forefront of donating funds to support temple construction, representing new sources of wealth to bolster a traditional institution. The history of patronage at this temple is worth recounting. The idea for its construction originated with the man who is now head priest of the institution. After visiting a Mahalakshmi temple in Bombay, he returned to Madras with the hope of building a temple dedicated to the goddess of wealth in south India.[46] To this end, he prepared drawings of the eight forms of Lakshmi, which he had printed and sold for a few rupees each. Thousands of copies were purchased by people who saw advertisements in the widely read Tamil magazine, *Kalki* (Hindus believe it is auspicious to place pictures of gods and goddesses in their homes). Along with several thousand rupees donated by wealthy philanthropists, the priest was able to buy a plot of land along the sea at Tiruvanmiyur.

The major support for the building, however, came from directors of a large mill complex (Lakshmi Mills) in the city of Coimbatore. The chairmen and managing directors of several other mill complexes both in Coimbatore and the city of Madras were also prominent at the consecration ceremonies of the temple held in 1976. The reasons offered by the head priest of the temple for the donation of 100,000 rupees by the millionaire director of the mill complex follow a traditional pattern.[47] The director, desirous of performing a devotional act for his patron goddess, Lakshmi, after whom the mill complex was named, sought the blessing of one of the great Hindu spiritual leaders (the Sankaracharya of Kanchipuram) and became the benefactor of the Mahalakshmi temple.

Yet temple patronage is not such a simple matter. In the twentieth century the focus of temple-centered activity has shifted from the countryside to the city. This is related both to the urbanization of south India since the 1920s and to political movements such as the non-brahmin movement of the 1920s and 1930s, which sought to de-brahminize temple management. Such movements encouraged brahmins, traditionally the priests and administrators of the large temple complexes of the south, to seek jobs in the major industrial cities of Salem, Coimbatore and Madras. One author argues that, for these reasons, the larger south Indian temples dating from the medieval period no longer gave the patrons who invested in them the ritual status they desired, and therefore the focus of investment shifted with migration patterns.[48] Along with these factors, the effects of the depression had an impact on the use of surplus wealth. With the increasing industrialization of south India after World War I, industry provided an alternative form of investment, yet it could not replace the ritual status gained from temple donorship. As in the past the temple legitimized the *nayakas* of Madurai and the merchant castes of early Madras, so today it remains an important ritual center for legitimizing wealthy newcomers. However, the scale of surplus wealth today can no longer compare with that of the pre-British period.

The patronage of the *nouveau riche* is also an important factor in the popularity of the temple. This is apparent not only in the Mahalakshmi temple but also in the tremendous growth of the Vadapalani Andavar temple in Kodambakkam, a Madras suburb and the center of the cinema industry in the twentieth century. In the late 1920s, the temple and its tank were renovated, and the public response to the call for funds was so great that a new royal gateway (*rajagopuram*) was built. Since this period the temple has grown in popularity, in large part because of its association with cinema stars who patronized it.[49]

Yet it is not merely the patrons of a temple, or its unusual design or size, that attracts the Hindu public today; of principal importance is the power of the deity to whom the temple is dedicated. Traditional deities with particular twentieth-century charisma such as Lakshmi, the goddess of wealth, and the elephant-headed god, Ganesh, are thought to bring the worshipper success and good fortune in troubled times.[50] One important factor contributing to the large numbers of devotees who visit the Mahalakshmi temple in Madras is the idea that the deity has great *shakti*, or power, and can answer the devotee's material as well as his spiritual needs. This is a product, in part, of the process of myth-building that surrounds the development of India's charismatic deities. At the Mahalakshmi temple, the goddess is linked with mother–goddess worship that began in pre-Hindu (Buddhist) times, reflecting her hoary and powerful history stretching down through the centuries. She is described as the mother with plentiful milk, and miracles are attributed to her.[51] One myth recounts the pilgrimage of a childless couple to her temple home, and their subsequent conception and bearing of an offspring. These are powerful images for the Hindu. Since temple-going calls for such little energy, but promises to give so much in return, the modern Hindu has much to gain by bringing his troubles to the goddess. One could argue that increasing religiosity in south India today is directly related to the problems of modern life. It is not only a response to materialistic pressures such as the need to pass exams, and to gain and hold jobs in a highly competitive labor market, but is also a response to the spiritual perplexity of 'modern life' that stems from such materialistic pressures. Further, the more people who come to a particular temple, the more sanctity the temple is believed to have; it therefore draws even more new devotees.

The temple, the neighborhood and the city

If one asks which temples have the most support in Madras City today, what immediately becomes apparent is that the most popular temples are all located in the suburbs. This leads us to the final area of investigation in this essay, the spatial and social location of the temple in relation to the *neighborhood*, and to the growth of the *city* as a whole. Whereas in the nineteenth century the most important temples in Madras were located near the heart of the city, today a devotee might travel to the suburban Vadapalani temple from his home near the ancient Parthasaraty temple in the center of the city, because the deity at Vadapalani is thought to have more power. What has made this possible is the twentieth-century revolution in transport. By the 1930s, both a bus service and electric tramway linked the central city with the outlying suburbs, and over the past forty years the bus system has been extended to keep pace with the physical expansion of the city.

In 1971, when I lived in Madras, the area where the Mahalakshmi temple is now located was an open beach, lined with fishing villages. There was a small Catholic church, and a few newly constructed flats for retired government servants. The municipal bus depot was located several miles away in the suburb of Adyar. When I visited this area again in 1977, a transformation had occurred: a bus depot was now located within one-quarter of a mile of the temple, allowing pilgrims and devotees easy access to the temple, and on Fridays and Sundays, when the largest numbers of people attended the temple, the buses were packed. Second, a paved road, traditionally called a *Rajavedi* (the king's road) extended to the temple entrance, and was flanked by shops selling all kinds of goods for temple *puja*, such as garlands of flowers, bananas, coconuts, incense, and a variety of souvenirs, including pictures of the deity. Third, a housing colony, Mahalakshminagar, has grown up near the temple, and here the head priest resides. Thus, the temple has played an important role in helping to define the neighborhood, a function historically associated with temples in India.

The industrial development of Madras, as well as its suburban expansion, are essentially post-World War II phenomena. After the war, the government of Madras (which owned substantial land in the city) encouraged the growth of cooperative housing societies in outlying areas, some of which already housed industrial estates. This was a common pattern in cities throughout south India. In this way, the area west and north of Mahalakshminagar developed in the 1950s and 1960s, and today, its residents are either middle- and upper middle-class employees of the government or retired professionals.[52] Cooperative construction also characterized the building of neighborhood temples to meet the spiritual needs of those living in the area, and families contributed a certain amount of their income, drew up temple plans, and hired *stapatis* to meet this end.

But the postwar period has also witnessed a tremendous population growth in the city as landless laborers have moved from the countryside in search of factory jobs. Between 1941 and 1971, the population of Madras rose from almost 800,000 to 2.5 million, and during the decade from 1951 to 1961, 37 per cent of the population growth could be attributed to migration.[53] As new migrants entered the city, they brought their religious beliefs with them. What is visually striking as one walks around the city of Madras is the number of small street shrines that have grown up in the recent decades. They consist of a single small room where the deity resides, and usually a gate that can be closed to protect the idol when *puja* is not being performed (Figure 4.6). The worship of folk deities has historically been associated with the lower castes, whereas Sanskritic deities like Shiva and Vishnu have been the purview of the higher castes. The prevalence of street shrines where popular deities can be worshipped on the way to work, or where the poorer classes can maintain their devotion to a village god or goddess, reflects a new mass form of urban Hinduism.

One interesting by-product of this practice are recent attempts of the Corporation of Madras to control the growth of street temples that tend to appear overnight in the middle of sidewalks. The first indication of an impending shrine is a brick placed on the sidewalk with religious markings on it. Next, a small box for the collection of donations appears near the brick. Once there are sufficient funds, a permanent room is erected, and a deity installed. Theoretically, in order for a street temple to be constructed the patrons must first obtain municipal permission. However, what was clear in discussions with municipal and temple-related officials was that the temple was part of the public domain, and ultimately there was little control over the emergence of such a religious institution. To demolish a street temple that already had popular support would be

4.6 Street temple, Georgetown, Madras City, 1977.
For description, see pp. 144–6.
(photograph by Susan Lewandowski)

virtually impossible without a tremendous public reaction.

Madras, therefore, remains a city of temples, in spite of its long period of secular rule. Street shrines define the areas of settlement of the poorer and more recent migrants to the city; neighborhood temples in the newly developing housing colonies provide a focal point for Hindu residents in the suburbs; the older pre-British and eighteenth-century temples define the original areas of residence in the central city, and the charismatic temples of the twentieth century mark the centers of modern pilgrimage networks.[54]

Conclusions

We began this investigation of the temple with the statement that Hinduism is a way of life. The twentieth century has witnessed a revival of Hinduism in urban India, and a shift from the ritual to the devotional path of salvation.[55] Some Hindus have argued that in the modern world the path of devotion is easier than that of strict ritual observance or meditation as a means of seeking ultimate union with Brahman. This has resulted in shortened versions, and in some cases omissions, of domestic rites. Marriage observances once conducted over a ten-day period have now been consolidated into a single day. Devotional worship characterized by visits to temples, the singing of religious songs and the celebration of festivals to charismatic deities has been coupled in the recent past with the emergence of a number of Hindu saints who claim to have been able to deal squarely with the trials of the modern world. These saints have led enormous devotional movements that have attracted followers throughout the sub-continent and in Europe and America, as in the case of Maharishi Mahesh Yogi. As one author stresses, 'the basic point is clear: the Hindu religious tradition is alive and well. Perhaps not in all its parts, for it never has been – nor has any other religious tradition. But there are centers of vitality and new growth, new efforts to engage the world or help men face its anxieties, new forms to meet new circumstances.'[56]

But, the religious tradition in India cannot be set apart from the culture. Hinduism is perceived as a cultural tradition; what is Hindu is Indian. One scholar conducting research in Madras City has asked his informants to list elements of urban cultural performance. Among those mentioned were *pujas*, sacred thread ceremonies and weddings, along with dance and music concerts.[57] A dance drama in the modern Music Academy of Madras begins with a *puja* performed by the dancer to the presiding deity. The intertwining of religion and culture is also apparent in the modern mass media, in films, in the theater and on the radio.

If we turn to the central religious built form of Hinduism, the temple, it is apparent that innovations have taken place, but they have been undertaken in

the name of a living tradition. Most Hindus would argue that modifications in
the built form resulting from monetary and spatial constraints have eliminated
the non-essential elements of temples, such as the subsidiary shrines and pillared
halls, that were a reflection of surplus wealth during the medieval period of
temple building; what we see now is a simplified, even purer, vision of the form.
The persistence of the basic temple form reflects the inherent relationship between the functions of the institution and the culture in which it continues to
thrive, a culture based, in part, on 'prescribed ways of doing things.'[58] The
model of the temple is essentially bound by the tradition. Yet, the religious
tradition has adapted and incorporated elements from the modern world to
strengthen itself, as modern technology (transport networks, engineering skills
and foundation techniques) is being used in support of this central- and
traditional-religious institution. Along similar lines, the spatial and social
location of the temple defines the neighborhood (new suburban housing
complexes) and the overall character of the city in ways that are analogous with,
though intrinsically different from, the pre-industrial past.

Although modern sources of wealth now finance the temple, patronage continues to reflect traditional patterns. The modern industrialist endows temples
and helps to renovate religious institutions not only because he receives spiritual
gratification, but also because it brings increased ritual and social status. As the
patron of the temple, he is treated as royalty, like the deity who is daily honored
in *puja* by a series of ritual acts that link the temple with a rich and varied
historical, yet living, tradition.

The Hindu temple continues to reflect the ideals of Indian society in the
twentieth century through its size, location and form; through the economic and
technological factors that have shaped its structure; and through the cultural
and religious beliefs, symbolic values and attitudes that remain a part of it. What
is apparent is that, as the needs of modern society have dictated social and
spatial change, the institution has molded its built form accordingly, but always
with the essentials of the tradition at its roots. Much can be learned about the
enduring quality of Hinduism, and the nature of the modernization process in
India, by examining the religious buildings and environments that exist in its
cities today, and by comparing them with the built environment of the past.

Notes and references

1 Thomas J. Hopkins, *The Hindu Religious Tradition*, Encino, California, Dickenson,
   1971, p. 1.
2 Bernard S. Cohn, *India: The Social Anthropology of a Civilization*, Englewood Cliffs, NJ,
   Prentice-Hall, 1971, p. 8.
3 There were originally five other primary civilizations: Middle American and

Andean, which have ceased to exist, and Mesopotamian, Egyptian and Cretan, which have undergone fundamental changes. See C. E. Black, *The Dynamics of Modernization*, New York, Harper & Row, 1966, pp. 3–4.

4   Hopkins, op. cit., p. 69.

5   Ibid., p. 110.

6   William T. deBary, *Sources of Indian Tradition*, New York, Columbia University Press, 1958, vol. I, p. 200.

7   Stella Kramrish, *The Hindu Temple*, Delhi, Motilal Banarsidass, 1976 (reprinted from 1946 edn), vol. I, preface. Much of the following discussion of form is taken from this two-volume classic.

8   Percy Brown, *Indian Architecture* (Buddhist and Hindu Periods), Bombay, D. B. Taraporevala, 1956, p. 57. This refers to a description found in the commentary, the *Satapatha Brahmana*, and from bas-reliefs of Barhut and Sanchi (second–first centuries BC).

9   This temple was built around AD 325. Charles Fabri, *An Introduction to Indian Architecture* (New York, Asia Publishing House, 1963).

10   Kramrish, op. cit., vol. I, pp. 3–5.

11   For a detailed discussion of different types of *mandalas*, see Julian S. Smith, 'Madurai, India: The Architecture of a City,' MA thesis, Massachusetts Institute of Technology, February 1976, chapter III.

12   Ibid., p. 22.

13   Kramrish, op. cit., vol. II, p. 357. This discussion is based on pp. 299–301.

14   Ibid., p. 299.

15   Brown, op. cit., p. 76.

16   Nelson I. Wu, *Chinese and Indian Architecture*, New York, George Braziller, 1963, p. 26.

17   The majority of temples built during this period were located not in cities but in village settlements, where the brahmin priesthood resided.

18   The following discussion is a revised version of Susan J. Lewandowski, 'Changing Form and Function in the Ceremonial and the Colonial Port City in India: An Historical Analysis of Madurai and Madras,' *Modern Asian Studies*, vol. II, no. 2, 1977, pp. 191–6.

19   Burton Stein, 'Integration of the agrarian system of south India,' in Robert Eric Frykenberg (ed.), *Land Control and Social Structure in Indian History*, Madison, University of Wisconsin Press, 1969, pp. 194–5.

20   J. P. L. Shency, *Madura, The Temple City*, Madura, CMV Press, 1937, p. 6.

21   Smith, op. cit., p. 70.

22   J. H. Nelson, *The Madura Country: A Manual*, Madras, Asylum Press, 1868, p. 93.

23   Binode Behari Dutt, *Town Planning in Ancient India*, Calcutta, Thacker, Spink, 1925, p. 326.

24   *Imperial Gazetteer of India*, vol. XVI, p. 405. There is also an important horizontal dimension for the temple occupies fourteen acres of land.

25   Wu, op. cit., p. 27.

26   Smith, op. cit., p. 69.

27   This idea is well developed in the work of Carol A. Breckenridge and Arjun Appadurai who argue that temple ritual defines the deity as royal sovereign. See

especially 'The south Indian temple: authority, honor and redistribution,' in Burton Stein (ed.), *The South Indian Temple*, New Delhi, Vikas, 1977.

28 Smith, op. cit., pp. 75–8.

29 This is a reference to the symbolic circling of the capital by the king mentioned in the *Agni Purana* and the *Manasara* which comes from the Hindu rite *pradakshina*, or delimitation of sacred space. Paul Wheatley cites examples of this rite in several south-east Asian cities. See *Pivot of the Four Quarters*, University of Edinburgh Press, 1971, p. 466. Dennis Hudson suggests that Tirumala Nayaka not only had two large cars constructed to pull the deities Shiva and Minakshi around the city of Madurai during the yearly festival celebrating their marriage, but also incorporated into the festival the coronation of Minakshi as queen of the city. 'Siva, Minakshi and Vishnu: Reflections on a popular myth in Madurai,' in *Indian Economic and Social History Review*, vol. XIV, no. 1, 1977, p. 11.

30 V. R. Ramachandra Dikshitar, 'Around the city pagodas,' in *The Madras Tercentenary Commemoration Volume*, London: Oxford University Press, 1939, p. 367.

31 R. A. Dayall, *Standing Orders*, G.O. 302, 11 July 1820. I would like to thank Carol A. Breckenridge for this reference.

32 *Madras Mail*, 1 November 1871, 'Temple Lands and Exeter Hall.'

33 Madras is the fourth largest city in India, after Calcutta, Bombay and Delhi, with a population of 2.5 million in 1971.

34 See Susan J. Lewandowski, 'Merchants, Temples and Power in the Colonial Port City of Madras,' in Dilip Basu and Thomas Metcalf (eds), *Colonial Port Cities in Asia*, Santa Cruz, University of California Press (forthcoming).

35 H. D. Love, *Vestiges of Old Madras*, New York, AMS Press, 1968 (reprinted from the 1913 edn), vol. I, p. 95.

36 *Census of India*, 1961, vol. IX (Madras), pt XI–D, pp. 155, 190. The temple owns about 150 shops and house sites in the central city, which annually contribute 175,000 rupees to the temple coffers and 582,000 rupees worth of ornaments, and it occupies two acres of urban land.

37 The following description is from personal observation, and K. Sundaram, 'Avani Kāṇā Alaimakaḷ Ālayam' (Unique Temple to the Wave Goddess) in *Sri Mahalakshmi Temple Mahasamprokshanam Souvenir*, 5 April 1976.

38 'Picturesque Madras shore temple for Mahalakshmi,' in *Sri Mahalakshmi Temple Mahasamprokshanam Souvenir*, 5 April 1976.

39 Specifically, Tiruchendur Muruga shrine in Tirunvelveli, Sone Somnath temple in Orissa and the Shore temple in Mahabalipuram.

40 The temple dimensions are 45ft by 45ft.

41 Interview with chief priest, Sri Mukkur Srinivasa Varadachari, Madras City, November 1977.

42 This is a reference to the new Ayyappa temple built in the suburb of Kodambakkam.

43 Brown, op. cit., pp. 79–80.

44 'Picturesque Madras Shore Temple.'

45 Personal interview with V. Ganapathi Stapathi, Mahabalipuram, January 1978. Also see history of *stapathis* of Madras State in *Census of India*, 1961, vol. IX (Madras), pt VII, A–V, chapter I.

46 Mukkur Srinivasa Varadachari, 'Jakatācāryarum Jakanmātāvum' (World Teacher and World Mother), in *Sri Mahalakshmi Temple Mahasamprokshanam Souvenir*, 5 April 1976.

47 'Picturesque Madras Shore Temple.'

48 See Richard Kennedy, 'Status and control of temples in Tamil Nadu,' *Indian Economic and Social History Review*, vol. 11, nos 2 and 3, June–September 1974, pp. 275–7.

49 For a discussion of the relationship between the *nouveau riche* and the traditional trustees of the temple (who were at one time both members of the temple management committee) see P. T. Rajan, 'The Tamils,' in *Justice Party Golden Jubilee Souvenir, 1968*, Madras, Justice Party, 1968, pp. 369–70.

50 Of the 288 temples under the administration of the Hindu Religious and Charitable Endowments Board in Madras City, 73 were dedicated to Ganesh (Vinayagar), and 75 to goddesses. *Census of India*, 1961, vol. IX (Madras), pt XI–D, p. 154.

51 Dr. R. Nagaswamy, 'Tirumakaḷ', in *Sri Mahalakshmi Temple Mahasamprokshanam Souvenir*, 5 July 1976.

52 Interview with D. K. Nambudripad, resident of Gandhinagar, 3 November 1977.

53 *Census of India*, 1961, vol. IX (Madras), part X–(I), Madras City Report, pp. 46, 53.

54 It is not known how many temples there are in the city of Madras today; however, of the 288 temples under the authority of the Hindu Religious and Charitable Endowments Board (HRCEB) (these include temples with some form of property), the majority (52 per cent) were located in the older divisions of the city, and less than 10 per cent in the post-1920 suburbs. This stands to reason, for the newer temples would have less of an endowment. What is also of interest is that approximately 66 per cent of the Madras temples under the HRCEB were built after the eighteenth century. *Census of India*, 1961, vol. IX (Madras), pt XI–D, pp. 153–4, 156.

55 Milton Singer, *When a Great Tradition Modernizes*, New York, Praeger, 1972, p. 149.

56 Hopkins, op. cit., pp. 139–40.

57 Singer, op. cit., p. 148.

58 See Amos Rapoport, *House Form and Culture*, Englewood Cliffs, NJ, Prentice-Hall, 1969, p. 4.

5 The apartment house in urban America

John Hancock

Like all building forms past or present, housing is above all a social statement about the people and culture in which it is found. It is a clue to how people in a historically unified territory perceive and work out their living arrangements with each other. While modernization affects housing's general character, culture is the major determinant of what gets built, for whom, how and why.

This chapter is an initiatory exploration of the increase and use of the apartment house in the United States. Neither its architectural nor its social significance has been much analyzed in scholarly literature: most studies of American architecture and urbanism rarely mention apartments. When they do, the term of reference is usually 'apartment houses,' the almost unconscious assumption being that these are limited or inferior types of dense housing in special areas of the city; more akin to resident clubs, tenements, public housing or 'vertical ghettos' than to desired homes. The neglect by scholars is itself an indicator to American housing attitudes. The most esteemed and the predominant type of American housing has always been the detached one-family 'home,' preferably occupant-owned and separated from neighbors by extensive green space on all sides; yet Americans from most social groups have been apartment dwellers at some stage of their lives – and increasingly this is the case. Within two generations of its appearance 110 years ago, the apartment house as a means of housing large numbers of people on rather small and valuable pieces of urban land became the major type of multi-dwelling in the United States.

As a social statement, the historic record of the American apartment house closely reflects persistence and change in American social order, status, bias and opportunity, as reinforced in the marketplace and the public arena. The forms and uses of apartment houses are dictated primarily by local governments and are developed primarily by private interests working for gain on the assumption that social wellbeing will naturally follow. In this chapter, I will examine what actually *did* follow, by looking at the transformation in the social functions of the apartment house, from that of serving a special type of great wealth, to fulfilling a limited demand for owner-occupied housing for the affluent, to being the major form of rental housing for all Americans.

Social segmentation as organizing principle in American life: the cities

The history of the American apartment house can be seen as a case study of segmentation affirmed and promulgated in an avowedly classless society. Although apartments house a wide cross-section of urban society, users past and present have at least two things in common: they are renters, and they are considered by society to be in an at best transient social state. Most of them have lived or intend one day to live in their own separate houses. Though neither the term 'apartment' nor the housing type is of American origins,[1] the social function of the American apartment house fully credits the word – for it shows how various groups are 'housed apart.'

Social segmentation is one of the oldest organizing principles in American life. It preceded and has reinforced functional segmentation and increasing specialization in the modernized economy. American development since the seventeenth century has featured segmentation that maintained order, stability and continuity amid increasing population growth, diversity, conflict and change.

Social segmentation was usually informal and began with the block in the small pre-industrial American city, since all major activities and people were in close contact in an area no larger than the present 'downtown' of today's big cities. The first large factories were located far out along waterways in the countryside. With adaptation to an inanimate energy base, population influx from throughout the world and related changes since the early nineteenth century, segmentation was given more sophisticated and formal legitimacy: as the city expanded upward and outward it also split into single-use zones of activity and sharply differentiated social territories – a trend which has continued and increased. In public and private development, economic growth at any social cost to neighborhoods in the way was the unifying – or, as it were, dividing – principle throughout; the order of social segmentation remained constant. People gathered or pushed into homogeneous blocks and neighborhoods made a necessary virtue of plurality, as the chief means to express their social differences and to protect and advance their group interests in the intense, uneven competitive struggle for 'success' in the United States. As Robert Wiebe says, 'What held Americans together was their ability to live apart. Society depended upon segmentation. From this elementary principle emerged a pattern of beliefs and behavior which was recognizably American.'[2]

The cities themselves underwent three basic changes in form from the beginnings of industrialization to the present. The nineteenth century's big industrial cities burgeoned several times in incorporated territory, and over ten times in population. By mid-century, most of them had already divided into separate factory, commercial and residential districts, the last further divided along neighborhood lines by class, income, ethnic, religious and racial group. Throughout the latter part of the century particularly, native white residents of downtown neighborhoods were priced out of and fled the booms in commercial development, with its concomitant soaring land values and influxes of factory-fodder immigrants – for whom many of the neighborhoods were rebuilt as cheap but squalid tenement districts within walking distance of the city's meanest jobs. As increasingly high-speed rail public transit lines were built along arterial streets from the central core to sub-centers formed at major intersections, those who could afford to do so relocated in newer but still dense residential districts around the inner city, and the city's elite built spacious new neighborhoods on choice in-town, peripheral and suburban lands – the beginning of our association of outward geographic mobility with upward social/economic mobility.

This divisive social legacy was reinforced as American urbanization assumed metropolitan dimensions in the early twentieth century. Between *c.* 1900 and 1940, urban space doubled again and urban population quadrupled; urbanites became the majority population (*c.* 1915); and politically independent suburbs became a permanent feature of metropolitan areas. The sharpest contrasts were still inside the central city. It had really become *two* cities: one for managers and one for workers, with an imbalance in privileges, services and infrastructure much like that in American- and European-planned colonial cities abroad.[3] An emerging elite alliance of business and government leaders aided by highly educated professional staffs encouraged the trend toward large-scale economic and urban development: control of the economy's ever larger and more centralized systems of financing, skilled labor, production, distribution and merchandising was only partly diffused by decentralized politics in the weak national–local network of government relationships which distinguishes the political structure of the United States from that of most other nations. In major cities, increased ground rents, property taxes and non-residential construction made living downtown unfeasible for most people. In Chicago, for example, central residential neighborhoods disappeared entirely, especially as black Americans and other poor native newcomers began replacing immigrant labor after 1915. Corporate headquarters were separated from factories and relocated in skyscrapers of the central 'Loop' near large department stores, city hall, banks, public media and related special services.

With downtown corporate buildings came tall luxury hotels and apartment houses along Lake Michigan, the north side of which was called the 'Gold Coast,' and which Carl Condit described as 'the solid strip of luxury that extends along the water's edge . . . [for ten blocks and in] unbroken walls to Lincoln

Park. . . .'[4] Behind these spread ten miles of tenement ghettoes, factories, tangled elevated and other rail lines, more apartments and one-family homes (Figure 5.1) until, thirty miles away, one reached exclusive suburbs connected to the city by inter-urban trains and later by automobiles on paved roads paralleling and filling the interstices of the rail lines.[5]

Residential segmentation was highly visible in this metropolitan stage of urbanization. In his study of 'urban villagers,' Herbert Gans found that the ecology of Boston's West End, an inner-city residential district of three- to five-storey wooden tenements and brick apartment building walk-ups, had been generally unchanged since the early nineteenth century when the first roads were cut through from downtown to the then farm areas. Bounded on one side by Boston's original and once largest skid row (an area of the destitute, homeless

5.1 Chicago: from slum to Gold Coast.
Most of these North Side buildings were constructed between 1890 and 1930: tenements by the elevated tracks, efficiency apartments beyond, tall luxury and palatial apartment houses along the lakefront at top.
(from Harold Mayer and Richard Wade, *Chicago: Growth of a Metropolis*, University of Chicago Press, 1969, p. 316. Courtesy of Gordon Coster Collections)

1960 to the present. The share of apartment unit construction in annual new housing starts tripled between 1900 (13 per cent) and 1971 (40 per cent), with the highest point in 1969 (42 per cent). However, this construction rate fluctuates drastically with major historic events, dropping in Chicago, for example, from a total of 37,000 units in 1927 to less than 1,500 in 1930. Apartments also vary widely from city to city in characteristic urban housing type, being about 90 per cent of the total housing in Manhattan and less than 10 per cent in Phoenix.[18]

Before the 1930s – except briefly during the First World War – all apartment houses were built by private developers. Apartment houses proved attractive forms of investment for insurance companies in the 1920s and for big corporations generally since 1937, with federal mortgage insurance, low-interest loans and accelerated tax write-offs subsidizing up to 90 per cent of investment costs. Like other home builders, apartment house developers have benefited from declining land costs as a percentage of total construction costs (from 40 to 20 per cent between 1890 and 1970), cheaper suburban lands being a major reason.

For all this, the private sector has never built inexpensive apartments or any other kind of housing for low-income groups, except mobile homes. Moreover, both the government and the subsidized private sector have displaced far more low-income housing and neighborhoods than they have built for these groups, especially the poor.[19]

Since the 1880s, zoning laws were enacted by local governments under state-delegated authority to regulate the uses of land (building uses, lot size, height, location, and sometimes density, parking and other conditions). Their purpose is to promote the general welfare, health and safety: above all, to prevent construction harmful to neighboring property. In actual practice, this authority was used by municipalities to zone on ever larger scales, to convert land and buildings to 'higher' (more profitable and tax-generating) economic uses, and to protect the *status quo* or even to 'down-zone' (and thus protect from apartment or other un-welcome incursions) areas with strong neighborhood organizations. Social discrimination in zoning, though declared unconstitutional in 1917 and again in 1948, remained possible, its prohibition unenforced and unenforceable until 1968.

The legal character of apartment house zoning was stated in 1926 when the Supreme Court first upheld zoning itself as a proper activity of local governments. In that case, the village of Euclid near Cleveland was allowed to prevent a realty company from building apartment houses on the same legal grounds that gave local governments the right to prevent business and related non-residential activity in residential neighborhoods. The Court held that[20]

development of detached house sections is greatly retarded by the coming

of apartment houses . . . that in such sections very often the apartment
house is a mere parasite, constructed in order to take advantage of the
open space and attractive surroundings created by the residential
character of the district. . . .

In other words, an apartment house was more like a business than a home; at
best it is a 'mixed' use in residential areas not zoned exclusively multi-family.
'Mixed' use is another term for transitional social character: apartments are
undesirable neighbors except in special circumstances. Some of these special
circumstances can be seen in the zoning history of Seattle, where 75 per cent of
the housing is single-home. Seattle's original zoning ordinance (1923, amended
1947) established six categories of use to be determined block by block, thus
affirming what already was in place, but granting variances with ease. The
present code (1957, amended 1965) reflects the belief that mixed uses are undesirable at larger scales too: blocks of similar use were combined into zones
subject to uniform regulations. Two new zones for tower and low-rise multi-
family residence have been added since 1965.[21] However, the whole process still
reflects the combined strength of market and upper-income residential behavior:
apartment houses are generally confined to the edges of 'stable' single-home
neighborhoods, to exclusive multi-family areas and to anywhere – block or
district – that a variance can be obtained, notably in the vulnerable lower-
income areas of the city.

Five major types of apartment housing emerged within this historic pattern of
social attitudes, market practices and government regulations. They are *palatial
apartments* for the rich, *luxury apartments* for the affluent, *owner-occupied apartments* for
the first two groups, *efficiency apartments* for the middle-class (median to moderate
incomes), and *subsidized apartments* for the low-income and poor. This social map
of apartment houses by income and tenure was further elaborated by the building types' chronology, appearance, amenities and unit costs, and by the
occupants' sex, race, and stage in the life cycle (age, family status, and health).

The earliest apartment houses, exclusively for the rich, were built alongside
mansions and elegant town houses in fashionable downtown neighborhoods of
the largest north-eastern and mid-western cities. Following the appearance of
Boston's Hotel Pelam (1857) and other upper-class apartment hotels, the prototype was the five-story Stuyvesant Apartment House (142 E. 18th Street, razed
1957) built in New York City in 1869 (Figure 5.2). Designed by Richard Morris
Hunt and financed by socialite Rutherford Stuyvesant, this was a type of Paris
flat originally known as the 'French flats' in reference to its fashionable European
antecedents. The building contained two balconied units per floor, each with a
chamber (bedroom) at either end of a long narrow hall from which emerged a
parlor (living room), a library or another bedroom, a dining room, one bath, a
kitchen and a windowless room for servants. (At this time, backyard privies were
still common in all parts of the city.)[22]

The first apartment house in Chicago was a similar building, known as the 'Flat' (1878 Erie Street, between State and Dearborn). These 'French Flats' also appeared in Boston, New York and elsewhere in the 1870s. The first-known newspaper reference to this building type was a New York ad in 1876 for a 'home in the elegant new "apartment house".'[23]

This modest entrance on the scene of a relatively new housing idea – that those who considered themselves above the working classes were willing to make their homes under a shared roof – caught on quickly, perhaps because these apartments provided accommodations about equal in size to fine small town houses at much cheaper maintenance and service costs. From the 1870s to the 1970s, *palatial apartment houses* were built in every expensive neighborhood of downtown Manhattan as far north as 82nd Street, around Central Park and especially on Park and Fifth Avenues. There were relatively few of this type of neighborhood: all of them were located downtown, mostly in Manhattan, or in Chicago along the Gold Coast.

The first buildings were not very spacious outside or in. Profligacy of available volume was expressed in high ceilings, stairwells, elevators, corridors and tiny

5.2 The Stuyvesant, New York City (1869, razed 1957).
Popularly named 'the French Flats' this building is believed to be the first apartment house in the United States.
(from Andrew Alpern, *Apartments for the Affluent*, McGraw-Hill, 1975, p. 13. Photo by Charles von Urban, courtesy of the Museum of the City of New York)

unused interior courts, with direct light and air only in rooms facing the court or the street. Typically there were two long narrow apartments on a 100ft by 100ft floor, with a common outside passageway to stairs or elevator. Many apartments occupied two floors. The ground floor was used for an entrance lobby, an elevator bank, and a superintendent's suite. Other servants employed in the building or by individual tenants lived in a half-basement or under the garret, and used a separate entrance from the street. Exteriors were elaborately finished in finely detailed stone and brick in the Classical and Second Empire styles favored by rich Americans in the Gilded Age. Annual rents were from $5,000 to $7,000 per floor, at a time (1890) when the average annual earnings in all non-farm industries and occupations was $486.[24]

By the 1900s, all palatial and many luxury apartments were identified by prestigious street addresses, not by the name 'apartment house.' Palatial apartments became taller and more spacious, had more rooms, private elevators and sometimes private street entrances – all on a scale of manorial elegance to which those who could afford it were accustomed. Apartment house sitings also changed from mid-block to corner to block-long locations with good views of parks, lakes, rivers and so on.

According to architect Andrew Alpern, 'certainly the largest and possibly the most luxurious apartment created anywhere'[25] was New York's 1107 Fifth Avenue (1926), a fourteen-story building on the former town house site of Mrs E. F. Hutton, who sold it on condition the builder recreate her town house exactly. Classified under New York law as a 'tenement house,' her fifty-four-room apartment on the top three floors of the building included a silver room, a wine room, cold storage rooms for flowers and furs, a private elevator, and an apartment for her parents; her concierge had a separate suite on the ground floor (Figure 5.3). Annual rent was $75,000 on a fifteen-year lease. The unit was converted into six smaller but still luxurious apartments in the 1950s. The general rent range of palatial apartments in the 1920s, about $30,000 to $40,000 per year, was high even compared with the price of individually owned 'luxury' class cooperative apartments like 1020 Fifth Avenue (1925), which originally ranged from $40,000 to $150,000 (for the duplex penthouse) plus monthly maintenance fees of $410 to $1,540.[26]

Changes in technology, taste and building regulations did not lessen the principles of social segmentation expressed in these apartment houses for the top 5 per cent of the American income pyramid. All the buildings were architect-designed, in every conceivable style – Gothic and Renaissance being favored in the 1920s. The ground and second floors were set off in monumental fashion from the relatively unadorned dwelling units which soared to rooftop penthouse rooms for servants. Since prospective tenants would not live on the ground floor, this space was rented for professional offices, exclusive retail shops and restaurants, entered by a separate door, usually from a side street.

The basic segmentation principles in the floor plan of palatial, and some luxury, apartments was well described in 1925 by an English architect, William Benslyn.[27] There was nearly total segregation of the three main functional areas: for entertaining, for family and privacy, and for service and servant quarters. At the center was the apartment's own elevator lobby, similar in use to the entryway of a private house. From this lobby, a foyer or reception room led to other doors or to separate hallways to each functional area. Entertaining and family rooms had generous outside views. Windowless kitchens, servants' halls and rooms were grouped in the center with their own hallway, which also cut off noise and smell and was used as a service entrance. Additional rooms for servants and other building employees were located in the basement or on the top floor near the vibrating, noisy central vacuum, heating and refrigeration machinery. As servants declined in availability in the 1940s, many 'lived out,' commuting from other parts of the city, though social and functional segregation has been maintained in these buildings and in each apartment.

Special apartment buildings for the rich have nearly vanished from New York

5.3 Architect's drawing of 1107 Fifth Avenue, New York City (1924). Mrs E. F. Hutton's fifty-four room apartment occupied the top three floors and was an exact recreation of her townhouse razed to construct this building. (from Andrew Alpern, *Apartments for the Affluent*, McGraw-Hill, 1975, p. 109. Harmon H. Gladstone, architect)

and other American cities today. 733 Park Avenue (1971) is one of the few contemporary examples of the mode. There are only twenty-eight apartments in this thirty-story cooperative constructed on the site of Senator Elihu Root's old brick mansion (built 1904). The least expensive apartment (nine rooms, four and a half baths) had an initial purchase price of $270,000; a same-size but more grandly laid out duplex penthouse was initially $526,000 plus a $37,635 annual maintenance charge.[28]

Luxury apartment houses for affluent income groups also became popular before the century's turn. In general, in this second form apartment houses were taller, had more units per floor, were stylistically more eclectic, had more variety of unit size and arrangement, were more numerous and were located in both city and suburb from the beginning. Luxury apartment buildings for the affluent, like the palatial ones for the rich, were architect-designed and usually were located in or near prestigious areas. Generally, they were the largest of all apartment buildings before the 1930s. A famous early New York City example is the Dakota (1884) (1 W. 72nd St; converted to a co-op 1961). Built near Central Park in a style described by a critic as 'Brewery Gothic Eclectic' and by one tenant as 'Middle European Post Office,'[29] this seven-story brick apartment house had a wine cellar, a baronial dining hall for private parties, a great lawn later made into tennis courts, and twenty units with rooms equal in size to those of large one-family homes. Servants had small individual rooms in the dormer (Figure 5.4).

Most luxury apartments were rented on a negotiable lease basis until the 1970s, but *cooperative ownership* for the affluent also began in the 1880s. One may speak in the same breath of 'luxury' and 'co-op' apartment houses, and later condominiums, because the fact is that only the affluent could afford either the amenity of location, design and construction of the luxury type of apartments, or the benefits of ownership of virtually any apartment that characterize the cooperative. One of the advantages of cooperative apartment ownership in the city was that residents usually controlled all activities allowed in the building, and signed contracts stipulating 'that no one may buy or rent in the building without the approval of the owners.'[30] This privilege of control is generally reserved for the affluent in America.

The architect/building firm of Hubert, Pirsson and Company was a pioneer in the development of cooperative luxury apartment houses. The firm created a series of joint stock companies in New York City known as Hubert Homes Clubs, and built duplex-unit apartments which might reproduce as closely as possible the feeling of a private home. A major part of the feeling stemmed from individual ownership of the unit occupied, for which was paid an initial sum ranging from $10,000 to $20,000, or about the price of an expensive private home (in 1900), plus a yearly maintenance and service fee of about 5 per cent. Land and building title remained with the joint stock company (in effect, with the firm). An early example was 121 Madison Avenue (1883; remodeled 1940), five duplex apartments each with four bedrooms, a dining room, kitchen, bath, and one or more small interior servant rooms with water closets.

Both luxury and cooperative apartment housing catered deliberately to a variety of well-to-do tenants, from single men to large families, with upper-class pretensions. The Chatsworth (1902) (346 W. 72nd St; annex 1906) in Manhattan is an example. The two separate buildings of eight and thirteen stories shared a common ground floor and entrance and a view of Central Park on one side and across to the Palisades on another side of the building. Units varied from one bedroom, living room, kitchen, bath and maid's room to fifteen rooms, four and one-half baths and laundry. 1 Lexington Avenue (1910) was a fashionable address for people who wanted to live in Gramercy Park but could not

5.4 The Dakota, New York City (1884).
This early and ostentatious luxury apartment house contained grand public rooms on the lower floors. An apartment tower was built on the adjacent space (originally a great lawn, later tennis courts) and the whole complex became a cooperative in 1961.
(from Andrew Alpern, *Apartments for the Affluent*, McGraw-Hill, 1975, p. 21. Courtesy of the Museum of the City of New York)

afford the costs of a private house there. The twelve-story building (one- and two-floor units) was next door to Mayor Abram Hewitt's house and across the street from a residence of famed socialite architect Sanford White.[31] Luxury apartments were considered ameliorative additions to fashionable neighbor-hoods; we will see later that all apartments were not so kindly received.

Luxury apartments constructed throughout the nation after the 1880s were generally small compared with the giant structures in the big eastern cities, and most such apartments everywhere by the 1920s no longer provided room for servants. Some very beautiful examples from the past still survive with elegance. The first apartment house in Atlanta was the eleven-story Ponce de Leon (1913) (75 Ponce de Leon Avenue), built in and still part of the city's downtown area where its curved facade and twin-roofed pavilions and minarets make it still 'Atlanta's most exotic skyline,'[32] even amid the huge towers of Peachtree Center and other commercial projects which now dominate the city.

The Century Apartments (1931) (25 Central Park West) was one of New York's last great pre-contemporary luxury apartment houses. The soaring thirty-one-story building with large windows, wrap-around corner balconies and a futuristic-looking set-back penthouse was designed to appeal to people who had to give up larger apartments after the Stock Market Crash in 1929. Alpern says it offered 'fifty-two varieties of accommodations . . . from one-room units with wrap-around terrace to an eleven-room suite with step-down living room and a private entrance from the street. It was the first apartment to provide the amenities of penthouse and duplex living to apartments as small as three rooms.'[33]

Most of these buildings were put up by speculating contractors who selected from a mishmash of pre-industrial styles from travel books, photographs and standard plans to achieve the most substantial image possible. Using the newest construction methods and varied facing materials, and putting the latest mechanical appliances in each unit, these developers occasionally produced some elegant buildings.

The work of Fred Anhalt in Seattle is an example. Anhalt, according to a recent study by Lawrence Kreisman,[34] was a designer, developer and promoter of 'the apartment home,' who in just three years (1926-9) 'may well have produced more "homes" of quality and distinction in Seattle than any other person.' He built small two- to four-story buildings modeled after Tudor and Norman country manors and Spanish Mediterranean villas and located on the city's most fashionable in-town residential hills. In a period over-saturated with apartments, he put up thirty buildings which are of such striking quality that they still stand out as the city's finest apartment buildings. His company designed, built, owned, and maintained (on twenty-four-hour call) these build-ings for small upper-middle-class households. Construction of each building took less than ninety days from site preparation to occupancy, and sometimes half that period. Each site was beautifully landscaped with a lush profusion of flowers, trees and shrubs; one building contained the first underground parking garage in a Seattle apartment. Rents, which included maintenance, were high for the time and place: $75–150 per month (averaging $113 against $83 investment costs[35]). The American banker's rule of thumb is that rents (or owner housing costs) should be no more than a quarter of total annual head-of-household income; Anhalt's lowest rental (at $990) was 75 per cent of the average annual earnings of all non-farm American employees in 1929 – just barely within the median income of lawyers, doctors, engineers and similar highly paid professionals.[36]

As early as the 1920s, developers had discovered that three- to five-room apartments were the most sought-after, even by the affluent. The reasons had to do with both costs and the growing unpopularity of apartment dwelling for affluent people with children. A seven-room luxury apartment in places like 9 E. 29th Street, Manhattan, rented for $4,000 per year, compared with three-room units in the same building for $2,000 per year.[37] Since the same ratios continue to be present, it appears that affluent people still choose apartments for much the same reasons: not so much the number of rooms as a fashionable address, excellent views, service, and being among people much like themselves. But, of course, there were also important incentives to own these units, as is now typically the case.

In general, luxury apartment housing is today distinguished from less expensive multi-dwelling not only by amenities and by the higher incomes and social status of its occupants but also by the feature of ownership. *Condominium ownership* is the newest and most rapidly growing form of apartment ownership. Each tenant owns his own apartment in fee simple, has common ownership of all public spaces with all other tenants, and is eligible for federal mortgage and insurance and tax benefits on the unit. Land ownership is sometimes separate from building ownership in this case.[38]

One of the advantages to developers in converting old apartment buildings into condominiums and selling them to individual residents is that condominiums are twice as profitable as rental buildings and often do not have to meet new building standards. For example, in Seattle between 1976 and 1978 sixty-three buildings totalling 1,800 apartments were converted to condominiums, displacing two-thirds of the occupants – many old, crippled, and long-time residents who could not afford down payments to buy their converted units.

Local business leaders and some politicians justify the 'condo' units as homes for people who want tax benefits and a first step toward establishing equity against the time they can afford to purchase a single home; but since condominiums units start at above $40,000, their purchase is beyond the reach of about half of Seattle's residents – though in this city median income is near the top of the national picture. Moreover, slightly more than half of the conversions were formerly low- and moderate-income rentals. The situation is so serious for these displaced groups that the city administration obtained a three-month moratorium on all condominium development and is now attempting to devise some means to prevent further displacement and renter ghetto-ization of below-median-income residents of Seattle.[39]

Today's luxury apartments are often on the scale of micro-cities. One of New York City's earliest condominiums is Olympic Tower (1974) (641 Fifth Avenue), a glass-sheathed forty-nine-storey tower containing eight expensive apartments per floor and duplex units on the top floors. At the base is a one-story building, a park-like shopping arcade, commercial offices, a wine cellar, a health club, and a stock quotation board.

The United Nations Plaza (1965) (49th St East of First Avenue) has two thirty-two-story apartment towers on a common six-story office and shopping base. The cooperative units in this building range in size from three and one-half rooms and bath to nine rooms with six and one-half baths. All apartments above the thirty-first floor are duplexes with curving staircases, woodburning fireplaces and private elevators. Original purchase prices were $27,000 to $166,000 plus annual maintenance and parking fees.[40] Today, the lower price will not purchase even the meanest converted condominium apartment in the nation.

Perhaps the best examples of the micro-city luxury apartment house are in Chicago, where Ludwig Mies van der Rohe led the way in rebuilding Lake Shore Drive into towering, shimmering urban villas with buildings like 860–880 Lake Shore Drive (1950–1), two twenty-six-story glass towers sited at right angles to the Lake and containing 580 apartments. They are mere dwarfs alongside Marina City (1964) (State and Dearborn Streets by the Chicago River), two sixty-two-story circular towers within walking distance of the Loop. Its site was purchased by the Building Services Employees Union, which invested its health and welfare funds to increase their return and to provide jobs for building service workers, few if any of whom could afford to live in these buildings. The first two floors contain the building machinery, shops, restaurants, bars, offices, a TV studio, a skating rink, a plaza and a sculpture garden next to a 700-boat marina. The next eighteen floors are a continuous helical ramp parking garage for 900 cars for the 896 apartments. The apartments begin on the twenty-first floor, high

5.5 Marina City, Chicago (1964–7). (Opposite page)
A contemporary example of luxury apartment house design, these micro-city towers also contain offices, services and parking and are within walking distance of city center and lakefront.
(from Carl Condit, *Chicago 1930–70*, University of Chicago Press, 1974, p. 70. Photo by Richard Nikel)

enough for unobstructed views and just above the greatest concentration of downtown air pollution. Every surface of the building is curved, every corner is rounded, and the whole exterior is covered with lead to deaden the sound of all outside noises, including rain[41] (Figure 5.5). Perhaps the most hierarchical of these micro-cities, but not the tallest in Chicago, is the tapered, diagonally-braced, dark glass 100-story John Hancock Building (1970) (875 N. Michigan Ave.). Public shopping and banking take up the ground floor area, offices are above, and the apartment lobby begins on the forty-fourth floor, with its lower-floor units reserved for one-bedroom and efficiency units, intermediate floors for two-bedroom units and top floors restricted to three- and four-bedroom units for maximum privacy, view and status.[42] An observatory and a restaurant occupy the top floors.

The development patterns resulting from the location of luxury apartments in the suburbs, beginning in the 1880s, bring to light some special segmentative features of this type of dwelling. Starting from scratch – or displacing at most some sparsely settled farmers – suburban luxury apartment developers initiated a pattern of segregation exactly mirroring that which already characterized the inner cities. Here were large parcels of relatively cheap land and even fewer restrictions on building and occupancy codes.

The first suburban luxury apartments went up in tree-lined, affluent old suburbs outside of Boston, New York, Philadelphia, Baltimore and Chicago nearly as fast as they did within those cities. In the suburbs, the attractiveness of apartments to tenants was the appeal of extensive natural surroundings, the contrast of quiet old upper-class, bedroom suburbs to the city, the resort-like provision of recreation facilities, and the new ease and prestige of commuting to offices in the central core in new cars on newly paved roads (which now supplemented the inter-urban trains and would eventually supplant trains in most parts of the nation). Characteristic of this type of apartment building were three developments outside of Baltimore: the Tuscany, the Lombardy, and the Garden Apartments, all four- and five-story buildings with wings or separate structures formed around a large courtyard. The Tuscany resembled a hillside private school or monastery, the Garden Apartments looked like a Mediterranean villa complex. All of these were built on undeveloped hilly woodland that did not appeal to ordinary speculators – builders of one-family homes.

Insurance companies built several suburban projects which were as large as whole suburbs themselves, or in fact became the nuclei of incorporated towns. Livingston (1927, Long Island) and Parkchester (1929), whose 12,000 units in six twelve-story buildings on 130 acres made it the largest development built in that decade, are examples. More typical was Alden Park (c. 1925) with six nine- to thirteen-story buildings, two separate garages, a restaurant, a swimming pool, tennis courts, a nine-hole golf course, large gardens, lawns and woods. Alden Park was owned and operated by three corporations, each handling a pair of the buildings and all owning the land corporation which operated the restaurant and recreation facilities. Suburban apartment densities normally were less than 400 people per acre – compared with, say, 1,200 persons per acre covering 50 per cent of the site of Knickerbocker Village near Central Park in New York.

Visionary new town and regional planners were kept very busy in the years between the world wars, designing two-story garden and low-rise walk-up apartments for single people and childless couples in the center of their 'new towns for the motor age' like Mariemont (1923, outside Cincinnati), and Radburn (1928, in New Jersey near New York), and the never-built Broadacres City scheme (1928–35). These plans were deliberately mixed so as to include white people from the middle and 'working' classes, though neither Mariemont nor Radburn, nor any other new town built before the 1930s except Kingsport (1916–23, Tennessee), contained units which either of these groups could afford.[43]

Suburban luxury apartment developments boomed in the 1960s: half of all new apartment buildings built since 1962 were located in the suburbs as a correlate to massive freeway construction. The case in Washington DC's suburbs illustrates the pattern that emerged around big central cities all across the nation. The amount of apartment building in Montgomery County, Maryland, and Fairfax County, Virginia, doubled between 1960 and 1965, maximum growth occurring twelve to fifteen miles from the federal triangle. The social result was predictable. The nation's capital became predominantly black and poor, the District's suburbs predominantly affluent and white, and several new patterns of apartment segmentation emerged: some suburban apartments were built exclusively for affluent 'singles' of both sexes under the age of thirty-five, others like Rossmoor Leisure World (Maryland) were built strictly for people over fifty-two years of age, and many excluded married couples with children on the grounds that the young were too disruptive or prone to vandalism.[44] In short, when the opportunity to flee social problems is coupled with fast transportation, new jobs and cheaper housing costs elsewhere, Americans take that opportunity to segment anew.

By far the largest number of multi-family dwellings are middle-class *efficiency apartment* houses. Less than seventy years ago, the majority of America's big city dwellers lived in middle- and lower-class multi-family housing: two- to three-family rental houses and apartments. In fact, palatial, luxury and resident-owned apartments together make up less than a quarter of the total number of apartments built in the United States since 1869.[45] Contrasting sharply to the apartments of higher-income groups, the majority of efficiency apartments are compact one- to five-room units in small walk-up buildings several stories high, covering half a block or less of land, and located in or near the city's middle- and lower-income residential areas and around commercial/industrial sub-centers; in the 1950s efficiency apartment houses began to appear in counterpart areas of the suburbs. Most are purely speculative developments built by contractors from standard plans, with few amenities and in the cheapest possible manner. Originally they were plain brick, sometimes wooden, structures with flat roofs and an overall boxy look. While until recently they lacked elevators, balconies, spacious rooms and landscaped surroundings, they have always had well-equipped kitchens, good bathrooms and safe heating systems, and they have always been cheaper than middle-income house rentals. These apartment houses were built on a scale and in a manner which did not disrupt existing patterns of segmentation: on the contrary, as they increased in number they made the patterns more visible and inalienable than ever.

Efficiency apartments were built in largest numbers between the 1880s and the 1930s. Chicago provides excellent examples, as it became an apartment city during this period. As one local newspaper reported in 1883, three- to five-story walk-up flats had risen 'as if by magic on every major street and cross street of the city.'[46] In that year alone, 1,142 of these apartment houses were constructed in Chicago, mostly on the edge of the inner city, across major streets and railroad tracks from immigrant and slum neighborhoods. By 1900 three times as many apartments as one-family houses were being built in Chicago; by 1928 the ratio was seven to one, and a great belt of mundane, three- to six-story apartment houses encircled the Loop and extended far to the south-west[47] (Figure 5.6).

The prototype floor plan was that of the two-room housekeeping unit in apartment hotels, large residential hotels for single affluent people which combined the functions and advantages of a hostelry with those of a private apartment. A typical housekeeping unit in such hotels had two rooms and a bath: a living room with a fold-up or disappearing bed and a combination buffet kitchen/breakfast room, plus a bath/dressing room. Adapted to walk-up apartments in the 1900s, this floor plan was popularized in the mid-west and on the West Coast as 'studio,' 'bachelor,' 'kitchenette' – euphemisms suggesting their efficiency, compactness and low rent.[48] The residential hills and regraded area near downtown Seattle, whose population grew from less than 50,000 to more than 250,000 people between 1890 and 1920, were dotted with these new efficiency apartment houses.[49] A typical example was the El Nido Apartments (c. 1915) (413–19 E. 13th Avenue), a three-story grey brick walk-up building with a small courtyard entrance on a street of apartment houses in a white middle-class neighborhood of single-family houses. The thirty-six units were all studio or one-bedroom apartments, each with a windowed kitchen the size of a walk-in closet opening to a high-ceilinged large-windowed living room and a small interior bedroom and a bath.

The quality of such apartments has been disputed. Condit feels that Chicago's apartments epitomized the banality and poverty of modern building: cramped, undecorative, minimal in service and spaciousness and surrounded by the noise and air pollution from arterial streets.[50] In Lewis Mumford's opinion, these buildings 'raised bad housing into an art. . . . The result of building apartments in New York and elsewhere was not cheaper rents for small units: it was smaller quarters without the cheaper rents.'[51] Rents for two- to four-room efficiency apartments in Seattle and New York in the late 1920s were from $30 to $609 per month as compared with rents of $50 to $80 in a six-room two-family house, $20 to $40 for one room with meals in a boarding house, $40 to $80 exclusive of meals in a good apartment hotel for single persons only, $10 per day for a first-class hotel room in Chicago's Loop, and $1,000 to $5,000 per year for luxury apartments anywhere.[52] At this time (1929) the average annual income of all non-farm employees was just over $1,200 per year.[53]

The efficiency apartment grew in spaciousness and amenity only with subsidies by the federal government, limited profit housing corporations or individual philanthropists. Experiments using these forms of substitution for profit were designed with specific middle-class social groups in mind.

The federal government led the way in setting design standards. In 1918–19

5.6 Middle-class apartment house district, Chicago (1934).
These three- and four-storey buildings exemplify the most common form of American apartment housing. While 90 per cent of those shown here were built in the 1920s, the form has continuing manifestations today.
(from Harold Mayer and Richard Wade, *Chicago: Growth of a Metropolis*, University of Chicago Press, 1969, p. 325. Lillian M. Campbell Collection, courtesy of West Side Historical Society, Legler Branch Library)

teams of outstanding planners, designers, engineers and experts in construction, financing and management were assembled to produce 'emergency' housing for white war-plant workers. Like the federal green belt towns of the 1930s, many of these wartime projects were later sold to the residents and were of such high calibre that they remain in high demand to the present. One example of the form later copied by private sponsors of subsidized middle-income apartment houses was the Black Rock housing project (Bridgeport, Connecticut), where three varieties of three-story buildings covered less than 50 per cent of well-landscaped wooded sites with fair amounts of open space for play, and pleasant window views. Several buildings, totalling forty units (of three to five rooms), were arranged on a block, with maximum density of 140 persons per acre. Exteriors were plain brick with flat roofs for drying clothes, and wooden back porches on all units.[54]

Limited dividend companies were chartered by state law for the express purpose of building better housing for the middle classes, but in order to prevent competition with private developers and lenders they were limited to paying investors a maximum annual return of less than 6 per cent. City and Suburban Homes Company (CSHC) (New York) was one of the nation's oldest and most successful of such companies. CSHC's apartment units (one to four rooms) were rented to young middle-class white single people and couples with small children for under $10 per room per month. With a less than 4 per cent vacancy rate, the Company paid an annual dividend of 4.2 per cent every year between 1898 and 1947, at which time its stock value had increased tenfold.[55] Operating under similar laws allowing them to invest 10 per cent of their assets in middle-class housing construction, insurance companies and other corporate investors subverted the apartments' original purposes when they found that by fixing annual profit at $5\frac{1}{2}$ per cent and charging double the CSHC rents they could attract more upper-middle than middle-income tenants.[56]

Individual philanthropists like Marshall Field III were only slightly more successful in solving the space problem, if not in meeting the most urgent housing demand. Marshall Field Garden Apartments (1930) were built in a low-income Italian neighborhood north of the Chicago Loop as a model white-only middle-class housing project meant to spur regular private investment in the renewal of the area. This experiment, the largest middle-income housing development in the United States before the Depression, included 628 apartments (three to six rooms) in ten interconnected buildings, a garage for 288 cars, twenty stores and a private grade school. The four- to five-story buildings were arranged on the edge of a superblock, leaving half the site in landscaped courtyards and playgrounds. Most tenants were young professional couples, just beginning their families, who could afford to pay monthly rents of $55–95 at a time (1932) when a third of the city's households had annual incomes below

$1,000. No immigrants or other people from the neighborhood lived in the project, and it failed to become part of the community.[57]

The difficulty of private investors, however well-intentioned, in building good middle-class apartment housing became even more apparent when philanthropists turned their attention to the black middle classes. Michigan Garden Apartments (1929) (46–47 Sts. Michigan and Wabash Avenues) was sponsored by Julius Rosenwald, perhaps Chicago's greatest philanthropist. Here, five-story brick walk-up buildings were joined as one unit around the edge of a superblock in the South Side black ghetto, with great interior spaces making the complex resemble a college campus. There were 421 two- to five-room apartments, fourteen stores, two nursery schools, and playgrounds. But since black Americans then as now made about half the annual income of their white counterparts in all occupations, the rents – even at $40–$60 per month with utilities included and $2–$3 Bonus Certificates for keeping apartments clean – made these apartments affordable only to the black upper (business and professional) and upper-middle classes.[58] A similar result came from John D. Rockefeller's sponsorship of cooperative ownership for the black middle class in the famous Paul Lawrence Dunbar Apartments (1928) in the Harlem ghetto of New York.[59]

The reluctance of the private sector to provide reasonable space and amenities to middle-class apartment dwellers continued to be demonstrated after the Second World War when the federal government financed and insured private buildings to redevelop rundown low-income and downtown areas of the cities. To protect the developers from the temptation of higher profits that would subvert the intent of development for the middle class, the government limited return on their investments to 6 per cent. In such subsidized development, the municipality purchased the land, demolishing many existing low-income apartments and other buildings, and sold it to the highest bidder, title and all (which meant losing city control of what was built for whom). The government's main purposes were to revitalize big business and stem the exodus of stable white upper-middle and middle-classes to the suburbs.

On the one hand, this resulted in the putting up of a few tall, well-landscaped and balconied middle-income apartment buildings, with more spacious units and a few amenities. An early prototype of this renewal endeavor was Lake Meadows (1952), built on 100 acres of slum land purchased by the Chicago Clearance Authority and cleared of its mostly black tenants to make way for ten twenty-story buildings containing two- to four-bedroom units for 2,003 middle- and upper-middle-class households (deliberately, and for a short time successfully, integrated), 1,300 cars, a shopping complex, open space, and a school. The redevelopment process displaced 3,600 low-income and poor families, none of whom could pay the new rents (three times higher than what they had paid), and a quarter of whom subsequently went into public housing elsewhere in this ghetto area.[60]

On the other hand, while urban renewal funds were building gleaming new skyscraper office, commercial and luxury apartment buildings in the cities and the suburbs, still the dominant type of efficiency apartment continued to be mean, small buildings put up by private speculators in middle- and lower-class neighborhoods. In Chicago after the 1950s, speculators began to favor little jerry-built wooden apartments known as 'four-plus-ones' in reference to dropping the ground floor to half-basement level so that the buildings conformed to the city's 55ft height limit for wood frame structures, thereby avoiding the more costly use of steel frame or concrete.[61]

The ill-famed social history of urban renewal through its demise in the late 1960s betrays an effort which became synonymous with black removal and the uprooting of large low-income families, the poor and the elderly generally in every city and town in the nation.[62]

It is a commonplace and unexamined smugness in the United States to associate publicly 'subsidized' housing with housing for the poor, elderly, crippled and racial minorities – a form of charity paid for by the middle classes and above. In fact, the opposite is true: since the 1930s the federal government has provided massive subsidies to housing the middle and upper classes – subsidies in the form of direct and indirect low-cost and long-term loans, home insurance, outright grants to big developers, and tax incentives – and only a pittance to low-income and poor people. Direct rent supplement, it is true, is a form of subsidy to those who most need it, but even that must be spent in multi-family rental housing, mainly in high-rise public housing projects.

The rhetorical justification for federal housing insurance, financing and construction programs lay originally on helping the 'one-third of a nation' ill-housed, ill-fed and unemployed in the 1930s; on providing 'a decent home in a suitable living environment for every American family' in the 1949 National Housing Act; and on doing the same 'for every American family now imprisoned in the squalor of the slums' in a suggested amendment to that Act made by a presidential housing commission in 1968.[63] However, the specific federal intent of all these programs since the 1930s was to stimulate large-scale economic growth, provide jobs, encourage home ownership for the middle classes, get rid of the slums, provide temporary housing of standards equivalent to that provided by the private market for the middle classes, and to transform Americans at the bottom of the social ladder into upwardly mobile citizens – primarily by the 'trickle down' effect of all the above.[64] Although the government has made innumerable and sometimes heroic attempts to create an essentially huge middle-class society without destroying the upper classes, it has also continually assumed that the American social system is working in this direction anyway, and should be encouraged, not altered fundamentally in approach. Thus, ironically, the term 'subsidized housing' refers in fact to the least subsidized people in the nation – the lower classes and the poor – and the government has made little effort to blunt popular charges that these groups are getting something for nothing, and indeed has paid little attention to the social implications of all public housing programs.

Historically, then, *subsidized apartment* housing for lower classes and the poor is the fifth and most recent social form of apartment housing. The effort began in the 1900s with normal speculative apartment building by private developers, all of whom produced slums, and by philanthropists and limited profit companies, all of whom failed to produce units within the range of even moderate income groups; and since the 1930s has been assumed primarily by the government. The result has been the formalization and completion of the ghetto-ization of the poor which had begun informally several centuries before.

The majority of lower-class American urbanites had lived in multi-family housing before and after 1869, but it was not until the beginning of this century that 'apartments' specifically by that name were built for them. When they were built, these apartments were physically very much like the tens of thousands of 'railroad flats' built before the palatial 'French flat' appeared in 1869 and the more numerous 'dumbell tenements' built after being suggested by housing reformers in 1879: three- to six-story wooden and then brick walk-ups for immigrants, the 'working classes,' and racial minorities, each building housing a minimum of four families per floor in a space as small as 100ft by 25ft – a housing unit one-eighth the size of a unit in the French flat. Like the tenements before them, these apartments in row after row covered 70 to 90 per cent of their sites and were built in the most run-down, badly serviced and deliberately isolated sections of the city, and gradually became the characteristic form of slum housing in most of them.[65]

In physical terms, the best subsidized apartments were built since the 1930s by the government, individual philanthropists and limited profit companies, although it has amounted to less than one-tenth of the total amount of low-income apartment housing in the United States. Most of this building was architect-designed and expertly managed, and clearly improved housing for the lower classes: providing more rooms and exterior space, modern kitchen and heating appliances, better lighting and air, and sound standards of construction, safety, and cleanliness. In aesthetic and social terms, however, the results were dreary uniform rows of barracks-like and high-rise elevator buildings, far more capacious than the small amount of slum housing replaced, but in ultimate effect extending the slum areas and setting them off more dramatically from other housing in the city than ever before. Before the 1950s, most of these apartments were small walk-up buildings covering about 50 per cent of the site; in the 1950s and 1960s they became twenty- to thirty-story elevator towers except in a few cities (Cleveland, Pittsburgh, Los Angeles, Seattle), covering as little as 10 per cent of the superblock sites – the Singapore effect. The same number of people as were stacked vertically in these towers could have been housed in two- to three-story garden apartments on the same amount of land and left 30 per cent of it for public space in shops, playgrounds, plazas and so on. These stark 'vertical ghettos' were often not racially integrated – deliberately not in Chicago between 1952 and 1968, when the practice was stopped by court order. They never proved attractive housing alternatives to the people who lived on these islands, surrounded by similar islands and by low-income neighborhoods – which often did not accept them any more than other neighborhoods more successful in keeping them out (Figure 5.7).

Nor did the tenants approve them enthusiastically. Indeed, the death knell of

5.7 Robert R. Taylor Homes, Chicago (1959–63).
One of the largest American public housing projects, this vertical ghetto is considered by some critics to be the worst example of federally funded low-income housing. It contains 28,000 poor people and extends for nearly two miles through the South Side slums. The low-rise buildings are schools and 'community' centers.
(from Carl Condit, *Chicago 1930–70*, University of Chicago Press, 1974, p. 156. Photo by Gates Priest, courtesy of Chicago Housing Authority)

the towering public ghettos may have sounded in 1972 when the federal government began dynamiting Pruitt-Igo (completely demolished in 1975), a prize-
winning public housing project (1956) in the slums of St Louis, which had been
turned into a battle region of damaged buildings and human lives by its
frustrated occupants and by criminal gangs from the surrounding slums.

Thus, far from mixing urban America's outsiders and newcomers across socio-
economic lines and exposing them to the daily workings of effective communities,
business, and government, subsidized apartment housing both public and
private shut off the poor from even these modest possibilities for learning about
and getting started toward mainstream America. The people who have lived in
these vertical ghettos have become more and more outcast over time, and their
Coventry is reinforced by government policy. Basic rents may be low (in
Chicago, for example, in 1976 these were $50 to $95 for a one- to five-bedroom
apartment; the average rent paid directly by the tenant was $54, with only the
difference made up by subsidy); however, families were not allowed to use their
subsidized housing budgets to find housing outside the projects. As Devereux
Bowly Jr writes in his case study, 'Public housing in Chicago was transformed
from what was hoped would be a temporary way-station for families moving up
the economic ladder, to a permanent repository for a whole underclass of
basically large, poor black families.'[66]

Who, then, benefits from segmentation of subsidized apartment house
dwellers? The answer seems clear from massive evidence of this most pervasive
form of apartment house segmentation. The direct beneficiaries have been
developers, lenders, housing specialists, city revenues and those who believe the
poor and lower classes of people should be set apart from the rest of American
society. It is unlikely that publicly subsidized housing provided a better opportunity to enter the American mainstream than the privately subsidized kind.

Summary: the popular ideology of who is housed apart

Like those of neighborhoods and cities, the social maps of apartment houses have
over time changed in form and function to follow changes in the social order of
the culture itself. Ethnicity, religion and sex appear today to be insignificant
indicators of social segmentation; and race may be diminishing as a factor,
although this is not yet clear. New categories of segmentation have emerged too,
particularly since the 1940s – the elderly, 'swinging singles,' and couples without
children, for all of whom special exclusive apartment houses have been built in
recent years. However, certain dimensions of who is housed apart have persisted
from 1869 to the present, the most notable of these related to the social status of
transience and to the social role of income in American society: all American
apartment dwellers have been segmented, many as if they were suspect citizens.

Some of these apartmenters are considered to be in transit to home ownership, the center of American society, and some are so powerful they need not worry about what other people think.

The social map of apartment housing since 1869 also indicates how market costs and public regulations reinforced American cultural principles of segmentation in the form, use, location, appearance and inhabitants of apartment houses. Today the availability of unsubsidized privately built apartment houses is diminishing for moderate income groups: not only because of rising rents as a proportion of total income, which have increased from 30 to 45 per cent for this group in recent years (1950–75);[67] and not only because apartment house landlords and other property owners in low-income and blighted neighborhoods are taxed by the city at twice the rate of stable middle- and upper-income single-home neighborhoods;[68] but also because these practices are honestly considered by both public and market leadership, including many planners and architects, to be ways of making or keeping the city a socially and environmentally desirable living place. There is no evidence that these or any other Americans will be content to live in any kind of apartments on a permanent basis, whatever the choices they may be left with. On the contrary: although a famous US senator, a wealthy heiress, an immigrant family, a poor black family, a young professional couple, an itinerant laborer, two swinging office workers, a single parent with children at home, an elderly woman on social security and all the other Americans who have been apartment dwellers are worlds apart in dwelling space and status, they generally agree with the popular ideology that separates all apartment dwellers from the rest of society: some are elevated, at the cost and to the disparagement of those underfoot.

Operating on the theoretical level of this ideology, students of housing market behavior have constructed a model of American housing choice as a *rational* selection based on one's stage in the life-cycle. The scenario appears thus: young single persons rent small apartments; young married ones without children rent slightly larger units; married couples with young children rent or buy a detached house; those with school-age children buy a larger house usually in the suburbs; older couples move to a smaller house or a condominium apartment close to a metropolitan center; the death of one spouse leads the other to live with relatives, or more likely, if very old, to go to a nursing home.[69]

On the popular ideological level – the level of expressed values and preferences and prejudices – the real meaning of the social order is much more explicit and accurate: apartment dwellers are second-class citizens. As Anselm Strauss found in a historical study of American urban imagery,[70]

> In the earliest days of the apartment house, it was argued in horrified
> tones that apartment living would destroy family life, and that it was, at
> any rate, not a proper place in which to raise children. . . . [Today] some

residue of antagonistic feeling persists. The apartment house also connotes a shallowness of social roots, a lack of community.

This view was reflected in laws like the 1901 Tenement House Act and the 1911 Multiple Dwelling House Act in New York City, which classified all apartments as tenements and later put apartments and hotels in the same category.[71] It was reinforced by court orders keeping apartment buildings out of residential neighborhoods in the city even before the Supreme Court upheld such restrictions in suburban villages. As Judge Kramer stated categorically, in 1920, apartment buildings not only spread infectious diseases, they also promoted immorality; thus 'the greater the proportion of private homes in the city, preferably occupied by their owners, the better the city in health, morals, peace and welfare.'[72] Popular magazines were consistent promoters of these views of apartment dwellers as social disease carriers. As the editor of *The Independent* stated in 1902,[73]

> It is not family affection . . . which we should expect to see destroyed by
> apartment house life and the habit of 'moving,' rather, it is neighborhood
> feeling, helpful friendships, church connections and those homely
> common interests which are the foundations of civic pride and duty.

Even the author of one of the first books on apartment house architecture (1929) began his study with the observation[74] that, although apartment houses are permanent,

> As a matter of fact, none of these buildings should rightfully be classed as
> a home. They offer living quarters to be sure, but they all lack the very
> fundamentals on which a home is founded. Of these, the most important
> is privacy. . . . in a building of six, nine or fifteen stories, where the plan of
> one floor is repeated exactly throughout the entire building, individuality
> is practically non-existent. . . .
> Rather than eliminating the home . . . these new types of multi-
> dwelling houses offer a new type of home . . . convenience might well be
> said to be its chief characteristic.

A few architect-planners were simply indifferent to the housing needs of most Americans, or held views similar to those of Edward Bennett, who worked on the first great American comprehensive city plan (Chicago, 1909) and on the first great regional plan (New York, 1925–9). In Bennett's judgment, the rule was 'House the people densely, if necessary, but conserve great areas for recreation.'[75] Henry Wright, designer of both regions and apartment houses, did not agree; but he too saw apartment house dwellers as transients in a building type, whose 'inception was brought about by the vaguely defined need of families whose habits were of a semi-transient nature, or by those who did not care to assume the responsibilities of the independent house, and yet neither desired nor could afford the luxury of hotel life.'[76]

These views of apartment dwellers as being culturally apart from the desired or 'real' America are still current in cities and suburbs. In 1973–6, Perin interviewed land-use decision makers – mortgage bankers, appraisers, developers, planners, architects, politicians, civic and neighborhood leaders – in terms of what *they* thought the public view of apartment houses was. The answers reveal what the leaders thought: apartments are acceptable on adjacent blocks, but should not be mixed within residential blocks because mixing is a transitional form of behavior that disrupts the stability of existing single-family neighborhoods. As one leader said, 'I don't think that the people in the subdivisions are objecting to their being apartments in town – they don't object to people *living* in apartments, they just don't want them living next to them.'[77] In a study of suburban neighborhood leaders in New Jersey, she found that they believe their suburban constituents dislike apartments because they are 'ugly,' packed together, and 'wild things go on there;' and they disliked apartment dwellers because they don't care about the community, don't fit in, drain community finances (requiring too many physical and social services), are transient and are socially undesirable. Only 2½ per cent of these leaders had any positive comments to make about apartment dwellers or their dwellings. Their views of publicly subsidized apartments, especially public housing, were more emphatic but in the same vein: almost 75 per cent felt that low- and moderate-income housing of any kind was ugly and unacceptable not only just on their block or in their neighborhood but in the whole community, because of the tenants' social and racial characteristics, their poverty, the conflicts they created, the slums and ghettos they created (where the poor should or could live was ignored, as well as who actually *created* the poverty and the conflict), the safety problems they created and their tendency to live together in non-family groups. About 4 per cent gave some positive reasons for the existence of such housing, but not in their neighborhoods.

A very strong belief among these suburbanites was the notion that apartment renters came from the city core. A study of 493 suburban garden apartment residents,[78] however, showed that less than 6 per cent had, compared with nearly 3 per cent of single-home residents – not a statistically significant difference.

One of the most interesting revelations of Perin's study was that leaders did not distinguish in their attitudes toward all apartment dwellers and renters. Renters were characterized by the leaders as non-permanent, 'poor,' 'carefree,' 'older,' 'liv[ing] differently,' 'not as conservative,' not indigenous to the neighborhood, 'gone tomorrow,' 'lazy,' not keeping up or caring about property (because they do not own it) and, in general, 'different.'[79] On the other hand, condominium apartment ownership by elderly people was fairly well regarded, though again not in one's own neighborhood, as a kind of 'reward for having naturally progressed through life's competitive hazards and its many dangers.' The renter, in contrast, 'not having progressed or upgraded, does not *deserve* those privileges.'[80]

Apartment dwellers themselves also have generally seen their position as transitional, according to various surveys, many of which are themselves biased against apartment dwelling. A 1927 Michigan survey of apartment residents,[81] constructed to determine 'if [there existed] a widespread tendency of the present generation to seek ease and comfort and avoid the responsibilities which the maintenance of a home entails,' found 36 per cent preferring city apartments to a single-family house in a garden suburb with parks, playgrounds, modern stores, public transportation within twelve minutes of their work, and equal housing costs. Since two-thirds of the respondents had no children, the authors concluded that apartment living tended to inhibit motherhood and that the women interviewed would, if they could, return to 1900s 'traditional American ideal of family life – the single house with the woman functioning exclusively as wife, mother and housekeeper.' At about the same time, another survey[82] of middle-class apartment dwellers in Chicago (half of them childless) found that they overwhelmingly preferred single-family homes because of the children's welfare, since apartments lacked play space. A 1978 survey[83] of 150 apartment dwellers on Seattle's Capitol Hill, ranging in age from nineteen to over seventy and mostly poor or low-income, finds that this belief is still widely shared among apartment dwellers regardless of economic condition.

In essence, apartment house dwelling seems to be a matter of choice only when people can make choices, and then primarily as a stop on the way to or from a private home. Americans segment whole areas on class and caste grounds right down to individual blocks, within them and even within buildings, although they do not use terms like 'class' and 'caste.' This is a statement about behavior in gross terms – not in the day-to-day social and personal relationships of individuals, which are much richer, more varied and finely textured than anything I have suggested here.

In the gross, however, socioeconomic class and caste prevail over any other factors in determining the social map of apartment buildings in the United States. The very rich have been able to stay in the center of the city and on the Gold Coast without much pressure to move, and with great ability to keep their own habitat – palatial apartments – quietly out of reach of all intruders. The affluent have less staying power in one place, although even luxury apartments in the suburbs have never aroused much public resistance from their peers in single-family homes, and virtually none from lesser endowed groups. The middle classes, like higher-income groups, have left their efficiency apartments as soon as possible, generally when the family began: their horizontal mobility, like the mushrooming of their neighborhoods, is impressive. The subsidized apartments of lower-income populations and poor people have remained where they originated, in increasingly isolated slum areas where people have the least choice of where and how to live, and where they are marooned by cultural practice and policy – a bitter subsidy. For the poor, above all, it is perfectly clear not only that Americans use space and building forms to differentiate themselves, but that in the United States to be poor is the highest order of social stigma. It is therefore pleasant to suppose that they are at best, like all other American apartment dwellers, merely in a state of transition – even if in that state they are, like most other apartment dwellers, neither here nor there in American society.

Notes and references

1 *OED* (1933, p. 381) dates the first English usage in London in 1641 and general use after 1751. See also H. W. Horwill, *A Dictionary of Modern American Usage*, 2nd edn, London: Oxford University Press, 1944, p. 10; Jacqueline Tyrwhitt, *High Rise Apartment and Urban Form*, Athens: Center of Ekistics, ACE Publications Research Report #5, 1968, pp. 1–5.
2 Robert Wiebe, *The Segmented Society: An Essay on the Meaning of America*, New York: Oxford University Press, 1975, p. 13.
3 Anthony D. King, *Colonial Urban Development: Culture, Social Power and Environment*, London: Routledge & Kegan Paul, 1976; and 'Exporting "Planning": The Colonial and Neo-Colonial Experience,' *Urbanism Past and Present* #5, Winter 1977–8, pp. 12–22; Thomas Hines, 'The Imperial Facade: Daniel H. Burnham and American Architectural Planning in the Philippines,' *Pacific Historical Review*, vol. 61, February 1972, pp. 33–53.
4 Carl Condit, *Chicago 1910–29: Building, Planning, and Urban Technology*, University of Chicago Press, 1973, p. 158.
5 Ibid., pp. 157–62; Harold Mayer and Richard Wade, *Chicago: Growth of a Metropolis*, University of Chicago Press, 1969, pp. 160–370; Roger Sale, *Seattle Past to Present*, Seattle: University of Washington Press, 1976; Sam Warner, *Streetcar Suburbs: The Process of Growth in Boston, 1870–1900*, Cambridge: Harvard University Press, 1962; Sam Warner, *The Urban Wilderness: A History of the American City*, New York: Harper & Row, 1972; Robert Wiebe, *The Search for Order, 1877–1920*, New York: Hill and Wang, 1967.
6 Herbert Gans, *The Urban Villagers: Group and Class in the Life of Italian-Americans*, Glencoe, Ill.: Free Press, 1962, pp. 5–24, 192–4, 313–7, quoted pp. 5–7.
7 *Houston: An Architectural Guide*, Houston: American Institute of Architects, 1972, pp. 1–119, quoted p. 57.
8 Warner, *The Urban Wilderness*, pp. 113–229; Edgar Kahn, Jr, *The American People*, Baltimore: Penguin Press, 1975; Berry Edmundson, *Population Distribution in American Cities*, Lexington, Mass.: Lexington Books, 1975.

9   *A Decent Home: The Report of the President's Committee on Urban Housing*, Washington: US
    Government Printing Office, 1969, p. 45.

10 US Bureau of the Census, *Historical Statistics of the United States: Colonial Times to 1970*,
    2 vols, vol. I, series A 288–319 (1790–1940), 1975, p. 41; *1974 Statistical Yearbook of the
    US Department of Housing and Urban Development*, Washington: US Government Print-
    ing Office, 1976, Table 222, March 1974, p. 227; *Background Report on Multifamily
    Housing Land Use Policies*, Seattle: Office of Policy Planning, City of Seattle, 1979, pp.
    7–9.

11 Edward Pessen, 'Equality and Opportunity in America, 1800–1940,' *Wilson
    Quarterly*, vol. I, Autumn 1977, pp. 136–42, quoted p. 142; Lester Thurow and
    Robert Lucas, 'The American Distribution of Income: A Structural Problem,' in
    Poverty in Perspective: A Critical Analysis of the Social Welfare Problem, ed. Ronald Dear
    and Donald Douglas, Skokie: National Textbook Co., 1973, pp. 109–24; Martin
    Schnitzer, *Income Distribution: A Comparative Study of the United States, Sweden, West
    Germany, the United Kingdom, and Japan*, New York: Praeger, 1974.

12 Edward Pessen (ed.), *Three Centuries of Social Mobility in America*, New York: Harper &
    Row, 1974; Stephen Thernstrom, *The Other Bostonians: Poverty and Progress in the
    American Metropolis, 1880–1970*, Cambridge: Harvard University Press, 1973; John
    Brittain, *The Inheritance of Economic Status*, Washington: Brookings Institution, 1977;
    Robert Lampman, 'Growth, Prosperity, and Inequality Since 1947,' *Wilson Quarterly*,
    vol. I, Autumn 1977, pp. 143–55.

13 *Historical Statistics*, vol. II, series N 238–45 (1890–1970), p. 646; series N 302–7
    (1890–1970), p. 651.

14 Robert Schaefer, *The Suburbanization of Multifamily Housing*, Lexington, Mass.:
    Lexington Books, 1974, pp. 3–4, 45–58.

15 Constance Perin, *Everything in its Place: Social Order and Land Use in America*, Princeton
    University Press, 1977, pp. 32–80.

16 Ibid., p. 32.

17 Ibid, pp. 59–80; Thurow and Lucas, op. cit.

18 *Historical Statistics*, vol. II, series N 156–69 (1889–1970), pp. 639–40; series N 238–45
    (1890–1970), p. 646; US Bureau of the Census, *Housing Construction Statistics: 1889–
    1964*, Washington: US Government Printing Office, 1966, table A-2 (1889–1962);
    Schaefer, op. cit., pp. 1–12, 125–7; Condit, op. cit., p. 162; *A Decent Home*, p. 116.
    The US Bureau of the Census differentiates urban housing only by the number of
    units per dwelling – usually employing the categories of one-, two-, three-, four-, or
    five-and-more -unit dwellings. A 'housing unit' is defined as living quarters regularly
    occupied by one household (a family or non-related individuals) having its own
    housekeeping facilities. All apartment houses at all levels of value and quality are
    included in this category, except residential units in non-residential buildings and
    converted units in existing dwellings. I have assumed that apartment houses are
    always the largest classifications of dwelling (i.e. from three to five-or-more units per
    building). By my definition, then, an apartment house is a building with at least
    three and generally a larger number of households living under one roof, arranged on
    at least two and usually more floors.

19 *Housing Construction Statistics*, table A-2 (1880–1962); *Historical Statistics*, vol. II, pp.

610–38; ibid., series N 1–29 (1915–70), pp. 620–1, series N 180–5 (1935–70), p. 641; and series N 291–300 (1934–70), p. 650; Chester Hartman, *Housing and Social Policy*, Englewood Cliffs, NJ: Prentice-Hall, 1975, pp. 67–84; Martin Anderson, *The Federal Bulldozer: A Critical Anthology of Urban Renewal, 1949–1962*, New York: McGraw-Hill, 1967.

20   *Village of Euclid* v. *Ambler Realty Co.* (1926); quoted in Perin, op. cit., pp. 47–8; see also Richard Babcock, *The Zoning Game*, Madison: University of Wisconsin Press, 1966; Seymour Toll, *Zoned America*, New York: Grossman, 1969; Warner, *Urban Wilderness*, pp. 23–37.

21   *Background Report*, pp. 4–6, 16–34.

22   Andrew Alpern, *Apartments for the Affluent: A Historical Survey of Buildings in New York*, New York: McGraw-Hill, 1975, p. 13. Douglas Tucci, *Built in Boston: City and Suburb 1800–1950* (Boston: New York Graphic Society, 1978).

23   *New York Herald*, 5 October 1869, Mayer and Wade, op. cit., p. 142; Tucci, op. cit.

24   Alpern, op. cit., pp. 1–159; William Benslyn, 'Recent Developments in Apartment Housing in America,' *Journal of the Royal Institute of British Architects*, parts I and II, (27 June, 18 July 1925), pt I, pp. 510–519; *Historical Statistics*, vol. I, series D 779–93. (1890–1926), p. 168.

25   Alpern, op. cit., pp. 108–9.

26   Ibid., pp. 102–3.

27   Benslyn, op. cit., pp. 510–13.

28   Alpern, op. cit., pp. 156–8.

29   Quoted in Alpern, op. cit., pp. 20–1.

30   Quoted in Mayer and Wade, op. cit., pp. 322–4; see also pp. 142–60.

31   Alpern, op. cit., pp. 14–19, 36–7, 68–9; Harold Vogel, *The Co-op Apartment: A Guide for Co-op Buyers and their Owners*, New York: Libra Press, 1960.

32   Kermit Marsh *et al.*, *Guide to Atlanta*, Atlanta: American Institute of Architects, 1975, p. 24.

33   Alpern, op. cit., pp. 130–1.

34   Lawrence Kreisman, *Apartments by Anhalt*, Seattle: City of Seattle Office of Conservation, Department of Community Development, 1978, p. 2.

35   Ibid., pp. 1–33.

36   *Historical Statistics*, vol. I, series D 722–7 (1900–70), p. 164; and series D 913–26 (1965–70), pp. 175–6.

37   Benslyn, op. cit., pt I, p. 514.

38   Samuel Paul, *Apartments: Their Design and Development*, New York: Reinhold, 1967, pp. 39–48; Carl Narcross, *Apartment Communities: The Next Big Market*, New York: Reinhold, 1968; Elizabeth Thompson, *Apartments, Town Houses and Condominiums*, New York: McGraw-Hill, 1975.

39   *Seattle Post-Intelligencer*, 3 April, 12 and 16 July, 30 August, 31 December 1978; 18 and 25 February 1979; Gregory Lipton, 'Evidence of Central City Revival,' *Journal of the American Institute of Planners*, no. 43, April 1977, pp. 136–47.

40   Alpern, op. cit., pp. 148–51.

41   Carl Condit, *Chicago 1930–70: Building, Planning, and Urban Technology*, University of

Part III

6 A time for space and a space for time: the social production of the vacation house

Anthony D. King

As a building to illustrate the theme of this book, the vacation house might seem an unpromising and inappropriate subject. Small, obscure and, as a proportion of the total built environment, numerically insignificant, only in the last decade – in the context of 'second homes' – has the vacation house become a subject of controversy.[1] Unlike the tower block or the multi-million-pound town hall, the vacation house is, by virtue of its function, often hidden from the everyday environment, part of the anonymous architecture seen at occasional times in the year.

Neither visually nor, apparently, socially or very politically significant, it is therefore not surprising that studies of its social or even architectural development are virtually nil;[2] and this omission might in itself be sufficient academic reason for this essay. Yet if one purpose of this volume is to ask what can be understood about society by examining its built environment, then studying the social production of the vacation house has an important contribution to make: it poses questions about the economic basis of society, about its forms of temporal organisation and about the ideas and beliefs which influence people's behaviour.

Strictly speaking, 'vacation house' is a contemporary American term for what earlier might have been called a summer cottage, cabin or seaside residence or today, in different places, a country cottage, holiday chalet, bungalow, *Ferienhaus*, *Zomerhaus*, *maison de campagne* or any of the large variety of terms which describe what is broadly, if not exactly, the same thing.[3] Though the term 'second home' masks important ideological and social properties expressed by 'country cottage' or 'cabin', the following definition of this phenomenon serves well enough for this chapter: 'the occasional residence of a household that usually lives elsewhere and which is primarily used for recreational purposes'.[4]

In this sense, for a minority at least, vacation houses have existed for centuries. Coppock refers to examples in ancient Egypt and classical Rome where wealthy Romans might have as many as fifteen 'second homes' for various periods of the year;[5] ancient Latin had a word for it, *aestivare*, meaning 'to spend or pass the summer in a place' (often a summer villa in the mountains).[6] In the seventeenth and eighteenth centuries, whether in Spain, Portugal, France, Germany, Italy, England, Turkey or China, evidence shows that the rich had luxurious summer villas or 'pleasure houses', often on country estates.[7] The English aristocracy owned country houses or villas round London as also did the Swedish nobility round Stockholm.[8] Travelling through Surrey and Essex of the 1720s, Daniel Defoe found the 'richest citizens' of London with two houses 'one in the country and one in the town'.[9] In mid-nineteeenth-century France, the *maison de campagne* was widely used by doctors, lawyers and merchants and even, in a more modest form, by shopkeepers and tradesmen.[10]

Yet all these were essentially for a small and affluent elite.[11] What this essay is concerned with is the emergence, on a *relatively* large scale, of the mass market, purpose-built (or converted) vacation house. To say 'mass market' implies neither majority ownership nor use. Studies suggest that ownership of second homes in selected industrial societies varies between some 20 per cent of all households in Sweden to 2–3 per cent in Britain with France (18 per cent), Denmark (10 per cent), Australia (5½ per cent), the United States (5 per cent) in between, although the percentage making use of them is obviously higher.[12]

Since the mid-1960s, increasing research has generated considerable data concerning the functions, social and spatial distribution, motivation for and extent of ownership of such second (that is, vacation) homes, as well as the problems they are said to generate.[13] The general assumption is that, given increasing economic growth and a free market economy, ownership will increase in the future, opposition from some host communities notwithstanding.

The conventional picture emerging from this research is as follows. The growth in second home ownership stems from three principal factors: greater disposable income, increased leisure (with shorter working hours and longer weekends and annual vacations) and higher rates of car ownership coupled with highway improvements. Because of the widespread occurrence of second homes in cultures as diverse as the Soviet Union and the USA and in equally varying geographic environments, the motives of owners, though varying from country to country, apparently have certain common causes. Though needing more precise definition, they include 'seeking compensation for city living', understood as escaping from perceived overcrowding, noise, traffic congestion, air pollution and the pressures of city life; self-expression; escape from routine and the need for change; capital accumulation; fashion-following; the achievement of leisure objectives which might be 'to get away from it all' by seeking isolation or to seek the company of others; to indulge in activities which need rural resources (fishing, shooting, hiking); to find a place for holidays and/or retirement, or for simple relaxation; to confer status; and to provide a setting for the renewal of familial values.[14]

This research, principally undertaken by geographers, has had two characteristics: so far, there have been almost no historical studies, and apart from the research by Ragatz and Clout,[15] there have been few attempts to develop a theoretical perspective. By adding a historical dimension and some preliminary theoretical comments, the object of this essay is to broaden the basis of the debate.[16] Putting the study of second homes in this larger context not only raises basic questions about the social development of the built environment but also corrects certain misconceptions in existing research.

It is, for example, generally assumed that 'the popularisation and proliferation of second homes is essentially a post-1945 phenomenon',[17] 'particularly of this last decade' (i.e. the 1960s), and only since then have they become more available to 'middle income families'.[18] It is also assumed (in regard to Britain at least) that, until the early 1970s, 'built second homes were mostly converted from existing buildings',[19] implying that purpose-built vacation dwellings were rare before this time, 'a relatively new feature in this country' and 'of comparatively little significance'.[20] Other misconceptions suggest that it is simply the shortening of working hours and the extension of annual holidays, rather than changes in the actual organisation of leisure time, which have led to the increase. Ideological factors, such as the spread of 'social isolation' and 'seclusion' as positive values among middle-class urban populations, or the increasing belief in and commitment to private property ownership, have also been neglected. It is further assumed that second homes are essentially a car-dependent phenomenon, an assumption that limits the understanding both of their development in the past and of their likely growth in the future.

All of these assumptions can be questioned. If the phenomenon is to be properly understood, the *significant* development and 'popularisation' of the vacation home must be traced to the late nineteenth and early twentieth centuries when virtually all the motivations listed above can first be identified. In assuming that purpose-built vacation homes are a recent development, existing research neglects one of the most important contributory factors to their growth, namely, technological developments in the prefabrication of housing, and also the development of a new dwelling type first introduced in industrial societies as a specialised vacation house – the bungalow. Nor was their use dependent on car ownership: access to the first mass vacation homes was achieved by using other types of modern mass transport, the train and bicycle; present-day owners make increasing use of air transport as, no doubt, will future ones.

Starting from current explanations of greater leisure, disposable income and improved transportation, therefore, this chapter suggests that the development of the mass vacation house can more adequately be understood by reference to four main factors: (1) the emergence of advanced industrial capitalism in the second half of the nineteenth century and the creation of an extensive economic surplus; (2) the increasing differentiation and specialisation of space and building form associated with this development; (3) changes in the social organisation of time consequent upon industrialisation and developments in transport technology; and (4) the more widespread social diffusion of the cultural and ideological beliefs of an elite. These more general theoretical themes are discussed in the first half of the chapter. They are then illustrated by reference to a case study, the emergence of the holiday bungalow and weekend or country cottage in England between 1870 and 1914. Finally, some comments on the contemporary vacation house suggest the relationship between social beliefs, behaviour and the built environment.

Differentiation and specialisation as characteristics of industrial capitalism

The two most basic facts about the mass vacation house are that it is an *additional* dwelling, and one built to accommodate activities pursued in *non-working free time*.

Central to capitalism, as an economic system, was the creation and selective appropriation of a surplus, an amount of wealth created by labour over and above what is necessary to satisfy society's basic wants. With the application of new forms of energy and mechanisation to labour during the Industrial Revolution, the size of this surplus was massively to increase and, according to Marx, to be appropriated by one section of society for the benefit of another.[21] In what Hobsbawm calls 'the Age of Capital' during the third quarter of the nineteenth century, an annually growing capital surplus was increasingly available for reinvestment, for example in railways, urban development and further industrialisation.[22]

Industrial capitalism, however, produced not only a surplus of wealth but also, for a sizeable minority, a surplus of time. While the development of factory production in the early nineteenth century meant, for the new working class, longer work hours and, in comparison with their agricultural forbears, a loss of traditional rural holidays, for the growing minority of capitalist employers and rentiers of industrial society it meant an increase of leisure. By the mid-nineteenth century there already existed a substantial class of the latter living on income from stocks and shares.[23] As industrialisation and the size of the surplus increased, as markets expanded and workers gained more control over their conditions of labour from the 1860s, increased prosperity and leisure became available to a larger proportion of the population, at first, the middle class and then, towards the end of the century, some of the skilled working class.

The most obvious environmental expression of these developments – surplus capital and surplus time – was in the new purpose-built leisure environments of the nineteenth century, the seaside resorts.[24] These, developing from the earlier socially elite practice of visiting inland spas, had grown especially from the mid-eighteenth century,[25] and by the first decades of the nineteenth were a principal location for aristocratic and upper-class leisure. With the rapid expansion of bourgeois society and developments in rail transport between the 1840s and 1860s, the seaside resorts were to provide one of the safest sources in Britain for the investment and circulation of surplus capital.[26] In a very real sense, therefore, the *functional* origin of the modern vacation home, if not its actual form or precise motivations, can be found in the terraces, squares or marine residences of the mid-nineteenth-century resort.

Two other features characteristic of capitalist industrial development are those of increasing specialisation and differentiation. In all societies, the creation of an economic surplus has led to greater social differentiation. This has been both *functional*, related to tasks, and *social*, related to status. In the simplest economies, for example, improved cultivation and the domestication of animals brought new forms of social organisation: greater productivity *per capita* released people from full-time food production to engage in other specialised tasks, as craftsmen, traders or priests. More obviously, the new techniques and processes of industrialisation, together with the vast surplus to which it gave rise, brought a new economic division of labour, with further specialisation and functional differentiation as well as social segregation.

Yet specialisation, as Durkheim and Simmel pointed out, was not just characteristic of the economic sphere but could be observed in all sectors of industrial societies, in government, law, science and the arts. In all spheres there was increasing differentiation of roles, activities and tasks, although, with the creation of larger social units such as states and classes, there was also re-integration.[27] Hence, differentiation was not incompatible with the formation of a class structure.

But the most immediate effects of industrialisation were on social stratification: the vast increase in the size of the surplus and its uneven distribution created greater inequalities; new industrial and scientific techniques generated a host of new occupations, each with its particular social status; and a vast growth in material culture (especially in housing and material consumption) allowed this stratification to be expressed in different ways. Thus, in comparison with the relatively simple modes of stratification in rural, agricultural economies of pre-industrial Europe, there emerged, in the late eighteenth and nineteenth centuries, a highly differentiated system of social stratification, not least manifest in the dwellings produced for different social class groups. The peasant's cottage, yeoman's farm, merchant's house and bishop's palace were superseded, in industrial society, by a range of residential forms differentiated according to cost, size, form, location, site, geographic setting and use. Only some of these criteria were, in the nineteenth century, expressed in the terminology used: the labourer's cottage, gentleman's villa, working-class tenement, mansion flats. The country bungalow or vacation house was, on one hand, evidence of the increasing tendency towards functional differentiation and specialisation in building form: on the other, it was simply another way in which social stratification was expressed in the built environment.

Differentiation and specialisation also characterised changes in the social organisation of time. The pre-industrial year of the rural peasant was divided according to nature's seasons and their associated activities, ploughing, sowing or harvesting; 'agricultural time' was task-oriented, not clock-oriented; holidays were literally 'holy days', religious fairs and festivals, often associated with slack periods in the agricultural year.[28] Alternatively, they were periods of non-work caused by inclement weather or the absence of paid employment.[29] The month, as its name implies, was decided according to the phases of the moon: the week, with no referent in nature, could – in different pre-industrial cultures – be of varying length, of four, five or six days, decided perhaps by the frequency of a market or, as in Christian societies, by religious observance.[30]

The pre-industrial day, like the year, was organised according to 'nature's time', the day's activities regulated by the advent of dawn and dusk or occasionally by tasks. For the peasant, time was not abstracted or rationalised, divided by watch and clock, but structured according to tasks, meals, events and places. Like the day and year, the entire life-span, or *lifetime*, was, in comparison with modern experience, relatively undifferentiated. 'In non-industrial societies, the repetitive patterns of human life and the world of nature provide the basic measures of time reckoning, the counters for verbalising the experience of duration.'[31]

Time, however, is also a social and cultural commodity,[32] a device, according to Bergson, invented by man to stop everything happening at once. Industrialisation brought a radical change in the social organisation of time and man's orientation to it.[33] It was, indeed, the differentiation and rationalisation of time which Weber saw as one of the fundamental characteristics of the spirit of capitalism.[34] 'Industrial time' is clock time, oriented by time-measuring machinery rather than the completion of a given task: the day of the early nineteenth-century industrial worker became increasingly organised by the clock and factory whistle.[35] With the diffusion of clocks and watches, urbanisation and the development of railways, there emerged a totally new orientation to, and organisation of, time, with 'local time' being suppressed in favour of 'London time'.[36] Railways and factory production meant that time was 'tabled', the day and week increasingly differentiated into socially and economically meaningful units.

After 1850 in Britain, urbanisation brought growing numbers under these industrial, capitalist and urban environmental influences. With increasing state intervention, the temporal organisation of economic and social life was regulated by legislation, the ten-hour day introduced in different trades and regions from the 1850s.[37] Later, 'shop hours' governed the duration in which economic transactions could take place, and technical and legislative change were to introduce such concepts as 'lighting up time', 'opening time' and 'closing time'. With the triumph of industrial capitalism in the later nineteenth century, the annual calendar of working life was steadily modified, the statutory 'bank holiday' established from 1871, the length of the working week reduced and, in different trades and regions over the following decades, an annual paid holiday introduced.[38] Like material wealth, however, such 'free time' was obviously inequitably distributed, itself a dimension of social stratification.[39]

This increasing organisation and fragmentation of time into carefully measured units, during the day, week, month and year, similarly extended to the life-span. Thus, Shakespeare's 'seven ages of man' have, in industrial society, become elaborated and statutorily defined according to a variety of criteria – medical, educational, welfare, social or economic – each with its own particular categories and nomenclature, brought into being by legislation, changing social norms, new scientific and social knowledge, all of which have helped place precise chronological limits on the age sets to which they refer. We thus now have a wide range of specifically differentiated populations, few of which existed a century ago: pre-natal, ante-natal, neo-natal, infant, junior, senior, adolescent, juvenile, teenage, adult, middle-aged, old, elderly, preretirement, retired, geriatric.

The total effect of these new orientations to time has been to create, within the hour, day, week, month, year and life-span, a whole new series of *temporal units* unknown to pre-industrial society; such standard units of time both reflect and regulate social rhythms.[40] And to anticipate the argument below, each new unit of time was frequently associated with a specialised location, building and geographic place, the segmentation of the day, for example, being 'symbolised for many people by the separation of various activities by location'.[41] As for the 'life-span units' we have the ante-natal ward, infant clinic, nursery class, junior school, juvenile court, teenage coffee bar, adult college, retirement resort, over-sixties club, old person's bungalow. Moreover, the development of some of these new temporal units has been dependent on a new spatial distribution of activities.[42]

Differentiation and specialisation in the economy, in society and in the organisation of time have been inextricably linked with (and indeed, often caused by) the development of a differentiated spatial (or geographic) environment: particular places have been reserved for particular uses, and special forms of building developed for specific purposes. As industrialisation made rural–agricultural and urban–industrial environments increasingly distinct, each developed markedly different patterns in their use of space. Within urban regions, further differentiation gave rise to functionally specialised towns,[43] where spatial divisions were based both on economic function and on social class. In London, the spatial segregation of residential areas, reflecting processes of social stratification discussed above, was already well marked in the early nineteenth century.[44] The industrial town developed its industrial, commercial and residential areas, with the central business district emerging in the later nineteenth century. The pre-industrial dwelling, whether farmhouse or weaver's cottage, previously housing both work and residence (and many other functions), was superseded by the factory or office and residential dwelling (as well as other new building forms). 'As corporations increased in complexity, so did the spatial separation of work experience. The new managerial and clerical functions occurred in partitioned offices and at times, in different buildings, often in different parts of the city.'[45] For the industrial worker, not only was working time increasingly distinct from non-working time but, with rising living standards and greater free time, positive 'recreation' was distinguished from other non-work activity. As stated more fully elsewhere,[46] this recreational time was increasingly accommodated, between 1850 and 1914, in the town, in the park, sports ground, music hall, pub, club house[47] and, with the development in transport technology, in the specialised recreational resorts at the seaside, where again new building forms, catering solely for leisure – the pier, promenade, pavilion, winter gardens and boarding house – developed.

To summarise, then, the economic transformations of industrial capitalism gave rise to new social formations, changes in the social organisation of time and a highly differentiated, functionally specialised building and spatial environment. These environments were stratified not only according to social class but also according to the times and seasons when they were used.[48] Walton, for example, has shown how, by the mid-nineteenth century, traditional Lancashire cotton town holidays, spent locally at the alehouse and fairground, were 'tamed', their place increasingly taken by the excursion to the seaside. 'The coming of factory discipline reduced casual absenteeism as employers attempted to impose a regular six-day and, later, five-and-a-half day week.'[49] In short, the temporal calendar of the pre-industrial workforce, linked to the local expression of leisure activities, was transformed into a modern pattern of annual holidays spent at a specialised working-class resort. By the 1880s, the purpose-built boarding house was catering for the specialised leisure needs of a working-class population.[50]

It is within this framework, therefore, that the development of the modern, purpose-built vacation house can be understood. It is a specialised dwelling type designed for a particular function, location, social group, time and, if possible, with a distinctive form and appearance. In these terms, the development of a specialised vacation house, at anything like a popular as opposed to an elite level, occurred in England in the last quarter of the nineteenth century. Here, its emergence is traced by the examination of lexical data supported by other evidence. As socially significant phenomena are generally named, it is reasonable to assume that the reality of the modern vacation house emerged when the terms 'vacation' or 'holiday house', 'weekend bungalow' or 'country cottage' were introduced. In Britain, both the terms and the reality of the 'bungalow' and 'country cottage' (understood with its present-day connotations), two prototypes of the modern mass vacation house, came into general use between 1870 and 1914.

The 'country cottage'

For most of its pre-industrial history, the term 'cottage' referred to a small, minimal dwelling which, by implication, housed the economically poorer agricultural or, later, industrial worker. The term, in fact, clearly demonstrates that certain house types were originally defined according to the economic and social status of their occupant: a cottage was the dwelling of a 'cottar', a peasant who held, under the feudal system, a given amount of land in return for labour.[51] In the nineteenth century, a cottage was generally a one- or two-storeyed dwelling 'ordinarily occupied by the humbler classes of society'.[52] The exception to this usage occurred in the late eighteenth and early nineteenth centuries when members of the aristocracy and urban elite adopted, in the 'ornamental cottage', a modified version of the peasant's dwelling. This practice, which generated some forty books of architectural designs between 1790 and 1810 and about the same number again in the following forty years,[53] stemmed primarily from ideological and aesthetic motives.

Thus, such a cottage might be built 'for a labourer and his family and intended as an ornamental object in a gentleman's grounds',[54] although others might be meant for retirement. Though some evidently had the function of a 'second home', this was apparently rare.[55] Elsam, for example, refers to 'gentlemen whose employments and business lie in the city' who are 'desirous of a villa or country seat a few miles out of town where they have an opportunity of relaxing in the most rational, useful recreations'.[56] Provision for such a need could be made by 'a small neat cottage fit for the retreat of a Merchant, within a few miles of the Metropolis, or the environs of any great town';[57] or, by 'a small villa suitable for the summer residence of a genteel family'.[58] For the clientele of these dwellings, retirement into the country was considered as 'an occasional retreat from the noise and ceremony, a relaxation from care and business'.[59]

While at least some of the modern motivations for the vacation house were, therefore, apparently present in the early nineteenth century, available transport possibilities kept it relatively close to the town and it was limited to seasonal (i.e. summer) use.

With this exception, then, the term 'cottage' retained its original meaning for most of the nineteenth century. In a school reader of 1881 a dialogue states: 'What is a cottage? Small houses in country villages. Who lives there? The farm labourers and other poor people.'[60] When the Oxford English Dictionary was first published in 1888, 'cottage' was defined in terms of its size, quality and the occupational characteristics of its inhabitants. It is 'a dwelling house of small size and humble character such as is occupied by farm labourers, villagers, miners, etc.' Yet significantly, there is also evidence of a change in social meaning: 'for some time past' the term had been in vogue 'as a particular designation for small country residences and detached suburban houses, adapted to a moderate scale of living . . . in this sense, the name is divested of all associations of poverty.'[61]

Yet for most, the social meaning of cottage was still associated with the 'lower orders'. Such interest as the middle class showed in the dwelling form was in the social and moral condition of its inhabitants or, by the aristocracy, in the provision of *rural* (not *country*) cottages for agricultural labourers. Neither the term nor the reality of the 'country cottage' in the modern sense, as a dwelling owned or rented for occasional middle class use in addition to the primary place of urban residence, can be identified before the later 1880s.[62]

The concept of the country cottage rests on three assumptions: it is a cottage defined according to *place* (i.e. 'the country') and not, as in previous common use, according to social or occupational status (labourer's, mechanic's, artisan's cottage) or design (ornamental, picturesque, rustic cottage). In this definition of place, 'country' is to be distinguished from 'rural', a term frequently associated with cottages in the nineteenth century, and suggests a different perception of both the country and the cottage. Finally, as a term describing a dwelling in the country, 'country cottage' is used in contradistinction to other terms used earlier in the nineteenth century such as 'country house', 'seat', 'residence', 'villa', and in this sense suggests a changed perception of a country dwelling dependent on size and, implicitly, on the social class who patronise it.

The term 'country', used to describe a particular cultural category of environment as distinct from 'the seaside' or 'the mountains' is significant in that it apparently originates in the Latin 'contra' (against) and is therefore defined according to town or urban criteria.[63] The specialised use of 'country' in contrast to 'city' began, according to Williams, in the late sixteenth century with increasing urbanisation and the growth of London.[64]

The idea of the rich and powerful having two or more dwellings, one in the city as the principal locus of social and political activity, the other in the country, for recreational use and as a symbol of power and status, common in many societies, had been well established in England since the fifteenth century and earlier.[65] It was this traditional elite which provided the model for the new aristocracy of wealth created by the Industrial Revolution, and for most of the nineteenth century the country remained the private 'leisure environment' of an aristocratic and wealthy commercial and industrial class.[66] Until the middle of that century, the majority of the population lived, worked and played in rural areas; for them 'the country', as a distinct and *preferred* location for leisure, had neither particular significance nor meaning. Only for an elite, moving between country and town, did it have a particular association with leisure, as well as a distinct social meaning.[67]

For the growing urban bourgeoisie, the principal settings for leisure were the developing seaside resorts which, with the odd exception,[68] catered almost entirely for a middle- and upper-middle-class clientèle. This division was still taken for granted in 1880. According to *The Architect* (1881),[69]

> the typical aristocrat is apt to despise seaside delights. He prefers to
> spend the autumn either at his own 'place in the country', or at the place
> of some friend, or abroad. [The seaside resorts were primarily] for the
> middle classes and though inferior people have also to be considered in
> these places, it is not to any appreciable extent.

In the last two decades of the century, this situation was to change. For the expanding urban middle class, with the aristocracy as a model for social emulation, the country was to become, in modern terminology, a recreational resource. The reasons were many. By the 1890s, not only was England the most urbanised country in the world, but people were aware of the fact.[70] By the late 1870s, the railway network practically covered the country:[71] with the help of improved road surfaces and better carriages, access to previously remote rural areas was gained. Rising profits from industry and commerce had inflated the size of the urban bourgeoisie, especially in London. Developments in shipping, American agriculture, refrigeration and other factors in an increasingly global economy had brought agricultural decline and, with growing emigration from rural areas, the decay of rural cottages in the last years of the century.[72] Not only the railway but, from the middle 1890s, the bicycle – or a combination of both – brought rural areas within travelling distance of the towns, far smaller in size than they are today.[73] Where the country had previously been the semi-private leisure environment of the elite, it now became more available to the urban middle class and even, in the early twentieth century, to the lower middle class. With 'the seaside', 'the country' was increasingly seen by these groups as a recreational resource providing respite from what were perceived as the 'growing strains of urban life'. It is in this context that *The General Register of Seaside and Country Quarters* is published in 1888 and, for a wealthy upper middle class, the journal *Country Life* begins in 1896.[74] And though the increasing use of the automobile (introduced in England from the mid-1890s) in the first decade of the century[75] stimulated the development of the country cottage as second home, the idea had been established well before. The first country bungalows and cottages were reached by rail, and where provision for transport was made in their design, it was for carriages and bicycles. However, together with all these factors, the particular reasons for the development of the country cottage were the articulation of an anti-urban ideology and, with gradual changes in the social organisation of time, the emergence of a new temporal unit – the weekend.

The emergence of the 'week-end'

In the social reorganisation of time consequent upon industrialisation, the week-end, as a socially differentiated unit of non-working free time, has emerged as one of the most important leisure institutions in modern society. Yet while geographers have studied perceptions of space, and anthropologists, cultural perceptions of time, surprisingly few historians have concerned themselves with temporal perceptions in the past or the way societies have organised time.[76] The emergence of the weekend has yet to be fully investigated.

The concept of the weekend, of either one and a half or two days from Friday night or Saturday noon to Monday morning of free 'leisure time', is relatively recent, and is associated only with industrial societies. It is obvious, however, that the weekend in this sense did not develop simultaneously for all social and economic groups. And though the emergence of the 'week-end cottage' was primarily a middle-class phenomenon, it is appropriate here (because of the apparent lack of discussion elsewhere) to include data on the development of the weekend for the larger, working-class, population. It is, for example, relatively easy to trace, by reference to the statutory limitation of working hours, the length of the working week and the introduction of the Saturday half holiday, for some working men in the industrial north to the 1840s, and in London from the 1850s.[77] The universal recognition of the institution, however, is more difficult to pin down: the full two-day weekend is, for instance, for the London worker, mainly a post-1945 phenomenon.[78] Yet by the 1860s, amusement for leisure had become 'an undertaking worthy of commercial exploitation'[79] and with the rise of the northern working class seaside resort during the third quarter of the nineteenth century there had developed the modern idea of the weekend as a period of leisure time spent away from the normal place of residence.[80]

Lexical recognition of this new temporal unit apparently occurs in the late 1870s: the first recorded use of 'week-end' is in 1879, and by 1900 the term had become commonplace. The geography of its use is clearly located in the new urban industrial regions of the Midlands and north-west England and the new leisure environments developed in response to them. Thus, in 1879 'in Stafford-shire, if a person leaves home at the end of his week's work on the Saturday afternoon to spend the evening of Saturday and the following Sunday with friends at a distance he is said to be spending his week-end at so and so'. In 1880 lodging house keepers in North Wales described visitors who came on Saturday and went on Monday as 'week-enders'; in 1887 a railway in Lancashire was advertising 'week-end tickets'; in 1889 the term was used 'for that kind of visit which north country people describe as a week-end'.[81]

Among the growing number of professional and white-collar employees, similar structural changes in working time were taking place: Lloyd's closed on Saturday afternoon in 1854; the civil service conceded the Saturday half-holiday in the 1860s and the Stock Exchange from 1874.[82] In 1901 a weekly magazine, the *Week-end*, was begun, aimed at the middle-class reader, its cover depicting a railway train, horse coach and car. It was for 'the man who spends the week-end in the cultured seclusion of his home; the man who runs out of town to the countryside; the family who pays a flying visit to the sea; the people who lazily loaf the hours away on the river'.[83] With almost 80 per cent of the English population urban in 1911, the 'busy toiler' in the now dominant world 'of commerce and industry' found his hours of leisure comparatively few, 'in the vast majority of instances restricted to that brief interval for relaxation which in modern parlance has come to be designated "the week-end"'.[84] In a steady secularisation of time, the weekend was replacing the Sabbath as a period to punctuate the month: for an upper-class minority at least, 'weekending' had become 'part of the British constitution'.[85]

In the majority of these examples, the new temporal concept of the weekend was defined in relation to place, a place different from the normal location of work and residence. The weekend was not simply a *duration* of time but also a spatial–temporal unit. The link was established by new modes of travel – the railway, bicycle and then the car. With the separation of work from residence, it had also a social dimension. The 'working week' was spent in town, in the company of office colleagues: the 'week-end', at home (or occasionally, at the 'cottage'), in the company of wife and children. That the term and concept were products of England as the first industrial society is indicated by their diffusion to other societies whose industrialisation followed that of Britain: in France (in 1906), where significantly, as 'le weekend', it was used as 'passer son weekend à la campagne'. It is, according to a major authority, 'un mot, un des rares, dont on peut dire qu'ils nous ont apporté une notion nouvelle'.[86]

Thus, with middle-class holidays away from home in the 1860s, a week's paid holiday for some manual workers gradually being introduced from the 1880s[87] and the weekend institutionalised by the end of the century, there were – within the context of surplus wealth – new 'social units' of time to be accommodated in the built environment.

The bungalow and weekend country cottage

The development of a purpose-built dwelling to meet these particular social, spatial, temporal and ideological needs of the expanding middle class took place in the last three decades of the century. The first bungalows built and named as such, speculatively built as a specialised seaside house for summer use, appeared on the north Kent coast, some two hours' journey by train from London, in 1869–70.[88] Though bungalows and 'seaside cottages' were being designed in the late 1870s, the earliest reference to 'country cottage' in the modern sense so far identified is in 1887[89] and to a 'week-end cottage' in 1904, although 'the evolution of the popular week-end cottage' had come about 'in the twenty years previous to this' (i.e. 1884–1904).[90]

Though the early bungalows and many small country houses built at this time had the function of second homes, many were mainly for summer use, though they were also being used for weekends by the 1890s and probably earlier. Thus, an estate of Sussex bungalows and small houses built in the late 1880s within easy rail distance of London were for 'people of moderate means in a city like ours where grime and smoke, bustle and hurry make us long for the country and its freshness where, at a small expense, we may pass a quiet week-end'.[91] At the seaside, the bungalow had developed in response to subtle value changes among middle-class urban populations. Early nineteenth-century resorts had been essentially social places, providing – in the assembly rooms, promenades, theatres, crescents and squares – opportunity for group enjoyment, social rituals and personal display. The bungalow was an early symbol of the rejection of this behaviour. It represented a search for solitude, a quest for quiet, and isolation from the city crowd. In this, it was essentially an *urban* house-type, performing a social function conceivable only when the links with community life (and the apparatus for sustaining them) could be taken for granted.[92]

From the late 1880s, the bungalow was to emerge as a specialised house type specifically developed for popular – as opposed to elite – use as a vacation house. It was, first and foremost, an *additional* or second dwelling, initially (1870–1900) for a wealthy urban middle and upper middle class; subsequently (1890–1914 and later) it was utilised by a far wider clientéle. In this, as in its form, location and site, it embodied and symbolised two principal characteristics of modern industrial capitalism: surplus wealth and surplus time. And at a time when the size of this economic surplus was greater than ever before, it also symbolised the vast inequalities in the distribution of wealth.[93]

The particular locations for which the early bungalows were designed, and the names by which they were known – seaside, countryside, riverside, hillside bungalows – demonstrate its use of location and site as a recreational resource. Its isolated setting, perched on a hillside or river bank, 'consumed' the space around; its overall design and layout determined by the requirements of leisure, relaxation and idleness. The essential element of the bungalow was its horizontality: early models were large, generally single-storey and often with a veranda all round. Here, as elsewhere, space was used for time-consuming, low-energy – generally horizontal – activities: billiards, boating, sleeping, sitting in the lounge, writing. It provided for the 'sedentary society',[94] the veranda accommodating the deck-chair (an invention of the 1880s), for gazing at distant

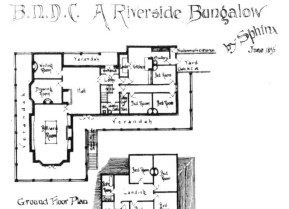

6.1 A horizontal container for the consumption of surplus free time: the bungalow as purpose-built vacation house, 1895.

Developed as a specialised form of leisure house, the first bungalows to be built and named as such in England were introduced at the seaside at the end of the 1860s. About the same time, 'French flats' were being built for the upper middle class in London and 'apartment houses' for a similar clientèle in New York. In subsequent years, the bungalow (with an earlier history in Asia) was to become the archetypical vacation house in much of the industrialised world.

(from *Building News*, 12 July 1895, p. 42)

views, and balconies for 'the matitudinal cigarette'.[95] Its internal spaces provided 'for comfort of the kind so needful in the bungalow after a pull on the river or a game or tennis'.[96] It was, in short, a purpose-built building for the consumption of surplus free time (Figure 6.1).

The ideology behind the development of such bungalows and country cottages was apparently little different from that of present-day second homes. These are said to be 'a desire for periodic escape from the pressures of an urban environment' and the search 'for places to which people like to retreat in privacy and isolation', 'the desire for self-expression and individuality . . . the urge to escape from the limitations of daily life . . . the need for change . . . the desire to rediscover and strengthen one's roots. Man needs to feel a tie not just to his fellow men but to history and to nature . . . he seeks direct contact with nature, with the elements, the historic and the primitive.'[97]

If these are seen to be the motivations of the 1970s, similar views can be found in the late nineteenth century: 'to have a country cottage, or better still, a bungalow . . . affords an attraction which warrants the necessarily frequent railway journeys to and from the shop or office during the summer months, while the family are enjoying the freedom of a countryside stay in some rural retreat.'[98] The 'object of a week-end cottage' was 'to afford a simple home, inexpensive in its first cost and in its upkeep, to which the busy man can run away from the turmoil of the town, and spend as much time as possible on both sides of the day that comes between Saturday and Monday'.[99] For the author of *Country Cottages: How to Build Them and Fit Them Up* (1905, and three further editions by 1910), 'the man who spends his week-ends at his own cottage or bungalow [would] . . . escape six counties overhung with smoke, escape the snorting steam and piston stroke.' He might also 'for two days out of seven, breathe pure air, eat wholesome food, take ideal exercise and enter into the new joys of knowing at first hand bird and beast, tree and flower.'[100] Another enthusiast, writing on 'week-end country cottages and how to adapt them' in *The Girls' Own Paper*, saw them as 'delightful little playhouses'.[101] In the first book of architectural designs devoted to the form (1906), the first sentence reads 'Those seeking the recuperative effects of the country as a remedy to the wear and tear of modern city life. . .'.[102]

By the early twentieth century, the country cottage and bungalow habit had filtered to a more middle-class and even lower middle-class clientèle. For these groups, the interest seems to have converged about 1904 with competitions for the design of weekend cottages in leading architectural journals[103] and an assertion that 'the week-end country cottage [had] arrived in England'.[104] Within a year it was being referred to as the 'country cottage craze'. And though not so prominent in provincial cities as in London, middle-class Glaswegians were weekending in Clydeside villages, Mancunians in Cheshire, Liverpudlians in Southport and those from Leicester, Yorkshire and Birmingham in the Charnwood Forest, Yorkshire Moors and Sutton Coldfield.[105] Though their motives were largely the same, they also included other factors, and these influenced the location, form and layout of the design.

For the second or even third generation of the bourgeoisie, both haute and petite, the comforts of urban domesticity – servants, social conformity, material wealth – as well as routine, had begun to pall. The result was 'a desire for the simple life' which 'now and then seizes on every brain-dweller in cities, living the life imposed by our complex civilisation'.[106] It was in simplicity that lay 'the very essence of the success of the week-end cottage'. It was, for the wealthy, a 'revolt against the tyranny of the town house, with its standing problems of servants and . . . burdens of cleaning and maintenance, entertaining on a scale which is "expected" and being more or less permanently at home'.[107] The motives were mixed: some were for solitude and isolation: others, for social recreation and the refreshment of a 'free and easy domestic life', the same, in fact, which had inspired the bungalow movement in the 1890s. Yet the actuality of 'the simple life' was relative, as much an ideology as a reality, the owners often surrounded with specially produced furnishings and fashions in the 'expensive simplicity' style.[108]

The function of the weekend cottage required that it be within a reasonably short rail, bicycle or motoring journey of the town, of the simplest design and contents so that, not only would it be easy to maintain, but it should not tempt intruders; and while being isolated, it should be accessible to town or village for supplies.[109]

Like the bungalow before it, the weekend country cottage was clearly a new building type, even if adapted from an existing labourer's cottage, specialised in terms of its location, function, social patronage and design, its proponents going to some lengths to establish its particular characteristics: 'This class of cottage is distinct from the artisan's home and ought to be recognised as essentially different.'[110] The 'weekend or middle-class cottage' had evolved 'in the past decade or two' from 'that of the humble labourer'; it 'belongs perhaps more to the bungalow house than the villa, and yet the intention is not entirely the same as the bungalow'.[111] The ideology behind the cottage required that it 'command an open prospect . . . and harmonise with the countryside and natural surroundings'.[112] The heightened urban consciousness of the time and the recurring notion of the 'disappearance of country life',[113] had given rise to a spate of books on romanticised versions of rural cottages, prompted by the notion, to quote one of them, that 'twentieth-century England, the England of the railway, the telegraph and the motorcar, is not the England of these old cottages'.[114] Such sentiments required that the ideal weekend cottage should have 'picturesque old English treatment inside and out'.[115] Two 'holiday home' cottages built outside Leicester in 1898 for a wealthy industrial family, 'before the term "weekender" became at all current',[116] had carefully simulated 'hand-plastered' walls. The functional requirements of such cottages included large family rooms, three or four bedrooms (for guests), a veranda, cycle storage space. Despite simplicity, it was assumed that one servant would be kept, though to maintain the illusion of privacy, 'the more she can be kept out of sight, the better'.[117]

There seems no easy way of knowing, on either a national or regional scale, either the total number of such vacation houses in the early twentieth century or the proportion of the population which had access to them. Quite clearly, architect-designed cottages, including competition designs for houses up to £500, were available only to a wealthy minority. Yet in the early twentieth century, the cheaper of the conventionally constructed, purpose-built weekend cottages and bungalows, depending on area, could be built for between £150 and £250, and existing cottages bought and converted for less in some areas.[118] Moreover, industrialised production, railways, and the development of new materials from the mid-nineteenth century (corrugated iron, 1830s; asbestos and Ruberoid roofing, 1890s) had revolutionised the production and distribution of prefabricated or 'portable' buildings.[119] Self-built holiday bungalows, sufficiently substantial for long-term occupation, were available for £100, although their location might be restricted by by-laws. By the early twentieth century, many companies were producing a variety of timber or corrugated iron and timber weekend houses and holiday bungalows, in some cases for as little as £60.[120] For the more enterprising, railway carriages could be bought and transferred to the beach for £15 and fitted up for not much more, depending on comforts expected.[121] As an indication of who might afford these various opportunities in 1906, professional salaries were between about £300 and £578, clerks' between £96 and £142 and manual workers' wages between £56 and £96 per annum. Professional, managerial and clerical occupations comprised some 2½ million (20 per cent of the employed male population) in 1911, though only about 277,000 had pre-tax incomes of over £200 per year[122] (Figure 6.2).

The patronage for the cheaper weekend cottage and more substantial prefabricated bungalow was, therefore, largely a middle-class, probably professional, phenomenon. And it was people from this group who, in 1905, had

6.2 Space for time: the prefabricated weekend cottage, 1905. (Opposite page) With the emergence of the 'week-end', prefabricated materials and ready transport transformed the habits of an élite into an aspiration for the middle class. The veranda (first introduced in name and form in England c. 1800) was to become an essential feature of the mass vacation house. For an urban population long removed from agricultural pursuits, and confined largely to office or house, it symbolised the attractions of 'outdoor' relaxation, a place for spending leisure hours.
(from Boulton and Paul, *Catalogue of Portable Buildings, . . .* , Norwich, 1906. By courtesy of the publishers)

BOULTON & PAUL, LIMITED,
Manufacturers, NORWICH.

No. 15. WEEK-END COTTAGE.

No. 15 PLAN.

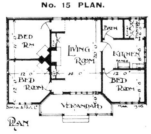

Brickwork foundations and chimneys, wood walls, Italian pattern iron roof.

FULL SPECIFICATION ON APPLICATION.

APPROXIMATE PRICE   -   **£285**

Carriage Paid to nearest Railway Station and erected by our men

visited the Cheap Cottages Exhibition, set up to investigate the possibilities of building cottages for rural labourers at less than £150, looking for weekend cottage plans on the cheap.[123] Yet one of the main advocates of the country cottage uses as his opening reference a £78 a year clerk searching the country on a bicycle to find a location for his country cottage.[124]

In brief, therefore, all the ingredients of the modern second home phenomenon had been established before the First World War. And while space does not permit discussion of the development of the mass vacation house in North America, the same influences can be identified from the 1860s in the growth of the summer cottage, cabin, and, at the turn of the century, the self-built bungalow and cottage.[125]

In the interwar years, obviously the most important influences on their growth were the vast expansion of car ownership, cheap fuel and roadway extensions. While there is no easy way of establishing the extent of middle-class ownership of second homes, whether converted cottages in the country or purpose-built bungalows by the sea, there is sufficient evidence that the phenomenon is worth investigating.[126] For lower middle- and even working-class vacation homes, the evidence is easier to establish. Many were self-built or made from the variety of prefabricated bungalow kits available from the 1920s.[127] It is mistaken to assume that such vacation homes were few or that their existence was not controversial. Whether described – by an aesthetic elite – as 'bungaloid growths' on the coast or as 'unsightly shacks' elsewhere, they were a major factor in the debate which resulted in planning legislation in 1932 which attempted to control both their location and their external appearance.[128] Such data demonstrate the error of defining second homes only as those which are 'permanent'; many self-built 'temporary' vacation houses built in the first forty years of this century have matured into permanent dwellings, their site, in some cases, now a flourishing permanent town[129] (Figure 6.3).

The contemporary vacation house

Literature on the modern vacation house has existed for over a century, even though the majority of purpose-built, often architect-designed, houses were destined for an unrepresentative elite. Yet if we accept that 'the established or ruling values of a society may be studied in their purest form by looking at its upper class',[130] this last section briefly examines a sample of the more recent literature.[131] It attempts to show, in no more than an impressionistic sense, how ideology, values and behaviour are reflected in the location, form and layout of the contemporary vacation house. If the past is any guide to the future, this is to what the majority aspire.

The ideological preference for 'nature' results not only in a preference for country or semi-wilderness locations, preferably with extensive views, but, in purpose-built houses, often with built-in features which integrate the 'indoors' and 'out of doors'. At its most extreme, whole walls and roofs are windows, giving extensive vistas of vegetation, or views of distant hills and beach. French windows, terraces, patios and, indoors, vast rambling plants, shut out society and bring in 'nature', eliminating the difference between indoors and out, devices explored in the 'bungalow craze' at the turn of the century. In conversions, functional openings for air or light are replaced by appropriately named 'picture windows'. In densely settled vacation areas, with other dwellings around, windows are high up in walls to give the illusion of solitude, of communion with the sky; in severe cases of over-crowded sites, vacation homes are of courtyard plan, their occupants turning their backs on the outside world to gaze at enclosed vegetation in the court. Where space is less restricted, living areas are located at first floor level, taking advantage of the 'view'. Similar values stress the use of artificially produced 'natural' materials – rough-cut timber, cane, grass matting, hand-woven fabrics: again, attributes of the late nineteenth-century, anti-industrial, 'simple life' ideology.[132] Only for the materially satiated did the 'simple life' have an appeal; the 'Great Outdoors' was attractive only if one had comfort within.

Whatever the varied motives for second homes, what is evident from the architectural literature are its many social functions. That the vacation house is essentially a mass phenomenon, generated by mass society, is manifest in the emphasis its owners place on originality and individualism. Here, cultural factors are important. Ideally, for the middle-class English owner, the vacation house is a converted stable, lighthouse, coastguard's or artisan's cottage, old church or schoolroom, with the left-over air of previous occupants providing an added nostalgia; if purpose-built, it should be 'original', different from all the others, offering 'a wholly different world from that of the house we live in'. 'What sort of feeling should a vacation house have? It should set up a certain spirit of fantasy, of relaxation, fun, escapism that would be inappropriate in a year-round residence.'[133] The house becomes an instrument of self-expression: a 'symbol of self',[134] yet also a symbol of status. Owning an inessential house is an important index of having arrived: people 'enjoy the distinction of having one'.[135] It is no longer a matter of excluding the herd but of belonging to it.[136]

In a society increasingly spatially, temporally and socially fragmented by work, commuting and leisure, or by role and generation, the vacation house provides the setting for a reassertion of familial activities and values.[137] In societies with high geographical mobility, such as in North America, the vacation house is thought to provide a relatively stable base to which far-flung kin return to renew familial bonds. For wealthy parents, it is an opportunity to keep adolescents in tow, yet independent of parental control. It is a place to share with visitors, entertain friends or simply use as hospitality. 'The whole purpose of the [Browns'] holiday house is to fill it with friends.'[138] In this

RAILWAY CARRIAGE CROSSING RIVER "ADUR" AT SHOREHAM BY SEA FOR BUNGALOWS.

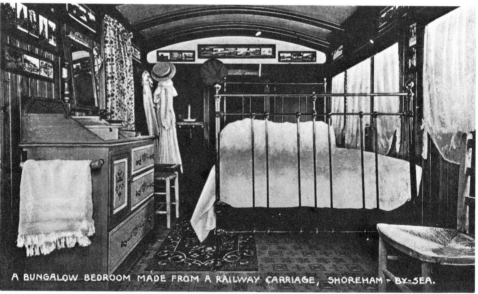

A BUNGALOW BEDROOM MADE FROM A RAILWAY CARRIAGE, SHOREHAM - BY-SEA.

6.3 Stages in the transformation of a temporary to a permanent settlement: the self-built bungalow, New Shoreham Beach, Sussex, c. 1910–75–80.
(by courtesy of the Marlipins Museum, Shoreham; photographs (1975, 1980) Anthony King)

respect, it becomes an extension of the business function, whether used as a setting for business deals or lent to clients as a tax-deductible 'perk'.

This emphasis on family or friends' activity, particularly if business associates are involved, heightens the need for the original, the unique, even bizarre, reflecting on the owner's individuality and status. It has also spatial implications. Accommodation is flexible, catering for eight, ten or even more occupants, twice the size of the average nuclear family. Indoors, the emphasis is on 'togetherness', conviviality and family-strengthening activities. This requires that communal space for relaxation, dining and talking is, compared with the 'first home', relatively large. As in the early upper-class bungalows, time-consuming activities require additional space: a bar, hobby room, library, sauna, swimming pool, solarium or patio. The presence of people throughout the day, and the temporary exchange of conventional sex roles, means that the preparation of food is integrated into eating–living areas, rather than isolated in a specific 'kitchen'. Yet 'the main difference between normal and holiday domesticity is the diminished importance of the bedroom . . . the living room becomes the sole *raison d'être* of the house when life is a series of fourteen-hour outdoor days.'[139] So pervasive is this assumption that, in one vacation house, there are no bedrooms at all. In this way, and by having no clocks in sight, the hosts seek to remove the sense of being disciplined by time. Guests 'talk the night away before going to sleep at six or seven on Sunday morning', supplied with rugs and cushions, and sleeping where they like. 'Because of the absence of the traditional bedroom, no one has a guilt complex.'[140]

Conclusion

With vacation houses in countries as far apart, both politically and climatically, as the USSR and the USA, it might seem that this is a universal building form or, at least, one with a function universally recognised. If so, it might support the idea that the universality of temporal units in industrial societies becomes reflected in the universality of built and spatial forms. The quantity of literature on the design of vacation homes is a reflection of those societies where their frequency is apparently greatest: Scandinavia, France, North America and Germany.[141] That there is little available literature in Britain on vacation houses in socialist or non-Western societies such as in Africa or Asia may simply show the parochialism of one's sources. It may also, however, confirm the obvious point: that the mass vacation house is most characteristic of highly industrialised, economically developed, capitalist, North American and European societies. But with the most widespread ownership in socialist Sweden and many in Yugoslavia, even this generalisation is suspect.

Yet there are certain cultural and ideological assumptions behind the acquisition of second homes in the Western world: that wealth for example, is best invested in this form of property rather than, as in parts of Asia, in jewellery, rural land or, as an investment for the future, in kin; also, that there is a purportedly anti-urban ideology which is expressed in a preference for particular cultural environments which have historically acquired meanings: the 'country-side', 'seaside' or 'the mountains'. And such environments, obviously, assume the existence of the geographical features which are the subject of these meanings in the first place.

Such assumptions can hardly be universal. Even with the penetration of international capitalism and the temporal reorganisation which accompanies industrial urbanisation, the vacation home as a means for leisure or capital investment may not be appropriate to the values or the family structure of African or Asian elites. Where second home settlements were built in such societies and are now used by a Westernised upper class (as, for example, in Indian hill stations), they were essentially European innovations, cultural environments which had social and political, as well as climatic and recreational functions.[142] Despite a growing wealthy middle and upper middle class in India, many of these classic 'vacation house settlements' have in recent years stagnated rather than grown. Whether the introduction of the seven-day week in urban Africa (by missionaries and wage labour), as well as 'annual vacations', has resulted in vacation homes for the rich, only research can prove.

The shift in terminology apparent from the 1960s, from 'holiday' or 'vacation homes' to 'second homes', '*résidences secondaire*' or '*Zweitwohnungen*', is evidence of a subtle and also ambiguous change in the perception of the phenomenon. In one sense, for critics the parameters are those of social justice, a concern that, where thousands are without homes and millions just rent them, a privileged minority own two. In the other sense, however, the ideology of consumption is unquestioned. Where 'the last metaphysical right, the right of property ownership'[143] is seen as fundamental, the acquisition of a second, vacation home becomes a positive goal: 'besides a second bathroom, second telephone and second car, many American families either own or are planning to acquire a second home.'[144] If investment is an important consideration, then the question of location can be almost secondary: 'anywhere can be a vacation pleasure to someone from somewhere else'.[145]

The vacation house as a special building, for use at a particular time and in a particular location, is a good illustration of the propensity for modern society to create organisational patterns and then for people to live within the strictures that such organisation imposes.[146] Though apparently 'free agents', we none the less live in a society whose social, spatial and temporal organisation is intricately structured, even if subject to change. In societies where capital accumulation and property ownership is encouraged, the further growth in ownership of vacation houses, with a long-established cultural tradition behind it – not only within the owner's own society but, increasingly, in other societies as well[147] – is, for the minority who can afford it, likely to continue, the need being met by new commercial developments. Because of the pressure to accumulate capital, the popularisation of vacation houses and their increasing acquisition and use become a significant influence on the way in which people spend their surplus time and wealth. It is not only that man exploits the environment: the environment which he builds also exploits man. If these concluding points are obvious, they none the less demonstrate the need for further study of the social development of the vacation house, not just over historical time, but also across cultures.

Notes and references

1   J. Barr, 'A two-home democracy?', *New Society*, 7 September 1967, pp. 313–15; C. L. Bielckus, A. W. Rogers and G. P. Wibberly, *Second Homes in England and Wales*, Wye College, University of London, 1972. Comprehensive bibliographies (on Europe) are in H. D. Clout, 'The growth of second home ownership: an example of seasonal suburbanisation', in J. H. Johnson, ed., *Suburban Growth. Geographical processes at the edge of the Western city*, John Wiley, London, 1974; and J. T. Coppock, ed., *Second Homes: Curse or Blessing?*, Pergamon Press, Oxford, 1977. See also D. White, 'Have second homes gone into hibernation?' *New Society*, 10 August 1978, pp. 286–8.
2   An exception is R. I. Wolfe, 'The summer resorts of Ontario in the nineteenth century', *Ontario History*, vol. 54, no. 3, 1962, pp. 150–60.
3   The terms 'summer house', 'weekend house', 'country house' and many more can be found in the main European languages in architectural literature from the 1920s and 1930s.
4   Quoted in Coppock, op. cit., pp. 139–40. The problems of conceptualising and

6.4   Weekend cottage as the idealisation of rural life, 1933. (Opposite page) The purpose-built dwelling illustrated here epitomises the ideology and social basis of the country cottage. Visual requirements dominate the design – the dwelling is to be looked at and looked from: outside, the thatched roof and hilltop setting hark back to an idealised rural past; inside, the shape of the living area is totally subordinated to the need of providing 'countryside views'. An excess display of material wealth in the 'town house' requires the 'very simple treatment' of the 'cottage'. In the small, three-member middle-class family for which it caters, sleeping space is provided strictly according to generation. The social isolation sought by the occupants became desirable only when the means for ending it could be taken for granted.
(from R. R. Phillips, *Houses for Moderate Means*, Country Life, London, 1936, p. 125. By courtesy of Hamlyn Group)

WEEK-END
COTTAGE

Peter Smith, A.R.I.B.A.,
Architect

GENERAL PARTICULARS: Occupying a site in the Berkshire hills, this cottage is very simply treated to serve the needs of two or three people. At the entrance is a small hall where the most is made of the space with built-in cupboards and flush doors. The living-room has a large bow window overlooking the country-side, and within this is a specially designed horseshoe dining-table and window seat, allowing the main space to be used as a sitting-room. At one end of the cottage is a bedroom 10 ft. square and at the other end a child's bedroom. A " Cozy " stove warms the living-room. In the tiny kitchen cooking is done by oil.

CONSTRUCTION: Walls of 11-in. cavity brickwork (light and dark red); roof thatched with wheat straw; windows, metal casements; glass ventilators to keep rooms aired when cottage is shut up.

BUILDING COST: £500 in 1933.

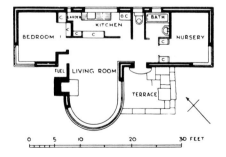

defining what is understood as a 'vacation house' and, more particularly, a 'second home', are well-known (see Coppock, op. cit., pp. 2–3) especially concerning the questions of permanence, ownership, frequency of occupation and actual built form. Is the nineteenth-century seaside terrace house, purpose-built for long seasonal letting, a vacation house or second home? How they are defined is obviously governed by the purpose for which the definition is needed, including historical research. In this essay the cultural assumption is made that 'vacation house' normally refers to a separate, detached dwelling.

5 Coppock, op. cit., p. 4.
6 N. Mitchell, *The Indian Hill Station: Kodaikanal*, Department of Geography, University of Chicago (Research Paper 141), 1972, p. 2.
7 F. Braudel, *Capitalism and Material Life, 1400–1800*, Fontana/Collins, London, 1974, p. 203.
8 M. Girouard, *Life in the English Country House*, Yale University Press, London, 1978, p. 6; Clout, op. cit., p. 103.
9 Clout, op. cit., p. 103.
10 Clout, 'Résidences secondaires in France', in Coppock, op. cit., pp. 47–62; p. 47.
11 Clout, 'The growth of second home ownership', p. 102.
12 Coppock, op. cit., p. 155.
13 Including outbreaks of cultural nationalism in the host environment (through arson and demonstrations) against second home owners. To suggest, as one reason for the growth of research since the 1960s, that university researchers increasingly used or, in some cases, owned second homes from this time is a hypothesis worth pursuing.
14 Coppock, op. cit., *passim*; Clout, 'The growth of second home ownership', p. 102.
15 R. L. Ragatz, 'Vacation housing: a missing component in urban and regional theory', *Land Economics*, vol. 46, 1970, pp. 118–26; 'Vacation homes in rural areas: towards a model for predicting their distribution and occupancy patterns', in Coppock, op. cit., pp. 181–94; Clout, 'The growth of second home ownership', and other essays.
16 The subject provides, for example, a rich field for time–space studies, with or without a Marxist perspective. See T. Carlstein, D. Parkes and N. Thrift, eds, *Timing Space and Spacing Time*, 3 vols, Edward Arnold, London, 1978; especially T. Carlstein and N. Thrift, 'Towards a time-space structured approach to society and environment', vol. 2 (*Human Activity and Time Geography*), pp. 225–63.
17 Clout, 'The growth of second home ownership', p. 102; Bielckus *et al.*, op. cit., p. 63.
18 Bielckus *et al.*, op. cit., p. 7; H. D. Clout, *Rural Geography*, Pergamon, Oxford, p. 69; although Coppock (op. cit., p. 4) suggests that 'the immediate predecessor of the modern concept of the second home is probably the shooting box of Victorian Britain and the summer cottage of the Atlantic coast of America'.
19 J. Dower, 'Planning aspects of second homes', in Coppock, op. cit., pp. 155–64; p. 15.
20 See Bielckus *et al.*, op. cit., pp. 65, 63, 139, 140.
21 A useful summary of the Marxist concept of surplus applied to urbanism is in D. Harvey, *Social Justice and the City*, Edward Arnold, London, 1973, pp. 230–1; see also

A. Giddens, *Capitalism and Modern Social Theory*, Cambridge University Press, 1971, pp. 24–34.

22 E. J. Hobsbawm, *The Age of Capital*, Weidenfeld & Nicolson, London, 1975, pp. 29 *et seq.*; E. J. Hobsbawm, *Industry and Empire*, Penguin, Harmondsworth, 1969, ch. 6.

23 Hobsbawm, *Industry and Empire*, p. 119.

24 Hobsbawm, *The Age of Capital*, pp. 203–4, 206.

25 J. A. R. Pimlott, *The Englishman's Holiday*, Faber & Faber, London, 1976; J. A. Patmore, 'The spa towns of Britain', in R. P. Beckinsale, ed., *Urbanisation and its Problems*, Blackwell, Oxford, 1970, pp. 47–69.

26 Hobsbawm, *The Age of Capital*, pp. 203–4, 206; J. Walton, *The Blackpool Landlady*, Manchester University Press, 1978, pp. 21, 49.

27 Harvey, op. cit., p. 222; Giddens, op. cit., pp. 26–40; E. Durkheim, *The Division of Labour*, Collier-Macmillan, 1964 (first published, like G. Simmel's *Social Differentiation*, in 1893).

28 J. Goody, 'Time: social organisation', in *International Encyclopaedia of the Social Sciences*, Macmillan, New York, 1968, pp. 30–42. On changes in the social organisation of time, see also J. Mbiti, 'The concept of time', in J. Mbiti, *African Religions and Philosophy*, Heinemann, London, 1971; W. E. Moore, *Man, Time and Society*, Wiley, New York, 1963; S. de Grazia, *Of Time, Work and Leisure*, Twentieth Century Fund, New York, 1962; G. Gurvitch, *The Spectrum of Social Time*, Reidel, Dordrecht, 1964; M. P. Nilsson, *Primitive Time Reckoning*, Oxford University Press, 1920; E. Zerubarel, *Patterns of Time*, Chicago University Press, 1979.

29 G. Friedmann, 'Leisure and technological civilisation', *International Social Science Journal*, vol. 12, no. 4, 1960, pp. 509–21; p. 510.

30 Goody, op. cit., p. 33; A. I. Hallowell, 'Temporal orientation in Western civilisation and in a pre-literate society', *American Anthropologist*, n.s., vol. 39, 1937, pp. 647–70; F. H. Colson, *The Week*, Cambridge University Press, 1926.

31 Goody, op. cit., p. 31.

32 P. A. Sorokin and R. K. Merton, 'Social time: a methodological and functional analysis', *American Journal of Sociology*, vol. 42, no. 5, 1937, pp. 615–29.

33 See especially E. P. Thompson, 'Time, work discipline and industrial capitalism', *Past and Present*, vol. 38, 1967, pp. 56–97.

34 Quoted in E. Zerubavel, 'Time-tables and scheduling: on the social organisation of time', *Sociological Inquiry*, vol. 46, no. 2, 1976, pp. 87–94; p. 88.

35 Thompson, op. cit.

36 N. Thrift, 'The diffusion of Greenwich Mean Time in Great Britain', Working Paper 188, School of Geography, University of Leeds, 1977. I am grateful to Nigel Thrift for other references on the literature of time.

37 J. H. Clapham, *An Economic History of Britain*, Cambridge University Press, 1938, vol. III, pp. 477–9; de Grazia, op. cit., pp. 192–8.

38 Paid holidays for manual workers began in the 1880s though were not general until after 1914. See Pimlott, op. cit., pp. 154–7; also A. H. Halsey, 'Leisure', in A. H. Halsey, *Trends in British Society since 1900*, Macmillan, London, 1972; on working hours in USA, see Friedmann, op. cit.; de Grazia, op. cit.

39 H. Wilensky, 'The uneven distribution of leisure: the impact of economic growth on free time', in E. O. Smigel, ed., *Work and Leisure*, College and University Press, New Haven, Conn., 1963, pp. 107–45.

40 Zerubavel, op. cit., p. 1.

41 N. H. Cheek and W. R. Burch, *The Social Organisation of Leisure in Human Society*, Harper & Row, New York, 1976, p. 29.

42 Cf. Carlstein and Thrift, op. cit., p. 260: 'the scope for temporal coordination of activities between different groups and individuals is to a considerable extent dependent upon the spatial layout and structure of society'. For the authors, 'this is an important research area'.

43 E. L. Lampard, 'The urbanising world', in H. J. Dyos and M. Wolff, eds, *The Victorian City*, Routledge & Kegan Paul, London, 1973, vol. 1, pp. 3–57, p. 40.

44 D. J. Olsen, 'Victorian London: specialisation, segregation and privacy', *Victorian Studies*, vol. 17, 1974, pp. 264–78; D. Cannadine, 'Victorian cities: how different?', *Social History*, 4 January 1977, pp. 457–82. See also Hancock, this volume, p. 153.

45 G. H. Singleton, 'The genesis of suburbia', in L. H. Masotti and J. K. Hadden (eds), *The Urbanization of the Suburbs*, Sage, Beverly Hills and London, 1973, pp. 29–50, p. 41

46 A. D. King, *Colonial Urban Development*, Routledge & Kegan Paul, London, 1976, p. 129.

47 H. Meller, *Leisure and the Changing City*, Routledge & Kegan Paul, London, 1976. For an analysis of contemporary trends see I. Appleton, 'Leisure and building policy', in I. Appleton (ed.), *Leisure Research and Policy*, Scottish Academic Press, Edinburgh, 1974, pp. 219–30.

48 H. J. Perkin, 'The social tone of Victorian seaside resorts', *Northern History*, vol. 11, 1976, pp. 180–94; J. Walvin, *Leisure and Society*, Longman, London, 1978.

49 Walton, op. cit., pp. 33–6.

50 Ibid., pp. 79, 111.

51 *OED*, 1933, under 'cottage'.

52 (Anon.), *A Dictionary of Daily Wants*, Houlston, London, 1859, and similar reference books.

53 B. Weinreb, *The Small English House: a catalogue of books*, Weinreb Architectural Books, London, 1977.

54 J. Gandy, *Designs for Cottages*, etc. John Harding, London, 1805, p. 7. Cf. also 'a cottage, to use the word in its literal sense, means a house of small dimensions, appropriated to the use of the lower class of people, but to buildings of this description the fashion of the present day has added one which bears a distinctive character and is known by the appellation of the ornamental or adorned cottage': W. Bartells, *Hints for Picturesque Improvements*, etc., J. Taylor, London, 1804, p. 4.

55 Only about half a dozen of the books listed in Weinreb's comprehensive catalogue give a clear reference to this function.

56 R. Elsam, *An Essay on Rural Architecture*, etc., for the author, London, 1803, p. 19.

57 W. F. Pocock, *Architectural Designs for Rural Cottages*, J. Taylor, London, 1807, p. 30.

58 E. Aiken, *Designs for Villas and Other Rural Buildings*, J. Taylor, 1808, plates IV and V.

59 J. Malton, *A Collection of Designs for Rural Retreats as Villas*, etc., J. Taylor, London, 1802, p. x.

60 (Anon.), *Things Indoors and Out*, Routledge, London, 1881.

61 J. A. H. Murray, *A New English Dictionary on Historical Principles*, Clarendon Press, Oxford, 1888.

62 Of the large number of architectural titles published on cottages, 1800–1900, only two (by J. Vincent, 1861 and J. L. Green, 1899) refer specifically to 'country cottages', yet these are still both on cottages for agricultural labourers. Though the term 'country cottage' does occur in the nineteenth century, it is comparatively rare and does not carry the meaning associated with it after the 1890s. Books on the 'country cottage' in the modern sense become common 1900–10. The first use of the term identified by the *OED* Supplement, 1972, as 'a country cottage fitted up for summer occupancy' (1881) refers to an American source.

63 R. Williams, *Keywords*, Fontana, London, 1976.

64 Ibid. See also the same author's *The Country and the City*, Chatto & Windus, London, 1973, especially chapter 1.

65 Girouard, op. cit.

66 M. Girouard, *The Victorian Country House*, Country Life, London, 1975.

67 The social meaning of 'country' continues. To help readers co-ordinate their social calendars, *The Times* publishes the dates and locales of forthcoming dances and cocktail parties. While some entries refer to the private address, club or just the city (e.g. 'in London', 'in Paris') a Capt Hoare indicates his intention to hold a dinner dance for his daughters simply 'in the country'. (7 July 1975).

68 E.g. Blackpool, Cleethorpes. See Walton, op. cit.

69 *The Architect*, 18 September 1881, p. 185.

70 A. F. Weber, *The Growth of Cities in the Nineteenth Century*, Cornell University Press, Ithaca, NY, 1967 (first published 1899), p. 144.

71 Pimlott, op. cit., p. 160.

72 J. T. Coppock, 'The changing face of England, 1850–1900', in H. C. Darby, ed., *A New Historical Geography of England*, Cambridge University Press, 1973, pp. 595–673; p. 596.

73 P. Thompson, *The Edwardians*, Weidenfeld & Nicolson, 1975, p. 295; on bicycling, see D. Rubinstein, 'Cycling in the 1890s', *Victorian Studies*, vol. 21, no. 1, 1977, pp. 47–72.

74 See also Girouard, *Life in the English Country House*, p. 303.

75 For a perceptive contemporary prediction of the effect of the automobile on cities and residential patterns, see the numerous references in *The Worlds' Work and Play*, 1903–6.

76 The main exception is Thompson, 'Time, work discipline and industrial capitalism'. See also L. Wright, *Clockwork Man*, Elek, London, 1968, p. 109.

77 Hobsbawm, *Industry and Empire*, p. 123; see also J. Myerscough, 'The recent history of leisure time', in Appleton, *Leisure Research and Policy*, pp. 3–16, p. 7.

78 M. Young and P. Willmott, *Family and Kinship in East London*, Penguin, Harmondsworth, 1957, p. 24.

79 T. Burns, 'Leisure in industrial society', in M. A. Smith, ed., *Leisure and Society in Britain*, Allen Lane, London, 1973, pp. 43–52; p. 45.

80 Walton, op. cit., pp. 27–31.

81 *OED*, 1933: 'week-end', like 'country-side', was at first hyphenated. With their

increasing use and familiarity in the twentieth century, the hyphen disappeared.

82 Burns, op. cit., p. 45.

83 *Week-end*, vol. 1, no. 1.

84 F. H. Farthing, *The Week-end Gardener*, Grant Richards, London, 1914, preface. The chapters (and schedules of work) are ordered according to the first, second, third and fourth weekend in each month rather than season or weather conditions – aptly demonstrating how the natural world is tamed to fit an urban industrial order.

85 'Does the smart set go to church at all? Where . . . and how do they spend their Sunday? . . . on the river, or in the motor or is it in bed? . . . nowadays everybody who is anybody has to be out of town in the Season, say from Saturday to Tuesday . . . there is no mention of Church at all, but only of walks or drives, or the stables, or golf, or else of bridge under the trees on the lawn, which means more than I need reveal.' B. Vaughan, *The Sins of Society* (sermons given in the Church of the Immaculate Conception, Mayfair 1906), Kegan Paul, London, 1906, pp. 65–8.

86 P. Dupré, *Encyclopédie du bon français dans l'usage contemporain*, Edition de Trévise, Paris, 1972, p. 2705.

87 G. Best, *Mid-Victorian Britain, 1851–75*, Panther, London, 1971, pp. 218 *et seq.*; Pimlott, op. cit., p. 160; Thompson, *The Edwardians*.

88 A. D. King, 'Social process and urban form: the bungalow as an indicator of social trends', *Architectural Association Quarterly*, vol. 5, no. 3, 1973, pp. 4–21.

89 'How Tankerville Smith took a country cottage', in R. Caldecott, *More 'Graphic' Pictures by Randolph Caldecott*, Routledge, London, 1887.

90 M. B. Adams, *Modern Cottage Architecture*, Batsford, London, 1904, preface.

91 R. A. Briggs, *Bungalows and Country Residences*, Batsford, London, 1891, preface.

92 A. D. King, *The Bungalow. A Cultural History and Sociology*, Routledge & Kegan Paul, London, 1981, forthcoming.

93 Thompson, *The Edwardians*.

94 H. Collins, 'The sedentary society', in E. Larrabee and R. Meyersohn, eds, *Mass Leisure*, Free Press, Glencoe, Ill., 1961, pp. 19–30.

95 *Building News*, 17 November 1905, p. 678 ('Building News Design Club on Week-end Cottage').

96 *Building News*, 1893, p. 6; also 'Country Cottages', *Country Life*, 11, 1898, p. 195.

97 P. Downing and M. Dower, *Second Homes in England and Wales*, Countryside Commission HMSO, London, 1973, p. 19.

98 *Building News*, 1893, p. 6.

99 'Week-end cottages', *The Studio*, vol. 31, 1904, p. 321.

100 'Home Counties' (J. W. Robertson Scott, subsequently proprietor of *The Country-man*). Preface by Henry Norman, MP, p. viii. The book included photographs, plans etc., of cottages and bungalows from £130 to £1,300. Heinemann, 1905. Most of it was first published in *The World's Work and Play*, 1904–5.

101 H. W. Burton, 'Week-end Country Cottages and How to adapt them', *Girls' Own Paper*, vol. 26, no. 1297, November 1904, pp. 92–3; p. 92 (the earliest identified reference to *weekend country* cottages).

102 J. Elder-Duncan, *Country Cottages and Week-end Homes*, Cassell, London, 1906 (2nd and 3rd impressions, 1912). This represented the top end of the market with designs

in three price brackets: £200–1,000, £1,000–2,000, £2,000–3,000; £175 was 'the lowest sum for which a middle-class country home can be erected' (p. 29).

103 'Week-end cottages', *The Studio*, vol. 31, 1904, pp. 321–34; *Building News*, Design Club, Week-end Cottage, 17 November 1905, p. 678.

104 Burton, op. cit., p. 92 who also refers to the phenomenon in North America.

105 Elder-Duncan, op. cit., p. 11.

106 Burton, op cit., p. 92.

107 G. L. Morris and E. Wood, *The Country Cottage*, John Lane, London, 1906, pp. 3–4.

108 A. Martin, *The Small House*, Alston Rivers, London, 1906, pp. 22–9.

109 Burton, op. cit., p. 92.

110 *Building News*, 1905, p. 678.

111 Adams, op. cit., pp. 16–7, 20. See also C. R. Ashbee, *A Book of Cottages and Little Houses*, etc., n.d. but *c.* 1905–6, p. 1.

112 *Building News*, 1905, p. 678.

113 Williams, *The Country and the City, passim*.

114 S. Dick, *The Cottage Homes of England*, Edward Arnold, London 1909, p. 12. See also the Batsford series of 'Old English Cottages and Farmhouses'.

115 *Building News*, 1905, p. 678.

116 Elder-Duncan, op. cit., p. 93.

117 *Building News*, 1905, p. 678.

118 See 'Home Counties', 1906.

119 G. Herbert, *Pioneers of Prefabrication*, Cornell University Press, Ithaca, NY, 1978.

120 E.g. various catalogues of W. Cooper, Old Kent Road, London, Harrison Smith, Birmingham; other companies listed in G. Herbert, 1978 and advertisements, 'Home Counties', 1906.

121 Holiday bungalows below £100 were in D. Allport, *Inexpensive Holiday Homes* (Wire Wove Roofing), 1896, 1905; P. N. Hasluck, *Cheap Dwellings Actually Built Costing £75–300*, Crosby Lockwood, London, 1907; Other books catering for the cheaper (i.e. below £200) market for the 'weekend cottage which has sprung into immense popularity during the last few years' were G. C. Samson, *How to Plan a House*, Crosby Lockwood, London, 1910.

122 G. Routh, *Occupation and Pay in Great Britain, 1906–60*. Cambridge University Press, 1965, pp. 52, 64, 67, 87, 91.

123 Elder-Duncan, op. cit., p. 17. It is worth noting that experiments in cheap – often prefabricated – housing for the deprived (not only in 1905 but in postwar Britain and today, in regard to housing for Third World cities) has, as a by-product, often stimulated interest in second, vacation, homes for the middle class.

124 'Home Counties', 1906.

125 My thanks are due to Clay Lancaster and especially Roy Wolfe, whose information on North American developments has been indispensable. According to Wolfe, the movement really got under way in the 1880s (personal communication, March, 1980).

       In tracing these developments, an important distinction might be made between the earlier 'summer cottage' of the elite and the conceptually different modern 'vacation home'. An early reference to the latter is Robert van Court, 'Vacation Homes in the Woods', *Independent*, vol. lxxii, June 6 1912, p. 1239. See also P. J. Schmitt, *Back to*

Nature, Oxford University Press, New York, 1969; B. Gill, *Summer places*, Methuen, New York, 1978; Roy I. Wolfe, 'Recreational Land Use in Ontario', PhD dissertation, Ontario University, 1956, pp. 500–11; King, *The Bungalow*, 1981 (forthcoming).

126 Modernising old cottages had, in 1939, 'become such a widespread craze that it is hard to find, within thirty miles of London, a genuine old cottage': A. Hastings, ed., *Week-end Houses, Cottages and Bungalows*, Architectural Press, London, 1939, preface.

127 King, 'Social process and urban form'.

128 See, for example, the various reports of the Council for the Preservation of Rural England on the Thames Valley (1929), Cornwall (1930), the Peak District (1932), Ryedale (1934), Buckinghamshire (1933) etc.; also W. Dougill, *The English Coast*, CPRE, London, 1936.

129 The best-known English example is New Shoreham, near Brighton, begun with a few railway carriages in the 1890s.

130 R. Dahrendorf, 'On the origin of inequality among men', in A. Beteille, ed., *Social Inequality. Selected Readings*, Penguin, Harmondsworth, 1970, p. 39.

131 F. R. Barran, *Ferienhauser*, Julius Hoffman Verlag, Stuttgart, 1961; G. C. Görlich, *Villette week-end e prefabricate*, Milan, Gorlich, 1961; H. Walton, *How to Build Your Cabin or Modern Vacation House*, Barnes & Noble, New York, 1964; P. Joye, *Votre Chalet*, Fribourg, Office du Livre, 1966; K. Kaspers, *Holiday Houses. An International Survey*. Thames & Hudson, London, 1967; B. Wolsinger and J. Debaigts, *Vacation Houses of Europe*, Tuttle, Vermont and Tokyo, 1968; R. Harling *et al.*, *House and Garden Book of Holiday and Weekend Houses*, Condé Nast Publications, London, 1968; *Architectural Record*, *Book of Vacation Houses*, American Heritage Press, New York, 1970 (2nd edn, 1977); A. Powell, *Your Holiday Home*, David & Charles, Newton Abbot, 1972.

132 See King, *The Bungalow*.

133 *Architectural Record*, op. cit., p. 110.

134 Clare Cooper, 'The House as Symbol of Self', Working Paper 120, Institute of Urban and Regional Development, University of California, Berkeley, 1971.

135 Walton, *How to Build Your Cabin*, p. 13.

136 R. I. Wolfe, 'About cottages and cottagers', *Landscape*, Autumn 1965, pp. 6–8.

137 R. I. Wolfe, 'Summer cottages in Ontario: purpose-built for an inessential purpose', in Coppock, *Second Homes*, pp. 17–33.

138 Harling *et al.*, op. cit., p. 36; or see the title of an article in *House Beautiful*, vol. 117, August 1975: 'A summer house designed for all ages where everyone's friends are welcome'.

139 Harling *et al.*, op. cit., p. 9.

140 Ibid., p. 36.

141 The *Avery Index to Architectural Periodicals*, Columbia University/Hall, Boston, 1976, lists approximately 560 articles on vacation houses between 1940 and 1976; the heaviest concentration begins about 1965–6. There are also significant numbers on 'weekend houses' in the 1930s.

142 King, *Colonial Urban Development*, chapter 7.

143 Wolfe, 'Summer cottages in Ontario', p. 30.

144 Walton, *How to Build Your Cabin*, p. 130.

145 *Architectural Record*, op. cit., p. 233. Hence, the practice of buying, for use as 'second homes', flats in converted inner city warehouses, terraced housing in industrial towns, or probably, in future, local authority dwellings now being sold off to their present tenants. 'Time-sharing' arrangements – the purchase of a lease giving access to a flat in modernised crescents at prestigious seaside towns for use at specified dates of the year – should also be seen in this light. With constant inflation, property is the best investment.

146 Cheek and Burch, op. cit., p. 71.

147 See, for example, the magazines *Homes Abroad* and *Homes Overseas*, with advertisements for second homes in Andorra, West Indies, Spain, France, North Africa, Sri Lanka, Greece, Malta, Cyprus, Italy, Germany, Portugal.

7 Places of refreshment in the nineteenth-century city

Robert Thorne

Eating and drinking are universal activities serving fundamental human needs. Yet, however essential they may be, they are circumscribed by rules and habits which govern what may be eaten or drunk, where and in whose company it can be consumed, and at what time or occasion. Patterns of consumption which in present-day Western countries are taken for granted and regarded as immutable may appear local and peculiar when set in historical perspective or contrasted with the customs of other countries. In every society the distribution and consumption of food and drink are expressions of particular values and relationships – the bonds between members of a family, the closeness or distance of friendships, the degree of respect shown to political, social or religious leaders.

The symbolic meanings attached to eating and drinking are especially evident at times of celebration: the giving of hospitality, the sale of goods or land, and the observance of rites of passage such as marriage and death. The rituals at these celebrations, and the taboos determining what is consumed, often have religious significance. The distinctiveness of the Jewish faith is in part expressed in a concern for the way in which meat is prepared, and the avoidance of certain kinds of seafood; Hinduism, Islam and Buddhism have equally strict dietary rules and customs. In this respect England – like the rest of Europe – is different. In comparison with other religions Christianity has never developed elaborate dietary laws, with the result that in Christian countries habits of eating and drinking have been determined largely by economic and social considerations. Differences of wealth and power have been marked by distinctions in the type, quantity and quality of food and drink consumed, as well as where and how it is prepared and taken: from the selection of the materials to the setting and conduct of the meal, each stage has reflected the social position of those involved.[1]

Anthropologists have long recognized the importance of these questions in the study of primitive societies, and some have joined hands with nutritionists and others in studying customs much nearer home. But their example has not been followed by historians, who have generally preferred to confine their interest in food and drink to the production stage. There have been many studies of the pattern of retailing and consumption in the critical years of the Industrial Revolution, and drink has been examined by historians interested in the temperance movement, but the social meaning of meals and drinking has been largely overlooked.[2] As long as historians have been interested primarily in problems covering the supply, cost and quality of food and drink, they have tended to push into second place the further set of problems which follow from these: when do people eat and drink, and who is present at the occasion? Do men eat with women? Is the activity confined to the nuclear family? How are guests and friends treated? Above all – and here the problem acquires an architectural complexion – where is the meal taken? This chapter is concerned mainly with the last of these questions, in particular with the buildings provided for public places of refreshment in nineteenth-century cities. But in order to reach an explanation of why such places developed, and whom they were intended to serve, it is necessary to refer back to the former questions – plus others – to establish the context in which the changes took place.

In the fragmentation of place and function which characterizes a modernizing society one of the surest indicators is the necessity for people to have meals away from home. At first, this is true for very few groups – administrators, soldiers and travellers. But the further an economy reaches beyond a subsistence level, and the larger the units of production become, the more likely it is that home and workplace will be separated and the working day broken up, making what was once the experience of minorities much more widely familiar. The speed with which activities once centred on the home are drained away from it is a measure of the pace of industrial change, and of urbanization, in a society. Towns, which traditionally met the specialized needs of the surrounding countryside – including the need for food, drink and shelter called for by travellers – are increasingly called upon to service their own population. In the British case, urbanization had reached a stage in 1801 where one-fifth of the population was living in cities and towns of 10,000 or more, places whose size and extent called for the provision of services on an unprecedented scale, including the provision of food and drink for those drawn away from home during the working day or travelling within the city at other times.

In the experience of industrialization and urban concentration Britain was the pioneer, a country whose cities granted the observer a dimension of urban scale and feeling unobtainable anywhere else, a way of living in the future, to be reported back to places following in the same path. In this transformation London held a special place. Before the Industrial Revolution it was conspicuous for its size, its population (in 1750 11 per cent of the total population lived in London), its dominant role as a consumer centre, and the symptoms it displayed of the beginnings of a marked spatial segregation. Although the heavy industries conventionally associated with the Industrial Revolution were developed away from the capital city, its leading position hardly changed, and the overall effect of the country's industrialization was to inflate its existing characteristics. From a population of under 1 million in 1801 it reached about 2¼ million in 1851, during which period it doubled in physical area. London was a conspicuous case of a change which, starting in Britain and western Europe, has gone on to affect almost every country across the globe. For that reason a study of where people ate and drank in the industrial city does well to concentrate on London, though with the reservation that, because of its special role as a capital city, generalizations founded on its experience may fit uneasily elsewhere.

The provision for eating and drinking in the 1860s

In most towns before about 1800 the setting up of a public house, a dining room or a coffee room required little equipment and seldom a special building. Public catering evolved from domestic catering for family, friends and visitors, and a room in the home, or the simplest adaptation of a domestic building, served well enough at first. A public house or tavern might be distinguished simply by a sign, and sometimes a lamp; an eating house by its display in the window of meat ready for cooking. Inside, patrons were confined to one or two ground floor rooms, the public house perhaps having the semblance of a serving counter in one of these. Strangers could be forgiven for their difficulty in distinguishing the building or its use.[3]

In the newly built-up areas of nineteenth-century cities special provision was made, for pubs at least, from the start.[4] Precocious in their size and number, these were much commented upon but they did not engender the kind of architectural debate given to other new building types of the time such as hospitals, prisons or workhouses. In part this may have been because they did not represent a new function, simply an old one in a new guise, and in part it may be attributed to the contempt with which they were viewed by the architectural and building press: in this they suffered through being designed by little-known architects and through being associated with the growing public alarm after 1830 over the level of drink consumption and its social consequences.[5] At the same time, the literature of social inquiry and reform, which often touched on architectural matters, shunned the investigation of these buildings or reported them only at second hand. In their design and layout public houses, eating houses and restaurants presented problems as interesting as those of other public or institutional buildings, but discussion about them, if it ever took place, went largely unrecorded. Even where architectural evidence survives – descriptions, plans, drawings and sometimes the buildings themselves – the intent behind the design has largely to be inferred. We are caught with a building type so ubiquitous and taken for granted, or by some so overlooked, that its meaning has been largely passed over.

Those who can be relied upon for evidence, though still not of the authenticity of those responsible at first hand for the buildings, are writers who, for one reason or another, could not take these changes for granted: travellers to whom the familiar was strange, writers of guidebooks forced to explain the obvious and autobiographers reflecting on changes witnessed in their lifetime. Three authors in this last category all remembered the 1860s as a crucial decade in the transformation of public life in London; a decade when, as one memoir writer put it, 'the rough element . . . was at its roughest', but when the possibilities of a better life were established, especially where public catering was concerned.[6] An army officer recalled that 'the fashion of dining out at restaurants had not taken root in those days, and the feeding resorts were few and good and very far between'; a theatre critic wrote that eating out was 'in a transition state in the 1860s'.[7] In the absence of better authorities these authors do suggest a time to catch changes at their most interesting: not at the opening stages in the public provision of refreshment, but at a time of significant shift in emphasis.

An examination of the range of places that were available for eating and drinking in the 1860s must take account from the start of problems in terminology. As many places were hard to distinguish from the shops and houses around, so the terms used to describe them blurred one with another. The author of the *Builder's Practical Director* (c. 1855) complained that 'the words tavern, inn, public house etc. do not appear to have any defined and very distinctive limits'.[8] He could have said the same of the terms 'coffee house', 'coffee shop', 'cigar divan', 'pastrycook' and 'confectioner'. Guidebooks, street directories and the decennial census all used slightly different systems of classification, some sensitive to new nomenclature, others keen to carry on with the old terms.

The tables of occupation in the 1861 census listed the most obvious groups engaged in public catering.[9] In London, the largest of these were publicans (6,867) and beersellers (1,977), whose premises ranged from the simplest beerhouse to the gin palace or gin shop prominent in the street for its use of gas, plate glass and expensive decoration. Whatever their past role or reputation, these houses had in common that – apart from those of the most superior kind, called 'taverns' – they served little more than alcoholic drink; the part of the pub called the 'tap room', where food that was brought in by customers could be cooked and eaten, was a dying institution. Apart from taverns, all such places were largely avoided by the more respectable classes. 'No person above the rank of a labouring man or artisan', G. R. Porter told a House of Commons committee in 1852, 'would venture to go into a public house to purchase anything to drink.'[10] Those who did go in, like the American theatre director, Stephen Fiske, were shocked to find 'women standing up at the counter and behind the counter', a contrast to the male exclusiveness of most refreshment places.[11]

The next most numerous group in the census returns were keepers of coffee houses (2,395), again a broad term which could refer to eating houses – sometimes called 'dining rooms' – or to coffee shops of the kind that had proliferated after the reduction of coffee duties in 1825, and which were as varied as the neighbourhoods they served. A description of 1863 pointed out the extremes that the term 'coffee house' could embrace, and the method used by those places which sought an exclusive clientèle: 'While some are handsomely finished saloons, where French café is served in china, where customers smoke cigars and play critically at chess, first dropping a shilling for admission, others are little better than mere barns, where you may see the navvy and the hodman importing their own provisions.'[12] Lastly, the census referred to innkeepers and hotel-keepers (649), a category including the keepers of coaching inns which had survived (though denuded of their traffic), hotels which were conversions of terrace houses, and purpose-built hotels such as the Great Western at Paddington (opened in 1854) and the Westminster Palace Hotel (1858). Although the use of the term 'hotel' had been introduced from France in the 1760s, the emergence of a distinct type of building of that name did not occur till the coming of the railways seventy or eighty years later: its development then went hand-in-hand with the expanding possibilities for travel and tourism which railways offered, and a demand among wealthy patrons for more private accommodation than inns could provide.[13]

To this outline classification should be added three other groups. First, there were the street salesmen of food and drink, whose occupation the census failed to distinguish perhaps because it so often merged, according to the season and state of trade, with that of general labourer. These, selling everything from hot eels to peppermint water, were numbered at between 3,000 and 5,000 in 1851. However, as theirs was an itinerant trade, yet to find permanent premises, they are precluded from consideration here.[14] At the other social extreme were gentlemen's clubs, occupying their own specially designed buildings, which had been established since 1815; for instance, the University Club (1826), the Athenaeum (1830) and the Travellers (1831). These were male preserves with a high entrance fee (£20–£30) and an annual subscription: only in the 1850s was the custom introduced of members entertaining their friends in the strangers' room.[15] Their membership was largely made up of aristocrats, members of Parliament and professional men for whom their location in the West End, near to Whitehall and the Houses of Parliament, was particularly suitable. Finally, also catering for the wealthy, were a few foreign (mainly French and Italian) eating places: Sablonière's, which had been established in Leicester Square in 1788, Bertolini's in St Martin's Street, and Verrey's in Regent Street, described as 'one of the nearest imitations of a café to be found in the metropolis'.[16]

London in the 1860s was, therefore, far from bereft of places for people to eat and drink. Yet those that existed, though so numerous, were in certain ways unsuited to a society increasingly sensitive to behaviour and contacts in public. The development of spatial differentiation and specialization which characterized the nineteenth-century city was not simply a function of its size and economic purpose but represented an unprecedented desire among the middle classes for segregation and privacy. On a large scale, the sorting out of London's social areas was well under way by the 1860s through the development of single-class suburbs on the fringes and the demolition of inner areas by the ruthless action of railway and road building and the quieter, though equally systematic, improvements carried out by ground landlords. At the same time specialization in services, retailing and entertainment was reaching a new level of sophistication.[17] The effect of this transformation was to reduce considerably the chance of arbitrary or alarming encounters as each class clung to its neighbourhood, at home and work, travelling between the two on suitably segregated transport.

The inadequacy of most places of refreshment was that their layout, based on the needs of an earlier period, failed to accommodate these changes. With the exception of the clubs they were essentially public places, open to any that could afford them; but in their design they made no allowance for that sense of the possibility of public embarrassment or shame which most dismayed their middle- and upper-class customers. While meals at home were, for those classes, growing more ritualized, with more courses, more implements and a greater concern about behaviour at table, meals taken away from home were conducted in a much less refined manner.[18]

The middle classes' avoidance of pubs can be attributed partly to a growing public opinion in favour of the restriction of alcohol consumption, but many were eager, as defenders of the pub pointed out, to buy drink to have at home. They shunned drinking in public as much because the drinking places provided little opportunity for social discrimination or privacy. The busiest pubs, on main roads or prominent corners, had been built or rebuilt in the early nineteenth century to a single- or two-bar plan in which the bar counter, set against the rear wall, faced a room without seats or other comforts. This was the type of interior most often illustrated in temperance propaganda – large, open and crowded with an alarming mass of people. Suburban pubs had a more traditional plan with its division into public bar, bar parlour and perhaps a tap room, and there was some seating. These divisions permitted a rudimentary kind of segregation – clerks, tradesmen and friends of the publican in the parlour, labourers and artisans in the public bar and tap room – but beyond that there was little chance for the drinker to distance himself from others.[19]

In the dining rooms, coffee houses and taverns this problem was reversed. These were laid out with two ranges of boxes or compartments along either side of a rectangular room each with a stained deal table and seating for six or eight people. Wooden or curtained partitions between the compartments lent an air of mystery to the interior (Figure 7.1). This arrangement can be traced back to the coffee houses of the late seventeenth and eighteenth centuries where the boxes, far from being exclusive, were intended to promote communal discussion between friends and strangers. Having paid his penny admission at the door, and had the rules of the house explained to him, a customer was free to go to any table and join in the conversation, uninhibited by the social standing of those present.[20] Joseph Addison described a variation on this ritual in the *Spectator* (1714):[21]

> I was Yesterday in a Coffee-House not far from the Royal Exchange, where I observed three Persons in close Conference over a Pipe of Tobacco; upon which, having filled one for my own Use, I lighted it at the little Wax Candle that stood before them; and after having thrown in two

7.1 Painting of the Cock Tavern, Fleet Street by Philip Norman.
This interior view, painted not long before the tavern was demolished in 1882, shows the kind of compartmentalised layout common in London eating houses earlier in the century. The plain interior contrasts sharply with the elaborate décor of the later West End restaurants (Figure 7.6). On the evidence of these illustrations, Purssell's Coffee Saloon (Figure 7.3) and the Cock Tavern, both at the 'business' end of the city, seem to have been generally all-male institutions.
(by courtesy of the Museum of London)

or three Whiffs amongst them, sat down and made one of the Company. I need not tell my Reader, that lighting a Man's Pipe at the same Candle, is looked upon amongst Brother-smoakers as an Overture to Conversation and Friendship.

This kind of experience, even if romanticized, is the one which attached to the compartmentalized layout. Such a layout could still, in the mid-nineteenth century, offer the thrill of a chance encounter with the famous or conversation with total strangers: the journalist George Sims recalled sharing a compartment at the Albion, Drury Lane with the author Augustus Hare and two of his colleagues on the day they apportioned some literary fees.[22] But it was just as likely that the arbitrary, levelling effect which attached to this plan would have far less agreeable consequences. What was apparently an ideal system for the preservation of privacy was, through a tradition of use, awkward and deterring. One effect of this deterrence was the retreat of some users, first to more genuinely private rooms upstairs and subsequently to purpose-built clubs elsewhere.

However the middle-class attitude to these buildings and their interiors is described, it can be doubly emphasized where women are concerned. In the matter of behaviour in public places, as in sexual behaviour, a double standard existed. Men could venture in public where women could not and might, it was supposed, be educated or toughened by contact with the varieties and extremes of urban life. Their freedom of action offered possibilities of either immorality or improvement, where for women there lay only disgrace.[23] In almost the same breath as they recollected the compartment system of eating houses, memoir writers referred to the exclusion of women from them. 'Their presence', wrote Clement Scott, 'would have been considered fast, if not disreputable.'[24] In 1851 some coffee houses were described as having rooms set apart where 'gentlemen may take their wives and daughters'; four years later an early guide to eating out in London identified thirteen places which had private rooms for ladies, though it suggested that the service in such rooms was likely to be grudging.[25] But for the most part women, especially when unaccompanied by men, were confined to pastrycooks' and confectioners' shops like the one where Miss Tox, in Dickens's *Dombey and Son*, sought refuge 'in a musty little back room usually devoted to the consumption of soups, and pervaded by an ox-tail atmosphere'.[26] The *Golden Guide to London* (1875) recommended eight such places for ladies. A year later the newly established *Women's Gazette* gave a fuller list of 'places in London where ladies can conveniently lunch when in town for a day's shopping, and un-attended by a gentleman': eight of these can be identified as confectioner's or baker's.[27]

The sight of such establishments crowded with women was not new. The *Epicure's Almanack* of 1815 listed a number in the fashionable West End, including Farrance's in Spring Gardens and Owen and Bentley's fruit shop in New Bond

Street, noted for its 'jellies, ices and liquors'.[28] One of the clearest signs of sexual division was the restriction put on where women could eat, and the limited range of refreshments available at the places open to them. By the 1860s, however, these places had become as obsolete as the male-dominated coffee and eating houses, not because of their inadequate facilities so much as because of shifts in the character of demand.

Although difficult to measure exactly, there seems to have been a growth in the institutions for leisure in London in the 1850s and 1860s. The best known of these – the rebuilt Crystal Palace at Sydenham and the South Kensington Museum – owed their genesis directly to the Great Exhibition of 1851, an event which gave a new dimension to the public life of the metropolis. The two decades also saw the foundation of other art galleries, museums and concert halls, an increase in the number of theatres and the quality of plays produced at them, and the beginnings of a transformation in retailing with the establishment of the first department stores.[29] There was more to attract visitors to London, and to draw Londoners away from home, especially the wives and daughters of middle- and upper-class families who had plenty of time to spare during the day. Gradual shifts in the timings of meals had extended the period when they could be out of the house. Earlier in the century such families had generally taken breakfast at about 10 a.m. and dinner, the principal meal of the day, between 3 and 5 p.m. Women could carry out their business and make visits between these two meals, needing no more than the soups and delicacies offered at pastrycooks to sustain them. But by the 1850s the time for breakfast had been brought forward and dinner pushed back, to between 5.30 and 6.30 p.m., giving lunch at mid-day a more established position in the timetable.[30] Men at work could take lunch at a coffee house or eating house, but for women wanting as substantial a meal while away from home there was no comparable provision.

The development of the restaurant

The emergence of a new type of eating place – a restaurant, containing separate public rooms, housed in a building designed for the purpose and often managed as part of a chain of such places – was not a clear-cut affair. Each of the elements which characterized such places can be identified well before the transformations of the 1860s. The first restaurant named as such was started in Paris in the 1760s: the number there reached nearly 3,000 by 1820.[31] In London the term was applied to foreign establishments in the early nineteenth century: the *Epicure's Almanack* (1815) referred to two 'restaurateurs' in Soho, both apparently from France.[32] Yet a change in terminology alone cannot be taken as evidence of innovation, especially in a field where the appeal of a new name could lead to its adoption in places where no material changes had been made. According to one source, the real innovator was not a Frenchman but John Simpson, whose Grand Divan Restaurant in the Strand, opened in 1848, was 'a revolution and a revelation' (Figure 7.2). Its notable features were first of all its layout – 'large tables and comfortable chairs in place of boxes and benches' – but also its equipment: 'abundance of clean linen tablecloths and napkins; plated forks and spoons; electro-plated tankards instead of pewter pots'.[33] In fact, the main room had open tables only along one side, retaining the traditional boxes on the other with a sideboard in the centre as was customary in older eating houses. The windows were separated by long mirrors, while on the opposite wall were reliefs set in gilt frames. The restaurant was sufficiently important to be noticed in the architectural press, its size and elaborate decoration setting it apart from those places which had a 'darkness "that is almost felt" '.[34]

7.2 Simpson's, the Strand.
The photograph was taken before the restaurant was rebuilt in 1903–4. The combination of compartments along one wall with separate tables elsewhere is as described at the time of the opening in 1848.
(by courtesy of B. T. Batsford and the National Monuments Record)

In the next decade the internal form of the modern restaurant was to emerge with the total abolition of compartments. This can be seen in an engraving of Purssell's Coffee Saloon in Cornhill (Figure 7.3), and it was also true of Sawyer and Strange's London Dinner in Fleet Street, opened in 1857. This had a number of different public rooms which were slotted into a building originally designed for another purpose – a familiar stage in the evolution of a new building type. Again, the use of separate tables was commented upon, as well as its 'air of quiet taste and comfortableness' in contrast to the 'dowdiness, and even squalour, of many well-reputed and largely frequented taverns'.[35]

The London Dinner was referred to as an imitator of Simpson's, as was the Wellington in St James's Street, a short-lived restaurant for which no architectural evidence survives.[36] To this list might be added Blanchard's in Beak Street, founded by a waiter from Simpson's; Carr's Restaurant, an addition to the King's Head Tavern in Fleet Street; the Café Royal in Regent Street, opened in 1865; and Gatti's in the Royal Adelaide Gallery, opened in 1862 by two brothers whose family had established themselves as confectioners the decade before.[37] This steady growth of new restaurants suggested an extensive new field for architects:[38]

7.3 Purssell's Coffee Saloon, Cornhill, 1849.
The all-male company, prominently displayed clock, newspapers, board games and general air of animated relaxation suggest the function of the coffee saloon as a meeting place for city businessmen. The generously spaced tables (without cloths) accommodate about six people.
(by courtesy of the Greater London Council Print Collection)

Dining-rooms are likely to give as much work to the profession as union-houses did a quarter of a century ago, baths and washhouses for ten years, and cemetery chapels lately, for the reconstruction of London and the demand for improvement are causing opportunities to be offered for this class of construction, though we are of the opinion it is yet only in the beginning.

None of these examples, interesting though they may be, is of enough substance to attract nomination as the arrival of a new building type. Although it is possible to recognize in their design and management a response to the changes in demand that were occurring at the time, as commercial businesses they were still small-scale. There were examples of caterers running more than one establishment, but London in the 1850s had no catering chain to compare with the Bouillons Duval set up in Paris from 1855 onwards.[39] The call for a similar enterprise in London existed – and the legal apparatus for setting up limited companies was introduced in Acts of 1855, 1856 and 1862 – but it was not until the 1860s that the full commercialization of catering began. The establishment of partnerships and limited companies to build and run restaurants, along with similar concerns in the hotel industry and retailing, was one of the most marked characteristics of that and the following decades: in the period 1866–74, 161 companies involved in the hotel and restaurant trade were registered.[40] The entrepreneurs most closely associated with this development were Frederick Gordon, a solicitor turned caterer, and the partnership of Spiers and Pond. They merit special attention as the innovators who made the most of the new opportunities that were emerging.

Gordon started in 1868 by taking a lease of Crosby Hall, a fifteenth-century building in Bishopsgate, and converting it into a restaurant. Reverence for the building's fabric inhibited the alterations made to it while on the same count providing a good excuse for not introducing a compartment layout: 'As a matter of policy the proprietors might have been induced to fit this truly great Hall with a series of "boxes", but to use a common expression, they, "could not find it in their heart to do it".' Instead the hall was laid out with separate tables and chairs designed in sympathy with the building's antiquity. The Council Chamber on the same floor became the 'Great Luncheon and Refreshment Bar', while the Throne Room above was adapted for more select dinners. In their publicity Frederick Gordon and Company laid less emphasis on the food they served than how they served it, employing waitresses rather than waiters, and the special provisions that they made to ensure that women would feel comfortable, including ladies' boudoir and retiring rooms with female attendants.[41]

From Crosby Hall Gordon went on to take an interest in two other buildings, the Holborn Restaurant and the King's Head Tavern in Fenchurch Street, both of which he remodelled to meet the increasingly sophisticated requirements of his clientèle. The Holborn had a ground floor saloon and grill room and three dining rooms above; the King's Head, a basement grill room, a luncheon buffet, luncheon bar, fish bar and tavern (called the 'American Stores') all on the ground floor, and two dining rooms above. Such a variety of facilities and food was a particular attraction for those who wanted to treat eating out as an enjoyable occasion, not just a necessity: the same kind of customers could also appreciate the attention Gordon gave to the decoration of his restaurants, especially the lavish use of 'art-tile painting' at the King's Head.[42]

Felix Spiers and Christopher Pond both emigrated to Melbourne, Australia, in 1853, where they established themselves in the catering business, one as partner in the Royal Hotel and the other as proprietor of the Shakspere Restaurant. They subsequently joined together in setting up the Café de Paris at the Theatre Royal. According to the booster booklet that they published about it, the Café had a main dining room with large communal tables at its centre surrounded by smaller, private tables; elsewhere there were billiard, coffee and news rooms. Though described as 'superior to anything among the restaurants of London', it was not sufficiently *avant-garde* to admit ladies.[43] Following this success the partners expanded their interest in catering and other enterprises before deciding to leave for London in 1863, where they were later credited with having 'effected a revolution in the English refreshment system'.[44]

For a partnership setting up in English catering for the first time there were two possibilities which promised a guaranteed business in return for a minimum of capital investment: the railway station buffet trade and the provision of refreshment at exhibitions. Spiers and Pond made their start in these two spheres. They subsequently took contracts at some of the places which most typified the development of public life in London, including the Royal Italian Opera House, the Horticultural Gardens in South Kensington and the Agricultural Hall at Islington.[45] At such places could be witnessed the new direction that society was taking as going out in public, and eating in public, became occasions to be delighted in for their own sake. In 1865–6 they established their first two restaurants which, in keeping with their earlier enterprises, were attached to the terminal stations at Victoria and Ludgate Hill. The one at the latter, called the Silver Grill, was located in the apparently unpromising setting of a railway arch. Into this were squeezed first- and second-class dining rooms, and dining rooms for ladies only, with everything 'on a club scale – glass, linen, food and decorations'. The grill itself, 'very like an elaborate shrine', was presented to the partners by well-wishers 'as a mark of appreciation of the reforms those gentlemen have worked out'.[46]

However, it was at the centre of the West End theatre and shopping district that Spiers and Pond made their major innovation. In 1869 they took a lease on a house in Piccadilly where they opened a set of dining and refreshment rooms to test the potential of such a location. That experience gave them the confidence to take the building lease of a plot nearby, the site of Webbs Hotel and the White Bear Inn, where they built the Criterion Theatre and Restaurant, opened in 1874. To maximize the publicity to be gained from such a project, they announced in the year that they took the lease their intention of holding an architectural competition for the design of the new building. The terms of the competition – not just the way the contestants were selected, but the fact that the winner had no guarantee of being granted the commission – ensured that the architectural press kept the scheme in its sights as it had done with no similar building before. The requirements put before the competitors gave a sense of the scale of activities which Spiers and Pond hoped to encompass: there was to be a hall in the basement capable of holding 1,000 people, a buffet and dining saloon on the ground floor, a grand hall for public meetings and concerts on the first floor and, at the top of the building, facilities for a photographer and an art gallery.[47]

The winning design, that submitted by Thomas Verity, is evidence of the transformation in the social life of London that had occurred over the previous twenty years.[48] There were to be three entrances to the building from Piccadilly. The principal one led to the vestibule, and beyond it to the grand staircase, both planned as areas of public parade: the two flanking ones led to the music hall in the basement and the buffet. Behind the buffet there was to be a smoking room, while to the right of the vestibule was a dining saloon: a further dining room was to be included at a lower level at the back of the building. The staircase led to the grand hall, or ball room, with two more dining rooms on an intermediate floor (Figures 7.4a, b). In the three years that the Criterion took to build no substantial changes were made in its design except for the decision, halfway through the project, to turn the basement hall into a fully fledged theatre.[49] In decoration Verity, like the architects employed by Frederick Gordon, chose to make extensive use of painted tile-work, which was thought to have the advantage of combining cleanliness with a feeling of richness and theatricality.[50]

The Criterion was sufficiently successful to require an extension only four years after its opening. At the same time Spiers and Pond were responsible for the reconstruction of the Gaiety Restaurant in the Strand and, harking back to their first ventures, the adaptation of the Mansion House Station Restaurant in the City. At the Gaiety, which like the Criterion was attached to a theatre, the accommodation included a grill room in the basement, a buffet on the ground floor, a table d'hôte on the first and a smoke room on the second, all once again sumptuously decorated with art tiles, mirrors and stained glass windows.[51] All these projects were discussed in a paper read to the Royal Institute of British Architects in 1878 by Thomas Verity, the first occasion that the Institute had looked specifically at the subject of restaurants.[52]

Reporting on London restaurants in 1879, the *Licensed Victuallers' Gazette* commented that the Criterion and the Gaiety 'stand on a special platform of

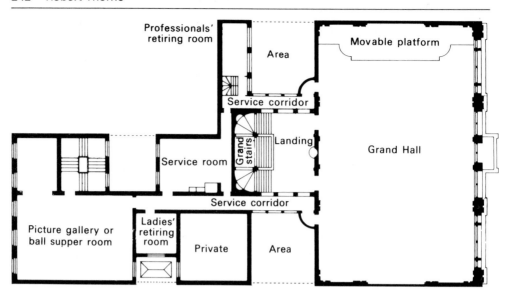

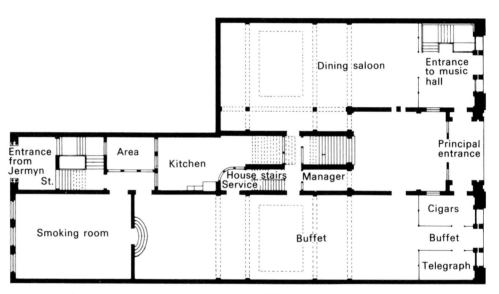

Ground Floor

7.4 Ground floor (a) and grand hall floor (b) of the Criterion, Piccadilly, 1871.
The plans are those of the winning entry to the competition.
(drawing by Alan Fagan based on *The Builder*, 8 July 1871, p. 526)

their own, and have no rivals in the way of popularity'.[53] Only the most vehement architectural determinist would insist that Spiers and Pond's achievement rested entirely on the design and layout of their buildings. Because they ran a chain of restaurants and refreshment rooms they were able, through centralized buying and stock control, to keep down prices and guarantee standards: they could also cross-check between establishments as a way of measuring customer demands and guarding against fraud. Yet descriptions of their work, even outside the architectural press, put as much emphasis on their buildings as on their management. The variety of accommodation provided at each restaurant and the lavish interiors were in keeping with the expectations of the time. The rooms were on a grander scale than those of any traditional eating house – the principal dining room at the Criterion was 80ft long, the bar at the Gaiety 100ft – and they had few claustrophobic sub-divisions. Their openness, enhanced by the brilliance of their tile-work decoration, offered a setting in which customers could appear in public while, seated at separate tables, still preserving an immediate territory that was private. Significantly, neither the Criterion not the Gaiety appears to have had separate ladies' dining rooms, though at both special attention was given to the cloakrooms built for them. The qualities which made the restaurants generally popular were ones which at the same time set ladies at their ease: in particular, the East Room at the Criterion established a reputation as a place where even the most timid women could eat while visiting the West End.[54]

The evolution of mass catering 1870–1914, and its impact on the public house

The success that Spiers and Pond and Frederick Gordon experienced rested on preconditions well beyond their making. Within the trade they may have learnt from the methods and appearance of pioneering establishments like Simpson's, but the scale on which they worked would not have been possible without a change in the character of demand. Both firms started out in a traditional field, one catering for travellers, the other for city clerks and businessmen, but both were carried further by the new needs of the time: more people having to travel further from their suburban homes, more attractions to encourage them to travel other than for work, and the growth of a 'habit of enjoyment' in the younger generation of middle-class families whose parents had been more earnest and domestic in their outlook.[55] The location of the Criterion in Piccadilly, near the Royal Academy, the Geological Museum, St James's Hall and the shops of Regent Street, was a sign of Spiers and Pond's awareness of this shift in trade, confirmed by their decision to incorporate a theatre in this building.

For a less affluent, lower middle-class and working-class clientèle the same set of needs was answered by caterers less well known. The forcing apart of home and work, already extensive because of London's size and spatial differentiation, was furthered by suburban expansion. The 1891 census revealed that in the previous decade the four places that had grown most rapidly in England and Wales were all suburbs of London, and the 1901 census told almost the same story. While thousands still walked to work, the development of suburbs beyond walking distance of central London, combined with cheap fares on trams and railways, gave the less well off an opportunity to join in a movement previously confined to the wealthy. The population of Greater London grew by slightly less than 50 per cent in the years 1875–95 but the number of journeys made by train, tram and bus increased by almost 300 per cent.[56] Such an increase is not to be accounted for simply by the commuting journeys of male heads of household. Some can be attributed to the growing number of women workers, notably shop assistants and, towards the end of the century, clerks and typists; and some were journeys for pleasure which the gradual improvement in real wages and hours of work made a more widespread possibility.

The requirements of the mass of people away from home during the day were for something simpler, and cheaper, than the table d'hôte dinner offered at the East Room of the Criterion. The achievements of those seeking to meet these requirements were more likely to be in production and management than in building design, and the architectural results of their efforts less remarkable: few of their customers were in a position to be as sensitive about the place where they ate as those whom Spiers and Pond attracted.

At the social level where the new mass caterers of the late nineteenth century hoped to operate the pub still held its own, despite its lack of comforts and the reluctance of publicans to serve any food beyond the most unappetizing snacks.[57] In varying degrees most of the innovators in mass catering were allied with the temperance crusade which, having embarked with the aim of curing the 'drink evil' through moral propaganda, now realized the desirabilty of providing alternative facilities to the pub. The attempt to 'see the devil cheated in his own colours' (as one campaigner put it) combined a real concern to meet an apparent demand with a mistrust that time spent away from home and workplace might be abused: so proselytizing was mixed with commerce, philanthropy with the search for profit.[58]

The most earnest of these institutions were the coffee houses and coffee public houses founded by temperance sympathizers in a movement which, starting in Dundee in 1853, spread to northern cities in the 1860s and so to London in the 1870s. In 1873 Dr Barnardo, famous for his work against child cruelty, opened the Edinburgh Castle Coffee Palace in a converted pub at Limehouse in the East End, following it three years later by the Dublin Castle in the Mile End Road. The People's Café Company founded its first house in Whitecross Street, Shoreditch, in 1875, and the Coffee Tavern Company its first in the Edgware Road in

1877. By 1884 London had 121 reformed coffee houses of various kinds offering tea, coffee, cocoa and other non-alcoholic drinks plus food, and providing reading and smoking rooms wherever the accommodation (usually in converted premises) allowed.[59] Most of the companies hoped to appeal to a working-class clientèle, though some set apart certain houses, or separate rooms, for a middle-class trade. They did not, however, cater for women, who made up only 6 per cent of the custom: even the Rose and Crown at the heart of the Knightsbridge shopping district was distinctly described as a 'Men's Coffee Palace'.[60]

Yet the temperance coffee houses were a short-lived phenomenon: the very earnestness of the movement was its undoing. Some companies, especially in the north, paid fair dividends for a few years, but in London many coffee houses disappeared as quickly as they had come: the Coffee Public-House National Society was attempting to sell off three of its houses as early as 1881.[61] Philanthropic enthusiasm was no substitute for expertise; the smell of missionary endeavour put off the very customers it was hoped to catch. After visiting a coffee palace in the East End the social investigator Charles Booth reported: 'Good food might excuse the texts, but the texts do not excuse bad food'.[62]

The more lasting achievement was of those who hid their temperance sympathies behind a thoroughly commercial facade. John Pearce ('We best serve ourselves by serving others best'), starting with a coffee stall off the City Road, established his first coffee bar in Aldersgate Street in 1880; by 1898 he was running twenty-three, plus twenty-nine restaurants of the British Tea Table Company, together serving 70,000 meals a day. Lockhart's Cocoa Rooms, of which there were twenty-three by 1884, served slightly less substantial meals but with the same concern for speed and cheapness: like Pearce, they formed a subsidiary chain called Ideal Restaurants to tap a more respectable trade.[63]

In the case of two other companies catering was closely associated with food processing and manufacture as befitted the scale of their operations. The Aerated Bread Company ('ABC'), incorporated in 1862, began as a chain of baker's shops selling a patent brand of bread before extending to the provision of light meals; J. Lyons and Company, who opened their first teashop in Piccadilly in 1894 and their first Corner House restaurant in 1909, moved in the other direction as they decided to expand the retail sale of the tea, ice cream and cakes that were so popular in their tea rooms.[64] Lyons, it was said, did 'more for the cause of temperance than almost anyone', and almost as much for a close ally of temperance, vegetarianism. Although there were about thirty-one vegetarian restaurants in London in 1897, their supporters complained that their success was prejudiced by the spread of ordinary cheap restaurants.[65]

The spread of reformed coffee houses, tea rooms and other cheap refreshment places offered an unprecedented challenge to the public house. It came at a time when the drink trade was feeling the impact of temperance opinion through local and national political pressures. In 1889 the Liberal Party added to its programme the policy of granting communities the option of deciding how many (if any) drinking places to have. Though its Bills to implement this policy were unsuccessful, its intentions were in part achieved through the growing stringency of licensing magistrates in granting new licences and renewing existing ones, and the increasing reluctance of landlords to see new pubs built on their suburban estates. Under this kind of threat, the response of publicans and brewers was to exploit what they had as vigorously as possible by rebuilding their pubs on a grander scale with layouts that would combine the most efficient service with the attraction of the widest range of clientèle. The most striking characteristic of these late nineteenth-century pubs was their multiplicity of small bar compartments, arranged around a long bar counter and divided by high partitions. Some compartments were approached by separate doors from the street, others gave off a common corridor down one side of the building: drinkers in one compartment were hidden from those in every other one, especially in those pubs which

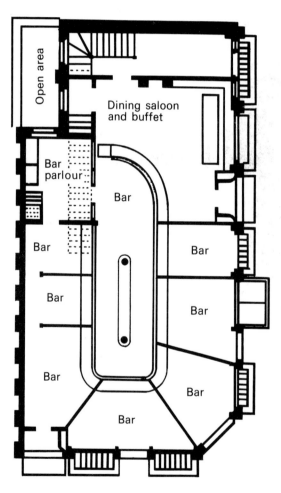

7.5 The Goat in Boots public house, Fulham Road, 1889: Ground floor plan.
This plan shows the layout of bar compartments around a central serving area typical of public house design of the period. The advantage of this kind of layout, in contrast to a more open one, was that it gave maximum privacy to those ashamed of drinking in public.
(drawing by Alan Fagan based on *The Builder*, 19 January 1889, p. 50)

had a screen on the bar counter itself partially obscuring the view from the serving area (Figure 7.5).[66]

Foreign observers were astonished by this compartment system. One German alluded to the possibility that it reflected the special subtleties of the class system: 'The people that patronise such a bar . . . divide themselves into six distinct and different classes, and the men in one compartment would think twice before consenting to rub shoulders with the men on the other side of the partition. This is typically English, exists in England only.'[67] A more mundane analysis was that by breaking the customers up into manageable groups the system enabled the publican to quell disorder and prevent it spreading through the whole building.[68] But these two explanations could have held true at any time earlier in the century, and do not of themselves account for the way in which compartments flourished and multiplied in its last three decades. The essence of this layout was that it secured privacy for the drinker at a time when the shame attached to drinking in public was acute, and for the publican it offered the opportunity of winning back some of the more respectable trade he had lost earlier in the century when his house had been literally too public. The compartments were particularly popular among women, whether accompanied by men or not, a popularity enhanced when some were set aside exclusively for their use. Typical of this attempt to attract a better-off female clientèle was the 'ladies only' bar introduced at the Royal Oak, Bayswater, in about 1900 with the specific intention of serving ladies shopping in the area.[69]

Conclusion

In the nineteenth century, as today, running a pub or a restaurant could be a precarious business, for in few towns did one such place hold a monopoly or serve an unfluctuating demand. A publican, restaurateur or coffee house proprietor had to be forever alive to the fickleness of his customers' tastes. The quality and price of food and drink offered, the type of service, and the location of the business all contributed to a successful formula: but even if that formula was found it could soon be overtaken by changing circumstances. The fact that so few examples of the types of building discussed in this paper can be seen today in an unaltered state is witness to the transience of enthusiasms in public catering: coffee houses, whether reformed or unreformed, are hard to find; Lyon's tea shops and Corner Houses have been closed; and nineteenth-century pubs have mostly been ruthlessly transformed. The survival rate of most other types of building from the same period has been much higher.

Of the many changes in taste to which caterers sought to respond, the hardest to define, and yet in many ways the most crucial, concerned people's perceptions of the most appealing setting for the meal or drink – whether it should be open or enclosed, communal or private, and how far divisions within the pub or restaurant were expected to mirror the social distinctions of the world outside. These were matters of particular importance at a time when many of those that caterers hoped to attract were especially anxious about whom they met and where. In this aspect of the trade, as in every other, the ingredients for success followed no immutable laws: a layout which seemed ideal for one set of customers at one time might seem singularly uninviting a decade or a generation later. The eclipse of

7.6 Prince's Restaurant, Piccadilly, photographed in 1896.
The opulent décor, monogrammed chairs, carpets, tablecloths, flowers, silverware and lavish fittings are evidence of the transformation of London's social life in the later nineteenth century as well as the expectations of the patrons. The high density of (separate) tables, apparently set for twos and fours, suggests a degree of patronage appropriate to the restaurant's location in the West End.
(by courtesy of the National Monuments Record)

the traditional eating house by the restaurant was in part because its compartment system offered the wrong kind of setting, enclosure too intimate. Yet when publicans and brewers sought to expand their trade they in a sense reversed the clock by introducing compartments which, though they were of a different character from those there had been in eating houses, gave the same impression of privacy. Similarly, while the openness of the earlier pubs was felt by many to be too exposing, the openness of the large restaurant with its separate tables dotted around the room was reassuring (Figure 7.6).[70]

These apparent contradictions do not imply that different layouts had no special meaning: the reports of contemporaries confirm that they did, that where people ate and drank mattered as much as what was served or how it was served. Rather, they confirm that the significance that attaches to an architectural form varies according to the social uses to which a building is put. The interest of places of refreshment is that, like other building types, they appear to have been a barometer of society's values and aspirations – in this case, one especially sensitive to the central concerns of the age.

As architectural meanings can change or reverse, so the public provision of refreshment in society follows no straightforward linear development. The presumption that an urbanizing society will have an increasing number and variety of places where people can eat and drink can be amply illustrated in the period under discussion, but the needs which produced the grand restaurant and the multi-compartment pub have not endured. To discuss why that is so requires a set of explanations as broad as those relied on in the interpretation of their original development: not just the changing attitude to the use of public places – the point stressed here – but shifts in the use of time and income, in the relation between home and work, and in the acceptance of different foods. A glance at any present-day guide to London restaurants indicates that the idea of eating out as an experience to be delighted in for its own sake, which first emerged in the nineteenth century, still flourishes: similar guides to pubs suggest that publicans' quest for a broader clientèle has, in the long run, succeeded. But in other respects provision has narrowed. Many businessmen who used to impress their clients by taking them to lunch or dinner at a restaurant now feed them in an office dining room or at home: families that once enjoyed a cheap meal at Lyons now rely on a take-away outlet. These and other changes may signal a decline in public catering which, if it continues, will make the developments discussed in this paper appear not only parochial but peculiarly time-bound. It may be that the second half of the nineteenth century was highly unusual in witnessing such an expansion in catering which, rather than being a stage in a long-term development, formed a unique episode. Only an exploration of a much wider chronology could establish whether that is so.

Notes and references

1 Mary Douglas, *Purity and Danger: an Analysis of the Concepts of Pollution and Taboo*, Routledge & Kegan Paul, London, 1966; Yehudi A. Cohen, 'Food. Consumption patterns', in David L. Sills, ed., *International Encyclopaedia of the Social Sciences*, Macmillan and the Free Press, New York, 1968, vol. 5, pp. 508–13.

2 Arthur J. Taylor (ed.), *The Standard of Living in Britain in the Industrial Revolution*, Methuen, London, 1975; John Burnett, *Plenty and Want*, Penguin, Harmondsworth, 1968; Brian Harrison, *Drink and the Victorians*, Faber, London, 1971.

3 'London eating-houses', *Chambers' Edinburgh Journal*, 24 June 1837, p. 173. The early evolution of the public house is outlined in Maurice Gorham and H. McG. Dunnett, *Inside the Pub*, Architectural Press, London, 1950, pp. 64–5. French historians of the *Annales* school have shown more interest in general patterns of food and drink consumption than their English colleagues: see Robert Forster and Orest Ranum, eds, *Food and Drink in History*, Johns Hopkins University Press, Baltimore and London, 1979.

4 The term 'pub' came into common use in the 1860s eclipsing the use of the abbreviation 'public' in referring to a public house.

5 This alarm was in part associated with the passage of the Beer Act in 1830, which permitted the establishment of a category of drinking place outside the control of the local magistrates. Although these beerhouses were not normally architecturally distinguished, it was thought by many that the competition they presented was one reason for the building or rebuilding of public houses in more splendid form (Harrison, op. cit., pp. 81–6).

6 George R. Sims, *My Life. Sixty Years' Recollecions of Bohemian London*, Eveleigh Nash Company, London, 1917, p. 320.

7 One of the Old Brigade, pseud. (Donald Shaw), *London in the Sixties*, Everett & Company, London, 1908, p. 168; Clement Scott, *How They Dined Us in 1860 and How They Dine Us Now*, London, n.d., *c.* 1900, p. 4.

8 (E. L. Tarbuck), *The Builder's Practical Director*, J. Hagger, London, n.d., *c.* 1855, p. 121.

9 *Parliamentary Papers*, 1863 (5597), LIIII, pp. 14–18.

10 Select Committee of the House of Commons on Wine Duties, *Parliamentary Papers*, 1852 (495), XVII, q 3817.

11 Stephen Fiske, *English Photographs*, Tinsley Brothers, London, 1869, p. 171.

12 'London coffee-houses, past and present', *Leisure Hour*, vol. xii, no. 21, March 1863, p. 187. For the spread of coffee houses see the Select Committee of the House of Commons on Import Duties, *Parliamentary Papers*, 1840 (601), v, qq 2738–824.

13 Christopher P. Monkhouse, 'The station hotel in the nineteenth century: the genesis of a building type', unpublished MA thesis, University of London, 1970.

14 Henry Mayhew, *London Labour and the London Poor*, London, 1851, vol. 1, pp. 158–212.

15 *London at Table*, Chapman & Hall, London, 1851, p. 9; 'Clubs and taverns', *London Society*, vol. ix, March 1866, pp. 269–70. There is evidence that among eighteenth-century clubs was at least one, Almack's, that was open to both sexes, the men electing the women and vice versa. In this, as in other spheres, the nineteenth

century was marked by more rigid social and sexual divisions (John Timbs, *Clubs and Club Life in London*, John Camden Hotten, London, 1872, pp. 73–6, 509–10).

16 *Survey of London*, Athlone Press, London, 1966, vol. xxxiii, p. 12; E. H. Malcolm, 'London coffee houses and their customers', *Tegg's Magazine*, vol. I, 1844, p. 124.

17 Gareth Stedman-Jones, *Outcast London*, Clarendon Press, Oxford, 1971, chapter 8; Donald J. Olsen, 'Victorian London: specialization, segregation and privacy', *Victorian Studies*, vol. xvii, March 1974, pp. 265–78; David Cannadine, 'Victorian cities: how different?', *Social History*, vol. 4, January 1977, pp. 460–6.

18 Etiquette books of the mid-nineteenth century which detail the rules to be observed when eating at home say little or nothing about eating in public: e.g., *The Habits of Good Society: a Handbook of Etiquette for Ladies and Gentlemen*, James Hogg, London, 1859.

19 Mark Girouard, *Victorian Pubs*, Studio Vista, London, 1975, pp. 40–5, 56.

20 Aytoun Ellis, *The Penny Universities. A History of the Coffee Houses*, Secker & Warburg, London, 1956, pp. 45, 86.

21 *The Spectator*, no. 568, 16 July 1714 (Everyman edn, vol. IV, Dent, London, 1945, p. 287).

22 Sims, op. cit., p. 96.

23 Richard Sennett, *The Fall of Public Man*, Cambridge University Press, 1977, pp. 23–4.

24 Scott, op. cit., p. 8.

25 *London at Table*, op. cit., p. 5; J. Gordon Lomax, *How to Live in London*, Hunt's Yachting Magazine, London, n.d., *c.* 1855, p. 8. George Augustus Sala described the attempt to 'change the eating-houses of Cheapside into pseudo "restaurants" with the introduction of private rooms for ladies' (*Twice Round the Clock*, Houlston & Wright, London, 1859, p. 142).

26 Charles Dickens, *Dombey and Son*, Penguin edn, Harmondsworth, 1970, p. 617.

27 *Woman's Gazette*, vol. I, August 1876, p. 174.

28 *The Epicure's Almanack: or Calendar of Good Living*, Longman, London, 1815, pp. 103, 182.

29 Alison Adburgham, *Shops and Shopping 1800–1914*, Allen & Unwin, London, 1964; Richard D. Altick, *The Shows of London*, Harvard University Press, Cambridge, Mass., and London, 1978, chapters 32–4.

30 Changing meal times are chronicled in Arnold Palmer, *Movable Feasts*, Oxford University Press, London, 1952, which is based mainly on literary sources.

31 Theodore Zeldin, *France 1848–1945*, Clarendon Press, Oxford, 1977, vol. 2, p. 739.

32 *The Epicure's Almanack*, op. cit., pp. 133, 150–1.

33 *Edmund Yates: his Recollections and Experiences*, R. Bentley & Son, London, 1884, vol. 2, pp. 156–7.

34 *Morning Post*, 11 October 1848, p. 1; *Builder*, 16 December 1848, p. 603; *Building News*, 25 September 1857, p. 1012. The original Simpson's, which was designed by a Mr Friend, was entirely rebuilt in 1903–4.

35 *Building News*, 18 September 1857, p. 980.

36 *Edmund Yates*, op. cit., p. 157.

37 *Evening News*, 21 August 1909, p. 4; 28 February 1910, p. 4; Nicholas Taylor, 'Rococo grill room', *Architectural Review*, vol. cxxxvii, April 1965, pp. 307–11; *Caterer*

and Hotel-Keeper's Gazette, 15 November 1906, p. 500.

38 *Building News*, 6 August 1858, p. 786.

39 Zeldin, op. cit., p. 741. A Frenchman visiting London in the mid-1850s found the provision of eating places, even for men, inadequate: 'London is really a city for the married. Home life here must have very real charms for the bachelor is not catered for at all' (Valerie Pirie, *A Frenchman sees the English in the Fifties*, Sidgwick & Jackson, London, 1935, p. 37).

40 H. A. Shannon, 'The limited companies of 1866–1883', *Economic History Review*, vol. IV, October 1933, p. 308. For a statement in the 1850s of the need for new commercial enterprise in catering see the speech made by the architect Arthur Allom reported in *Land and Building News*, 11 October 1856, p. 708.

41 *Crosby Hall*, Frederick Gordon, London, 1870. Although Gordon stressed the innovation of having waitresses, they were quite common in earlier eating houses ('London eating-houses', op. cit., p. 173).

42 *Building News*, 7 February 1879, pp. 157–8; *Licensed Victuallers' Gazette*, 16 June 1877, pp. 377–8. The Holborn Restaurant was subsequently rebuilt 1883–5. Frederick Gordon went on to become a hotel proprietor (among his hotels were the Grand Hotel, Trafalgar Square, and the Metropole, Northumberland Avenue) and business magnate (Derek Taylor and David Bush, *The Golden Age of British Hotels*, Northwood Publications, London, 1974, chapter 7; *Financial Times*, 24 March 1904, p. 3).

43 *Opinions of the Press on Messrs Spiers and Pond's Management of the Café de Paris, Melbourne* etc., Melbourne, Australia, 1861, pp. 1–12. I have to thank the La Trobe Librarian of the State Library of Victoria for sending a copy of this booklet to me, as well as supplying other information on Spiers and Pond.

44 *Caterer and Hotel Proprietor's Gazette*, 15 October 1881, p. 188. Spiers and Pond's most noted enterprise outside the field of catering was promoting the first English cricket tour of Australia in 1861–2: they also tried to lure Charles Dickens out to give his famous readings (Bryan Morgan, *Express Journey 1864–1964*, Newman Neame, London, 1964, pp. 129–33; *Notes and Queries*, 25 May 1912, p. 404).

45 'Genii of the cave', *All the Year Round*, vol. XIX, 28 December 1867, p. 62: Agricultural Hall Company, *Report of Directors*, 1869.

46 *All the Year Round*, op. cit., pp. 62–4; *City Press*, 6 January 1866, p. 3.

47 *Builder*, 24 December 1870, p. 1023. I am extremely grateful to Anne Riches for her help in tracing the evolution of the Criterion scheme.

48 *Builder*, 25 March 1871, p. 220; *Architect*, 25 March 1871, pp. 155–6.

49 *Architect*, 24 January 1874, pp. 45–6.

50 *Building News*, 14 November 1873, pp. 530–1.

51 Thomas Verity, 'The modern restaurant', *RIBA Transactions*, 1878–9, p. 91; *Caterer and Hotel Proprietors' Gazette*, 7 December 1878, pp. 133–4; *Architect*, 16 November 1878, p. 274.

52 Verity, op. cit., pp. 85–92.

53 *Licensed Victuallers' Gazette*, 31 May 1879, p. 343.

54 *The Lady*, 27 September 1888, pp. 277–8. Another part of the Criterion, the Long Bar, had a reputation of being exclusively male (W. Macqueen-Pope, *Goodbye Piccadilly*, Michael Joseph, London, 1960, pp. 320–1).

55 T. C. Barker and Michael Robbins, *A History of London Transport*, Allen & Unwin, London, 1963, vol. 1, pp. 201–8; Peter Bailey, *Leisure and Class in Victorian England*, Routledge & Kegan Paul, London, 1978, pp. 57–9.

56 Barker and Robbins, op. cit., p. 208.

57 *Licensing World*, 20 June 1903, p. 476; *Caterer and Hotelkeepers' Gazette*, 15 March 1909, pp. 149–50.

58 *Builder*, 15 April 1871, p. 277.

59 Girouard, op. cit., pp. 171–6; E. Hepple Hall, *Coffee-Taverns, Cocoa Houses and Coffee Palaces*, S. W. Partridge, London, 1878, pp. 52–89.

60 Hall, op. cit., p. 103; *Dickens's Dictionary of London*, Macmillan, London, 1885, p. 84; H. A. Page, pseud. (Alexander Hay Japp), 'Coffee palaces', *Good Words*, 1877, pp. 678–9.

61 *City Press*, 16 April 1881, p. 6.

62 Quoted in T. S. and M. B. Simey, *Charles Booth, Social Scientist*, Oxford University Press, London, 1960, p. 65.

63 Royal Commission on Liquor Licensing Laws III, *Parliamentary Papers*, 1898 (8694), XXXVI, qq 33657–92; *Caterer and Hotel Proprietors' Gazette*, 15 October 1884, pp. 230–1; 15 October 1912, pp. 560–1.

64 D. J. Richardson, 'J. Lyons and Company Limited: Caterers and Food Manu-facturers, 1894 to 1939', in Derek Oddy and Derek Miller, eds, *The Making of Modern British Diet*, Croom Helm, London, 1976, pp. 161–72.

65 Royal Commission on Licensing 1929–31, minutes of evidence 8 January 1930, q 5, 802; Charles W. Forward, *Fifty Years of Food Reform*, Ideal Publishing Union, London, 1898, pp. 103, 106–7: I am most grateful to Julia Twigg for various references on vegetarianism.

66 Girouard, op. cit., pp. 57–73.

67 *Daily Mail*, 15 June 1909, p. 6.

68 Arthur Shadwell, *Drink, Temperance and Legislation*, Longmans, London, 1902, p. 204.

69 *Licensed Victuallers' Gazette*, 3 January 1902, p. 9; *Licensing World*, 18 March 1902, p. 163. For an example of the alarm caused by women using pub compartments see the correspondence in the *Daily Telegraph*, 24 September 1892, p. 3.

70 At some late nineteenth-century country houses meals were served at small, separate tables as in a restaurant. In such an exclusive environment the main motive for having such an arrangement cannot have been a fear of arbitrary social mixing. Rather, perhaps, house-owners were following what was thought to be a fashionable trend regardless of the reasons for its establishment in the first place (Mark Girouard, *The Victorian Country House*, Clarendon Press, Oxford, 1971, p. 50).

8.1 Interior of the Bank of England, London, early nineteenth century.
Within the classical framework of the palace is the office technology of the
period, fixed schoolroom desks, inkpots, notes on hooks, baskets. High-
status clerks work in a high-status environment. Compare this with the
Ninoflax office (Figure 8.13).
(by courtesy of the National Monuments Record)

8 Office buildings and organisational change

Francis Duffy

Buildings betray what we value. Offices in particular reveal the values of those who build them and work in them. No one who passed down the main street of Casterbridge had any doubts about which corn merchants or bankers or solicitors considered themselves of weight and prominence. It is equally easy to detect in any plan of an office interior layout which shows furniture as well as room size those managers who have been powerful enough to appropriate spatial as well as organisational influence.

What image best captures the capacity of buildings to reflect society? Buildings are like mirrors, but like grotesque distorting mirrors, since they exaggerate some features of life and diminish others. Some aspects of social relationships, such as rank, are expressed in spatial terms in an almost unambiguous fashion. Yet this is certainly not always the case. What appears to be a predictable correspondence between space and society can be contradicted, inverted or transformed into another medium. Nothing can be taken for granted. Less like mirrors than the surface of a lake, buildings reflect – but not for long, and even then distort as much as they depict. There are at least two causes of confusion. The first is that buildings can be used to say things about society which, if not lies, are statements of aspirations or propaganda rather than facts. Hitler and Speer, as they drew plans for a new Berlin, knew this.

The second cause of confusion is that buildings themselves are not a neutral medium: they have the capacity, because of the images they project and through the powerful associations which cling about them, to acquire a significance which transcends and transforms what they contain. Gibbon's[1] description of the moment 'at Rome, on the 15th of October, 1764, as I sat musing amidst the ruins of Capitol, while the barefooted friars were singing vespers in the Temple of Jupiter, that the idea of writing the decline and fall of the city first started to my mind', captures the significance invested even in ruins.

An agenda for research

Office buildings have changed our cities; office work has revolutionised our society. Manhattan or Frankfurt or the City of London are evidence of the enormous impact the office has had upon our lives. How can we explain these spectacular aggregations of expensive building materials?

Despite distinguished contributions to parts of the story, the history of the development of the office as a social system has still to be written. We have a handful of company histories[2] which give a glimpse of how companies were accommodated. There is pioneer work[3] on the development of office technology and some interesting work on the history of white-collar unions.[4] An inherent difficulty in writing the history of the office building is that for historians the distinction between the office as a building or collection of buildings and the activities of an enterprise is hard to justify.

For architects, the history of the office building has been partially studied, but largely as a by-product of an interest in certain architects' careers or technical developments such as the invention of the elevator and the steel frame which made the skyscraper possible.[5] The history of the office building as a reflection of changing office organisations and the basis on which they came to exist has hardly been attempted.

The difficulties are formidable. We have no full theoretical understanding of the way in which buildings relate to office organisations. We do not know which aspects of building form – height, width, degree of enclosure, richness, texture – related to which aspects of organisational life. Why do rich stockbrokers work three or four of them together in a shared office while partners in accountants' firms work in single rooms? Is it technology, or social structure, or simply tradition which explains such habits? Without explanation it is very hard to avoid either exaggerating or minimising the significance of a particular building for office organisations. Moreover, data are scarce and not fully worked over. It is hard, for example, to find plans which show how buildings were used since few architects have ever interested themselves in this aspect of their *own* buildings let alone of buildings in general. It is hard enough, as Banham has shown (in *The Architecture of the Well-Tempered Environment*), to explain such non-constructional aspects of office design as air-conditioning. Finally, the office as a focus for social and economic history has not yet proved attractive to historians. The groundwork for a coherent explanation of the relations between developing office organisations and changing office buildings has yet to be prepared.

All this is required: knowledge of building design as well as of organisational structure; a comparative understanding of economic, social and business development in the major industrial societies; a grasp of economics, organisation theory and sociology; a trained historical imagination.

The introduction of the study of office buildings into the social and economic history of office organisation could make important contributions to our understanding of aspects of modern society. In office buildings, unlike in factories, schools and shops, there is a close correspondence – at least on a functional level – between each worker and that small area of space which is his and his alone, his desk, chair and workplace. Like traces of some primitive form of life, the remains of workplaces and the enterprises which were the aggregates of many workplaces are still evident in the form of the buildings in which they used to labour. Workplaces were clustered together to become whole leases or buildings, while the workers combined into many various shapes and structures of organisation. The clerks are gone now. Lupin as well as Mr Pooter is dead. But the office buildings which were designed to meet their need and foster their fantasies still exist and still contain their ghosts. Despite the considerable difficulty of relating building form to social life, because of the importance of the workplace it should be traceable in a particularly pure and simple form in office buildings.

Office space is found in units of every size, from the tiny solicitor's office to great monuments of industry like the Shell Centre on London's South Bank, which contains over forty-two acres of space. It is therefore possible to make comparisons between all manner of social and organisational units and their use of space.

The study of office space focuses attention in a particularly acute way on a vast section of the economy and working population which is otherwise hazily and inadequately defined. That a special form of accommodation was set aside for these workers gives them a more effective and all-embracing definition than the technical label 'clerical' or the social tag of 'white-collar'. Because of this spatial perspective questions about modern society can be raised in a sharpened way. To explain why certain buildings came to be we need to know a lot about the people who worked in them.

The final advantage is that the physical office, although inadequately recorded and photographed, adds a vast amount of data to the study of changes in organisation. Buildings and their interiors are rich in evidence and could be to social historians what a dig is to an archaeologist, or a tribe's artefacts are to an anthropologist.

A method for this chapter

As a practising architect rather than historian, I must leave to others the preparation of a comprehensive history of how office building has reflected organisational form. However, on the basis of some reading and a little experience, three fragments of the kind of history I should like to see might be attempted. Underlying these attempts are such general questions as 'Why isn't all office space always the same?' and 'If office design does change, why does it?'

Obviously, office buildings have changed in many ways in the last one hundred years. Each generation of new enterprises seems to have had its own organisational and technological problems to solve. In more precise terms, my questions become:

1   What were the prevailing social ideas about relationships in office organis- ations and, indeed, in society at large?
2   To what extent does the form of office buildings and office interiors reveal changes in office technology and office organisation?
3   To what degree is the form of office buildings and their interior arrangements dependent upon available building construction and real estate practice?
4   What is the more powerful agent of change in office design: internal factors related to building use or external factors to do with building technology or real estate practice?

Some definitions are necessary. First, a sharp distinction is customarily made in office design between the *building*, that is the main structural and core elements designed to last for many years, and the *interior*, including internal spatial divisions, the furniture, fittings and furnishings which make an office inhabitable and which are frequently renewed. This is a relatively modern distinction and should be used with care in connection with early buildings.

Office technology covers the tasks performed in the office, the machines and equipment needed to carry them out, the flow of work and the pattern of communications between the parts. This is the system engineer's way of looking at the office. In contrast, *office organisation* is the manager's or union's view of the office as a complex of relationships between people, some powerful and others weak. What is it that holds the office organisation together when so many forces tend to pull it apart? In what ways can a manager design his organisation to improve its effectiveness? What impact does industrial democracy have upon organisational structure? These are the kind of questions which have been debated throughout the century by men like Fayol, McGregor, Jacques and Mayo.[6] Some social scientists would argue that it is necessary to consider technology and organisation together as aspects of a *socio-technical* system.

Building construction covers the materials and methods available to the build- ing industry, to build, for example, steel frames up to forty storeys high or to air-condition spaces 100 metres deep. *Real estate factors* are the conditions under which office properties are bought, leased and valued.

These four major factors seem to have been the most important influences on the design of offices. Office technology and organisation relate directly to building users and are therefore internal factors. Building technology and real estate relate to users through the medium of agents who are not directly under their control and who intervene only intermittently in their organisational lives. They are therefore external factors. The relationship between external and internal factors is critical.

Three contrasted cases

To examine the play of these factors upon the office building, three contrasted pairs of buildings have been selected. Each pair is roughly contemporary; each example reveals something of the way technology or organisation or building construction or real estate practice has had an impact upon the form of the office.

The Sun Life Insurance Company Office and Oriel Chambers, 1849–64.
The Exchange is one of the great prototypes of the office – a kind of marketplace where, instead of buying and selling goods, complex financial arrangements are set up. Lloyds' coffee shop was where insurance risks were calculated and cover negotiated. Lloyds Exchange is now a vast hall where, in benches which are not too different from those in the original coffee house, hundreds of brokers and syndicates transact their business. Round the edges of Lloyds have grown up other parts of the insurance industry which have had to find a way of accommodating themselves.

A relatively well documented example of an insurance company's office building history is that of the Sun Life Insurance Company,[7] founded in the early eighteenth century and the world's oldest insurance office. The 'technology' of a fire insurance office at this time involved various people:[8]

> besides the clerks, busily engaged in filling in policies, receiving
> premiums, and paying claims, a small staff of Collectors or, as they were
> called after 1791, Messengers, and Collectors, was needed to deliver and
> take directions for London policies, to collect the premiums on them from
> those who did not pay in person at the office, to deliver and bring in
> letters, and to affix the firemark to insured premises.

Above these members of staff were the treasurer, secretary and the managers, who exercised control over the capital structure of the company, the clerks' business activities, and other aspects of business through a series of general meetings and sub-committees.

Until the early nineteenth century, the company had always leased buildings in close proximity to the Royal Exchange. In 1849, however, it moved into new architect-designed premises. These were designed by C. R. Cockerell, whose elder brother John was one of the Sun's managers[9] and who had earlier designed two other insurance offices in London.

It is worth noting that this new building, which cost over £1,000 per workplace and a total of £55,842, including the cost of the freeholds, was built for an organisation which, by modern standards, was extremely small and, again by today's standards, growing only slowly. This can be seen from the data in Table 8.1.[10]

TABLE 8.1*

| Department | Number of staff, including head of dept | | |
	1806	1866	1880
Accountant	9	15	15
Secretaries	2	9	10
Town	4	7	8
Country	4	11	21
Duty	1	1	–
Craig's Court (branch near Charing Cross)	5	5	5
	25	48	59
Messengers	1	8	10
Total	26	56	69

* The table is only in respect of the departments existing in 1806; by 1880, the creation of the Foreign, Guarantee, Surveyor's and Classification Departments had brought the total number of head office staff to just over 80.

What kind of a building was thought appropriate by the Sun Insurance Company? It was still relatively unusual and, therefore, a sign of some prosperity for a company to build its own offices. Location and presence seem to have mattered a great deal and perhaps more than any other factor. But this was the Sun's building; its robust classical detailing hardly removed it from its palazzo prototypes, although it was thought necessary to slip in two unclassical extra floors (Figure 8.2). There seems little contradiction between the serene mercantile hierarchy of the Sun Insurance Company in which the secretary (who originally had chambers in the building), the managers, the clerks and the messengers all took their places, and a building form which took the Piano Nobile for granted. Nor is there any difficulty in fitting such an organisation of small stable groups of six to ten clerks into a plan not far removed from that of a fine house, with its sequence of great rooms, in the most fashionable parts of London such as Berkeley Square (Figure 8.3).

The organisation of the Sun Insurance Company might be seen as a small

8.2 The Sun Insurance Office, London, 1849.
The Sun built its own offices in 1849. The form that the firm found appropriate was the palazzo, although extra storeys had to be added. Despite
some pressure to maximise site value, the main thrust was to express
corporate solidity.
(from *Architectural Review*, vol. 12, October 1902, p. 137; photograph: The
British Architectural Library–RIBA, London)

household. Because of their skills, which were scarce and hard to replace, clerks had a high status in the early nineteenth century. Charles Lamb, for example, was such a clerk in East India House, retiring in 1825 on a pension of £450 a year.[11] Dickens[12] catches the atmosphere of different businesses as well as the subtle relationship between space and status:

> Between Mr Dombey and the common world, as it was accessible through the medium of the other office – to which Mr Dombey's presence in his own room may be said to have struck like damp, or cold air – there were two degrees of descent. Mr Carker in his own office was the first step; Mr Morfin, in his own office, was the second. Each of these gentlemen occupied a little chamber like a bathroom, opening from a passage outside Mr Dombey's door. Mr Carker, as Grand Vizier, inhabited the room that was nearest to the Sultan. Mr Morfin, as an officer of inferior state, inhabited the room that was nearest to the clerks.

8.3 The Sun Insurance Office, London, built 1849; mid-twentieth-century photograph.
As this photograph shows, there is little functional differentiation at this period between the home and office; a fireplace for heating, the bureau for storage – only the seating arrangement hints at office use.
(by courtesy of the National Monuments Record)

In the early nineteenth century, according to Pevsner,[13] office buildings were first built to be let. In the view of the architect, Edward I'Anson,[14] such buildings were a relative novelty in the 1850s. This I find hard to believe in the face of evidence such as the building history of the Sun Insurance Company, the commercial development in Newcastle-upon-Tyne by Dobson in the 1840s or the longstanding example of lawyers' accommodation in the Inns of Court. Most of these speculative lettable offices are hard to distinguish in external form from the purpose-built Sun Insurance Company. The Oriel Chambers in Liverpool (1864), both in plan and elevation, is sharply different.

Oriel Chambers are *chambers*; that is, the building was designed to provide small suites of accommodation for very small firms. The two- or three-man office must have been a far more typical form of accommodation than the purpose-built Sun office providing for forty or fifty people. These small offices were absolutely right for the Dickensian world of the Cheeryble Brothers or Ralph Nickleby, small entrepreneurs, financiers or professional men, each supported by one or two indispensable clerks. Such small units could easily be accommodated in domestic structures, as Grays Inn shows very clearly. What is remarkable about Oriel Chambers is that the architect, Peter Ellis, seems to have wanted neither the Georgian, domestic-cum-college solution of the Inns of Court nor the normal sub-palazzo façade with all its implications of the one proud organisation standing alone. Oriel Chambers,[15] both in plan and elevation (Figures 8.4, 8.5), is almost programmatically modular – a neat aggregation of small undifferentiated units, which is exactly what it is. This is the novelty of Oriel Chambers: not only is the plan a succession of small office suites which are highly adapted to the needs of small businesses, but the façade also carries the same message.

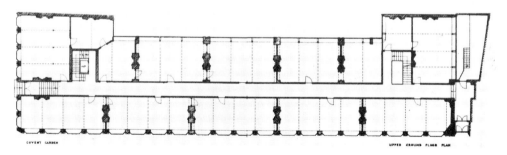

8.4 Oriel Chambers, Liverpool, 1864: floor plan.
The plan shows how this building was designed to be divided into small separate units, each with its own fireplace: ideal for small enterprises and professional men.
(from *Architectural History*, vol. 1, 1958, p. 87; photograph: The British Architectural Library–RIBA, London)

8.5 Oriel Chambers, Liverpool, 1864: elevation.
The novel feature of Oriel Chambers is that its modular planning, adapted
for the use of small organisations, is expressed straightforwardly in the
facade, without either classical dress or the metaphor of the college.
(by courtesy of *Architectural Review*, vol. 119, May 1956, p. 269; photograph: The British Architectural Library–RIBA, London)

Neither palace nor college, Oriel Chambers created a stylistic precedent for countless office buildings.

The Larkin building and the Guaranty building (1894–1904)

The most important fact about the Larkin building (Frank Lloyd Wright, Buffalo, 1904) is that it was built for a mail order house. The mail order company is typical of the new kinds of enterprise which sprang up towards the end of the nineteenth century and depended upon three essential preconditions: the economies of scale which vast coordinating purchasing could achieve, excellent communications for ordering and distribution, and, finally, a large, malleable, well organised and above all cheap workforce capable of handling quickly hundreds and thousands of minute transactions. The Larkin building is an office built by a corporation to accommodate hundreds of clerks. The scale of the operation was entirely different to what had been usual earlier in the nineteenth century: the technology was far more routinised and factory-like; the employees were low in status, and the corporate owner was more dominant.

It is no accident that the Larkin building was used to illustrate an exemplary, if anonymous, 'modern office building' in one of the many handbooks for office managers published in the United States at the beginning of the century.[16] In a sense, both the building and these handbooks are products of the same movement, the application of 'scientific management' principles developed in industry to the growing clerical workforce. Employees were seen as so many units of production who responded only to financial reward. The task of the manager was to break down any operation into its simplest constituent parts and achieve great productivity by the application of scientific methods. This is how machines were designed; so also could the office be run. In 1911, the editor of *Industrial Engineering* noticed that[17]

> in handling the successive instalments of *Motion Study*, he [the time and motion pioneer, Frank Gilbreth] became more and more impressed with the possibilities . . . [of applying] . . . some of these principles in his own office. Naturally, the first point of attack is . . . where the greatest saving can be accomplished. In our case, it happened to be the outgoing mail.

Many American handbooks[18] on office management published at the beginning of the century give detailed instructions on how to plan the office, relate adjacent departments, calculate areas and take paper flow into account:[19]

> It is occasionally necessary to trace the path of a piece of work, visualizing not only the steps but the parts of the office through which it passes. This can be accomplished by constructing an isometric . . . in the example shown a very radical rearrangement of the office was found necessary . . .

and the chart was therefore prepared to convince all concerned of the waste involved in the faulty arrangement.

Such an approach is a far cry from Charles Lamb hidden among his ledgers in East India House. The scale of the operation is much larger, the proportion of young women employees is very high, the level of clerical skill required much less, the techniques of handling information far more developed, the use of office machinery far greater. We do not know enough about these changes except that they were very rapid and were first employed in the United States.

The typewriter was developed in the USA in the early 1870s. In 1879 Remingtons sold 146 machines; in 1881, 3,300 and in 1890, 65,000. In the same year, the YWCA in New York introduced the first course in typewriting. Similar rapid growth characterised the use of the telephone. Two years after the granting of a patent to Alexander Graham Bell in 1876, the first telephone line was in operation between Boston and Cambridge, Massachusetts. By the end of the century there were one million telephones in use in the United States.[20]

The Larkin building is an original building not only because of its design but as evidence of the same rapid commercial growth. In comparison to all earlier office buildings, it is vast, probably accommodating several hundred people. Early office prototypes were based, like the Sun office, either on the palace-like model of grand, sequential spaces or on simple repetitive spaces like Oriel Chambers. The Larkin building is different. Just as it is one building externally, so internally it is one space proclaiming the unity of organisation (Figure 8.6). Slogans on the walls affirmed corporate values. Within this organisation every-one takes his place. This is apparent not only from the tight and rigid planning of the desks but by the seats themselves, which are pivoted from the desk allowing only a minimum of movement: an eloquent statement of the abdication of free-dom on the part of the clerks in the early years of 'Taylorism' (Figure 8.7). A similar example of this application of scientific ideas to the rationalisation of space and activity can be seen in the way in which filing cabinets are built into the balustrades and outer walls and become an architectural feature in their own right. The absence of small enclosed spaces possibly resulted from the

8.6 Larkin Company Administration building, Buffalo, New York, 1904.
(Opposite page)
The increased size, complexity and regimentation of organisational life is apparent in this interior. Corporate values are expressed in slogans. The workforce is highly regimented; women work here, but are sharply segre-gated from the men. To the left, the supervisor can see all. Office technology is advanced for the date of this photograph.
(photograph by courtesy of the Museum of Modern Art, New York)

8.7 Clerical desk, Larkin Administration building, Buffalo, New York, 1904.
Here, design control is in league with work study; the seat hinged to the
clerical desk restricts freedom of movement, saves space, is entirely
rational, and effectively expresses the degradation of the clerk.
(from *Prairie School Review*, vol. 7, no. 1, 1970, p. 17; photograph: The
British Architectural Library–RIBA, London)

mechanical ventilation which, at this time, could cope with high spaces in department stores and theatres but not small rooms.[21] However, it might also suggest the new importance of supervision. 'It is not easy to decide what positions or persons in an organisation are entitled to such distinction'.[22] According to early twentieth-century office manual writers, privacy was frequently overstressed. 'The modern metropolitan bank has already almost abandoned private offices and major executives are located in the open on an officers' platform.'[23]

What is not clear is whether the absence of small offices resulted from ventilation problems or organisational demands. Whatever the answer, the Larkin building evidently conformed to a widely held ideal about business:[24]

> The office, to some extent, should be an expression in physical form of the organisation of the business . . . that is, it should show the lines of authority, the separation of functions, and the direction of work through the different departments.

Far less is known about another type of office building at this time which is, at least in its external form, as spectacular as Larkin. This is the skyscraper. By the late 1880s there were many buildings in Chicago and New York which were colossal versions of the tiny speculative office building such as the Oriel Chambers of the 1860s. Instead of a built area three or four times the area of the site, the Chicago skyscrapers had achieved a ratio of 1:20 by the end of the century. This was possible because of the development of steel frame construction from the 1860s, and the elevator. At a more fundamental level these buildings were the result of a real estate market in which the key factor was that building costs were less significant than the cost of the land. The economic forces which governed the size of the Sun Life Assurance Building in the 1860s were certainly not the same as those which drove Chicago developers onwards and upwards.

In other ways the speculative Chicago office buildings of the 1880s and 1890s, unlike the Larkin building, were not innovative in office use. They were designed on exactly the same principle as Oriel Chambers, aggregations of small rooms for small firms. The critical problem for the architect was to invent forms which mastered both great bulk and the endless repetition of similar windows.

The skyscraper, obviously, was a product of real estate practice and technology. If not the result of a change in the size of organisation, it was perhaps a reflection of the growth in number of different enterprises. This was apparently seen by one of the most prominent skyscraper architects, whose career was provided by these developments, Louis Sullivan: 'an indefinite number of storeys of offices piled tier upon tier, one tier just like another tier, one office just like all the other offices – an office being similar to a cell in a honey-comb, merely a compartment, nothing more'.[25]

8.8 The Guaranty building: Buffalo, New York, 1895.
Cell upon cell: realtors found it possible to make money by maximising the
use of sites in the central business district. Architects served them by in-
venting ways of congregating many small offices into buildings that
expressed some general sense of business grandeur.
(from J. B. Burchard and A. B. Brown, *The Architectures of America*,
Gollancz, London, 1967, pp. 178–9. By courtesy of the publishers; photograph: The British Architectural Library–RIBA, London)

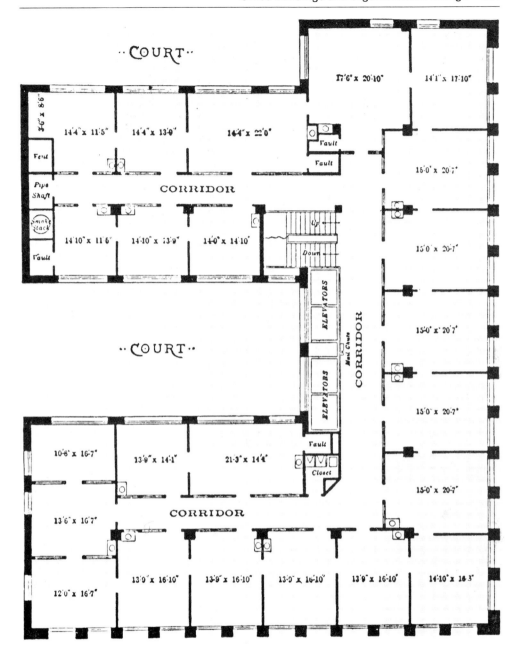

8.9 The Guaranty building, Buffalo, 1895.
What appears to be a complete block turns out in plan to have a back as
well as a front. A court is needed to light and ventilate many small rooms –
exactly the same kind of U-shaped plan as was used for hotels.
(from John D. Randall, *Buffalo and Western New York Architecture and
Human Values*, Buffalo, NY, 1976. Privately published)

These early skyscrapers were probably let to small firms, each not much larger than those at which Oriel Chambers were aimed. The difference was that the basic unit of accommodation could be multiplied endlessly. This is evident from the plans of original buildings such as the Reliance (1895), the Monadock Building (1891) and the Garrick Building (1892). Even buildings of deeper plan such as the Fischer Building (1896) could easily be subdivided into small units of office accommodation.

The Guaranty building can be allowed to sum up this great development in real estate practice. Despite its mass and apparent unity, its twelve U-shaped storeys provide a very large number of small offices on a very restricted site (Figures 8.8, 8.9). The contrast with Larkin, built nine years later in the same city, could hardly be greater.

The Seagram building, New York, and Ninoflax, Nordhorn (1954 and 1963)

The office building is a building of work, of organisation, of transparency, of economy. Bright spacious working areas, open, unpartitioned, zoned only according to the organism of the company.[26]

Despite these fine words of the 1920s, the evidence seems to point to the architect of the Seagram building being more interested in the formal possibilities of reflective glass than any real organisational requirements or actual developmental possibilities. When this architect was able eventually to build an office skyscraper – in New York in 1954 – the result is extremely refined but nevertheless entirely local, as much a product of New York or Chicago real estate practices as Sullivan's Guaranty building of 1895 (Figure 8.11). Like the Guaranty building, each floor apart from the podium is quite small; but by 1956 total air-conditioning was possible and even small rooms could be controlled quite separately from all other spaces. Because of this, internal rooms and therefore a relatively deep space are possible within a compact plan form. In this respect alone the Seagram building is different from Guaranty. However, in all other ways, and particularly in the vision of the office as one building with one entrance which is eminently capable of being sub-divided and let off in many small units, it is the same. To an architect, the relatively unimportant details of the façade allow Seagram to be distinguished from Guaranty. Inside things are not quite the same.

The experience of moving from floor to floor in the Seagram building is surreal. Within the immaculately detailed bronze frame, the very blinds of which are controlled to reduce accidental variety in external appearance, there exist as many as twenty different firms, each occupying at least one floor. Each of these tenants acting within the normal conventions of New York real estate practice has fitted out or rather decorated its own floor in its own way. One firm is a glass company and celebrates its product with elaborate display. The law practice of an eminent senator radiates wealth and solidity. Only one architectural practice reveals the building as the architect conceived it. Moving by elevator from one floor to another is to move from one wildly different corporate world to another (Figures 8.11, 8.12).

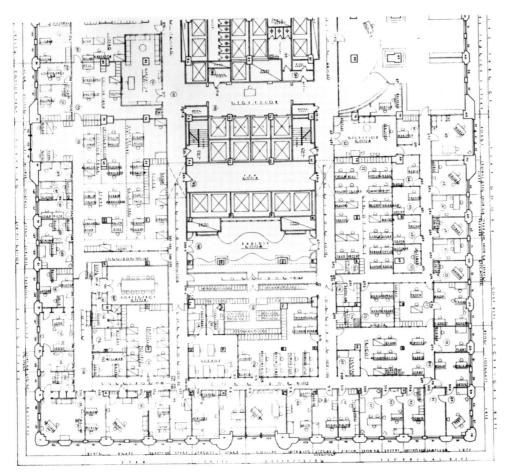

8.10 Empire State building, New York City, 1940: part plan of section from window wall to building core.

By the mid-1930s, air-conditioning made it possible to stack together not just small businesses in speculative offices in the city centre, but whole clerical factories as big as the Larkin building itself.

(from K. Ripnen, *Office Space Administration*, McGraw-Hill, New York, 1974, p. 46; photograph: The British Architectural Library–RIBA, London)

While the Seagram building was being built in the early 1950s in the United States, a far more spectacular development in office design was taking place in Germany. This was the invention of *burolandschaft* or office landscaping, an attempt to achieve an organic freedom both in organisational and building form without precedents or constraints.

The origins of office landscaping lie outside architecture. The basic ideas stem from management consultancy. These have three diverse origins. First, the basic Taylorist ideas of scientific work study with their immense impact on the Larkin building in the early years of the century; second, attempts to translate into a relaxed and status-free form of layout the 'human relations' thinking

8.11 Exterior of the Seagram building, New York City, 1953.
Despite its refinement and the addition of air-conditioning, the Seagram building is exactly the same product as the Guaranty building. Even the practice of the major space-user naming the building remains.
(by courtesy of *Bauen und Wohnen*, January 1959, p. 128; photograph: The British Architectural Library – RIBA, London)

which superseded Taylorism and which emphasised the importance of non-instrumental aspects of work, such as smiling and addressing staff by their first names; third, the cybernetic idea of the office as a kind of communication device or control system. These ideas were developed as part of the management consultancy movement of the 1950s. They were applied in particular by the Schnelles who invented the unforgettable imagery of random desk arrangement, plants, relaxation areas and light, portable furniture. Less known is that this form of layout was made possible only by an advance in building technology: the potential, for the first time in Europe, of using air-conditioning to make deep space habitable. Even more obscure is that such radical advances in building form were possible in the German real estate tradition with its emphasis on custom-built buildings.

The Ninoflax office is a typical early example of a *burolandschaft* building (Figure 8.13). It is the administration building for a textile company in Nord-

8.12 Seagram building, New York City, 1953: interior of Management Office.
The specialised environment of corporate culture. Note the alliance between business and art: as earlier the Bank of England had adopted classical motives, so Seagram's management borrows the art of Jackson Pollock. Highly specialised design services are available to create this image.
(by courtesy of *Bauen und Wohnen*, January 1959, p. 7; photograph: The British Architectural Library – RIBA, London)

horn, a small town on the Dutch border. Most activities are clerical. The offices are entirely open-plan (Figure 8.14); the building form and constructional grids are non-orthogonal, breaking the modular discipline which marks the Seagram building. Standards are uniform and high. Unlike Seagram with its different tenancies, the building is a product of organisational ideas in a particularly obvious way, and is almost a diagram of a large clerical organisation run with a certain management style. No deviation is tolerated from the corporate style. It is also the product of a real estate tradition which values the importance of custom-built offices almost to the exclusion of speculative development. This basic condition ensured that architect's ideas would be subordinate to the ideas behind *burolandschaft*. Building forms were moulded to express the intentions of the client. The final conditioning factor was the industrial climate of the time, in which staff discipline and obedience could be relied upon and senior manage-

8.13 Ninoflax offices, Nordhorn, West Germany, 1963: interior.
The final solution of the human relations philosophy: the undermining of privacy goes hand in hand with comfortable working conditions. Low-status clerks in a high-status environment.
(by courtesy of *Deutsche Bauzeit*, vol. 64, no. 9, 1964, p. 1361; photograph: The British Architectural Library–RIBA, London)

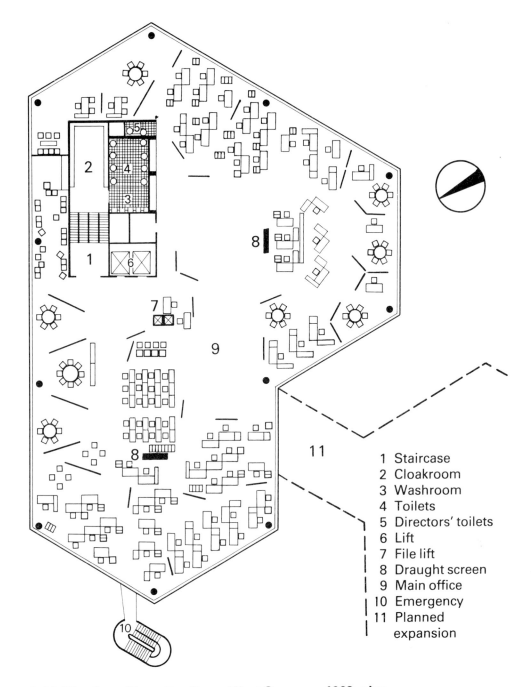

1 Staircase
2 Cloakroom
3 Washroom
4 Toilets
5 Directors' toilets
6 Lift
7 File lift
8 Draught screen
9 Main office
10 Emergency
11 Planned
   expansion

8.14 Ninoflax offices, Nordhorn, West Germany, 1963: plan.
The random low-density layout reflects an attempt to express a flexible
management style as well as the low criticality of real estate factors in
Europe.
(by courtesy of *Deutsche Bauzeit*, vol. 64, no. 9, 1964, p. 1362)

ment were able to adopt 'advanced' policies without question. Open layout as well as open management were imposed from above.

These conditions no longer prevail in northern Europe. With increasing scepticism about office landscaping, tougher attitudes to real estate practice and, above all, a new attitude among employees who are far more anxious to negotiate about the physical working environment, Ninoflax and hundreds of other similar buildings have become obsolescent within ten years.

Conclusion

To compare three pairs of buildings is not enough. Other examples could have been used to make different points and to mark different stages in the history of office buildings.

Offices are not the same. Measured by practically any scale, Oriel Chambers and Ninoflax, Guaranty and Seagram, Sun Life and Larkin vary enormously – in size, in site coverage, in relative emphasis on exterior and interior, in subdivision, in lettability, in relation to the outside world. Why do they vary?

Office organisation and office technology – the internal factors – have clearly played their part. Without the spectacular growth and change in office size and organisation since the beginning of the nineteenth century, the huge office complexes of today would be inexplicable. Even today, the increasing impact of participation, or, more fundamentally, the shift of power from management to staff, is making office landscaping an untenable concept in northern Europe. A form of planning of which the openness and completeness reflect powerful centralised management thinking cannot be reconciled with the new ability of staff to negotiate about the physical conditions they would like to appropriate for themselves such as partitions, access to windows, and privacy. Centraal Beheer, an open plan office for an insurance company in Holland, and famous for the intervention of staff in design – painting their own walls, bringing in posters and even pets – marked the end of the period when total management control was possible.[27] Current anti-office landscaping and highly cellular projects in Scandinavia are the direct consequence of new participative labour laws.

The most interesting crux in this history is the conflict between these internal organisational factors and external real estate forces. Unlike North American projects, European buildings have generally tended to reflect architectural or stylistic trends and, in more recent times, managerial fashions rather quickly and accurately. This is because of the relative weakness of the external forces. From Mies van der Rohe's glass skyscraper to the Pirelli building and Centre Point we can observe European buildings which are an imitation of American practice without the tough grip of real estate rules which pervades American offices. In Ninoflax and other open-plan buildings we see the direct impact of managerial fashion on building forms.

In the United States, despite the enormous fertility in organisational ideas, external real estate factors have tended to be dominant. Buildings have been seen as negotiable commodities first and objects of use secondarily. This is obvious in the impact of land values on building bulk in Chicago and New York and later in the strong emphasis on modular construction which is designed to make subdivision and sub-letting easy. These disciplines, which are practically universal in the United States, are even now relatively little understood in Europe.

Why external constraints were weak in one context and at one time, and strong in another can be explained only in terms of fundamental economic forces. Explanations of why, within these constraints, certain building forms were possible and preferred must be undertaken through an understanding of the structure and organisation of business society. When both levels of explanation, external and internal, are exhausted, we can then begin to ask questions about the particular design contribution of Ellis, Sullivan, Wright, Mies van der Rohe. How much freedom these architects enjoyed within the economic and social circumstances of their time is open to question. In many ways they had little freedom and their design energy was expended on relatively trivial details. The buildings discussed here tell us far more about the societies which built them than about their architects.

Notes and references

1 Edward Gibbon, *Autobiography*, Oxford University Press, 1950, p. 160.
2 Such as P. G. M. Dickson, *The Sun Insurance Office, 1710–1960*, Oxford University Press, 1960.
3 H. A. Rhee, *Office Automation in Social Perspective*, Oxford, Basil Blackwell, 1968.
4 David Lockwood, *The Black Coated Worker*, London, Unwin University Books, 1969.
5 This is still so in Nikolaus Pevsner's very useful section in *A History of Building Types*, London, Thames & Hudson, 1976.
6 A useful review of modern organisation theory is A. S. Tannenbaum, *Social Psychology of the Work Organisation*, Belmont, California, Wadsworth, 1966.
7 Dickson, op. cit.
8 Ibid., p. 123.
9 Ibid., p. 114.
10 Ibid., p. 123.
11 Letter to Wordsworth, 6 April 1825: George Woodcock, ed., *The Letters of Charles Lamb*, London, The Grey Walls Press, 1950.
12 Charles Dickens, *Dombey and Son*, London, Chapman & Hall, 1848, vol. 1, p. 207.
13 Pevsner, op. cit., p. 214.
14 Quoted by Pevsner: Edward I'Anson, 'Some notice of office buildings in the City of London', *Transactions of the RIBA, 1864–85*, pp. 31–6.
15 Well illustrated in *Architectural History*, vol. 1, 1958.

16 L. Galloway, *Office Management: Its Principles and Practice*, New York, The Ronald Press, 1918.
17 From the introduction by R. Thurston Kent to F. B. Gilbreth, *Motion Study*, New York, Van Nostrand, 1911, p. xii.
18 E.g., L. P. Alford, *Management's Handbook*, New York, The Ronald Press, 1924; W. H. Leffingwell, *Office Management: Principles and Practice*, Chicago, A. W. Shaw, 1925; T. W. Schulze, *The American Office: Its Organization, Management and Records*, New York, The Ronald Press, 1914. T. W. Schulze, *Office Administration*, New York, McGraw-Hill, 1919.
19 Leffingwell, op. cit., p. 148.
20 Data from Rhee, op. cit.
21 See Reyner Banham, *The Architectures of the Well Tempered Environment*, London, Architectural Press, 1969, pp. 86–92.
22 Leffingwell, op. cit., p. 292.
23 Ibid., p. 293.
24 Schulze, *Office Administration*, p. 148.
25 Louis H. Sullivan, 'The tall office building artistically considered', from *Kindergarten Chats*, New York, Wittenborn Schulz, 1947; originally published 1896.
26 Mies van der Rohe.
27 Reviewed by F. Duffy, *Architects' Journal*, 29 October 1975.

Part IV

9 Vernacular architecture and the cultural determinants of form

Amos Rapoport

Introduction

It might validly be asked why the primitive and vernacular design, and hence the origins of the built environment, should be studied. One important answer is that the ability to make correct analyses and decisions depends on having valid theory. To be valid, however, theories and concepts must be based on the broadest possible sample, yet most of what passes for theory in planning, design and even man–environment studies (MES) is based only on the high-design tradition, ignoring folk environments, although these constitute by far the majority of all built environments. Moreover, the high-style elements – the monumental plazas, buildings and complexes – that environmental history has usually studied can be fully and properly understood only in the context of the vernacular matrix which surrounded them, and to which they were related, at the time they were created (Rapoport, 1964–5; 1969a).

At the same time, such theories also tend to be based on the evidence from the Western tradition, neglecting other cultural milieus and hence, again, ignoring most of the built environment. Finally, and this is particularly true in man–environment studies, these theories are largely based on recent research which neglects the historical dimension, particularly the remote past and the past in non-literate and non-Western traditions. This becomes particularly problematic in the light of the antiquity of built environments. Hominids, such as the Upper Pliocene *Australopithecines*, apparently built shelters: semicircular stone elements which may have been either windbreaks or bases for huts were found in Olduvai Gorge, Tanzania, going back approximately 1,800,000 years (Leakey, 1963). These sites seem to have been well established by that time and this suggests that the use of a *home-base* is a fundamental feature of human behavior in comparison with other primates (Isaac, 1972; 1978). In part, the *non-shelter function* of such construction – for example, marking place and home – is probably at least as important (if not more so) than its role as shelter. After all, even animals make places, mark locations, engage in ritual behavior, structure time – and even build (e.g. Hediger, 1955; Wynne Edwards, 1962; Von Frisch, 1974). In fact, animals seem to order the environment by abstracting and creating schemata (e.g. Von Uexküll, 1957; Peters, 1973), i.e. cognitive representations of the world as it is and, in the case of humans, as it *should* be.

It thus becomes clearer why hominids and humans who, more than other animals, need places to meet, to share food, to have private territories, should have differentiated among spaces and places from earliest times. Distinctions are first *known*; humans then *describe* them through language, and finally *make* them through building. In this sense language and environments are related: both express the cognitive process of making distinctions, reflecting the tendency of the human mind to impose an order on the world through schemata and naming. One can, therefore, look at built environments as physical expressions of schemata and cognitive domains: *environments are thought before they are built* (Rapoport, 1975a; 1976a,b). Many examples of all these processes could be given both from the remote past and the ethnographic literature (e.g. Rapoport, 1980a,b).

It is therefore imperative to consider man–environment interaction both through time and cross-culturally in order to trace regularities and patterns and also in order that any generalizations which are made might be valid. Generalizations based on limited samples are suspect. The broader our sample in space and time, the more likely we are to see regularities in apparent chaos and to understand better those differences which are really significant. We are then more likely to see patterns and relationships which are the most significant things for which to look.

The ability to establish the presence of such patterns might help us deal with the problem of constancy and change by establishing certain base lines of human behavior, some of which may be evolutionary (Hamburg, 1975; Dubos, 1966; Tiger, 1969; Tiger and Fox, 1966, 1971; Fox, 1970; Boyden, 1974). If people, as a species, have particular characteristics, if human beings have done certain things for a very long time, there may be very good reasons for it (e.g. Rapoport, 1975b; 1976b; 1977). It is, therefore, imperative to broaden the sample in the ways described above so that we can understand constancies as well as changes – particularly since our own culture stresses change to an inordinate degree. Moreover, if apparent change and variability are an expression of invariant processes this is also extremely important because the *reasons* for doing apparently different things remain the same. Thus, apparently unrelated forms and apparently different ways of doing things may be equivalent in the sense that they aim to achieve the same objectives. They may be the result of similar mental processes or may be transformations of each other.

To use a physical example, consider three urban forms: a dense city of courtyards, a low-density urban fabric of widely separated houses, and a city made up of 'urban villages' composed of highly homogeneous populations with strong social links. These appear to be very different indeed, yet all can be shown to be mechanisms for controlling unwanted interaction, that is, for reducing information overload and stress, for modulating interaction and for achieving desired levels of privacy (Rapoport, 1977, p. 339).

More generally, this kind of analysis can tell us something about the *purposes* of the environment. Built environments are more than shelter. Even in cold climates which make stringent demands for shelter and protection, one finds great variability. This ranges from minimal shelter in Tierra del Fuego, through fairly low levels of protection among some American Indian dwellings in Wisconsin and Minnesota to the highly developed shelter of the Eskimo (Rapoport, 1969a). Built environments, in fact, have various purposes: to shelter people, their activities and possessions from climate, from human and animal enemies and from supernatural powers; to create a humanized, safe space in a profane and potentially dangerous world; to establish place; to stress social identity and indicate status; and so on. Socio-cultural factors in the broadest sense are thus more important than climate, technology, materials and economics in influencing built form. In any situation it is, of course, the interplay of all these factors which best explains the form of environments. No single explanation will suffice because environments, even apparently humble dwellings, are more than material objects or structures: they are institutions, basic cultural phenomena.

It is in this context that vernacular architecture will be considered in this chapter; that is, not for itself (much as many observers find it appealing as a product), but as a process, for what it can tell us about man–environment interaction, and how an understanding of it can help develop the kind of theory needed. Therefore vernacular design will be used as a point of entry to more general problems, and, since the framework described clearly deals with one particular aspect of man–environment interaction, vernacular design will be considered here in terms of the insights it can provide about the relationship between culture and form. It will be used to analyze a particular aspect of the relation of culture and the built environment (cf. Rapoport, 1980c).

I will begin by discussing the three terms of the title.

Vernacular architecture

I have tried elsewhere to define and describe vernacular design as part of a typology which comprises primitive, vernacular and high-style (or grand-design) environments with modern architecture seen as a special case of the latter (Rapoport, 1969a). This classification neglects an important and interesting problem, namely, where does modern popular design (suburbs and roadside strips) belong? In this chapter I will continue to neglect it.

Vernacular design can be described either in terms of a *process*, of how it comes to be, or as a *product* – a resulting environment having certain characteristics. Concentrating on the process, the important point is not that it is created directly by the users, without architects, but rather, that vernacular design is achieved through the application of a system of shared rules. This is much more significant. In effect, vernacular design is best defined as being based on the use of a model with variations and differing from primitive design in the extent of the variations. The model is not questioned and is self-evident for any given group. It is accepted and adjusted to specific requirements and this makes it very specific to its context and place (Rapoport, 1969a, pp. 4–5). Since the model is shared and widely accepted, the resulting environments communicate clearly to their inhabitants; that is, they represent lexical rather than idiosyncratic symbols (Royce, 1965). Since in humans symbolic behavior generally is central, and since artifacts, including buildings and settlements, are one type of symbol which make concrete the immaterial, spaceless, timeless nature of values, meanings and the like (Sorokin, 1947), this is important in itself. But it is even more important in terms of man–environment theory. If we conceptualize environments as settings which provide cues for behavior and which need to be decoded in order to be understood (i.e. a form of non-verbal communication: Rapoport, 1977; 1978a,b; 1980c), then such environments clearly indicate which occasions they house, who should do what, when, with whom and in what context. Although I will return to this point later, the characteristics described also imply that vernacular environments are culture-specific and thus have a close link to the culture in which they occur.

Culture

Anthropologists agree about the centrality of 'culture' in defining humanity. Beyond that, however, they disagree much more, so that definitions of culture abound. In 1952 Kroeber and Kluckhohn produced a sizeable book reviewing concepts and definitions of culture, and since then many more have been proposed. A new book, including those more recent proposals, would be significantly larger.

For our purposes, however, it is enough to note that all definitions fall into one of three major categories. The first of these defines culture in terms of a way of life typical of a group; the second defines it as a system of symbols, meanings and cognitive schemata transmitted through symbolic codes; the third defines it as a set of adaptive strategies for survival, related to ecology and resources. Increasingly, these three views are seen not as being in conflict but rather as complementary. Thus, in terms of our interests, the designed environments of particular cultures are settings for the kind of people which a particular group sees as normative and for the particular life-style which is significant and typical for that group and distinguishes it from others. In creating such settings and life-styles an order is expressed, a particular set of cognitive schemata or 'templates' representing some vision of an ideal is given form – however imperfectly; finally, the life-style, the symbolic system and the environment may be part of the group's adaptive strategies within their ecological setting.

In this chapter one particular view of culture, its relationship to environment, will be stressed – what might be called a 'cognitive congruence model', suggesting that environments and life-styles both reflect certain ideals and images, that is, are both shaped by cultural 'templates' and are also approximations to the cognitive schemata held by people in a culture. In this, two of the three views of culture are emphasized: those dealing with ways of life, and with schemata and symbolic meanings. This is because these two are related: settings house particular life-styles, and both environments and life-styles, as we shall see, result from choices among alternatives which are based on common schemata. In general, the third major category of definitions of culture, that stressing adaptive strategies within particular ecological settings, will be ignored.

At the same time, all definitions of culture include certain common elements, a core as it were, which may be adequate for our purpose. Such a generalized definition suggests that culture is about a group of people who have a set of values and beliefs which embody ideals and which are transmitted to members of the group through enculturation (although there may be the pan-human regularities already briefly mentioned). These beliefs lead to a world view – the characteristic way of looking at the world and, in the case of design, of *shaping* the world. These ideals also create a system of rules and habits which lead to systematic and consistent choices. These rules, therefore, both reflect an ideal and create life-styles and built environments. After all, these latter are generally the result of individual decisions and acts of many people which none the less add up to a recognizable whole. If the ordering systems or 'codes' are known it is possible easily to identify cities as Indian or Italian, landscapes as Australian or Mexican. Habits, manners, food, roles and behavior also result from such sets of rules. Given adequate knowledge, all these elements show, or should show, regularities resulting from the common underlying schemata and the fact that they form a system. If understood, they should be mutually illuminating since both environments and behavior are not random but ordered.

Such sets of rules apply, for example, to the use of urban space, so that we find two clear traditions, one where urban space is used for many activities and another where such activities are prohibited. In other words, different groups will decide, on the basis of such rules, which behavior is appropriate in what setting, thus relating environments and behavior – whether these be streets, front or back regions, dwellings, or other settings (Rapoport, 1969a; 1977). Culture can then be seen as a habitual set of choices which reflect an ideal human being, an ideal life and, hence, an ideal environment. In this way these choices are also a way of mediating between human beings and the natural environment, of dealing with the fundamental human activity of contrasting culture and nature.

Culture and vernacular design

I have argued in more detail elsewhere (e.g. Rapoport, 1976b; 1977) that any artifact can be seen as the result of a series of choices among various alternatives. The design process, that is the shaping of any kind of environment, can also be seen as a series of choices made from a set of alternatives. *How* these choices are made, what is included or excluded, and how various elements are ranked in terms of high or low value leads to the specific environment. The purpose of the successive applications of various criteria is to approximate, as far as possible, the schemata and ideal images of the culture. This helps to explain the fact that environments which result from many individual decisions nevertheless add up to recognizable wholes, and also serve as appropriate settings for behaviour.

In primitive and vernacular situations there are fewer initial choices than there are today (where, one might argue, there is almost an excess of choice). The choices available depend partly on ecological and partly on cultural constraints so that most possible alternatives are just not considered. For example (using the ethnographic present), Pueblo Indians 'know' before they begin that the outcome will be a communal dwelling – the shape follows; Navaho, on the other hand, 'know' that they will live in clusters of individual, widely spaced dwellings (*hogans*): the materials, shapes and number in the cluster follow. We also often eliminate alternatives without considering them (Rapoport, 1969b; 1977). Furthermore, the outcome of such systems of consistent choices is what we call *style*. Both architectural and life-styles result from consistent inclusions and exclusions of possible alternatives. In the case of environments it is, of course, this process which makes possible the recognition of cultural landscapes already discussed, the consistency of particular historical periods of design, the specificity of vernacular architecture, architecture in specific locales, the recognizable style of individual architects or schools of architecture or the stylistic changes traceable in contemporary architecture which a content analysis of architectural journals quickly reveals.

Vernacular design, then, serves as a model of the design process generally which is broadly applicable once the specifics of the situation are understood. At the same time, it also reveals the specific characteristics of vernacular design, its consistency of choices and thus its close link to the culture. In such design we find settings for particular life-styles which, because of this close agreement, communicate clearly the expected behavior through noticeable and legible cues (Rapoport, 1977; 1978a,b). We will return to this point; at this stage it is important to stress the fact that in traditional cultures there is a close congruence between conceptual and physical space. There is thus a good fit between physical space and behavior; there is a clear communication, whereas in contemporary situations there is non-congruence and consequently unclear communication.

If we conceptualize the built environment as encoding cognitive schemata which then need to be decoded in order to produce appropriate and congruent schemata in the minds of users, then one could say that the process works extremely well, efficiently and clearly in vernacular situations and either badly or not at all in modern settings. Thus, we can obtain insights into the functioning of the built environment as a system of non-verbal communication, with cues which need to be noticed, and understood (and which one then needs to be prepared to obey) by analyzing primitive and vernacular environments.

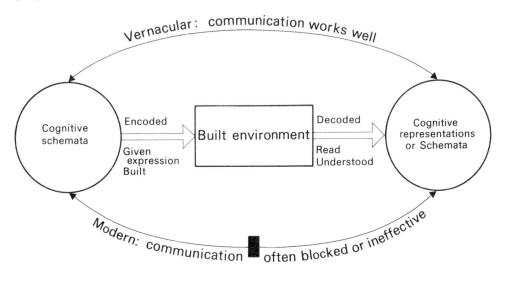

9.1 (based on a drawing in Rapoport, 1977, p. 109)

One way of looking at man–environment interaction through time and cross-culturally, therefore, is in terms of the degree of congruence or non-congruence (since the two extremes of complete congruence or non-congruence are equally unlikely) between physical and human systems. It can be suggested that one way of distinguishing vernacular and primitive from other types of design is precisely in terms of the *higher degree of such congruence*. This has clear implications, once again, for why these forms of design should be studied.

When we consider the criteria used in the choice process, vernacular and primitive design can often be distinguished by the distinct nature of the criteria used. For example, ritual considerations may be more important than economic, known technology is not necessarily used or given priority, originality and novelty are avoided and so on. But such design can also be distinguished in terms of two other types of congruence. First, in primitive and vernacular situations there is extremely high congruence in criteria used by all members of the group (recall that the model is shared and not questioned); second, as a result, the environments which result from these choices come to identify the group. One could thus rank various forms of environments, from primitive, through vernacular and traditional high-style to modern, in terms of the diminishing degree of congruence among the schemata held in common by the group. Additionally, in the case of traditional settings, one often finds that environments of the little and great traditions (Redfield, 1956) (i.e. vernacular and high-style environments), are based on similar schemata. What is different is the degree of elaboration, the complexity of the symbolism and so on (e.g. Stahl and Stahl, 1976). This implies a higher degree of congruence among the schemata underlying the various forms of environments and, once again, a much higher level of legibility and communication among them. It also implies a link between the high-style and vernacular forms in traditional environments.

This discussion of congruence suggests that vernacular environments become very good indicators of culture and thus provide the most useful point of entry for studying that relationship at the theoretical level. In this connection vernacular is more useful than primitive design (useful as that is): first, the degree of differentiation and hence similarity to our own culture is greater and the models thus more applicable; second, since vernacular is distinguished from primitive partly by its awareness of high-style design and also of other groups (Rapoport, 1969a, p. 4), it follows that models derived from it have more general applicability. On the other hand, the study of primitive situations is essential, both to trace origins and also to understand the complete gamut of possibilities.

One of the implications of our discussion of culture, and the use of concepts such as life-styles and sets of rules, is that, as it stands, a concept such as culture is too broad to relate to environmental design. It is, therefore, useful to consider how it might be reduced to more manageable elements. One proposal (Rapoport, 1973; 1976b, p. 25) is that culture typically leads to a particular world view. World views reflect ideals and lead to choices, but they are still difficult to use, particularly in relation to environments. Values are one aspect of world views and, while easier to identify and analyze, are still rather too complex, at this stage, to link directly to built environments. Values are frequently embodied in images, and these can, and have, been studied. But values result in particular life-styles, the ways in which people characteristically make choices about how to behave, what roles to play and how to allocate resources. This has been used successfully in relation to artifacts and built environments, as in the concept of *genre de vie* in French cultural geography, in environmental design research (e.g. Michelson and Reed, 1970) and in marketing and advertising. One can further argue that activities (if they include latent aspects) and activity systems may be an even more specific aspect of culture with which to begin certain types of culture–environment analysis (e.g. Rapoport, 1980c).

At this stage, however, another point needs to be made: in order to be useful, concepts such as 'environment' and 'form' also need to be analyzed. I therefore turn to a discussion of the third term of the title – form.

Form

The concept of form needs to be discussed in some detail because it is used here in a specific sense. A phrase like 'the form of the environment', like 'culture', is too broad to be useful in clarifying relationships. Therefore, the term 'environment' must be discussed before considering 'form'.

It has already been implied that all man-made environments are designed in the sense that they embody human decisions and choices and modify the world in some purposeful way. In that sense, since there are few places left on earth which have not been altered in some way, much of the earth is really designed – although the schemata, the choices made and the criteria used in these choices vary. Designed environments obviously include places where forests have been planted or cleared, rivers diverted or fields laid out in certain patterns. The placement of roads and dams, pubs and cities are all design; roadside stands and second-hand car lots are as much designed environments as glamorous office blocks and cultural centers. The work of a tribesman burning off, laying out a camp or village or building a dwelling is as much an act of design as the planner's or architect's act of dreaming up ideal cities or creating beautiful buildings. This is clearly a much broader definition of design than is common, but it is an essential one.

This seems clear enough, but when we say that these are all designed environments what do we mean by 'environment'? A number of conceptualizations have been proposed which have two things in common. First, they discuss the environment in terms of a number of components, that is they subdivide the term (much as 'culture' was subdivided above). Second, these components deal with both human and physical aspects; as implied by our discussion of the congruence of social and physical space, one cannot discuss merely the physical or built environment (e.g. Rapoport, 1977). Before I discuss the last of these, it can also be suggested that the environment can be seen as a series of relationships between things and things, things and people, and people and people. These relationships are orderly, having a pattern and a structure: the environment is no more a random assemblage of things and people any more than a culture is a random assemblage of behaviors and beliefs. Both are guided by the schemata or templates which organize both people's lives and the settings for these. These patterns and organizations thus have commonalities, which are seen most clearly in primitive and vernacular situations. In the case of environments the relationships are primarily, although not exclusively, spatial: objects and people are related through the various degrees of separation in and by space. But when environments are being designed, *four* elements are being organized: communication, time, space and meaning (Rapoport, 1977). For our purpose in discussing form, space and meaning are the most important, so we will first briefly discuss communication and time.

The specific organization of space, meaning and time reflect and influence the *organization of communication*. Who communicates with whom, under what conditions, how, when, where and in what context is an important way in which built environments and social organization are related. Both are culturally variable: the nature, intensity, rate and direction of interaction vary, as do the settings appropriate to various forms of interaction and the defenses used to control and modulate it. Thus, if people notice and understand the cues in the environment identifying particular settings, they know how to behave appropriately; the context and the situation are established (Rapoport, 1978b). Of course people also need to be prepared to act appropriately – a problem not encountered in traditional cultures but not uncommon in ours. But if the cues are not noticed, or, if noticed, are not understood, appropriate behavior becomes impossible. As already intimated, the legibility of cues and the clear communication by settings are typically found in vernacular situations. Thus, once again, vernacular provides the clearest examples of the model operating effectively.

Communication can also be controlled by the *organization of time* – people live in time and the environment is also temporal, reflecting and influencing behavior in time. The organization of time may be understood in at least two major ways. The first refers to large-scale, cognitive structuring of time such as linear flows versus cyclic time; future orientation versus past orientation (e.g. Doob, 1971; Yaker *et al.*, 1971); the future as an improvement over the past versus the future as likely to be worse (e.g. Kearney, 1972). It can be shown that these influence behavior and decisions and, through those, environments (cf. Rapoport, 1980c). Such time structuring also influences how time is valued and, hence, how finely it is subdivided into units. Thus, we advertise watches as being accurate to within seconds a year, whereas in traditional Pueblo culture a week was the smallest relevant unit (e.g. Ortiz, 1972). Such differences clearly influence the second major way in which cultural differences in the organization of time can be considered – the tempos and rhythms of human activities: the number of events per unit time and the distribution of activities in time (day and night, weekday and restday, seasonal, sacred and profane times, etc.) respectively.

Tempos and rhythms distinguish among groups and individuals who may have different temporal 'signatures' and they may also be congruent and incongruent with each other. Thus, people may be separated in time as well as, or instead of, space, and groups with different rhythms occupying the same space may never communicate. Groups with such different rhythms may also conflict as when one group regards a particular time as for sleep, and hence quiet, while another as one appropriate for noise and boisterous activity (Rapoport, 1977). Cultural conflicts and problems may often be more severe at the temporal level than at the spatial although the two interact: people live in space–time.

Design at all scales, from regions to furniture groupings, and relationships among people can be seen as the *organization of space* for different purposes and according to different rules which reflect the activities, values and purposes of the individuals and groups doing the organizing. At the same time organizations of space also reflect ideal images, representing the congruence (or, in cases where the system ceases to work, the lack of congruence) between physical space and social, conceptual and other kinds of space (Rapoport, 1970; 1977). This great variety of possible types of space, and the fact that different groups often 'see' space differently, makes any definition of space difficult. Intuitively, however, space is the three-dimensional extension of the world around us, the intervals, distances and relationships between people and people, people and objects, and objects and objects. Space organization is, then, the way in which *these* separations occur and is central in understanding, analyzing and comparing built environments. I have argued elsewhere (Rapoport, 1976b; 1977) that space organization in this connection needs to be seen at a higher level of abstraction than is customary; that one is concerned with relationships among domains, people and the like. Space organization is, therefore, independent of shape and is a more fundamental property of environments than shape, the materials which give it physical expression and other similar characteristics. In fact, space organization in this sense I regard as the essential aspect of form, although shape, materials and the like are also extremely important but are more usefully seen as an aspect of the *organization of meaning*; this can then be separated from the organization of space, both conceptually and in fact, and form can be understood in terms of the interplay of these two systems, with an increase of clarity and utility.

While space organization itself expresses meaning and has communicative properties, particularly in primitive, vernacular and other traditional situations, meaning is often expressed through signs, materials, colors, shapes, size, furnishings or landscaping. If we conceptualize spatial organization primarily as the organization of fixed feature elements (Hall, 1966), then meaning is often expressed through the organization of semi-fixed feature elements. People themselves, their dress, hair styles, proxemics, kinesics and other non-verbal behaviors, are aspects of the non-fixed elements of the environment. In contemporary situations where people generally do not directly shape their environment, these semi-fixed elements become particularly important, playing a major role in personalization and other ways of expressing individual and group identity and status. This is reinforced by the fact that behavior and the organization of non-fixed elements is frequently reflected rather quickly in changes in the semi-fixed elements, whereas fixed-feature elements remain unchanged or change very slowly. Although in traditional settings meaning systems coincided with spatial organization (which is why archaeology 'works'), the former may represent a separate, non-coinciding, symbolic system as it frequently seems to do in modern cities where eikonic and symbolic meaning systems may become semi-independent of the spatial system (Venturi, *et al.*, 1972; Choay, 1970–1; Carr, 1973).

Thus, both spatial and other systems of cues may identify settings, which then become indicators of social position, ways of establishing group or social identity and ways of indicating expected behavior. But this is only so if the cues communicate, that is, if they are comprehensible and can be decoded (Rapoport, 1977; 1978a,b). As already discussed, this process works particularly well in vernacular environments, partly because the various systems are congruent: they then reinforce one another, redundancy is high, and meanings are clearest and strongest; low congruence and redundancy, or conflicting systems, lead to environments which communicate less clearly (as do those where there is no agreement about the meaning of cues, or where the cues are not noticeable or are incomprehensible). For example, there are situations where location in urban space, say centrality, indicates location in social space and others where it does not (Stanislawski, 1950; Rapoport, 1977). There are also reversals, so that in the United States today central location often indicates low status and is seen as undesirable, whereas in Italy it still indicates very high status and is most desirable (Schnapper, 1971).

In all these cases a misreading of the code will lead to false conclusions and inappropriate behavior. Even when spatial location communicates, this is usefully reinforced by other cues: the kinds of people, shops, levels of maintenance, front/back behavior, planting, colours and many other noticeable differences (Rapoport, 1977). It may also, as in parts of Latin America, be stressed further by street layout, for example, regular in the center and irregular at the periphery; and the materials used, such as man-made at the center and natural at the periphery, with the former in each case indicating higher status (e.g. Richardson, 1974). In such situations the message is much clearer but, once again, this depends on culture-specific codes; in the last example, the code stresses the distinction between the basic conceptual domains of culture (high status) and nature (low status). High congruence among these systems is thus desirable because social communication among people is helped by the meaning of settings, by communication from the environment to people.

The purpose of organizing space and time is to organize and structure communication, for example, interaction, dominance, avoidance, and this is done partly through organizing meaning. In organizing these four variables which link life-style and environment, choices are made and alternatives eliminated, and these choices tend to lead to approximations of images or schemata as already discussed. These organizations can also be seen as physical expressions of cognitive domains (Rapoport, 1976a,b, 1977). In other words, built environments encode, give expression to and, in turn, influence social, cognitive and other environments.

In traditional, and particularly vernacular, environments the organization of these four variables was more uniform and coincided more. For example, temporal organizations were more uniform because they were based on natural diurnal or seasonal cycles, or on universally accepted ritual calendars. Temporal and spatial organizations also worked together. Among Australian aborigines, for example, darkness and the location of fires in front of each family's dwelling meant that people could not see each other at night. This was used to develop a particular system of conflict resolution through verbal means which depended on the congruence of darkness and the spatial organization of the camp. When lighting is introduced, or the spatial organization of the camp is altered, this system tends to break down with consequent increases in stress and aggression (Hamilton, 1972). Also, in traditional situations there was much greater sharing of meanings and the cues which communicated them. Most people agreed about these and, at the same time, the meaning/space congruence was strong and clear. Communication was much more predictable, being fixed and prescribed, enforced by sanctions, and related to membership in various groups; the organization of the other variables coincided and further expressed and reinforced this clarity. Such environments, therefore, communicated clearly the appropriate behavior, and people could easily respond to their reading of the environmental cues. In other words, if we consider design as the encoding of information then users easily decoded it.

While environments are not determining and do not elicit fully automatic responses (they present some choices), appropriate settings do restrict the range of responses – they make certain behavior more likely; they guide and constrain behavior. In fact, most of culture consists of habitual, routinized behavior which, in many cases, is almost automatic; the cues and rules of settings which are understood help elicit these appropriate responses (Rapoport, 1978b; 1980c). This process operates particularly effectively in traditional cultures and settings. Cultures and settings could, in fact, be ranked on the basis of how well these processes operate, and, once again, a rationale is provided for beginning with primitive and vernacular environments.

Effects of broadening the sample

This chapter began by discussing the importance of broadening the sample of environments on the basis of which generalizations are made. Environments must be examined cross-culturally and through time, and as full a range as possible should be included. Approached in this way, many topics become clearer and change their character.

The approach is basically 'anthropological' in the sense that we become aware of the ethnocentricity and specificity of the ways in which we do or look at things by comparing them with other, preferably very different, examples, which are remote in time or culture. Thus, if we compare standards – whether of heating, lighting, stair designs or storage – in various cultures, even today, we quickly learn that what appeared to be based on hard data is highly variable and influenced by culture (Rapoport and Watson, 1972). If this approach is extended to the discussion of environmental quality more generally, then the definition of slums and the viability of squatter settlements become much more open questions, and one's approach to these issues changes markedly (Rapoport, 1977). If we similarly apply this insight about the relativity of environmental quality and standards to 'improvements' to traditional dwellings and settlements, one quickly comes to realize that such 'improvements' may have disastrous consequences; they may, in fact, change environments for the worse (Rapoport, 1980c). Clearly, the outcome of such analyses is in line with our initial discussion; looking at a broader sample does seem to change the conclusions drawn about man–environment theory.

Consider privacy as an example. When one reads the architectural literature on privacy one finds that the definition of this concept is highly ethnocentric; that the major mechanism for achieving it which is considered is based almost exclusively on the use of physical devices, and that vision is the major sense considered. In fact all three of these characteristics are highly ethnocentric. The following discussion derives from a consideration of a much broader sample. As with the discussion of form, it seems clear that privacy is an aspect of the organization of communication. Considering various examples, one finds that privacy is best defined as the control of unwanted interaction with other people (which involves information flows among them). This definition also relates well to certain ethological parallels; in other words, it is of great generality. More importantly, though, for our discussion is the fact that 'unwanted' and 'interaction' are both culturally variable terms. Moreover, the mechanisms used, i.e.

how one avoids interaction, once defined, are also variable; one can suggest at least five or six major mechanisms which can be used.

The first of these mechanisms is the use of *rules*, for example manners, avoidance, social hierarchies. This method works by making behavior fully predictable so that unwanted interaction becomes 'impossible'. A striking example is provided by the Yagua Indians, on the Peru–Brazil border, where there is an absolute rule that turning away from the center of the dwelling indicates that one is 'no longer present' and even infants have this privilege (Rapoport, 1967). This has ethological parallels – e.g. among Australian bush turkeys (McBride, 1970), showing the continuity of mechanisms. Another mechanism consists of *moving away*, used by nomads (Rapoport, 1978c). In some cases *psychological means* may be used, such as internal withdrawal, trances (as in Samoa), feigning sleep (as among the Lapps), or depersonalization. Activities may be structured in *time* so that particular individuals and groups do not meet or meet under clearly defined conditions which then become fully predictable. Another mechanism is *spatial separation* and the last in our list, *physical devices*, such as walls, doors, locks, curtains and other design mechanisms, which can be conceptualized as privacy filters. The equivalence of the last two was discussed earlier in connection with the three urban fabrics and has been studied in some detail cross-culturally (King, 1976).

These mechanisms could be further discussed. Some of them are rather striking, such as the use of uncurtained windows in Holland indicating that there is nothing to hide and hence that one should not look (e.g. Bailey, 1970) and other examples might be given from China, Japan, and elsewhere (Rapoport, 1977; 1978d). In most cases, of course, multiple mechanisms are used, but various groups stress particular ones and the use of inappropriate mechanisms can lead to major stress. This is so in the case of nomads who can no longer move away (Rapoport, 1978c) or of people in a culture which relies on physical divides and spatial separation who are obliged to use temporal mechanisms (Harrington, 1965). All these mechanisms have the same purpose: to avoid unwanted interaction by controlling who interacts with whom, when, where and in what context (Rapoport, 1976b), and privacy can be of the individual or the group. Finally, in each of these cases different sense modalities are involved, not just vision, and they operate in two directions – one does not want to see or be seen, smell or be smelled, hear or be heard.

This brief summary discussion, based on a broader sample than customary, seems to lead to a much more useful view of what privacy is and how it can be achieved. It also seems to lead to a greater realization that behavior and environment cannot be separated but form a system. How well such mechanisms work also seems related to culture and the clarity of cues in the setting. Once again vernacular environments show very striking examples. In Australian aborigine camps women frequently sweep the ground around the windbreak in a 30ft diameter circle (Hamilton, 1972). This change in the character of the ground marks an important boundary – one between the public camp and the private family space. In moving from the 'outside', public space of the desert (and the various parts of the desert 'belonging' to a particular group), to the 'semi-inside', semi-public space of the camp, to the 'inside', private family space, there are no walls or barriers, but these transitions are important and there are rules of passage for negotiating them; they are not easily passed even though invisible.

In Latin America (for example, Colombia), in dwellings in squatter settlements there are clear rules about who can penetrate and how far. These boundaries are not always indicated by solid walls. Sometimes, very subtle indications such as bead curtains or a small change in floor level are used (Foster, 1971). In older farmhouses in Norway one often finds a particular beam in the ceiling which marks the point at which visitors must stop and be admitted. Up to that point, although actually in the room, they are regarded as being outside and in semi-public space rather than the private space of the dwelling itself. This 'waiting for admission' is very similar to what happens in the aboriginal camp, the bedouin tent – or, once again, among certain animals, such as baboons.

If transitions are important it must be because there are differences in domains. We have just discussed admissions rituals; socially, there are rites of passage to mark social transitions and these often have environmental equivalents. Architecture makes manifest such transitions which have social and conceptual significance; as said earlier, environments are thought before they are built. Walls, gates, doors, thresholds and the like mark transitions not only between public and private but also between domains such as inside/outside, sacred/profane, or men/women. Hence their importance. Even more important is the very fact of differentiation of various kinds. Thus, another way of looking at primitive, vernacular and other environments is in terms of the degree and extent of differentiation. If we look at the cultural origins of architecture (Rapoport, 1980a) we find increasing differentiation, from identical huts, to huts which vary in size or decoration but not use, to the development of specialized buildings which then become more clearly differentiated. Later still, we find more differentiation – from one room to many rooms for different purposes; from dwelling and work combined to separation of dwelling and work; from house and shop combined to a separation of those, then specialized work and shop settings and so on. The many building types discussed in this book themselves indicate degrees of differentiation not found in primitive and vernacular environments.

In dealing with domain differentiation, the striking fact about the examples is that apparently very simple environments may be highly divided conceptually and these divisions may be indicated either not at all physically – or only in very subtle ways. Examples of the former phenomenon will be found in the Berber house (Bourdieu, 1973), the Ainu house (Ohnuki-Tierney, 1972) and many others; we have already discussed the second. An example which shows both extremely clearly is the single-room Maya dwelling, 23ft by 20ft, which is a single room yet is conceptually divided into sacred and profane areas and men's and women's areas (Vogt, 1969). Many other such examples could be cited.

Given these findings, why is it possible to say that architecture is much more than a means of modifying the microclimate, i.e. much more than just shelter? Why should built environments have developed, why have forms become so highly elaborated and differentiated? This is the last point which needs to be discussed: what are the possible purposes of the built environment?

The purposes of the built environment

Architecture can provide settings for certain activities, remind people of what these activities are, signify power, status or privacy, express and support cosmological beliefs, communicate information, help establish individual or group identity and encode value systems. It also separates domains. While all these things can happen conceptually, and while subtle cues can often communicate, the tangible expression of all these things helps. It produces concrete metaphors for the ideals and beliefs of groups, providing concrete images, *mnemonics*, for important things. These can be important landscapes so that, although sacred places can be merely known, as among Australian aborigines (Rapoport, 1975a) they become more clearly identified when marked, e.g. when temples are built, both reinforcing the relation of deity to landscape and reminding people of this relationship (e.g. Scully, 1962). It also does this for behavior: when physical cues identify a setting, people are reminded of the context, the situation and hence of the expected, and culturally appropriate, behavior. If one of the purposes of the culture is to help people to coact efficiently, then environments help in that process (Rapoport, 1978b).

If we use the notion of behavior as drama, it follows that the proper settings and 'props' make it easier to play appropriate roles (this seems central in the work of Goffman and Barker). It is thus both useful and efficient to express settings physically, to remind people how to behave and help them behave. Consider a performance – ritual, dramatic or everyday. Clearly it can take place anywhere where there is enough room for actors and audience. However, it is useful to mark that place in some way. Australian aborigines lay out ritual grounds, prepare them, erect elements which act as 'scenery' and decorate their bodies into 'mobile architecture' (Rapoport, 1975a). The next step is to set aside a permanent place with the proper relationship of participants, reflecting notions of how performances should be and how people should behave.

Or consider shopping. At first, a market is just a spot which becomes a place when used. It may then become permanent, in a specific location and with the ground cleared. Then shades or stalls may be added, communicating 'trading' and its various latent functions. We then find bazaars, markets and shops where bargaining occurs, then department stores and supermarkets where there is no bargaining behavior. In each setting behavior is different – and the setting helps to communicate the context and thus elicit the appropriate behavior.

Thus, buildings and settlements are ways of ordering behavior by placing it into discrete and distinguishable places and settings, each with known and expected roles, behaviors and the like. The more roles, the more behaviors, the most distinct settings. This is one reason for increased differentiation, indicating and making visible differences among places and their associated behaviors. Built environments thus communicate meanings to help serve social and cultural purposes; they provide frameworks, or systems of settings, for human action and appropriate behavior. In the built environment, therefore, distinctions are crucial. They exist as cues for the understanding of other things. This helps explain why latent functions are frequently more important than manifest functions; people frequently do the same things, but they *mean* different things. Moreover, the more complex and differentiated the group the greater the help from the built environment. In a small, isolated group *knowing* settings may be enough, whereas later settings need to be marked and differentiated. Finally, even that is not enough and we find verbal and eikonic signs – meaning systems – distinct from the built environment and superimposed on it to increase the redundancy and hence the clarity of the messages.

By making visible the distinctions among places, built environments communicate information about the spatial, temporal, social and other forms of the ordering of society. Such settings communicate preferences, hierarchies and life-styles; they also communicate the nature of the domains into which the environment is organized. But as domains become more numerous, and behaviors more differentiated, so also do settings. Recall that the physical expression of differences is a useful mnemonic which reminds people about behavior, among other things. The total system of settings reminds them of the appropriate relationships among behaviors and sequences of behaviors. This also follows from the fact that people live in space–time and have complex activity systems associated with specific other activities and people. Thus, cultural differences lead to different combinations of activities, roles and situations and hence to different systems of settings for those. Of these a very important one is the house-settlement system: one cannot separate buildings and settlements (Rapoport, 1969a; 1977). It is not altogether clear what a particular setting is or does, unless one considers associated settings. After all, in the built environment (as in language) meaning is often established through contrasts and oppositions. In fact, taking such a systems view may show that, for example, defining a dwelling is far from obvious if we think of it in terms of activities and where they occur. Similarly, to return to the example of privacy, this is central to the understanding of how privacy mechanisms work. It is also part of the reason why high-style elements must be considered in their vernacular matrix.

Conclusion

Clearly all the processes discussed operate very efficiently in traditional situations with small, relatively homogeneous groups sharing values, world views, life-styles and agreeing about the meaning of cues and appropriate behaviors. For example, a !Kung Bushman woman takes only forty-five minutes to build a shelter. But frequently she will not feel like building a shelter at all and will simply put up two sticks to symbolize the entrance without actually building the shelter. This allows the family to orient themselves and know which is the men's or women's side of the fire (Marshall, 1960); this also allows others to know the relation of dwelling to camp. Clearly, this is a mnemonic which is not essential since occasionally the women may not even bother with sticks, although they are helpful. The greater redundancy of the information, the easier it becomes to achieve congruence between physical form and behavior. It also makes it easier to teach appropriate behavior to children through the environment (Rapoport, 1978a).

At the same time the environments of such groups are more responsive and communicate more clearly. Thus, in M'Buti pygmy camps, huts are changed around so that the relationship of doors, and the presence or absence of 'spite fences', expresses the relationships among people and the absence or presence of communication (Turnbull, 1961). While the group is small enough to *know* who is angry or friendly with whom, the built environment, because it is so responsive and because its meanings are so clear, becomes a most useful mnemonic.

As the nature of the group changes, these various processes work less well and the mnemonic function becomes more important. Settings can no longer be known; settings no longer elicit appropriate behavior in almost automatic ways, nor do subtle cues effectively constrain and restrict the range of responses. While much of culture still consists of habitual, routinized behavior which is often almost automatic, the number of such cultures is much greater and more varied, the range of choice in behavior repertoire greater than in traditional situations and the response is therefore *less* automatic, consistent and uniform. Given these changes, one can argue that the role of built environments becomes more important. This greater importance follows from the fact that in larger groups less is known about others and, at the same time, many traditional cues – clothing, hair styles, facial scars and the like – either disappear or lose their ability to communicate the location of people in social space, for example because they tend to be used randomly rather than systematically (Lofland, 1973; Rapoport, 1977).

Under these conditions, clearly, other cues – including environments – become more important. Since environments are less responsive, however, and because they communicate less effectively, their redundancy must be much greater; the cues less subtle.

Here is the key to the question of the purpose of the built environment and the increasing differentiation of settings. The elaboration of physical elements is necessary to achieve higher redundancy so as to communicate more effectively; the development of specialized settings, by restricting the range of behavior in any one setting, also helps settings communicate by reducing their ambiguity. Here is the central lesson of the cultural determinants of form as understood through a consideration of vernacular design.

Paradoxically, as the importance of the built environment has thus grown, its effectiveness in this process has greatly diminished; clearly, our environments fulfill these functions very much less well than primitive and vernacular ones. If we are to be able to do better we must understand those conditions and situations where it does work well.

Here also, an analysis of vernacular environments would seem to be indicated. It would thus appear that much more study of the origins of the built environment and of vernacular environments – broadening our sample in time and cross-culturally – seems critical for the development of valid man–environment theory.

References

Bailey, A. (1970), 'The little room', I and II, *New Yorker*, 8 and 15 August 1970.

Bourdieu, P. (1973), 'The Berber house,' in Mary Douglas, ed., *Rules and Meanings*, Penguin, Harmondsworth, pp. 98–110.

Boyden, S. V. (1974), 'Conceptual basis of proposed international ecological studies in large metropolitan areas,' mimeo.

Carr, S. (1973), *City Signs and Lights: a Policy Study*, MIT Press, Cambridge, Mass.

Choay, F. (1970–1), 'Remarques à propos de semiologie urbaine,' *Architecture d'Aujourd'hui*, vol. 42, no. 153, December 1970–January 1971, pp. 9–10.

Doob, L. W. (1971), *The Patterning of Time*, Yale University Press, New Haven, Conn.

Dubos, René (1966), *Man Adapting*, Yale University Press, New Haven, Conn.

Foster, D. W. (1971), 'Housing in low income barrios in Latin America: some cultural considerations,' paper presented at the 71st Annual Meeting of the American Anthropological Association, Toronto, December 1971, mimeo.

Fox, R. (1970), 'The cultural animal,' *Encounter*, vol. XXV, no. 1, pp. 31–42.

Hall, E. T. (1966), *The Hidden Dimension*, Doubleday, Garden City, NJ.

Hamburg, D. A. (1975), 'Ancient man in the twentieth century,' in V. Goodall, ed., *The Quest for Man*, Praeger, New York.

Hamilton, P. (1972), 'Aspects of interdependence between aboriginal social behaviour and spatial and physical environment,' Royal Australian Institute of Architects seminar on low cost and self-help housing in remote areas, Canberra, February.

Harrington, M. (1965), 'Resettlement and self-image,' *Human Relations*, vol. 18, no. 2, May, pp. 115–37.

Hediger, H. (1955), *Studies in the Psychology and Behavior of Animals in Zoos and Circuses*, Butterworth, London.

Isaac, Gl. (1972), 'Comparative studies of Pleistocene site locations in East Africa,' in P. J. Ucko *et al.*, eds, *Man, Settlement and Urbanism*, Duckworth, London, pp. 165–76.

Isaac, Gl. (1978), 'The food sharing behavior of protohuman hominids,' *Scientific American*, vol. 238, no. 4, April, pp. 90–108.

Kearney, M. (1972), *The Winds of Ixtepeji: World View and Society in a Zapotec Town*, Holt, Rinehart & Winston, New York.

King, A. D. (1976), *Colonial Urban Development*, Routledge & Kegan Paul, London.

Kroeber, A. L. and Kluckhohn C. (1952), *Culture: A Critical Review of Concepts and Definitions*, papers of the Peabody Museum, Harvard University, Cambridge, Mass., vol. XLVII, no. 1.

Leakey, L. B. (1963), 'Adventures in search of man,' *National Geographic*, vol. 123, January, pp. 132–52.

Lofland, L. H. (1973), *A World of Strangers*, Basic Books, New York.

Marshall, L. (1960), '!Kung bushman bands,' *Africa*, vol. 30, pp. 325–55.

McBride, G. (1970), 'Social adaptation to crowding in animals and man', in S. V. Boyden, ed., *The Impact of Civilization on the Biology of Man*, Australian National University Press, Canberra, pp. 142–6.

Michelson, W. and Reed, P. (1970), *The Theoretical Status and Operational Usage of Lifestyle in Environmental Research*, University of Toronto, Centre for Urban and Community Studies, Research Paper 36.

Ohnuki-Tierney, E. (1972), 'Spatial concepts of the Ainu of the north-west coast of southern Sakhalin,' *American Anthropologist*, vol. 73, no. 3, June, pp. 426–57.

Ortiz, A. (1972), 'Ritual drama and the Pueblo world view,' in A. Ortiz, ed., *New Perspectives on the Pueblos*, University of New Mexico Press, Albuquerque, NM.

Peters, R. (1973), 'Cognitive maps in wolves and men,' in W. Preiser, ed., *EDRA 4*, Dowden, Hutchinson & Ross, Stroudsburg, Pa., vol. 2, pp. 247–53.

Rapoport, Amos (1964–5), 'The architecture of Isphahan,' *Landscape*, vol. 14, no. 2, Winter, pp. 4–11.

Rapoport, Amos (1967), 'Yagua or the Amazon dwelling,' *Landscape*, vol. 16, no. 3, Spring, pp. 27–30.

Rapoport, Amos (1969a), *House Form and Culture*, Prentice-Hall, Englewood Cliffs, NJ.

Rapoport, Amos (1969b), 'Facts and models,' in G. Broadbent and A. Ward, eds, *Design Methods in Architecture*, Lund Humphries, London, pp. 136–46.

Rapoport, Amos (1970), 'The study of spatial quality,' *Journal of Aesthetic Education*, vol. 4, no. 4, October, pp. 81–96.

Rapoport, Amos (1973), 'Images, symbols and popular design,' *International Journal of*

Symbology, vol. 4, no. 3, November, pp. 1–12.

Rapoport, Amos (1975a), 'Australian aborigines and the definition of place,' in P. Oliver, ed., *Shelter Sign and Symbol*, Barrie & Jenkins, London, pp. 38–51 (originally, in a different form, in W. Mitchell, ed., *EDRA 3*, vol. 1, Los Angeles, 1972).

Rapoport, Amos (1975b), 'An "anthropological" approach to environmental design research,' in B. Honikman, ed., *Responding to Social Change*, Dowden, Hutchinson & Ross, Stroudsburg, Pa., pp. 145–51.

Rapoport, Amos (1976a), 'Environmental cognition in cross-cultural perspective,' in G. T. Moore and R. G. Golledge, ed., *Environmental Knowing*, Dowden, Hutchinson & Ross, Stroudsburg, Pa., pp. 220–34.

Rapoport, Amos (1976b), 'Socio-cultural aspects of man-environment studies,' in Amos Rapoport, ed., *The Mutual Interaction of People and Their Built Environments*, Mouton, The Hague, pp. 7–35.

Rapoport, Amos (1977), *Human Aspects of Urban Form*, Pergamon, Oxford.

Rapoport, Amos (1978a), 'On the environment as an enculturating medium,' in S. Weidemann and J. R. Anderson, eds, *Priorities for Environmental Design Research*, EDRA, Washington, pp. 54–8.

Rapoport, Amos (1978b), 'On the environment and the definition of the situation,' paper given at EDRA 9 conference, Tucson, Arizona (mimeo).

Rapoport, Amos (1978c), 'Nomadism as a man-environment system,' *Environment and Behavior*, vol. 10, no. 2, June, pp. 215–46.

Rapoport, Amos (1978d), 'Culture and the subjective effects of stress,' *Urban Ecology*, vol. 3, no. 2.

Rapoport, Amos (1980a), 'On the cultural origins of architecture,' in A. J. Catanese and J. S. Snyder, eds, *Introduction to Architecture*, McGraw-Hill, New York.

Rapoport, Amos (1980b), 'On the cultural origins of settlements,' in A. J. Catanese and J. S. Snyder, eds, *Introduction to Planning*, McGraw-Hill, New York.

Rapoport, Amos (1980c), 'Cross-cultural aspects of environmental design,' in I. Altman, J. Wohlwill and A. Rapoport, eds, *Culture and Environment*, Plenum, New York.

Rapoport, Amos and Watson, N. (1972), 'Cultural variability in physical standards,' in R. Gutman, ed., *People and Buildings*, Basic Books, New York, pp. 33–53 (originally in *The Transactions of the Bartlett Society* (London), vol. 6, 1967–8).

Redfield, R. (1956), *Peasant Society and Culture*, University of Chicago Press.

Richardson, M. (1974), 'The Spanish American (Colombian) settlement pattern as societal expression and as behavioral cause,' in H. J. Walker and W. G. Haag, eds, *Man and Cultural Heritage* (Geoscience and Man, vol. 5), Louisiana State University Press, Baton Rouge, pp. 35–52.

Royce, J., ed. (1965), *Psychology and the Symbol*, Random House, New York.

Schnapper, D. (1971), *L'Italie Rouge et Noire*, Gallimard, Paris.

Scully, V. (1962), *The Earth, the Temple and the Gods*, Yale University Press, New Haven, Conn.

Sorokin, P. A. (1947), *Society, Culture and Personality*, Harper, New York.

Stahl, A. and Stahl, P. H. (1976), 'Peasant house building and its relation to church building: the Rumanian case,' in Amos Rapoport, ed., *The Mutual Interaction of People and Their Built Environment*, Mouton, The Hague, pp. 243–54.

Stanislawski, D. (1950), *The Anatomy of Eleven Towns and Michoacan*, University of Texas Press, Austin.

Tiger, L. (1969), *Men in Groups*, Random House, New York.

Tiger, L. and Fox, R. (1966), 'The zoological perspective in social science,' *Man*, vol. 1.

Tiger, L. and Fox, R. (1971), *The Imperial Animal*, Delta Books, New York.

Turnbull, C. M. (1961), *The Forest People*, Reprint Society, London.

Venturi, R. *et al.* (1972), *Learning from Las Vegas*, MIT Press, Cambridge, Mass.

Vogt, E. Z. (1969), *Zinacantan: A Maya Community in the Highlands of Chiapas*, Belknap Press of Harvard University, Cambridge, Mass.

Von Frisch, K. (1974), *Animal Architecture*, Harcourt, Brace, Jovanovich, New York.

Von Uexküll, J. J. (1957), 'A stroll through the world of animals and men,' in C. H. Schiller, ed., *Instinctive Behavior*, International Universities Press, New York.

Wynne-Edwards, V. C. (1962), *Animal Dispersion in Relation to Social Behaviour*, Oliver & Boyd, Edinburgh.

Yaker, H. M. *et al.*, eds (1971), *The Future of Time*, Doubleday, Garden City, NY.

Contributors

Francis Duffy

Architect/Principal, Duffy, Lange, Giffone, Worthington, Space Planners & Architects, London. Harkness Fellow, Princeton and Berkeley, 1967–70, Leverhulme Fellow, 1977. Doctoral research on the social organisation of office space, Princeton University. Author of *Office Planning* (Dunbar, 1965); *Planning Office Space* (Architectural Press, 1976, with Cave and Worthington). Contributor to *Environment and Planning*, *EDRA Proceedings*, *Architects' Journal*, etc. Teaches occasionally at the Architectural Association and at Cambridge University.

Adrian Forty

Lecturer, Bartlett School of Architecture, University College, London. Read Modern History, University of Oxford and History of Art, Courtauld Institute, University of London. Contributed unit ('The Electric Home') to Open University course on *History of Architecture and Design, 1890–1939* (Open University, 1975); other writings in *Architectural Association Quarterly*, *Architectural Review*, and in M. Banham and B. Hillier (eds), *A Tonic to the Nation* (Thames and Hudson, 1976), and the *London Journal*.

John Hancock

Professor of Urban Planning and Environmental Studies, University of Washington, Seattle; also member of Japan Studies and American Studies Faculties. Editor, *America's Planners: A Century of Social Change and Conflict* (in preparation, 1980); author of *American Urbanisation Past and Present: Bibliography* (Doshisha University, Kyoto, Japan, 1978); *John Nolen* (Cornell University Press, Ithaca,

1976) and other writings on American planning history, the city in South Asia and related issues in development and planning.

Anthony King

Associate Senior Lecturer, Sociology and Environmental Studies, Brunel University. Author of *Colonial Urban Development* (Routledge & Kegan Paul, 1976); in preparation, *The Bungalow: A Cultural History and Sociology* (Routledge & Kegan Paul). Contributor, A. Rapoport (ed.), *The Mutual Interaction of People and Their Built Environment* (World Anthropology Series, Mouton, 1976), *Sociology, Ekistics, Architectural Review, Medical History, AAQ,* K. Ballhatchet (ed.), *The City in South Asia* (Curzon Press, 1980), G. E. Cherry (ed.), *Shaping an Urban World* (Mansell, 1980), etc.

Susan Lewandowski

Assistant Professor of History, Amherst College, Mass. Chairperson, Asian Studies Program. Author of *Migration and Ethnicity in Urban India* (1979); contributor, D. Basu and T. Metcalfe (eds), *Colonial Port Cities in Asia* (University of California Press, 1979); also to *Modern Asian Studies, Journal of Asian Studies, Charitram,* etc. Doctoral research on urban development in South Asian cities, University of Chicago.

Amos Rapoport

Professor of Architecture and Anthropology, University of Wisconsin-Milwaukee. Previously taught at University of Melbourne, at Berkeley, University College, London, and at the University of Sydney. Author of *House Form and Culture* (Prentice-Hall, 1969); *Human Aspects of Urban Form* (Pergamon, 1977); editor, *The Mutual Inter-Action of People and Their Built Environment* (World Anthropology Series, Mouton, 1976) and of *Australia as Human Setting* (Angus & Robertson, Sydney, 1972). Has written over eighty articles in the field of man – environment studies in various journals and contributed to several books.

Andrew T. Scull

Associate Professor of Sociology, University of California, San Diego. Author of *Decarceration: Community Treatment and the Deviant. A Radical View* (Prentice-Hall,

1977). Read PPE, University of Oxford. Doctoral research (Sociology, Princeton) published as *Museums of Madness: The Social Organisation of Insanity in Nineteenth-Century England* (Allen Lane and Penguin Books, 1979). Other publications in *European Journal of Sociology, Politics and Society, Social Problems, Economy and Society, Social Science and Medicine, Psychological Medicine*, etc.

Robert Thorne

Historic buildings officer, Greater London Council. Previously worked for Stanford University following study at the University of East Anglia and the University of Sussex. Author (with Alan Crawford) of *Birmingham Pubs, 1890–1939* (Centre for Urban and Regional Studies, University of Birmingham, 1974), *Liverpool Street Station* (Greater London Council, 1978), *Covent Garden Market* (Architectural Press, 1980), and contributor to *Architectural Review*.

Heather Tomlinson

Currently Tutor for Open University Arts Faculty and for National Extension College, Cambridge. Formerly Fellow, Institute of Historical Research, University of London. Doctoral research on administrative development and architectural design of prisons in nineteenth-century England, University of London. Articles in the *Bulletin of the Institute of Historical Research, Journal of Consumer Studies, Prison Commission Journal*.

Index

Page numbers printed in italics refer to illustrations.

aesthetic criteria, 6, 7
Africa, 17, 23, 216, 217
agriculture, 10, 24, 25, 203; task-oriented year, 198
Aikin, John: *Thoughts on Hospitals*, 74
alienists, 14, 44, 45, 50, 58n31
Alpern, Andrew, 162, *163*, 166
Amazonia: *molucas* house types, 4
Ambrose, P. and Colenutt, B., 25
America, 1, 5; housing choice, 19, 151, 158, 180; rival penal experiments, 96, 97; social segmentation in city life, 152–3; process of industrialization and urbanization, 157; inequality in distribution of wealth, 157; cultural stability, 167; housing tenure and debt, 157–8; social distinction between owners and renters, 158, 182–3; Stock Market crash, 166; ghettoization of the poor, 177, 179, 184; ideal of family life, 183; second home ownership, 194, 225n125; scientific management, 265; domination of real estate factor, 279; hospitals, 81, 93n54
Americans, black, 153; percentage in black suburbs, 156
animals, ordering of the environment, 284
anthropology, 3–4, 9, 204, 228, 257, 286
Apartment houses (US), 2, 10, 13, 24; social segregation function, 19, 132, 152, 172, 179; perceived lack of community and social roots, 20, 175, 181, 182; major type of multi-dwelling, 151; dictates of its forms and uses, 151–2; mandatory zoning codes, 156,

159–60; socio-economic character of 'renters', 157–8, 160, 182–3; financial aspects for developers, 159; five socio-economic types, 160–79; palatial (rich), 160, 161–4, 183; luxury (affluent), 160–8, *165*, 176, 183; owner-occupied (rich and affluent), 160, 167–8, 170–1; efficiency (middle-class), 160, 171–6, *173*, 183–4; sub-sidized (low income and poor), 160, 175–9, 183–4; rents, 162, 164, 167, 172, 173, 175, 179, 180; segmentation principles, 162ff., 180–3; cooperative ownership, 164–5, *165*, 168, 175; condominium ownership, 167–8, 183; micro-cities, 168, 170; corporation-owned, 170–1, 174, 177; population distribution, 171; siting, 172, 177; federal government designers, 173–4, 175, 176–7, 179; philanthropic enterprises, 174, 175, 177; for black middle classes, 175–9; acceptability, 178, 181; changes in social maps, 179–80, 183; transient population, 179–83; influence of children on choice, 183
Apartment houses, named blocks: Alden Park, 170–1; Black Rock, 174; Century, 166; Chatsworth, 165; Dakota, 164, *165*; El Nido, 172; French Flat, *161*, 177; the Garden, 170; Mrs Hutton, 162, *163*; Hubert Homes, 164; John Hancock, 170; Lake Meadows, 175; Lake Shore Drive, 168; Livingstone, 170; Lombardy, 170; Marina City, 168, *169*, 170; Marshall Field, 174; Michigan Garden, 175; Olympic Tower, 168;

Parkchester, 170; Paul Lawrence Dunbar, 175; Ponce de Leon, 166; Pruitt-Igo, 179; Rossmore Leisure World, 171; Stuyvesant, 160, *161*; Robt. R. Taylor, *178*; the Tuscany, 170; United Nations Plaza, 168
architects, 28; professional identity, 6, 17, 78, 81; social power, 15; specialisms, 81; of apartment house, 160, 162, 163, 164, 166; of Hindu temples, 141; of hospitals, 80, 83; of office buildings, 256; of prisons, 17, 110
architectural determinism, 17
architectural psychology, 7
architecture, 2; and social factors, 4, 6, 27; history, 6; narrow criteria in evaluation, 6, 7; purpose-built, 14, 96–7, 99; and classification, 46; differentiation in cultural origins, 298
architecture, institutional, *see under* hospitals; prisons
architecture, vernacular, role of shared cultural rules, 27, 286; amalgam of behaviour and environment, 27; groups involved in its creation, 28; majority of built environments, 283; and man–environment interaction, 285; in context of design, 285, 288–91; and relationship between culture and form, 285; classification, 285–6; a process or a product, 286; relationship to culture, 288–91; distinguished from primitive, 289–90
aristocracy: and Palladian villa, 15, 72; and voluntary hospitals, 67, 72; summer villas, 194, 202; and seaside resorts, 196–7; ornamental cottages, 201, 202,

aristocracy – *contd.*
  222n54; of wealth, 202; model
  for social emulation, 203, 210;
  country house meals, 253n70
Armstrong, R. B., 25
asylums, *see* lunatic asylums
Australia: aborigine society, 27,
  295, 297–8, 299, 301; second
  home ownership, 194; Spiers
  and Pond, 240; first English
  cricket tour, 252n44

bachelor apartments, USA, 172
bachelor houses, Trobriand
  Islands, 4
Bailey, A., 297
Baker, Herbert, 3
Banham, Reyner, 21, 256
bankers, as accreditors of citizen-
  ship, 158
banks, 5, 12, 269; Bank of
  England, *254*
Barnardo, Dr: Coffee Palace, 244
behaviour: deviant/insane identification, 14; new patterns
  resulting from socio-economic
  and cultural changes, 23;
  institutionalization, 23;
  influence of ideologies and
  beliefs, 193; social beliefs and
  the built environment, 196,
  295; table manners, 233; in
  public places, 235; men/
  women double standards, 235,
  236; and problem of constancy
  and change, 284; 'drama'
  concept, 299
beliefs, religious/social/cultural,
  1, 3, 9, 10, 16, 28, 30, 69, 104,
  112, 130, 139, 144, 152, 193,
  196, 287; *see also* religion;
  values
Bell, Luther: the asylum as
  instrument of treatment, 45
Bellers, John, 41; economic cost
  of ill health, 66; and hospitals,
  66, 67
Bennett, Edward (city architect-
  planner), 181
Bentham, Jeremy, 40, 140;
  utilitarianism, 95; panopticon,
  112; and prison reform, 113
Bergson, Henri, 198
Bierstedt, R. *et al.*, *Modern Social
  Science*, 9
Blackburn, William: and prison
  reform, 95
Booth, Charles, 245
Bourdieu, P., 299
Bowly, Devereux, Jr: Chicago
  public housing, 179
Briggs, Asa, 6
Britain: prisons, 2; occupations of
  workers in primary, secondary
  and tertiary sectors, 25; second
  home ownership, 194; pioneer
  in urbanization and industrialization, 229

British Medical Association,
  80–1
Buddhism, 228
Buildings: as socio-cultural
  products, 1; factors governing
  their appearance, 1; functions,
  1, 6; symbolic meaning, 3;
  reflect distribution of power, 4;
  socio-religious influences, 4;
  response of occupants, 6;
  discrete units in built environment, 6; history of, 6; emphasis
  on materials and technology, 6;
  effect of socio-economic
  changes, 6–7, 14; extensive
  terminology, 21–3; cultural
  influences, 27; institutional
  approach to their study, 29;
  stages in their creation, 30;
  social importance of new types,
  30; purpose-built, 13, 14, 21,
  25, 29, 39, 45–8, 57, 69, 194,
  205, 236; therapeutic function,
  74; sound-proofing, 99–100;
  expressions of values, 255;
  capacity to reflect society, 255,
  257; ways of ordering
  behaviour, 300; services,
  16–17, 100–11
built environment: as socio-
  cultural product, 1; relationship with society, 1, 8, 21, 193;
  historical development, 2, 9;
  inclusions in concept, 2; socio-
  cultural, psychological aspects,
  4, 5; economic and political
  influences, 5; codes and
  systems ordering, 27; and
  behaviour, 27, 300; expressions
  of cultural rules, 27, 287;
  influence on social and
  cognitive environments, 27;
  elements involved in their
  design, 27–8; communicate
  meaning, 28, 300–1; relation to
  social organization, 28, 193;
  results of cultural trans-
  ferences, 29; relationship to
  environment,   287–8; non-
  shelter functions, 283;
  socio-cultural purposes, 285;
  encode cognitive and social
  schemata, 289, 295; purposes
  of, 299–301; communicate
  spatial, temporal and social
  information, 300; need for
  differentiation, 300; *see also*
  architecture; environment
built form, building form: and
  social forms, 1, 3, 20; and
  socio-cultural variables, 4, 8; a
  province of urban geography,
  5; social factors effecting
  change, 11, 12; socio-historical
  study, 12; identification of
  'firsts', 13, 21; traditional, 13;
  and commensality groupings,
  22; socio-economic criteria, 22;

and units of time, 22; industrial
  and pre-industrial, 28;
  expressions of ideological
  conflicts, 31; embodiment of
  social ideas, 94; functional
  differentiation under industrial
  capitalism, 198
bureaucracy, 15, 25, 62
burolandschaft, 274
business organizations, 23, 25;
  scientific management, 26; and
  central city sites, 200

California, Southern: megalo-
  polis, 156
capital, 24; accumulation of, 217,
  218; surplus, 20, 29
capitalism, industrial: and
  segregative approach to
  insanity, 14, 39; creation of
  surpluses, 20–1, 196–7;
  development in England, 39–
  40; development of city under,
  5, 25; dependence on labour
  force, 41; and work ethic, 67;
  characterized by differentiation
  and specialization, 196, 197;
  inequitable division of 'free
  time', 199; penetration of international capitalism, 217;
  socio-economic transformations, 14, 200; transformations of cultures under, 29
Carr, S., 294
caste system, *see* India
Castells, M., 5
cemeteries, 10, 30
central business district, 25, 153,
  200
charity, 62, 67; asylums, 42,
  57n24; St Luke's Hospital,
  57n24
China: care of the sick, 62;
  continuous civilization, 124;
  summer villas, 194
Chingleput district, Uttiramerur
  temple centre, 139;
  Mahabalipuram school of
  architecture, 141
Christianity: socio-economic
  factors and commensality, 22,
  228; and care of the sick, 63;
  education in prisons, 107;
  overarching ecclesiastical
  structure, 126; absence of
  dietary rules, 228
churches, 5, 10; asylum chapels,
  53; associated prisons, 112
cities: colonial, 153; social
  structure in, 30; reflect
  distribution of power, 4; socio-
  economic, political systems,
  4–5; changing spatial
  organization, 22, 24;
  cosmopolitanism, 23;
  commercial refreshment
  houses, 23; aggregates of built
  form, 24; central business

districts, 25, 200; land and property speculation, 25; unassociated with growth of asylums, 39; and problem of migrants, 68

cities (US): absence of cultural variables, 5; effects of industrialization and population increase, 153; politically independent suburbs, 153; imbalance in managers/workers areas, 153; residential segmentation, 164–6, 179; inner city slum housing, 156; location and social status, 294; Atlanta, 166; Baltimore, 170; Boston, ecology of its West End, 154–5, Hotel Pelam, 160, apartment houses, 161, 170; Chicago, 159, 'Gold Coast', 153–5, 161, 183, tenement ghettoes, 154, 178, 179, French Flats, 161, apartment houses, 168, 170, 172, 173, 175, skyscrapers, 269; Cleveland, Euclid village, 159–60, 177; Houston, 155, 158; Los Angeles, 156, 177; Manhattan, 159, 161, 165; New York, apartment houses, 162–6, 168, 170, 171, 173, 175, 207, skyscrapers, 269; Philadelphia, 158, 170; Phoenix, 159; Pittsburgh, 177; San Diego, 156; Seattle, demography, 156, zoning history, 160, apartment houses, 166–8, 172, 173, 183, centre ghettoization, 168, 177; Capitol Hill, 183; St Louis, 179; Washington, DC, 171, predominantly poor black population, 171

class, see social class

classification: of eating places, 23, 231; of hospitals, 16; of insane, 14, 45, of prisoners; see also social class; terminology

Clive, Lord: temple donations, 136

Clout, H. C., 195

Cockerell, C. R., 260

Codes, 27, 287, 292–6

Coimbatore Hill complex: and Hindu temple sponsorship, 142

colonialism: and effects on built form, 3, 136; effect on Indian community, 4; categorization of the sick, 16; English club, 29; US city compared to planned cities under, 153

commensality: and caste system, 22; social groupings, 22, 23; built form, 22–3

commercialization, 25; and segregative approach to madness, 14, 39; of amusement and leisure, 204; of catering, 239

communication: element in space organization, 25, 27–8, 292; prevention in prison buildings, 99–100, 104, 117n22; control by organization of time, 292; through temporal and spatial organization, 295

community, the: changes in moral boundaries, 14; control of deviance, 38, 49; treatment of derelicts and troublesome, 50; health centres, 11, 13; 'lack of', 20, 181

comparative studies, 4, 8, 9, 28

Condit, Carl: residential segmentation, 153–4; apartment housing, 172, 178; Chicago 1910–29

Cooney, E. W., 19

Coppock, J. T., 193, 218n4

council estates, 15

country/city cultural distinction, 202, 203

Crawford, William, 97, 98, 99, 102, 113, 116n9

crematoria, 30

criminal, the: treatment in prison, 14; use of classification, 58n36, 95; increase in capital offences, 94; transportation, 94–5; utilitarian remedy, 95; low educational attainment, 107; detention of dangerous offenders, 115

criminal law, 94, 95

cross-cultural research, 4

cultural geography, 3

cultural imperialism, 29

cultural nationalism, 220n13

culture, 1, 3, 4, 5, 6, 8, 11, 22, 28; relationship to form, 3, 27, 29, 146–7, 151, 285; and socialization, 10, 11, 24; complementary categories, 286–7; as a way of life (life-style), 286, 287, 290; a system of symbols and meanings, 286, 287; a set of adaptive strategies for survival, 286; centrality in defining humanity, 286; relationship to environment, 287; creation of rules and habits through ideals, 287, 288; and vernacular design, 288–91; habitual and ritualized behaviour, 295; influence on comparison of standards, 296

Dance, George, 57n24

Daniels, P. W., 25

Davidoff, L., 24

decision-making: socio-cultural assumptions, 31

Delgado, A., 25

Delhi, Old and New, 2, 3, 4

Denmark, second home ownership in, 194

Denyer, S., 4

design, 12, 117; socio-religious influences, 4; identification of 'firsts', 13; comprehensive conceptualization, 27, 283; elements involved in creating environments, 27–8; definition, 291; and organization of space, 293; encoding of information, 295; see also architecture, vernacular

deviance, social control of, 13, 38; categories, 14, 41; treatment of the insane, 38, 41; institutional/segregative approach, 39, 41–2

dietary and ideological factors, 23; vegetarianism, temperance, 229, 244, 245

disease: 'miasmic' theory of infection, 15, 79, 84, 100; germ theory, 82, use of antisepsis and ascepsis, 82; quarantine regulations, 66

distribution of income, resources, 12, 157, 167–8, 173, 206, 210

doctors, 28; growth of social position and power, 15, 62, 72–3, 77; influence on hospital building and design, 15, 62, 73, 74, 75–8, 81; failure to cure madness, 48, 49–50; and hospital management, 62; and eighteenth-century hospitals, 67, 72–3, 75; criteria of success, 73; struggle for professional status, 73; hospital appointments, 73; private practices, 73–4, 75; relationship with patients, 74, 76, 77–8; teaching methods, 76; governors and consultant relationship, 77; and pavilion plan, 80, 83–4; interest in clinical research, 84; hierarchical division between consultants and practitioners, 84, 85, 93n53

domiciliary care for the sick, 62, 69

Doob, L., 292

Douglas, Mary: Rules and Meanings, 27

Dubos, R., 284

Duffy, Frank: and purpose-built environments, 21, 26–7

Duly, F., 4

Dumont, L., 22

Durkheim, Émile: The Division of Labour, 197

dwellings, dwelling form, 4; and culture as a way of life, 4; and institutions, 9, 13; distinction by culturally significant criteria, 22; conceptual division of single room, 299; see also house; housing

Dyos, H. J., 6

East India Company: temple endowments, 136–7

eating and drinking: socio-cultural considerations, 22, 228, 233; social groupings for, 23; eating away from home, 22, 229, 244; public facilities, 22, 24, 229, 231–6, 240–3; expressions of values and relationships, 228; socio-economic determinants, 228; and separation of home and workplace, 229, 244; results of industrial change and urbanization, 229, 244; evolution of public catering, 230–43; coffee houses and taverns, 231, 232, 233–5, *234*; street salesmen, 232; gentlemen's clubs, 232, 233; ritualized meals at home, 233, 251n18; compartmentalized layout, *234*, 235

economics, the economy, 9, 10; new social needs, 11, 12; changes in building form, 18, 20; structural change to post-industrial society, 24–5; dominance of tertiary sector (finance), 25; and wage earners, 40; and second homes, 194; surplus, 19, 20, 24, 29, 196, 197, 217–18, invested in temples, 142, 147; *see also* capitalism; industrialization; labour; mercantilism; political economy

Eden, Sir William: and criminal law reform, 95

education, 5, 9, 107; transference from church to state, 29

Ellis, Peter, 263, 279

energy, 3, 12, 152

environment(s): influence on inhabitants, 4; man–environment studies (MES), 7, 283, 284, 289–90; new social needs causing changes in, 11; need for system of rules, 16; man-made, 20, 29, 291; purpose-built, 21, 27, 30; 'thought' before it is 'built', 30; distinction between rural-agricultural and urban-industrial, 199; basic cultural phenomena, 285; settings providing cues for behaviour, 286; form of non-verbal behaviour, 286, 287–8; relationship to culture, 287; superiority of vernacular over primitive, 290; a series of patterned interrelationships, 291–2; variation in conceptualization, 291; effects of broadening the sample as basis of organization, 296–9; *see also* architecture; buildings; built environment; built form

ethnicity, nationality: and commensality, 23

Europe: separate prison system, 17; army hospitals, 66; 'second homes' for the wealthy, 193–4

Evans, R.: penal architecture, 16, 17, 57n27

factories, 5, 10; effect of discipline and units of time, 200

Fairweather, L.: 'The evolution of the prison', 116

family, the, 29; common social institution, 9; related associations and building forms, 10, 13; control of deviance, 38, 49; and health care, 66; *see also* kinship

finance capital, increasing dominance, 25

Fitzgerald, M. and Sim, J., 16, 17

form: concept of, 27, 291–6; as organization of meaning, 293

Forty, Adrian, 7, 15, 20, 29

Foster, D. W., 298

Foucault, M., 6, 16, 91, 92

France: *maison de campagne*, 193, 194; 'le weekend', 205; the café, 232; Paris restaurants, 236, 239; *see also* hospitals, French

funeral homes, American, 29

Gans, Herbert: ecology of segmentation (Boston), 154–5

gender, sex, as criteria of classification and stratification, 16, 20, 23, 160, 216; *see also* men; women

geography, geographers, 3, 4, 5, 6, 21, 195, 204

Gerth, H. and Mills, C. W., 25

Gibbon, Edward, 255

Giddens, A., 221n21

Girouard, M., 6, 23

Goffman, E.: and a 'learning situation', 46, 299

Gordon, Frederick (hotel entrepreneur), 239–40, 252nn41, 42

government, institution, 10, 15; *see also* state

Hall, E. T., 293

Hambury, D. A., 284

Hamilton, P., 295, 298

Hancock, John: study of US apartment house, 19, 27, 30

Harloe, M., 5

Harrington, M., 297

Harvey, D., 5, 220n20

Hediger, H., 284

Henriques, U. R. Q., 95

Hinduism: cosmological ideas, 15, 124–5, 130–1, 132; religious continuity, 18, 19; relationship to temple complex, 18, 19, 124; cultural diversity, 123–4; sacred and secular cohesion, 124; revivalism, 124, 146; devotional path of salvation,

124, 126, 146; a way of life, 124, 137, 146; socio-economic hierarchy, 125, 134; theistic development, 125, 126; performance of *puja*, 125, 126, 127, 144, 145, 146; British impositions, 136; sacred numbers, 138; belief system, 139, 141, 143–4; new movements and saints, 145–6; dietary rules and customs, 228; gods and goddesses, 137, 139, 140, 142, 143, 150n50; Brahmanic priesthood, 126, 127, 131, 132, 133, 142, 148n17

Hindu temples, *see* temples, Hindu

historical research, 4, 204, 228, 229, 256; and built environment, 6, 28; limited in application to 'great architects' and 'housing', 7; need for interdisciplinary approach to socio-cultural relations, 8, 28

Hobsbawm, E. J.: and capitalist economy, 20, 21, 24, 196

holidays, 198, 199, 200, 205

Holland: Central Beheer open plan office, 278

hospitals, 5, 10; social functions, 13, 15, 62, 68–9, 70; treatment of the sick, 14, 62, 67–9; rapid growth in buildings, 15, 61–2, 63, 65; motivation of founders, 15, 29, 61, 63, 65–9, 72, 78; role of social class, 15, 16, 70, 84, 85; secularization, 29, 63; and mental illness, 37; lack of scientific expertise, 61–2; management structure, 62, 65, 67, 72–3, 75; alleged causes of death, 62–3, 90n5; closures at Reformation, 63; run by private individuals (voluntary), 63, 65, 66; out-patients and home visiting, 66–7, 75, 76–7, 85; and sick poor, 67–9; administration of sick relief, 68–9; areas of moral reform, 69, 72; interior spatial organization, 69–70, 84–5, 88, 93n65; staff hierarchy, 70; and medical profession, 73–4, 75; segregation of patients, 65, 75–6, 76; medical schools, 77; means to professional advancement, 78, 79, 85, 88; paying patients, 85, 88; influence on powerful consultants, 85; remain medical territories, 88

hospitals, American: Johns Hopkins, Baltimore, 81, 93n54

hospitals, architecture of, 74: Palladian style, 15, 69–72, *71*; pavilion plan, 15, 61, 66, 81–2, *83*, 92n45; mansion style, 61, *83*; office block, 61, 84, *89*; ward

layout, 63–5, *65*, 70, *71*, 74, 75, *76*, 77–80, *79*, 85, *86*, *87*, 88
hospitals, French, 62; religious character, 63, *64*, *65*; civic authority, 72; lack of medical prestige, 72; spatial arrangements, 75; doctor–patient relationship, 77; Charité Hospital, Paris, 63, *64*, *65*; Hôtel Dieu, 75, 78; pavilion plan, 78, 79
hospitals named: Glasgow Western Infirmary, 86, *88*; London, 16, 70, *71*; naval, Portsmouth and Plymouth, 66, 75, 78; Newcastle-upon-Tyne Infirmary, 75, *76*, 78; Radcliffe Infirmary, 68; Royal Northern, *87*; St Bartholomew's, 63; St Thomas's, 63, 72, 78–9, *79*; University College, 81, *88*, 93n54; Winchester, 69
hotels: seaside boarding houses, 24; US residential, 172; commercialization, 239; Great Western, Paddington, 232; Westminster Palace, 232
house form, 24; social stratification, 10; domain differentiation, 298–9; *see also* dwelling
housing: relationship to social stratification, 5, 7, 10, 15, 20; defined by ownership and tenure, 19–20; multi-storey flats, 19; socio-cultural statement about its environment, 151; settlement system, 300; US, 156, 174; subsidized, 176–7; *see also* apartment houses; vacation house
housing classes, 5, 20
housing sociology, 7
Howard, D. L.: *The English Prison*, 115–16
Howard, John, 45; notes on UK and European prisons, 95; and sites for reform prisons, 57n27
Howe, A., 16
human relations school: and office design, 26, 274–5, *276*
Hurd. G., 25

I'Anson, E., 263
ideas, 1, 10, 16, 17, 27; social distribution, 31, 193
ideologies, institutional, 14, 43, 44, 94, 96–9, 105, 113, 115; and architect-planning, 15; and penal reformation, 16; and built form, 31; regarding apartment house, 179–84; of vacation house, 195, 196, 209, 212–13, 217–18; *see also* knowledge; science
Ignatieff, M., 16
Illich, I., 17, 26

imagery, urban, 5
imperialism: influence on built form and environments, 17–18, 29; assumed transference of ideas and values, 29
imprisonment: supersedes hanging, whipping, etc, 84, 95; debate on its purpose and achievement, 95, 114, 115; use of in medieval period, 116n2; *see also* ideologies
income, *see* distribution
India: caste system, 3, 22, 125, 145; culture, 18, 22, 123–4; impact of British Raj, 47, 217; influence of Islam, 124; Pallava period, 131; urban planning, 132
industrialization, 11, 12, 28; shift of workforce from primary to tertiary sector, 25; geographical scope, 39; alleged increase in crime, 97; and US cities, 156, 157; influence on social organization, 196–7; reallocation and organization of time, 198–9, 205
Industrial Revolution, 39, 196, 202, 229, 230
insanity: social organization in nineteenth-century England, 14, 38; transferred to medical science, 14; segregative approach, 14, 45, 48; a burden on market economy, 40; exclusion from workhouses, 42; parsimonious treatment, 50–6; in prisons, 109
institutions: and study of society, 9; growth and differentiation of, 9; related associations and building forms, 9, 10, 11, 27, 29; and private leisure, 21, 236; emphasis on consumption, 21; diachronic and synchronic approaches, 27; cultural variations, 28–9; importance of spatial organization, 28, 30; cultural/functional relationship, 147
International Journal of Urban and Regional Research, 5
Isaac, G.I., 284
Islam, 124, 228
Islamic house, 10, 13

Jackson, A. A., 6
Jebb, Joshua, 99, 110; and prisons, 113
Jews, diet and religion, 23, 228
Journal of Architectural Research: and built form study, 8

Kailasa, Mount, ritual ascent of,139
Kalman, H. D.: 'Newgate Prison', 110, 118n26
Kanchipuram, 136; the Sankaracharya, 142

Kearney, M., 292
King, A. D., 4, 15, 17, 21, 27, 29, 30
kinship, 9, 10; and house types, 4; *see also* family
knowledge: increasing fragmentation, 7; associated institutions, 10; cultural 15, 28; development of specialized, 17; generation in relation to society and buildings, 20; scientific, applied to buildings, 26, 62, 67; social context and distribution, 7, 31
Kramrish, S., 128

labour, 11, 26; percentage shifts in employment, 25; attitude of prison inspectors, 102, 117n17; new economic divisions under industrialization, 197
labour market: and categories of deviance and poverty, 14, 41; motivation of hospital governors, 15, 20; and capitalist production, 20, 41
Lamb, Charles, 262, 266
Lancet, the, 81
land, US valuations, 156, 159, 167, 269, 279; speculation, 25; *see also* real estate practice
landscape, 3, 6, 274, 278
language, relation to environment, 284; *see also* terminology
Larson, M. S., 17
Latin America, street layout, 294; boundaries in squatter areas, 298
law, the: and temporal organization of socio-economic life, 198–9; Inns of Court accommodation, 263
leisure: a social institution, 9, 13; private institutions, 21; organization of time, 22, 198–9; and second homes, 194, 195; increases due to factory production, 196; purpose-built environments, 196, 200; uneven distribution, 199; the annual holiday, 200; settings of urban bourgeoisie, 203; emergence of the 'week-end', 204–5, 224n85; temporal/spatial concept,295; growth in institutions, 236
Lewandowski, Susan, 18
Local Government, 82, 159
location, 1, 2, 5, 6, 12, 18, 26; of asylums, 37, *54*; apartment houses, 152–4, 160, 164, 170, 171, 172, 177; hospitals, 69; offices, 26, 259, 270; restaurants, 232, 240, 243, 246; temples, 18, 124, 126–7, 131–2, 134, 138–9, 143, 147; vacation houses, 206, 208, 209, 212, 217
Loffland, L. H., 302

London: consumer and cultural activities, 24; an 'office city', 25; residential/spatial segregation, 199–200, 233; French flats, 207; industrial transformation, 229–30; provisions for eating and drinking, 230–6, 239, 244–5; suburban increase, 244
lower classes, and dependent groups, 40
lunacy, trade in, 42, 43; 'reform', 42–5
lunatic asylums, 10, 18; and control of deviance, 13, 38; emergence of purpose-built, 14, 38–9, 42–8; and classification as a means of control, 14, 45–6, 58n36; effect of economics on numbers and conditions, 14, 48, 50–6; self-perpetuating systems, 14–15, 48–9; 'receptacles for storage of imbeciles', 15, 54; role in organization of labour, 20; spatial organization, 28, 30, 45; community based alternatives, 37; social forces behind their emergence, 38; recipients of sufferers from mental illness, 38–9; charity institutions, 42, 57nn23, 24; reform movement, 42–5, 56; to be state supported and inspected, 43–5, 57n27, 58n31; role of architecture, 45, 74; treatment of patients, 43, 44–5; mechanisms for controlling conduct, 45–6; numbers to be accommodated, 46, 48, 50; ideal siting, 48, 54; the superintendent, 49, 53, 59n58; basic architectural types, 50–6; corridor, 52; pavilion, 53, 54; hours of detention for incurable cases, 56
lunatic asylums, named institutions: Bethlem, 42, 57nn23, 24, inter-patient communication, 45; Caterham and Leavesden, 46, 53–4, 54, floor plan, 55; Cheshire County, 48, 49; Claybury County, 15, 46, 50, ground floor plan, 47; Colney Hatch, 52, 53, facade, 52–3; Gloucester County, 51; Lancashire, 48; Middlesex, 48, 51, 52; Suffolk County, 50–1; Retreat at York, 15, model for reformers, 43, 44, 49, ideal siting, 59n44
lunatics: increase in numbers certified 1844–1904, 48; failure of doctors to effect a cure, 48, 49, 59n49; overwhelmingly lower class, 49; public belief in their violence, 50; see also madness
Lutyens, Edwin, 3

McBride, G., 297
madhouses: use of chains and manacles, 14, 42; Victorian 'loony bins', 37; synonymous with built form, 38; trade in lunacy, 42, 43; the keepers and maniacs, 43
madness, segregative approach, 14, 39; emergence of professionalism, 14; control by classification, 14; early opinions on, 42; changed treatment, 42, 43
Madras: modern urban city, 136, 149n33; impact of British rule on Hinduism, 18, 136–7; new pattern of urbanization, 18, 136, 137, 142, 144; change from horizontal to vertical circumambulation space in temple, 18; disappearance of processional streets for Jagannath temple cars, 18; changes in location, scale and form of temples, 124, 136–7; number of temples, 143, 146, 150nn50, 54; suburban location, 143–4; housing societies, 144; new migrant population, 144, 146; street shrines, 144–6, 145; cultural activities, 146; Kodambakkam suburb, Vadalapalani and Ayyappa temples, 143–4, 149n42; Mahalakshmi temple, influence of its built form, 138, 139, urban pilgrimage centre, 138, 143, shrine decoration and mythology, 139, 149n39, shore location, 139, 140, 142, dimensions, 139–40, 149n40, history of patronage, 141–2, mother-goddess worship, 143
Madurai city: unitary planning, 131–2, 134; layout, 132, 133, 134, 137; brahmin community houses, 132; sacred and secular aspects of the city, 134; kingly circumambulation at coronation, 134, 149n29; Koodalazhagar temple, 139; legitimization of Nayakas, 142; Minakshi Temple, 124, 130, horizontal circumambulation space, 18, emergence from stone temples, 131, dedication to Siva, 131, 134, gate towers (gopurams), 132, work of Nayakas, 134, annual festival cycle, 134, 149n29, plan, 134, 135, impact of British, 134, 136
magistracy: and small asylums, 48, 57n27; and incurable pauper-lunatics, 50; corruption and apathy over prisons, 95, 113, 118n33; control of drinking places, 246, 250n5
Mahalakshminagar, 144

Maharishi Mahesh Yogi, 146
Malthus, Thomas: and promotion of poverty, 40, 41
management: and office design, 26, 255, 278; new spatial arrangements, 200; scientific, 265; consultancy movement, 274–5
man–environment studies (MES), 7, 283; and interaction, 284, 289; diagrammatic representation, 289; and congruence or non-congruence between physical and human forms, 289–90
Marriott, O., 25
Marshall, L., 301
Marx, K., Marxism, 5, 57n16, 196, 220n16
Mason, B. M. and Thompson, A., 21
Mayer, A. C., 22
Mayhew, Henry, 110, 232
meaning, spatial organization, 293, 295
medical science: and insanity, 14; and hospitals, 62, 67, 73–4
men, single apartments for, 165; see also bachelor; gender; women
menstrual lodges, 4, 129
mental illness, 37, 38, 45
mercantilism, 66
Michaelson, W. and Reed, R., 291
middle and upper middle classes, 23; domination of cultural life, 40; use of hospitals, 62, 88; desire for privacy, 233; and public refreshment places, 235–6; changing mealtimes, 236; see also social class
Middle East, 29
Minakshi Sundaresvarar, temple, 132
monasteries: and hospitals, 63
motor car: and second home ownership, 194, 195, 203, 212
Mount Kailasa (Meru): home of the gods, 130; ritual ascent of, 139
Mumford, Lewis, 6; on bad housing, 172–3

National Health Service, 16, 85, 88
neighbourhood: and apartment houses, 19, 152, 155, 179–89; temple as focus of, 143–6; disappearance of in American city centre, 153
Nightingale, Florence: nursing reform, 80; 'ward', 79, 82
nomenclature, spatial, 13, 27; see also terminology
Nurses, nursing: religious orders, 63; home visiting, 66; social hierarchy, 70; and dying

patients, 77; and pavilion plan, 80, 83
Nyaka, Tirumala, 149n29

office buildings and blocks, 5, 15; real estate practice, 26, 258, 259, 269, 272–3; cultural variation in type, 28–9; change cities, 256; relationship between internal and external factors, 259; the skyscraper, 256, 269–72; Guaranty building, 270, 271
offices, 10, 12, 15; growth of in towns, 24–5; most typical work environment, 25; socio-economic development, 25–6; social basis of design, 26; organization and technology, 26, 254, 256–9, 265, 275; open plan, landscaped, 26, 276, 278; variation in spatial allocation, 256, 257; relationship between space and status, 262; importance of supervision, 269; scientific principles, 265–6, 266–9; shift in power from management to staff, 278; new participative labour laws, 278
offices, named: Bank of England, 254; Central Beheer open plan, 278; Guaranty Building, 270, 271, 272; Larkin Building, 269, 278, socio-economic environment, 265–6, 267, regimented organizational life, 266, 268; Ninoflex, Nordhorn, 272, invention of burolandschaft, 274, 275, 276, human relations philosophy, 276, 277, 278; Oriel Chambers, 259, 263, 266, 269, 278, small office suites, 263, office plan, 263, facade, 263, 264, 265; Royal Exchange, Lloyd's, 259; Seagram Building, NY, 278, use of reflective glass, 272, architecture, 272, 274, air-conditioning, 272, 274, management interior, 275; Sun Life Insurance Co., 269, 278, staffing, 259, 260, 263, architecture, 259, 260, 261; 263, 266, interior, 262
Ohnuki-Tierney, E., 299
Oliver, P., 4
Ortiz, A., 292

Pahl, R. E., 5
Palladian mansion, prison, hospital, asylum compared to, 15, 61, 69–70
Perin, Constance: social status and house tenure, 20, 157–8, 182–3
Pessen, Edward: inequitable distribution of wealth, 157
Peters, R., 284

Pevsner, Nikolaus, 263; History of Building Types, 6
philanthropy, and hospitals, 66–7; and housing, 174, 175; and low income groups, 177
Pickvance, C., 5, 21
planning, 2, 4, 6, 8, 28, 132, 171, 212, 283
political economy of cities, 5, 8, 25
polity (civil government), 9, 10, 11; see also government; power; state
Polyani, Karl, 40
poor, the: distinction between able- and non-able bodied, 14, 41, 42; relief systems and administration, 39, 40, 41, 62, 67–8; dependent groups, 40; numbers in receipt of relief, 40; rise of institutionalism, 40, 41–2; categorization, 41; and hospitals, 62, 63; work ethic, 67, 82; dealing with the sick, 67–72; attribution of idleness, 68; distinction between deserving and undeserving, 68
Poor Laws, 41, 44
population: source of national wealth, 66; differentiation by age limits, 199; tables of occupation, 131–2
power, economic and political: reflected in variation in city and building form, 4, 5, 15, 18, 25, 29, 31; cultural variations in expression, 5; transference from lay to professional control, 16, 90; changing relationship in office design, 26; opposition to concentration in the state, 44
'primitive' societies: eating and drinking, 228; shelter building, 283, 285; use of a home base, 283; space-time organization, 295; rules for ensuring privacy, 297, 301
Pringle, Sir John: Diseases of the Army, 74, 75
Prison Commission, 114, 118n39
Prison Discipline Society, 97
prisoners, 14; emphasis on reform, 16, 17, 58n36, 95, 96, 97, 105, 107; classification, 16; deterrence through terror, 17, 111, 112; assumed characters, 95, 112; segregation against class corruption, 96, 97, 107; communication between, 97–8; maintenance of health, 108, 109; solitary eating, 109–10, 112; recidivism, 115; disciplinary measures, hard labour, 98, 114; silence, 97–8, 117n22; solitary confinement, 16, 30, 96, 97, 112, 118n35; transportation and penal

servitude, 118n34
prisons, 5, 10, 13; relationship between ideologies and architectural form, 16, 26, 58n36, 94, 99ff.; 'separate system', 16–17, 94–6, 113–14; administration, 16, 104, 113, 114, 118n39; exclusion of aural and visual stimuli, 17, 99; emphasis on moral reform, 17, 97, 99; acoustic control, 17, 100; concentration on security, 17, 97, 100, 104–5; role in organization of labour, 20; spatial morphology, 27; nineteenth-century survivals, 94, 97; reform movement, 95–7; evangelical v. utilitarian ideas, 95, 97; rebuilding after 1820s and 1830s, 95, 97, 99–100, 116n6; state of ideological confusion, 96; inspectorate, 97–8, 110, 113; role of chaplain and chapel, 98, 99, 105–8, 108; task of warders, 104, 107; financing, 113, 118n34; obstacles to progress, 114–15
prisons, architecture of: prevention of communication, 99–104, 105, 117n22; cell construction, 99–100, 101, 102, 104, 105, security, 104, 105; radial construction, 103, 104, 105, 106; chapels, 105, 107; Gothic style, 110–12, 111; post-Second World War, 114
prisons, named institutions: Aylesbury, 104; Bath, 118n32; Blunderstone, 115; Clerkenwell House of Detention, 106; Derby, 16, 102; Ely, bishop's, 118n33; Gloucester, 118n33; Hereford, 102; Holloway, 110, 111; King's Lynn, 102; Lincoln, 108; Millbank, 99–100; Moabit (Berlin), 17; Newgate, 10, 110, 57n24; Northallerton, 102; Nottingham, 102; Pentonville, 17, 101, 106, 107, 109, model construction, 99, 102, 104, 106, 107, 109, 110; Peterborough, liberty, 118n33; Portsmouth, 110; Reading, 110; St Albans, 96; Strangeways (Manchester), 103, 110; York, 118n33
prisons (US), 97, 100
privacy: in refreshment places, 24, 233, 234, 243, 249, 276; in vacation house, 210; in offices, 26, 269, 278; and spatial segregation, 30; ethnocentric definition, 296; and organization of communication, 296–7; methods of achieving, 297–8
private sector, 159, 174–5, 176, 177

professionals, professionalism: increased social power, 15, 16; alliance with state, 17; ceremonial eating functions, 23; lay organizations and, 26; creation of specific cultural knowledge, 28; *see also* architects; doctors; human relations school; psychiatrists
property: rights, 30; ownership, 217–19; speculation, 26
Provincial Medical and Surgical Association, 80–1
psychiatrists, 14, 28, 58n31
psychology, architectural, 7
public houses: social functions, 23, 230, 233, 247; association with public alarm, 230, 233, 250n5; numbers and types employed, 231–2; middle-class avoidance, 233; interior design, 233, *246*, 249; non-alcoholic alternatives, 244, 245; rebuilding on grand scale, 246–7; and changes in taste, 247–9
Pulicat, Madras and Dutch settlements, 136
punishment, debate on nature of, 95, 112, *see also* prisoners

race: as criterion of classification and stratification, 16, 20; racial minorities, 153, 156, 160, 175–9, 182
Ragatz, R. L., 195
Ramakrishna Mission, 123
Rapoport, Amos, 4, 6, 14, 21, 22, 23, 24, 27, 284–301 *passim*
Ravetz, A., 6
real estate practice, 26, 258, 259, 269, 272–3, 276
refreshment places: nineteenth-century, 10, 13, 15; in Victorian London, 22; Thorne's pioneering essay, 22, 24, 228–49; influence of finance and business organizations, 23, 24; social meaning of changes in table arrangement, 23, 24; commercial provision, 23, 240–3; social factors affecting interior form, 24, 28, 233, 234; and needs of the time, 24, 243; terms used to describe, 231–2; in seventeenth and eighteenth centuries, 234–5; commercialized catering, 239–43; barometers of society's values and aspirations, 249; gentlemen's clubs, 232, 233, 250n15; social class and gender, 232; teashops, ABC, 245, Lyons, 245; transport caff, 23; foreign, 232; *see also* public houses; restaurants
Reid, I., 20
religion: social regulations, 228; common social institution, 9,

10; related associations and building forms, 10, 11, 29; and care of the sick, 63; and 'separate' prison system, 98–9, 105; and organization of time, 198; *see also* Christianity; Hinduism; Jews
religious beliefs: represented in settlement form, 3; changes creating new social needs, 11; and prison rebuilding, 16, 98; and commensality, 23; and hospital buildings, 29
research laboratories, 11
residential areas, social stratification, 10; and spatial segregation, 199–200
restaurants, 21; emergence of modern form, 24, 236–43; practice of dining out, 231; decor and layout, 234, 237, 238, 239, 240; architecture, 238–9; caterers and catering, 239–43
restaurants, named: Blanchard's, 238; Café Royal, 238; Carr's, 238; Criterion, 24, *242*, 243, 252n54; Gatti's, 239; King's Head Tavern, 236; Prince's, *248*; Purssell's Coffee Saloon, 234, *238*; Sawyer and Strange's London Diner, 238; Wellington, 238
Rex, J. and Moore, R., 5, 20
Richardson, M., 294
Rockefeller, John D.: and black cooperative apartments, 175
Rosenwald, Julius (housing sponsor), 175
Royal Institute of British Architects: terminology of building forms, 21; paper given on restaurant design, 241
Royce, J., 286
rules, social/cultural, 13, 16, 22, 27, 29, 109, 220, 287, 290, 293; *see also* culture
Russell, William W. (prison inspector), 97, 116n9; and separate system, 97, 98, 99–100, 113; attitude to labour, 102

Salem, S. India, 142
Saxon-Snell, Henry, 81, 83
Scandinavia: cellular office projects, 26, 278
Scheflen, A., 23
Schnapper, D., 294
Schnelles, the: and office management, 275
scholarship: 'aesthetic' motives in evaluation, 7; influence of disciplinary specialization, 7; influence of social background, 7
schools, 5, 10; instruments of education, 74

Schwartz, B., 25
science, 11, 15; medical, applied to hospital design, 73, 74
scientific management, 265, 274, 275
Scotland, Cornton Vale women's prison, 115
Scull, Andrew, 67; study of insanity, 14
Scully, V., 299
second homes, *see* vacation house
segmentation, social, *see* social stratification
Seringapatam, loot of, 138
settlement form, 3, 300; relation to culture, 4; and social form, 24; Hindu street shrines, 146; vacation house, 217
shops, shopping, 5, 21, 24, 144; department stores, 236; role of the market, 299–300
Simmel, G.: *Social differentiation*, 197
Simpson, John, *237*, 238, 243, 251n34
Smith, Adam: and relief for the able-bodied, 41
social change: and new building types, 23
social class, and built environment, 5, 12; expressed in dwelling terminology, 197; in spatial location, 294; in relation to apartment house, *see* apartment house; asylum, 45, 49; eating places, 231, 232, 233, 235, 236, 243, 245, 247; hospitals, 15, 16, 70, 84, 85; vacation house, 194, 206, 208, 209, 210–11, 212; *see also* middle class; social stratification; upper class; working class
social control: institutions for, 10; essays related to, 13; architecture and built environment as means of, 31
social differentiation: in nineteenth century commercial houses, 23; and class structure, 197
social forms: relationship with built forms, 1, 2, 3, 9; institutionalization, 23; reflected in cities, 24
social ideas, 8
social mobility, US absence, 157, 179
social organizations: expressed in spatial form, 3; influence of culture, 4; represented in care of the sick, 16; and built environments, 28; influence of technology, 30; changes due to industrialization, 198
social stratification: reflected in housing type and quality, 5, 158; common to all societies, 9,

10; related associations and building forms, 10; and hospital design, 15; and organization of the sick, 16; and high rise blocks, 30–1; increase due to industrialization, 197, 200; social segmentation in American city, 152–8, 162, 163, 180, 183

Society: effect of change on built environment, 1; effect of ideologies and socio-economic factors on buildings, 1; and urban development, 5; relationship with built environment, 8, 20, 193; study of through its institutions, 9ff.; and care of the sick, 16; control of deviance through built forms, 13, 31, 38; propensity to create socio/spatial/temporal organizations of constraint, 22; organization of time, 22; redefinition of moral boundaries, 38; based on class structure, 40; dependence on segmentation, 152; encouragement of property ownership, 217–18; impact of office work, 256

Sociology, 8, 9, 21; urban, 5, 7; of architectural knowledge, 7; housing, 7

Sorokin, P., 286

South-East Asia, de-urbanization policies, 25

South India: extension of Nayaka rule, 134; influence of British arrival, 136; medieval temple centre, 139; traditional construction, 141; changes in patronage, 141–2; urbanization, 142; industrialization, 142, 144; impact of depression, 142; increasing religiosity, 143; housing estates, 144; see also temples, Hindu

space, definition and organization, 293; fundamental property of environment, 293

space–time concept, 205, 295, 300

spatial arrangements: within houses, 6, 12; differentiations by humans and hominids, 284

spatial forms, 27; relationship to social forms, 2, 3, 4, 12, 13

spatial organization, 28, 30; relationship to social variables, 4; and built form, 8, 195; and new forms of socio-economic organization, 18, 199–200; traditions in utilizations, 287, 291

spatial segregation: a principle of social life, 30; achievement of privacy, 30; residential representation, 199–200; expresses meaning, 293; ways

of indicating expected behaviour, 294; nomenclature, 13

specialization: in knowledge, 7; as characteristic of industrial capitalism, 21, 196–201

Spiers and Pond (catering entrepreneurs), 240–3

Stacey, M., 5

Stahl, A. P., 290

Stanislowski, D., 294

state, 17, 20, 29, 43, 44, 66, 82

Strauss, Anselm: and urban imagery, 5; and apartment dwellers, 180–1

style, architectural, 6, 7, 13, 162–4, 288

suburbs, suburbanism, 19, 23–4, 171, 244; UK, 233; US, 156–7, 170, 182; India, 143–4

Sun Life Insurance Co., 269, 278; staffing, 259, 260, 263; architecture, 259, 260, 261, 263, 266; interior, 262

supermarkets, 12, 15

surplus, see capitalism; economics

Sweden, second home ownership in, 194

symbolism, 3, 4, 13, 17, 19, 124, 126, 134, 213, 286

Tamilnadu, 124, 141

taxonomy, of building types, 21–2; see also classification

Taylorist ideas, scientific work studies, 274, 275

technology, 8, 84; effect of developments on socio/behavioural/architectural patterns, 11, 23, 30, 112–13, 124, 149, 195; transference between cultures, 31; and the office, 26, 254, 266; and 'second home' developments, 195, 210; creation of social inequalities, 197; 'prefabricated' or 'portable' buildings, 210, 211

temples, Hindu, 10, 13, 123; cosmological ideas, 15, 124, 130, 131, 132, 134; socio-economic/political functions, 18, 19, 131; legitimization of status, 18, 131, 132, 138, 142; influence of British on administration and form, 18, 136–7, 141; change from horizontal to vertical ritual spaces, 18, 138, 139; disappearance of processional streets, 18, 137, 140; absence of brahmin residential quarters, 18–19, 140; investment of surplus economic wealth, 19, 126, 131, 136; catering for suburban expansion, 19, 124, 140; symbolize religious values, 19, 124, 126; position of priest-

hood, 126, 127, 131, 132, 148n17; rite of circumambulation, 127–8, 131, 141, 149n29; role of patronage, 131, 136, 141–3, 147; expansion of ritual and ceremonies, 132, 134; changes in urban built form, 136–7, 140–1; de-Brahminization of temple management, 142–3, 150n49; role in development of neighbourhood, 143, 144, 146, 147; and the city, 146, 147, 150n54; main built form of Hinduism, 146; reflect ideals of Indian society, 147

temples, Hindu, architecture of, 126–7, 129; geometrical design, 127; the ambulatory, 127–8; waiting halls, 128, 130, 140; subsidiary shrines, 128, 130, 149; evaluation, 128–30; outer gateways, 128, 131, 132, 139; culmination of Dravidian architecture, 131; Durge, Aihole, 128, 129; Kailasanatha, Kanchipuram, 128, 129; Sanchi, 128, 129

Tenon, J. R.: and Paris hospitals, 64, 65, 74, 75

terminology, SFB index, 21–2, 27, 197, 201–2, 204; Madurai street names, 132, 152, 184n11; eating places, 231–2

'Third World', 18, 31, 225n123

Thorne, Robert, 20, 22, 23, 24, 27

time: social organization, 22, 195–6, 198, 204; creation of surplus due to industrialization, 196–7; task-v. clock-orientated, 198; influence of transport, 198; the law and its socio-economic organization, 198–9; fragmentation into measured units, 199, 292; and spatial distribution of activities, 199–200, 292; working and non-working, 200; emergence of the week-end, 204–5, 210; large-scale cognitive structuring, 292; tempos and rhythms, 292–3

Tiruvanmiyur, shore temple site, 142

Tollet, Casimir, 81

Tomlinson, Heather: and prison organization, 16–17

transport, 124; and large commercial restaurant, 23; improvements, 56n12; and Hindu temple attendance, 143–4; and US city life, 153; and access to vacation houses, 195, 197, 203, 205, 212; and organization of time, 198; and access to the country, 203

tribal man, villages, 4, 29

Trobriand islanders: bachelor houses, 4; menstrual lodges, 4, 29

Tuke, Samuel: and York Retreat, 58nn28, 29

unemployed/employed boundaries, 41

United States (US), *see* America

universe of meaning, 13

universities, commensality social divisions, 23

upper classes: and poverty, 40; and institutionalism, 41; and hospitals, 62; and seaside resorts, 196–7; and country cottage, 209; as embodying ruling values, 212

urbanization, 2, 180; and social development, 5; conflict due to social stratification, 5; interest groups, 5; new patterns in India under British Raj, 18; ethnography and eating place behaviour, 23; and eighteenth-century hospitals, 69, 91n25; influence on US city structure, 157; functionally specific towns, 199; behaviour of bourgeoisie, 203, 204, 205, 206, 209; location and social stratification, 294

US Bureau of Census, 185n18

USSR, 25, 194

vacation houses, 10, 12, 13, 15, 18, 20; relation with built environment, 21, 28, 193, 195; socio-economic/cultural factors governing their development, 21, 193, 195, 196–8, 201, 203, 206, 208, 213, 216; second home controversy, 193, 201, 203, 206, 208; definition, 193, 219n4; mass market, purpose-built, 194, 195–6, 200–1, 213; opposition from host communi-

ties, 194, 220n13; common motivations, 194, 201, 203, 205, 208, 213; influence of technology and prefabrication, 195, 210, *211*, 212; and increase in functional differentiation and specialization, 197–8; aesthetic condemnation, 212; contemporary ideology, 212–13; shift in terminology to 'second home', 217; the bungalow and week-end country cottage, 193, 195, 196, 197, 200, 201, 205–12, *207*, classes catered for, 206, 208, 209, 210–211, 212; location and site, 206, 208–9, 212, adaptations, 209, 210, *214*, accommodation, 209–10, 216, prefabricated conversions, 210, *211*, 212, *214*, *215*, idealization of country life, 218, *219*; the country cottage, basis of concept, 202, use of by elite, 202–3; the seaside resort, 196–7, 200, 203, 204

values, 6, 7, 10, 22, 30, 180, 195, 196, 249, 255, 286–7, 290, 293, 299–300

van der Rohe, Ludwig Mies, 165, 278, 279

Vedas, the (sacred scriptures), 125, 131, 140

Venturi, R., 294

Verity, Thomas, 241, *242*, 243

Vishvanatha (Nayaka ruler), 18, 131, 132

Vogt, E. Z., 299

Von Frisch, K., 284

Von Uexküll, J. J., 284

wage labour system, 40, 41

Walton, I., 24, 200

Weber, M., 25, 197

week-end, *see* time

Wiebe, Robert: *The Segmented Society*, 152

Williams, R., 202

women: in employment, 23, 239, 244, 266; London attractions for, 24; and nursing profession, 80; prisons for, 115; access to public refreshment places, 235–6, 239, 240, 243, 251n25, 253n69; change in mealtimes, 236; commune, 30; *see also* gender; men

work: methods of compulsion, 41, 'ethic', 41, 62; outcome of capitalism, 67

workhouses, 14, 39; and punishment of idleness, 40, 68; authoritarian structure, 40; separation between indigents, 41, 68; eventual population, 41–2, 68; exclusion of insane, 42; administration of relief, 68; separate infirmaries, 82; asylums for infectious diseases, 82; Boards of Guardians, 82; Infirmaries, St Marylebone, 82, *83*

working class, 39; effect of industrialization on leisure, 196; organized by clock and factory whistle, 198; paid holidays, 199; seaside boarding houses, 200; emergence of 'week-end', 204; public catering provisions, 243–4; non-alcoholic coffee houses, 245

Wright, Frank Lloyd, 265

Wright, Henry: and apartment house dwellers, 181

Wynter, Andrew: and asylums as 'lumber rooms', 49

Yaker, H. M., 292

York Retreat, 43, 46, 49

Zones: single use, 152, 155; zoning laws, 156, 159